Being challenged in life is inevitable,
being defeated is optional.

—Roger Crawford

SPINNING FORWARD

Successfully
Redefining Life
from a
New Perspective

Doug Hamlin
with Rick D'Errico

Cover and text design by Beth Farrell
Cover and text layout by Frankie Lee

Sea Script Company
Seattle, Washington
info@seascriptcompany.com
www.seascriptcompany.com

ISBN: 9798749929959
Library of Congress Control No.: 2021909435

First Printing May 2021

Printed in the United States

Cover photo: One of Doug's longest serving chairs.
Thousands of miles in the air and on the ground.

SEA SCRIPT COMPANY
BOOK PUBLISHING

TABLE OF CONTENTS

Printed book and eBook available at:

www.Amazon.com

To contact the author:

Doug Hamlin
Spinforward, LLC
doug.hamlin@spinforward.com

FOREWORD

Every year since the inaugural "Journey Along the Erie Canal" bike ride in 2013, I've pulled back from the rest of the riders four miles from the finish line at Jennings Landing in Albany, N.Y. I do this because I need a few minutes to myself, just to reflect on the previous 10 days and 360 miles of this journey and all of the family and friends who took part to make the event so special. I am so thankful for each and every one of them because, as much as I hope to ride in this event for many years to come, father time is catching up with me and I don't know if it will be our last ride together.

As I slow my bike to a crawl and the other riders shrink in the distance, I begin to get emotional thinking about these friendships and one rider in particular. His name is Doug Hamlin. A quadriplegic and former CEO and well-respected businessman in the Capital Region, Doug is the first individual with a disability like me to take an interest in the annual ride along the Erie Canalway Trail. And he is the only such person to ride the full 363.4 miles with me.

Doug and I first met in the passenger waiting area at Albany International Airport in 2010. We were both catching a flight to Chicago by way of Baltimore. From there I was headed to Sacramento, California where I was a last-minute replacement for a keynote speaker who had cancelled just six hours earlier. Doug and I exchanged brief hellos before our flight boarded and agreed to talk some more during our layover in Baltimore.

When we arrived in Baltimore, I told Doug about my plans to start a company to mentor people with disabilities who were struggling to find jobs. With an unemployment rate at a staggering 70%, I wanted to do something about it. I knew of Doug and the sale of his company, VersaTrans, to Tyler Technologies two years earlier and could use a mentor with his business skills to help me with my new company, Our Ability, Inc. As it turned out, Doug could use my expertise as well, as he was planning to leave his role as president of the VersaTrans division of Tyler to get into public speaking, something I had been doing for quite some time.

We had a good conversation and agreed to meet again soon over breakfast in the small Albany suburb of Delmar. To our astonishment, we lived just one mile apart in Delmar, which was home to VersaTrans for many years. Somehow our paths had never crossed, but Doug and I quickly made up for lost time and became very good friends. As I had hoped, he also became an invaluable counselor and guide to me and my fledgling company. To have as a mentor someone disabled like me, who was also very successful in growing a business, was extremely helpful to me.

Very soon, Doug became more and more involved with Our Ability. Around the same time, my wife Andrea convinced me that I should bike across New York State to raise awareness for the hundreds of thousands of disabled people without jobs. So I talked to Doug about the idea sometime in January 2013, and he agreed to take part in a meeting with the Canal Corporation that runs the New York State Canal System.

The Canal people thought we were nuts, but they green-lighted the bike trip anyhow, and I quickly began making preparations for the late June event. Things got out of control pretty quickly, however. We had disability groups, sports groups and sponsors all requesting to take part, and we hadn't even biked one mile yet. I was also being asked to speak at various stops along the way. I needed help, so I asked Doug if he could assist with the logistics and do what he's always done, which is be supportive of what I'm doing. It was a lot to ask since Doug was not a logistics person. Like me, he was a CEO and a leader, not a COO. But he said he'd do it.

Sometime around March 1, Doug's competitive spirit got the best of him and he asked if he could train with me, his goal being to bike a few miles with us each day along the Canalway. "Of course," I said. I was thrilled to have some company. So I did half of my training with Andrea running alongside me and half with Doug. Unfortunately for Doug, he had this large, cumbersome, "granny" bike and could only ride about half my speed. My bike wasn't much better, it was just lower to the ground and easier to push. Andrea and I would watch Doug push that old, heavy scrap of metal with everything he had and he just couldn't get it to move very fast. I could sense his frustration growing. Here was a man who had been successful at virtually everything he'd done, even with his disability, and now he looked nearly helpless.

The following year Doug had a much smaller, sleeker bike built to do exactly what he wanted it to do, and it was like night and day compared to the year before. Now, he could ride every mile with us, and he did that all the way through 2017.

That Doug was able to find a way to conquer the Erie Canal is a testament to his inner-drive and his amazing ability to be present in the moment, no matter what the obstacles or distractions. Whatever he's doing, he doesn't give off the appearance of worry. He engages whomever he's with at the time and in that moment. He knows his limitations better than anyone I've ever met, and he's comfortable in his existence. That combination of being able to be present with whomever you're with and comfortable with who you are, I don't know if I've ever seen that in anyone else.

Doug is the most normal person with a disability that I've ever met. He is successful at business and with his family and friendships. He is a faithful man. If you were writing a bio about Doug, you wouldn't even mention his disability. That's how normal an existence he's lived, despite everything he's had to endure. You can't ask for anything more if you're an individual with a disability. I would love it if my bio didn't include my disability or mention that I was a congenital amputee. I can only hope to accomplish what Doug has achieved in business and in life.

I'm so glad that Doug is telling his story and documenting his own personal journey in this book. In the time I've known Doug, I've learned so much from him, not just about business, but about life and relationships and how to interact with people. He really has an amazing knack for connecting with others and making them feel at ease. He makes you feel as if you're the most important person in the room.

Whether you're someone with a physical or mental disability, someone who's down on their luck or a young aspiring executive or entrepreneur, you will learn so many valuable life lessons from reading this book. And you'll also be much better equipped to succeed in business or whatever it is you want to accomplish in life.

Doug teaches us the most valuable lesson in life: Shit happens to all of us. It's how you deal with it that defines who you are. Doug has embraced who he is, not what he was. To have all of those athletic skills and youthful dreams snatched away from him in an instant had to be difficult. I was born with my disability, so I had no other choice but to adapt. I can't even imagine what it'd be like to be able-bodied and then lose it all so suddenly. But Doug never wallowed in self-pity. He learned how to become the best version of himself he could be, and I think that's why so many people gravitate to him. No doubt he's benefitted by having great friends and two very strong women in his life (his wife Pam and sister Priscilla), but they've also benefitted by him being such a great man. You, too, will benefit from reading this man's inspiring and educational story.

—*John Robinson*, CEO, Our Ability, Inc.
www.ourability.com

Better to spin forward than to look back.

Introduction

When I first thought about writing a book, I envisioned it to be a collection of anecdotes about business travel in a wheelchair. I was spending countless hours in airplanes, rental cars, airports and hotels, and eating more Grand Slam breakfasts at Denny's than I'm comfortable admitting.

Doing all of this from the perspective of a wheelchair user provided any number of stories, some humorous and some not, to fill a short book. Like the time in Chicago when I lost my chair because this adorable but confused Filipino couple thought my $3,000 custom ride was the airport chair they had requested upon landing. After an hour or so, airline personnel found it floating around baggage claim. Thankfully it hadn't left the airport!

Then there was the time in Los Angeles when I was stranded on the plane for 90 minutes because the ground crew failed to come assist me off the plane. I did okay, though. I had a delightful conversation with the flight attendant who was required by law to stay with me until help arrived. She also happened to be the attendant who served me drinks on the five-hour flight. We shared pleasantries and learned a bit about each others' lives, and she helped me with my carry-on bag once I finally departed. Later, when I got to my hotel room and opened the bag, out tumbled 20 or so airline vodka bottles!

She had remembered my preference and found the perfect way to compensate me for my inconvenience.

I realized that as I traveled more and talked to others that EVERY business traveler has a ready list of a hundred or more stories to share. While they are fun to tell at cocktail parties, they don't necessarily make a compelling book with a message.

The bulk of the work on this book took place between January and September of 2020. In that time, the world was consumed with the COVID-19 pandemic which took the lives of hundreds of thousands and sickened millions more people here in the United States alone. Literally overnight we were locked down, quarantined at home and forced to face a world that bore no resemblance to the one we were accustomed to or were planning for. The U.S. was additionally distracted by one of the most divisive presidential campaigns in modern history. This added to the unease and thickened the haze of our view of the future.

On August 20, 1983, I faced an immediate and irreversible assault on my clear and optimistic view of the future when I came down headfirst on a trampoline breaking three bones in my neck and leaving me paralyzed from mid-chest down. I was 23 years-old. What had started as a bright sunny day celebrating my sister Priscilla's birthday on the lakeshore was ending on a medevac helicopter with Priscilla calling my parents to deliver the devastating news.

The elements of your challenge are probably entirely different. You may have a mental or physical disability, or you may be facing the realities of substance abuse, a divorce or a problem with your parents or children. Whatever is clouding your vision of the future, my hope is that these pages will tell you a story about confronting adversity with a positive attitude. Between the ages of 23 and 29, I lost my ability to walk and both of my parents to colon cancer. Yet in that same period of time, I married my soulmate, earned a graduate degree and began a career path that would one day make me a CEO.

I knew almost immediately after I landed on the trampoline that my life had changed forever. I looked at my hands, but they seemed disconnected from my body. I couldn't feel my legs at all. This was bad. I knew to stay as still as possible and I insisted that no one touch me. My mind flashed on images of hospital beds and wheelchairs. I'd seen enough after-school specials about injured athletes to understand that people lived through these things and found ways to adapt but at that particular moment, all I could think about was: Let's get the professionals here and not make this thing worse than it is.

I've always been an optimistic person. I believe that was instilled in me at a young age by two loving parents and a very stable middle-class upbringing in the suburbs of upstate New York. My father worked for IBM and my mom stayed at home with the kids. I learned that if you worked hard and did the right things, good fortune followed.

I literally landed in the spinal cord injury unit at Erie County Medical Center at 8 p.m. that night and began making relationships with doctors and nurses I had no idea existed a few hours prior. Our family knew something about hospitals having spent countless hours in them with my father as he battled cancer. He was diagnosed 15 months before my accident. Now I was on the other side. I was the one looking up at the docs and my family trying to understand what they were saying and searching for the real meaning behind their words. We had learned that you really need to look out for yourself in this environment. Hospitals are machines with a lot of moving parts and limited compassion. Thus, my sister immediately inherited the role of advocate, a role she shined in for the next 91 days.

I was hospitalized for nearly six months. This consisted of three months of acute care in Buffalo and three months of rehab near my hometown of Albany. It was hard at first. I would wake up every morning and have that very brief second of ordinariness—you know, the one before your brain fully engages and you think it's just another normal day. Business as usual. Then the reality of what happened would come crushing down as I realized that someone would have to bathe me in bed and feed me breakfast.

Eventually a routine emerged and I learned what my "new" body could and could not do. I also learned what physical therapists do. They worked me HARD! One day my entire assignment was to figure out how to dress myself and then transfer myself from my bed to a wheelchair. It took 90 minutes! When I finally settled in the chair, my therapist said, "Ok, now spin forward." (Meaning, put your hands on the wheels and give them a push.) That phrase, "Spin forward," stuck with me. It's optimistic, reflects some fun action and results in progress. It's how I have always looked at life— forward. I don't spend a lot of time dwelling on the past and lamenting "what might have been."

I was six weeks into a new job as a software engineer when I got injured. It was the kind of job I could return to when I recovered enough. Through God's good graces or the luck of the universe, whichever you prefer, the company was run by a gentleman named Roger Creighton, who saw immediately that by holding my job for me he could play a crucial role in my recovery. He did that, and I am eternally grateful.

Once I realized that I had that job to return to, my outlook got progressively more optimistic. I worked harder and harder to get out of the hospital. Finally, in April of 1984, I rolled through the lobby and out the door of Sunnyview Rehabilitation Hospital, independently, in a shiny, sporty new wheelchair. I never looked back.

I married my wife, Pam, the following September. Five weeks after that, my dad lost his 30-month battle with cancer. Needless to say, it was a year of ups and downs. I continued to learn even more about how to face adversity. I grew to realize, for me anyway, managing challenges and grief is a team sport. I learned how to accept help from others and not feel guilty about it. I also learned how to help others and provide a shoulder of support when needed.

Five short years later, my mother would fall to the same disease. This was heartbreaking and sadly "familiar" at the same time. I leaned hard on my friends and family once again. As I reflected on my parents' short lives (Mom was 55, Dad 51) I began to formulate a vision that included our enjoyment of the retirement that my parents never got.

I began to make choices that always looked forward. I was able to have three "careers" inside the same company. When presented with a career path choice, I always chose the option that would bring me closer to senior leadership and majority ownership. I worked both with and for some amazing people. I was president by 2000 and CEO by 2003. Some would tell me that doing it in a wheelchair was inspiring to them. I'm glad about that, but I never really thought about it as a goal. I was laser focused on growing the company and maintaining its culture.

I learned how to travel (a lot!) in my wheelchair. I learned how to ask for what I needed and educated people along the way. I learned that management and leadership are entirely different things. Management takes skill; leadership takes guts. I learned most of all that I own my place in the world. I can decide to be optimistic and grab the future, or I can get stuck on what sucks. I've done both. The former is a lot more fun and productive.

As I sit here in my dream house on my favorite lake in Skaneateles, New York, I can't help but be amazed at how the stars aligned. My challenges and my response to them have made me who I am today—the very best version of myself. To thank everyone who helped me along the way would be impossible. But hopefully this is a start.

As you read this book, try and find the parts of the story that are similar to yours. Parts of your journey may intersect with mine and, hopefully, you can find solace, inspiration or both in my approach to certain challenges.

Finally, this tale is not all about me. It's about relationships. It's about the little things people said to me in the quiet moments that helped me see the world as full of opportunity rather than dread. It's about spinning forward.

—*Doug Hamlin*, President, Spinforward, LLC
doug.hamlin@spinforward.com

For Pam
Without you, there is no story.

ONE

THE ACCIDENT

Life's challenges are not supposed to paralyze you,
they're supposed to help you discover who you are.

—Bernice Johnson Reagon

"I want to go home," I thought to myself. I didn't really mean it, but this trip was far different than what I had anticipated.

It was June 24th, 2013, Day 2 of the inaugural "Journey Across the Erie Canal" bike ride, a 363-mile trek across New York State's Erie Canal to raise employment awareness for people with disabilities. We were in the village of Lockport, N.Y., following a grueling 22-mile first leg—I was able to ride only half that distance—and now the ride's organizer, John Robinson, and I were facing an even more difficult 27-mile second leg in 90-degree plus heat.

It was in this city on the banks of the Erie Canal that I realized this nearly 400-mile trek was going to test not just my endurance, my physical abilities or even just my will. It was going to test me to the core of who I am and what I am about.

Part of me wished I could just pack up and shove off. But I knew I would never do that. Not after the 30-year journey that had brought me to this point. For it was on a similar hot summer day in 1983 that I found myself confronted with a much more daunting and life-altering set of circumstances.

And I didn't back down from that challenge—I didn't really have a choice.

To understand my story, and to understand why I was so driven to bike a few hundred miles in what was essentially a poorly modified wheelchair with a handcrank, you have to go back to the weekend that changed my life forever. August 19, 1983, was a pretty non-descript late summer day as far as I can remember. I had worked a full day at Roger Creighton Associates—a leading transportation planning and engineering firm based in Albany, N.Y.—and planned to take an Amtrak train west to Buffalo to celebrate my sister Priscilla's 26th birthday that weekend.

I was looking forward to the train ride and being able to sit in the bar car without having to focus my eyes on the road for four-plus hours. It's as if I didn't have a care in the world. This was in the days when, at 23, I could smoke half a pack of cigarettes, have a few beers and still get up early the next morning, run six miles—and feel great. Now, just writing that sentence makes me sick (and a little nostalgic).

I arrived that night to celebrate Priscilla's birthday, the details of which escape me. She was living with a couple of girlfriends and we pretty much had what I'd call an old-fashioned social evening together. It was the next day, Saturday, August 20, 1983, that would forever change the trajectory I was on. I got up early that morning, went on that six-mile run and got ready to leave for an all-day outing at the home of one of Priscilla's friends about an hour southwest of Buffalo on Lake Erie. At the time, Priscilla was working at toy manufacturer Fisher-Price in nearby East Aurora, and much of her social network was made up of Fisher-Price colleagues. Needless to say, they were a fun bunch.

The day had an ominous beginning to it. I had been swim-

ming in the lake and diving off this floating dock, generally showing off to some of the attractive women within close
proximity. (Once a little brother, always a little brother.) Somehow, in the midst of scaling the dock, my right leg slipped and
got wedged in between the wooden slats, preventing me from
pulling myself up and out of the water.

I can't explain how it happened, but suddenly I found
myself under water and in dire straits, desperately gasping for
air each time my head bobbed and peaked above the water's
surface. But it was a losing battle. At one point, I could barely
keep my head above water and I began to think, "It's going
to take something drastic to get me out of this jam." I even
contemplated breaking my leg in order to free myself from the
dock so I could breathe again.

Then, seemingly out of nowhere, a wave shook the floating
dock violently enough to free my leg. And as quickly as I had
gotten into this potentially life-threatening jam, I was free.
The scare had passed and life was good again. In retrospect, I
probably should have left well enough alone and headed back
to my sister's place or, at the very least, cooled it on the stunts.
Instead, I stayed and enjoyed the company of some 50 people
who were wringing the most out of the waning days of summer.

At some point, some activity that was taking place along
the side of the house caught my eye. There was a trampoline
there and people were taking turns jumping, some higher and
with more flare than others. Naturally, I took it as a challenge—
or an opportunity, at least—to show some folks how to really
work this thing.

I was very comfortable on a trampoline, having trained on
them during my diving days in high school. So when it was

my turn, I started off slowly, giving those gathered around the trampoline a glimpse of some of my style—like swiveling my hips or sweeping a leg underneath my body between bounces. Then, I decided to do a simple backflip. You see backflips, especially layout backflips, are way cooler than your run-of-the-mill forward flips, and while I hadn't performed this particular trick on a trampoline before, I had done hundreds off diving boards. Basically, you raise your head, look back, start the rotation as you leave the board, lock your body straight, and let it ride, soon you see the water, your legs come around, and you splash down. How different could this be?

So I started jumping, climbing higher and higher in the air until I reached a height I thought was sufficient enough to demonstrate my simple trick. Then I started into my flip, keeping my body as stiff as a board. My feet rose toward the sky and I hung upside down in midair. Then, my backflip lost all momentum. My body stopped rotating and my feet stopped coming around, leaving me confused and helpless as I began to plunge headfirst like a missile toward the trampoline. I had neither the instinct nor the time to correct the situation.

As my head crashed into the trampoline, it jerked forward and I heard a loud snap in my neck. As soon as I came to rest on the trampoline, my instincts told me something very, very bad had happened, and that my life may have just changed forever. As I lay on my back, looking into the sky, I glanced at my hands and could see them, but they felt disconnected from my body. I couldn't control them or much of anything else. I told those gathered around the trampoline not to touch me as Priscilla, who thankfully had not seen the accident, rushed to my side. She was scared and concerned but did her best to keep me calm.

The accident ignited a series of events that took on a life of their own and I was merely along for the ride—a ride I didn't want to take. If there's one thing I do consistently well in my life it's mitigate risk and control outcomes. At that particular moment, I could do neither. I knew, lying on that trampoline, that my life had changed, likely forever, and I couldn't do a damn thing about it!

Two emergency medical technicians arrived soon after and gently climbed onto the trampoline to talk to me. Of course, I had no idea what they were asking. I was too focused on the excruciating pain in my neck and odd sensations throughout my body. The pain grew agonizingly worse with each workers' movement on the unstable surface. The EMTs rolled me onto a backboard, stabilized my neck in a brace and removed me from the trampoline and into an ambulance. It would be at least six weeks before I would look in any direction—other than straight ahead.

The 15-minute ambulance ride to the nearest emergency care facility brought new intensifications of pain. When we arrived and entered the emergency room, it was readily apparent to everyone that the facility was ill-equipped to handle the type of injury I just suffered. So the EMTs advised me that they were transporting me to the Erie County Medical Center in Buffalo (ECMC), which had a fairly good spinal cord injury unit. Those were the words they used, "spinal cord injury." I knew the accident was serious the moment I heard the loud snap. And based on the pain I was experiencing and the way the EMTs were treating me, I was fairly certain I had broken my neck. But it was still hard to hear those words, "spinal cord injury."

I told the emergency workers that I couldn't handle another long ambulance ride, so they summoned a helicopter and in the summer dusk, I was whisked off to Erie County Medical Center. I had always wanted to ride in a helicopter; this just wasn't how I wanted to do it. Still, it was a much better ride than the ambulance. Thirty-two years later, in 2015 I would take a much more enjoyable helicopter ride on a tour of the Big Island in Hawaii with my wife. I have much fonder memories of that ride.

Throughout this whole ordeal, including the 45-minute-or-so helicopter ride to the medical center, I remained conscious and without pain medication. Emergency personnel wanted me to have clarity of mind so that when I arrived at the hospital, I could answer a lot of weird questions such as: Can you move this? Or, do you feel this?

At that point, I had no feeling from the neck down with the exception of some slight tingly sensations in my right hand. I had no dexterity in either hand and I had no feeling in the nether region, either, even though at one point one of the hospital staff asked me, "Do you know you have an erection right now?" For which I responded with a joke that I won't repeat.

As it turns out, the C4, C5 and C6 cervical vertebrae at the base of my neck had been fractured and dislocated, and my spinal cord bruised, not severed. This is what they refer to as an "incomplete" spinal cord injury, and it is why I would eventually experience some movement and various levels of sensations around my body to this very day (versus having no feeling at all). Think of it as a partially clogged pipe. Like many traumas, spinal cord injuries have some degree of swelling of the cord and, as that swelling subsides, some functions and sensations return to the body. In rare cases, you can even regain full functionality. I wasn't that fortunate, but I was able to regain full strength and sensation in both arms about four to six weeks after the incident.

For comparison, the late actor and director Christopher Reeve severed, or transected, his spinal cord and he suffered a "complete" injury. Reeve shattered the C1 and C2 vertebrae in his neck when he was thrown off his horse during an equestrian event in May 1995. The violent nature of his headlong fall did severe damage to his spinal cord, and thus he lost all sensory and motor function below his shoulders, including the ability to breathe on his own. Reeve's injury also occurred higher than mine, closer to the base of the skull, and the higher the injury on the spinal cord, the more dysfunction. Basically, those few centimeters may have saved me from being completely paralyzed.

By definition, I am a quadriplegic because all four extremities are affected. I am paralyzed from the mid-chest down, but I can move my right leg to a very minimal degree and my right hand can do everything. My left hand, however, works more like a C5 quadriplegic hand, in that my thumb doesn't move and I cannot grip or hold objects with it. My right leg has a fair amount of muscle "tone" (semi-voluntary stiffening or contraction of the muscles) to create some stability. I have very limited sensation and muscle tone in my left leg.

Upon arriving at the hospital that evening, I was immediately whisked into the emergency room where I was met by several trauma specialists. I don't recall much else about the first few hours in the hospital, other than it was your standard Saturday night in the ER (i.e., very busy) and that Priscilla was by my side the whole time.

As I was in the ER, the doctors decided they needed to better stabilize my neck, and thus put me in this framed apparatus that looked more like a form of torture popular during the Middle Ages. This contraption, commonly used for patients with spinal cord injuries, was called a Stryker frame. It involved cervical tongs, a half-circle frame made out of aluminum that wrapped around the back of my head and two threaded spikes—yes, spikes—about 3 inches long that were drilled about a half- to three-quarters-of-an inch into my skull.

But wait, it gets better. As if having two spikes drilled into my head wasn't enough, attached to this aluminum half-circle frame was a rope attached to a heavy weight that was used to stretch—yes, I said stretch—my neck and stabilize my head. The goal was to provide traction and stability and eliminate the need for a brace, and believe me, you can't move with this thing attached to you!

I would be on this Stryker frame for 10 long days, recuperating and awaiting surgery in a ward-like setting with a dozen other guys who had suffered spinal cord injuries. What they did with patients strapped to this Stryker frame was simply medieval. It was for my own good, of course, but in addition to the unfamiliar headwear, every two hours I was turned over like a pig on a spit roasting over an open fire. They did this to prevent pressure ulcers, or bedsores, since I was unable to feel any such pressure nor was I able to move to alleviate any discomfort.

For two hours I would lay on my stomach counting specks on the floor tiles, then for the next two hours I'd be on my back counting holes on the ceiling tiles. For more than 200 hours I would alternate between staring at the floor and the ceiling tiles, comparing and contrasting the dots on both in an attempt to pass the time.

This was when I began a series of what I call "recalibrations." Just 12 hours before my first twirl on the Stryker frame, I was a carefree, athletic young software engineer with few worries and limitless possibilities. Now my body didn't respond to any commands and I was strapped in. My world was reduced to counting floor and ceiling tiles. Somehow that had to fill my day.

Every so often, when I was on my back, I was given these prism glasses which allowed me to see most everything in the room around me and watch television, even though my head was facing the ceiling. There were only a few of these glasses available and you'd only get them for two-hour periods, but boy it was like an inmate getting time off for good behavior when I got my hands on a pair. These things were like gold!

Even worse than being flipped like a hamburger, I couldn't feed myself. I am a fiercely independent individual, and I don't like others doing for me what I can do for myself. It's human nature, I guess. But now, even the most simple of tasks were embarrassingly out of my control because I couldn't move my arms or use my hands. Others had to feed me, including Priscilla and her friends and my soon-to-be fiancée, Pam.

Like anyone would in my situation, I went through the entire grieving process in the hours and days (and months and years) after the accident. This included feelings of anger and some denial. I grieved my previous life—the life of that independent, active and athletic guy who ran, swam, played golf and skied. I was scared, confused and sad that I may not ever be able to do those things again. And I experienced a few "why me" moments too, especially during the seemingly endless days on the Stryker frame.

Leading up to surgery, the medical team was very diligent about telling me that this procedure would not "heal" me. A successful outcome was not that I would be able to walk again, but that they would be able to stabilize my neck. I got that. I fully understood the purpose of the surgery was to fix my neck, not cure me. That's not to say I didn't fantasize about being completely healed and able to walk again. I did periodically have what I referred to as "walking dreams," in which I was fully able-bodied—as if nothing had ever happened. Those were tough in the beginning, because I'd be very sad and angry when I woke up. But I knew the grim reality of the situation, and I was adapting to that new reality.

My neurosurgeon was Dr. Thomas Doolittle. No, not that Dr. Doolittle! He was in his early thirties, not much older than I, which was something that took some getting used to for my parents.

The surgery took more than six hours. Dr. Doolittle and his team made two incisions near my hip, carved off some of the bone from that hip and then applied the bone graft material between the vertebrae at the back of my neck. They then wrapped the vertebrae together with wire to hold them in place while the bone graft healed. The result was all three of my vertebrae were fused together, limiting my ability to turn my head too much to the left or right, and my head is bent slightly forward.

The procedure has changed over the years and is less invasive today than it was nearly 40 years ago. I have a big, giant scar on the back of my neck, but today the doctors take an anterior approach to get to the vertebrae from the front of the neck, through the throat area, instead of the back. The vertebrae are much more accessible this way as they can be reached without disturbing the spinal cord.

After the surgery, I remained on the Stryker frame, but only for a period of a few days when I graduated to the Philadelphia Collar—an extremely tight neck brace that immobilized my neck but allowed me to be freed from the Stryker/Tong combo. This would be the first of what would be several "graduations." When you know you have a long road to recovery ahead of you and you're not sure where you are headed or what you will encounter next, graduations, even small ones, become a big deal. They did for me, anyway.

Reflecting back on the day of the accident and the days that followed, I drew a tremendous amount of strength from whom and what had constituted my life so far—which you'll read about in the chapters ahead. I also recall thinking about my dad and his struggle quite a bit. My father had been diagnosed with colon cancer about 15 months prior to my accident and had gone through countless hours of chemotherapy and "bad" days, and yet he NEVER complained. In fact, soon after we had been given the news of his dire condition at his bedside, we all began to cry (Dad included). After just a few moments he said, "That's enough, we're moving forward." If he could move forward and face his situation with such dignity and strength, I thought, why couldn't I?

I'm sure I was in a bit of shock immediately following the

accident, and that numbed me somewhat to everything that was going on. I do, however, believe that the full impact of my accident was quite real to me almost immediately. I began to balance the "maybes" or "what ifs" with my natural instincts. I have a mind that adapts to the current situation, whatever it is, and begins to solve problems. And that's exactly what I started to do.

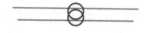

TWO

DAYS FOLLOWING THE ACCIDENT

Friends make everything easier. If you want to succeed at a challenge,
involve your friends. They have an amazing capacity to lighten
physical, emotional, and mental burdens by simply being there.

—Richelle E. Goodrich

Out of sheer exhaustion, I'm not sure how long I slept once I got settled into my hospital room. When I woke up, I had one of those experiences where a new reality hits you all over again. You wake up with a "clean slate" for the day, and then you realize, "Oh yeah...that happened."

"OK," I thought to myself. "I'm still here. I guess I'm doing this." Another recalibration.

My greatest source of strength those first few hours and days came from my faith and the people that surrounded me. I don't know if I would've made it without the grace of God and the amazing support of family and friends and even a few acquaintances who turned out to play pivotal roles in my recovery.

My mother, father and sister Priscilla were my core. There are no words to describe how they were the glue that held me together. I needed them all now more than ever. Backing them up were countless friends and family that snapped into emergency mode to get this big supporting cast in the place they needed to be—by my side.

There was my Uncle Jim (mom's brother) and Aunt Marilyn, who received the call from my mom explaining that I had been in a terrible accident, and that it didn't look so good. They immediately called my father Mo, picked him up in Saratoga, where he was singing for a chorus event, and drove him to our lakefront cottage in Skaneateles—about 30 minutes outside of Syracuse—where he met up with my mom. Very early the next morning, Mom and Dad arrived at Priscilla's and made the short trip to the hospital. En route, Priscilla made sure they were prepared for what they were about to see, which couldn't have been easy.

When my mom showed up that morning, she sobbed. I can only imagine what that must have felt like for her, seeing her baby boy helpless on a Stryker frame, tongs in his skull, staring straight ahead. It reminded me of the time we got the news about my dad's cancer. We all cried for a moment until Dad said, "That's enough, let's move forward."

As she looked down at me, I said, "Don't cry Mom." But she did, and I started to cry, then Dad...and Priscilla.

My mom was a very intelligent, driven woman. How she was able to get through that most difficult time, with my father also ill with colon cancer, I'll never fully know. When she approached the operating neurosurgeon, Dr. Thomas Doolittle, to learn more about the surgery I would be undergoing, he was adamantly clear with her that the surgery would not restore all of my functionality and allow me to walk again. He did not want to give her any kind of false hope. The goal of the surgery was to fuse the bones in my neck together to stabilize it. I got that. So did my mom, although she didn't need to hear him say it with so much emphasis. According to Priscilla, she looked him in the eye and said, "I understand what you're telling me." In other words, "Shut up!"

Also among the first to visit me was my youth pastor, Drew Mann, and his family. Drew was an instrumental figure in my life from the time I was 12. He's the one that taught me how to work with colleagues and kids as a camp counselor. He guided me through early relationships with girls. He helped me grow up. By 1983, our relationship was no longer adult-to-kid or pastor-to-congregant. He was a trusted friend, mentor and guide.

Drew and his family upended their annual summer vacation in Weld, Maine to be by my bedside, making the 12-hour trip in only nine hours. In 1983, the only way to contact Drew during his vacation was to put a message in his mailbox at the local post office. Fortunately, he decided to check his box just a few days before their departure. He discovered a note from the church secretary in my boyhood home of Endicott, New York urging him to call her immediately, which he did. She said, "Doug's hurt. He's asking for you."

It's times like this that you know—really, really know—who your friends are. I didn't create this "test" to do that, but looking back it amazes me the efforts people made to support my family and me during these early, bewildering hours.

Years later, I told Drew this at his retirement party. I needed him to be there and to tell me that it was okay to be mad at God and the world, but also to seek His strength. I remember him telling me that this was the one time he put his clergy sign on his dashboard to fend off a speeding ticket if he got stopped.

Priscilla's small apartment in Buffalo was Command Central during the early days, and from there the Manns headed to the hospital. When Drew and his family arrived at the door to my room and saw me, facing the floor, they paused. Was this the opportune time to come in? Or should Drew go in all alone? His daughter Ryan had her own ideas. A precocious 5-year-old, she plunged in, running across the room and diving head first a la Pete Rose under the bed. And something magical happened. You see, Ryan and I had a unique relationship. For whatever reason she had given me the nickname "Mustard," which I found both confusing and endearing. She slid under the bed, looked up, and said in her sweet child's voice: "What are you doing up there, Mustard?"

I laughed. Then we all cried. And then we prayed, and we talked and talked some more.

The next day I was visited by perhaps the most important person in my recovery, my soon-to-be fiancée Pamela. On the night of the accident, I asked Priscilla to call Pam. Priscilla was a bit confused, which is understandable, as Pam and I had just recently gotten back together after I had foolishly broken things off in the spring of 1982 to sow my wild oats. (Pam still calls this my "weird" year.) I guess Priscilla figured I'd screw it up again and thought it strange to be calling a soon-to-be ex-girlfriend-again with such horrible news. But I was adamant that she call Pam, and the next morning I brought it up again.

Priscilla was still reluctant. Pam was different from the other girls I had dated. She had spent time up at the cottage with my family. Priscilla felt a connection with her that she hadn't with any of my previous girlfriends. My parents felt it, too. They enjoyed getting to know Pam and having her around. In fact, Pam later told me that the most difficult part about breaking up was not that she wouldn't see me anymore, but that she wouldn't be able to hang around my family anymore. Even my father was upset at me!

That Sunday morning around 10 o'clock, Priscilla called Pam with the news.

"Doug's been in an accident," she said. The news hit Pam hard, and she began shaking involuntarily from head to toe. She wanted to know if I was going to live. Priscilla assured her that I was, and that I was going to pull out of it okay. At that point, she hung up the phone. Here was a man she loved, someone she felt destined to spend the rest of her life with, and now all of that was in question.

"I remember sitting on the couch with my mother," says Pam, "and just crying and saying, 'I don't know if I can do this.' My mother assured me, 'You can do this.'"

Pam and I finally spoke on the phone, and the tears flowed again. We knew we were headed toward a future together. What form that took, or where, was not fully defined, but the college kid stuff had morphed into an adult relationship with promise. Would that all change?

The morning Pam was due to visit the first time, I asked my mom to brush my teeth for me. The what-ifs melted when Pam walked over to me and crawled under the rack and onto the floor so that she could see my face, and kissed me (thus, the tooth brushing). Pam was somehow "reaffirming" that I was still the same guy she always knew and fell in love with—the only difference was how I would get around. At that moment, I was lifted up emotionally. To know there was a partner here who did not question her ability to look forward, helped me to do the same. Pam is a person who "assumes things will be fine." I needed that. Her visit filled me with a lot of optimism for the future.

Among the other people to visit that day was Dave Gonino, one of my best friends from college. Dave, Artie Banks and I met the very first day of our freshman year at the University at Albany in August 1978. We've been close ever since. We were in suites of six across the hall from each other at our UAlbany dorm—Artie and I in one suite and Dave in the other. Truth be told, we really functioned as a suite of 12. We looked out for each other and bonded in various subgroups at various times.

When Artie became a Resident Assistant (RA), he needed a pair for the other room in his suite. Dave and I slid right in, and the three of us would live together for the next three years, including in an off-campus apartment our senior year.

Dave, Artie and I are "I'll be right there" friends. We have supported each other through the divorces of Artie's and Dave's parents, the illness and death of Artie's dad, and the passing of my parents. We were best men at each others' weddings—all of this before we were 30. With few exceptions, for the past 35 years we've managed to stage a boys' weekend at one of our houses. For three wonderful days, we grant ourselves the right to act 20 again, smoking cigarettes, drinking too much vodka, tequila and beer, and telling stories from the old days.

When word of my accident reached Dave and later Artie, they both wanted to be there for me. And they were.

People know exactly where they were and what they were doing when JFK was assassinated and when the Towers fell on 9/11. Some personal events have the same kind of impact, and for some people, including Dave, my accident was such an event.

Dave was a regular at the Saratoga race track that summer. He was there that Sunday afternoon when he got the news from his father, Joe, about my accident. Joe assured him that I was okay, but the news was too much for Dave to absorb all at once and he blanked out for a short while. After a bit, he got in his car and drove to Buffalo, his mind racing the entire 300 miles as he sped along the New York State Thruway toward Priscilla's and then, Erie County Medical Center.

During that emotional five-hour drive to Buffalo, all kinds of rapid-fire thoughts blasted through Dave's head. "Was my best friend in the world going to die?" "What was his life going to be like moving forward?" "What am I going to say to him when I get to the hospital?" "How do I help him?"

When he walked into the hospital the next day, however, all of those fears quickly disappeared. There was all of this noise coming from one of the rooms down the hall—people talking and, most of all, laughing—and that's when Dave knew everything was going to be okay. My family and closest friends always try and keep things lighthearted, even in the most difficult of times, and we found ways to do just that in the hospital.

Dave would be the first one to tell Artie about my accident. Artie was living in Florida at the time on a four-month assignment selling encylopedias door-to-door. Artie had spent his summers throughout college doing this and it gave him the foundation to be a great, self-motivated salesman and executive. That said, we teased him unmercifully about his unique summer job.

As much as it killed Artie, he was near the end of his assignment and he wasn't able to come visit right away. He did call me a few days after my accident, and we chatted briefly. I told him that I was getting very good care at the hospital, and that I was enjoying all of the attention I was getting from the parade of visitors to my room. He said that the moment he made his last sale he'd come up and visit. True to his word, he was there the first week of September, where we had a good laugh about his book-selling career. (We still laugh about it today).

Dave and Artie connected me to my pre-injury life. I don't recall us talking a lot about my situation. We talked about real-life stuff—love interests, stories from our new careers, etc. And we laughed...a lot! Whether it's a defense mechanism or just a part of who I am, finding levity in a situation has always been a part of my problem-solving method. That doesn't mean that I don't get sad, especially when I think about what "might have been," but my life has been so blessed that I'm convinced my "might have been" may well have been worse if not for the accident.

Of all the visitors I had in the hospital after my accident, none was by my side longer or more often than Priscilla. Because I was immobilized for so long and unable to look around, I got really good at discerning sounds. The sound I anticipated most happened between 5 and 6 p.m. every day when the elevator swished open and high-heeled shoes clicked along the terrazzo floor some 50 yards away. My sister was here.

For 91 consecutive days, Priscilla came to my bedside after a long day at work and would end her days with me, leaving at 9 p.m. most nights. Priscilla carried the load for our small family. Mom was torn between two hospitals, dealing with my dad's cancer battle 200 miles away, and managing her own career. My sister and I had always been close, but these visits brought us even closer.

We'd always have dinner together which, for me, started

with hospital food being fed to me, eventually graduating to real food that Priscilla would bring with her from the outside. We talked, watched TV or just sat in silence. There was no pressure to keep up a conversation all the time. We laughed and we wept, either for my dad or me and my predicament.

There would be many other visitors during those 91 days. I had a regular date to share beers and watch Monday Night Football with another college friend who lived nearby. Others, mostly friends of Priscilla, would materialize at just the right time with real food, a newspaper, a joke or two, or even a foot massage from heaven. Thanks largely to their collective love, friendship and support, I began to realize that this unfortunate accident may not be the end of the world, but the start of something new.

THREE

WE'RE ENGAGED?

Until further notice, celebrate everything.

—Cheena Wright

When young people get engaged today, they plan full-blown productions. Scripts are written, scenarios are painstakingly choreographed and videos produced set to just the right music.

There was nothing remotely romantic about my proposal to Pam. Then again, I never expected to propose in a hospital room with a broken neck, my head stabilized in a hard, plastic "neck brace on steroids" called a Philadelphia collar, and my body paralyzed from the mid-chest down. Dropping to one knee was not an option. The truth of the matter is, I didn't even make a formal proposal. Our engagement was born out of a mutual discussion we were having about the future. It was as if it happened without either of us knowing it at the time. But that didn't seem to bother Pam because here we are today, happily married for nearly four decades.

I'm not sure love at first sight is a thing, but that's not how it happened for Pam and me. Ours was more of a gradual love story, maybe more like love at second or third sight. I first met Pam during the winter of my freshman year at the University at Albany, at a bowling alley of all places. I was part of a beer, er, bowling team, and Pam was a substitute for the team we were playing against one night. It was a cordial first meeting. There were no bells, no fireworks.

During my sophomore year, I would run into Pam periodically while doing my rounds in the cafeteria, where I happened to work alongside Pam's friend and roommate, Donna Murphy (known to all as "Murph"). Pam and I would strike up casual conversations, but nothing more. That all changed that spring when I had my first intimate date with Pam, along with 18,000 other people! Back in the day, UAlbany held what it called "Mayfest." It was, in my estimation, a most brilliantly conceived idea—eight hours of free music, beer and hot dogs that started at noon on the first Saturday in May. It's been described as UAlbany's annual springtime end of semester frolic and we took our responsibility to do so quite seriously.

The list of Mayfest headliners has been pretty impressive over the years, and has included Bruce Springsteen, U2 and Squeeze. The headliners for that year's Mayfest were David Bromberg and David Johansen (a.k.a. Buster Poindexter years later)—not exactly Bono or The Boss, but not too shabby for 1980. Back then, the event was held on a grassy lawn, now occupied by the Science Library, and required a large blanket or two. I attended the concert with Dave, Artie and the better part of our softball team, which was cleverly named "The Sultans of Swing" after the famous Dire Straits song.

We had played a game earlier that day, and it just so happened that Murph and Pam had come to watch the game because they knew some guys on my team. Murph had mentioned to Pam just that morning that there was this cute guy in the cafeteria (her words, not mine) that she should get to know, so when she pointed me out during the softball game you might say that the stars began to align for later that day.

After setting our blanket down, I looked up and noticed that just two blankets away were Pam, Murph and friends from their dorm suite. This time, when our eyes made contact, it was different. There was a spark. It was just a feeling but when I looked at her, I instinctively knew that this day was going to be different. And it was! At some point, Pam walked up behind me and casually "stole" the straw cowboy hat I had worn to the concert. I took this as a huge "Go" signal. We spent the entire day together listening to tunes, drinking beer and making out at the Campus Center. As Mayfest came to a close, we went to our separate dorms for a few hours and then reconnected later to go out downtown with friends.

Thus began what would become a blossoming summer romance. I was midway through my college career and I didn't have a job so Mom took pity on me and "hired" me to work on our family cottage in Skaneateles, some three hours west of Albany. The family had purchased the Cape Cod gray cottage two years earlier during my last year in high school. It was a rather small, simple cottage—600 square feet—but friends and extended family were always welcome and on some occasions, we might host as many as 25 people there. This was especially true each Memorial Day, Fourth of July and Labor Day when our small family and friends would gather to commemorate the start, middle and end of the summer.

Although Pam and I had just really begun to date, we were at that point (you know, that point) where being apart for even a few days was simply not an option. So I'd work at the cottage during the day, painting and performing other light repairs, call it quits around 3:00 in the afternoon, clean up and drive the three hours to Albany where Pam had an apartment and was temping as a Kelly Girl at the State Department of Education. The following morning, I'd head back to the cottage and start the cycle all over again. It sounds crazy to drive six hours back and forth each day, but I was young and in love, and my brain had yet to fully develop. It was a magical summer and Mom was none the wiser (I convinced myself) that I wasn't spending every waking moment at the cottage. Remember: This was 1980, which meant no cell phones, no texts and no FaceTime app.

I was drawn to Pam for more than just her looks. To this day, she has an innate compassion about her, caring about her students as their teacher, helping older folks and her close friends, nieces and nephews. It is one of those intangible qualities that draws two people together. She also had a good sense of humor (still does) and we shared a lot of common interests and friends. Oh, and she was a good party girl, too, which back then matched well with my interests and priorities.

Pam's home life was much different than mine, however. Instead of living in an IBM suburb, she grew up in rural Cherry Valley, N.Y. (not too far from Cooperstown and The Baseball Hall of Fame), where her parents, Norman and Marilyn Mollen, grew their own vegetables. Pam was the oldest of four siblings, which included two sisters, Diane and Kristine, and a brother, Jim, whereas I was the youngest of two. My dad worked at an office and was home every night for dinner; Pam's dad was a research scientist at the Lindsley F. Kimball New York Blood Center in New York City. He headed to New York on Sunday evenings on a Greyhound bus, stayed in a one-room flat in Queens where he had a lawn chair, TV and a hot plate, and returned late Thursday or early Friday morning after working four very long days.

Neither of our fathers graduated from college, yet both became accomplished, valued professionals, and garnered respect from their bosses and peers. Their work and their families were very important to them.

Pam and I dated that summer and throughout our junior and senior years. Then, I did a very stupid thing. I broke up with her. Why? Because I was 22. I had some wild oats to sow, I guess, and did so throughout the balance of 1982 and into 1983—my aforementioned "weird year."

The summer after graduating college, I landed the same job I had in high school at Friendly's Ice Cream (that made my mom and dad so proud after four years of college!), working about 60 hours a week. I had moved out of the apartment I shared with Dave and Artie, who went their separate ways, and moved in with a group of girls who had an extra room in their downtown Albany apartment on Warren Street. It would be another summer full of partying.

Pam and I didn't officially get back together until just two months prior to the accident. Dave and I had gone to visit Pam and her friend Kelly at their apartment on Sycamore Ave., and that evening served to "reintroduce" us. Basically, I got wise and Pam, bless her heart, decided to give me another chance. I guess I had sown my wild oats, but more importantly, I had come to the realization that I never had, nor ever would have, a better relationship than I had with Pam. I was pretty empty emotionally, and I needed her.

Things were really clicking between Pam and me in August

of '83, and I was planning for us to have a romantic dinner at The Krebs on Labor Day weekend, a local restaurant not too far from the cottage. The Krebs is an institution in Skaneateles. Founded in 1899 by Fred and Cora Krebs, this fine dining establishment has served three presidents—both Teddy and Franklin D. Roosevelt and Bill Clinton—as well as some notable celebrities, including ABC news anchor David Muir and the Baldwin brothers (Alec, Daniel, Billy and Stephen). Known for its seven-course meals and famous prime rib, The Krebs was where Skaneateles families, including my mom's, would go for a "special" family meal. This was where I wanted to propose to Pam.

Instead, Pam had to settle for my hospital room. And no engagement ring. I had planned to get a ring prior to Labor Day, as well as ask Pam's dad for his daughter's hand in marriage, but neither happened.

It had to be extremely difficult on Pam knowing how all this could've gone down, and how it wound up. It's not how anyone would picture that big day. We'd been talking about getting married earlier in the summer, after attending several weddings of college friends, and were very much aligned on a future together. And then I had to go and show off and break my neck, leaving Pam to ponder what could've been. It's every girl's desire to walk down the aisle and have a magical wedding before their family and friends. I wanted that for Pam, too. Yet we were able to look past those disappointments toward the anticipation of being together.

One mid-October day, about seven weeks after the accident, we were having a mutual discussion in my hospital room about our future and us living together, and what that would be like with my disability. We talked about the idea of getting married, sort of in the abstract at first, and in the context of everything going on. At some point, it must have all clicked because we looked at each other and said, "Did we just get engaged?" And we both responded with a quick "Yes." There was no proposal—from either of us. Instead, the question kind of popped itself.

At that point, our attention turned to our parents. Mine were having dinner in Buffalo that night with Uncle Jim and Aunt Marilyn, and Pam's parents were in Cherry Valley. I recall both of us thinking: "What are our families going to think?" Were they going to think we were nuts? Try and talk us out of our plans or convince us that we were being naïve and didn't know what we were doing? Would they be angry or worried?

As it turns out, it was none of the above. They were overjoyed by the news and shared in our celebration. There was only happiness and delight in our decision. Now, I can't say whether conversations outside our room had a different tone, but I don't think so. I never heard a negative comment about our marrying each other. Just the contrary. They were thrilled for us.

I shouldn't have been surprised. We'd been together for a long time, albeit with some false starts along the way. I joked sometimes, only half kidding, that my dad liked Pam more than me! At one point early in our dating relationship, I remember telling him that I was coming to the cottage alone as Pam and I were on the outs. He responded by saying he'd rather see her than me. He knew I was making a mistake.

My mom and sister Priscilla did offer Pam several off-ramps, and I'm glad they did, and especially glad Pam didn't take them. On one of Pam's initial trips to the hospital my mom told her, "We will not think any less of you if you decide this is not for you." Priscilla echoed Mom's sentiment, adding that Pam needed to do what was best for her future.

But Pam was resolute. She never thought for a moment about leaving me, that it just wasn't an option. She said there were so many things she loved about me and that she looked forward to having a great life together. And she was very convincing.

Would I have done the same if the roles had been reversed, and it was Pam bound to a lifetime in a wheelchair? I would love to unequivocally say "Yes." But do I know that for sure? I just don't know. I was 23 and full of myself. I loved her and would have been right by her side, but for the long haul? Boy, I hope so.

It might sound crazy that I even contemplated proposing to Pam just weeks after suffering from this life-altering accident. I hadn't even mastered the wheelchair yet and here I was asking Pam to be my wife. So, indeed, it was crazy. On the other hand, it's what 20-something-year-olds do. We didn't take the longer view on things. We were happy to enter the unknown with gusto, ready to tackle whatever came our way. At least it was that way for us.

The reality is that getting engaged was our way to commit to one another. We'd only just recently reunited, but I think deep down we knew we'd end up together. By deciding that we would get married, we were also saying, "Yep, we are going to get past all this and we're going to have a life and let's just focus on that."

At that moment, despite my circumstance, I knew just how baseball legend Lou Gehrig felt when he said, "Today, I consider myself the luckiest man on the face of this earth." Pam probably saved my life—at least, emotionally. Could I have moved forward with my life without her by my side? I think so, but without her full support and her mutual optimism about the future, I'm sure it would have been an emotional struggle for me for a very long time. With her by my side, I was genuinely very excited about the future and very optimistic looking forward. I felt like I could live a somewhat normal life, which was something I felt quite uncertain about when lying on that trampoline.

I was indeed the luckiest man on the face of the earth, although the "luck" I feel now is exponentially greater because of the awesome life we built together.

FOUR

Rehab and Departure

*And once the storm is over, you won't remember how you made
it through, how you managed to survive. You won't even be sure
whether the storm is really over. But one thing is certain. When you
come out of the storm, you won't be the same person who walked in.
That's what this storm's all about.*

—Haruki Murakami

As you understand by now, I have a generally optimistic
outlook. I'm also a realist. I knew that I wasn't walking out of Erie County Medical Center on my own two feet.
Sometime during my three long months there, I did begin to
visualize leaving under my own power...in a wheelchair.

In my first 10 days in the hospital, I had regularly been
spun like a rotisserie chicken and had undergone six hours of
surgery to fuse my neck back together. That was the medical
stuff. The real rigorous stuff was still to come, as I had yet to
meet the therapy sisters—occupational and physical.

Occupational therapy had nothing to do with preparing
me for the workforce. Instead, it prepared me to be human
again and to execute the activities of daily living (ADLs) in
some adapted way. As my neck stabilized and healed from
surgery, my next step, so to speak, was to move from acute
treatment to rehabilitation, where I was going to learn how
to live with this "thing" I now had to embrace—my disability.

This was another stage, another transition, another
graduation. A few weeks earlier, I was in shock, not able to
even think about living the rest of my life with a disability.

But now I was ready (mostly because they told me I was) to take on some of these new challenges. Occupational therapy focused mainly on fine motor skills and ADLs, such as eating, bathing, shaving, using the bathroom, etc. I had to learn how to perform these tasks anew—all of which I took for granted prior to the afternoon of August 20, 1983.

Initially, I was presented with blocks and simple puzzles to put together to assess how well my hands worked. That didn't go well. Another recalibration of expectations. During the first six weeks or so after my accident my hands functioned like those of a typical C5 quadriplegic. I had very limited finger movement and no thumb activity. This made holding a fork, comb, toothbrush or anything at all impossible without some adaptive equipment, or the help of a family member or friend.

My first attempts at feeding myself came about 10 days into my hospital stay, and it was at once embarrassing, humiliating and hysterical. I really did look like a 2-year-old after I was done, especially on spaghetti night! Initially, I was just eating with my hands. It was good practice to try to pick up items and deliver them to my mouth, although I wasn't always successful. My hands weren't working properly. It was as though I knew what I wanted them to do but I just couldn't get them to behave. This got to be very frustrating, but eventually motivating.

After a time, I tried to use an adaptive device that my therapist gave me to feed myself. It wrapped around my right hand and allowed for a utensil to be inserted into the palm of my hand. It worked to some extent, although it still proved very challenging to keep the food from getting all over myself, the dinner tray or my bed sheets.

Then, happily, I began to get some return of function in my right hand. This is not unusual as swelling to the spinal column dissipates, but it is neither predictable nor guaranteed. It was one of those things that just happened. One day my brain sent signals to my hand and they got through, where the day before they had not. My hand was weak, but it worked. I began to deliver food to my mouth the way I did before my accident and hold a pencil (or someone else's hand) and grasp my bed covers. It was a special moment. I still couldn't grasp any objects with my left hand—nor can I to this day—but I have devised ways to use this hand as a stabilizing device and hold things by bracing them against my body or my right hand.

Being able to regain the use of my right hand was monumental, but it did little to alleviate my anxiety or struggles to manage some of my other bodily functions. A spinal cord injury like mine affects sensation and mobility below the level of the injury—which, in my case, is from the mid-chest down. This includes limb movement as well as bodily functions. I have no control over my bladder or bowel function. Yes, that's as potentially gross and demeaning as it sounds. It meant being catheterized four to six times a day in the hospital and learning how to catheterize myself, which I still do. It also meant I had to be given a suppository every other day to stimulate my bowels and force them to evacuate—in bed, while a nurse assists and cleans.

The graduation to actually transferring onto and using a toilet took as long as eight or more weeks after the injury. That's a long time for a 23-year-old to feel like an infant with a dirty diaper!

Over the years I've had to train my body and become adept at both stimulating and suppressing my need to go to the bathroom. It's a process that persists to this day, and it is by no means foolproof. Bladder and bowel accidents do happen, sometimes in public with no ability to do anything but sit in the mess until I can get to a toilet and a shower. This has instilled in me a constant "what if it happens here" vigilance. To this day, wherever I am, I always have an escape plan in mind and a cover story ready. I got to know my body very well. I was determined to live a normal life, not defined by a disability. This drove me to pay attention to every signal from my body that I could and learn how to manage it.

The hardest adaptation I had to make was when I started flying frequently for work. About twice a month for a period of 15 years, I was traveling somewhere in North America. Talk about a recipe for disaster! Here I was in an airplane seat that I can't get up from, with no way to get to the airplane rest room. Fortunately—or you might say out of necessity—I would dehydrate for up to 12 hours prior to any flight to be sure my bladder was empty. That wasn't too hard to do. The bowel part was a little trickier.

I worried A LOT about having a bowel accident on an airplane. The humiliation associated with that, especially the inability to move and the impact on surrounding passengers, would have been unbearable. I worried about that so much at the beginning that I thought it might become self-fulfilling. I talked to my doctor about this and I remember saying, "I just wish there was a pill I could take that would ensure that I wouldn't poop when I didn't want to." He said: "There is. It's called IMODIUM®. Sometimes I tell little old ladies to take it and they don't poop for a week!" He was right, and I have gotten very good at understanding how this drug affects my body. I sometimes say that Imodium helped my career. I would not have been able to travel like I did without the reassurance it provided. (Author's note: don't try this without consulting your doctor!).

I've also had to get comfortable with wearing an external catheter and urine collection bag on my left leg. This can make for some interesting conversations on airplanes. I remember one particular flight shortly after 9/11 when the traveling public was both nervous and hyper-alert. I was sitting in seat 1A, one of my favorites (first class/window/bulkhead), on an early morning flight. Typically, with bulkhead legroom, I sit with one leg crossed at the ankle over my other knee. This day, it was my left leg that was up. That's where I wear my leg bag, and it exposed the small blue twist valve I use to empty it when necessary.

Before we took off, I could see the man next to me having a conversation with his wife across the aisle. He kept glancing at me. Finally, he leaned over to me and asked what the device was under my pant leg, because his wife was afraid it was something of nefarious intent. I calmly explained that it was not, in fact, a bomb, but a urine collection device. This was a natural conversation and I put them at ease. Frankly, I'm not even sure they knew I used a wheelchair since we were already on the plane. Maybe they thought it was a convenient travel strategy.

I frequently have TSA officers look at me quizzically when they discover the bag. If it's full I let them take a good close look. We all lost our "right to privacy" getting on a plane a long time ago. I learned fairly quickly that I could treat these incidents as reasons to be angry and annoyed at people, or as opportunities to educate them. I've chosen the latter.

With a little medication and a lot of discipline, I've learned how to gain control over my bodily functions. It's really just a matter of having a regular routine and being quite precise about when I use the bathroom. I even have to arrange my travel schedule and board meetings around it. I have to think ahead to plan for these basic functions.

Early on, this process took a toll on me emotionally. Here I was, 23 years-old, and I was back in diapers. How long would this go on? This was one of the things I despised most about my time in the hospital and rehabilitation: I hated not knowing how long certain phases were going to take and not knowing what was around the corner. I couldn't picture what life was going to look like. I'm a planner and a long-term thinker, and this uncertainty was not compatible with my mindset. How was I going to live my life, day in and day out, for the next decade or two or three?

Physical therapy was another matter. This is where strength and conditioning come into play. The physical therapist is more like a drill sergeant, challenging you to do more of everything—to take your wheelchair farther, lift heavier weights and so on. This felt natural to me as it harkened back to my coach/athlete relationships.

One of my first challenges was simply to get out of bed and into the wheelchair—and vice versa. That's not as easy as it may sound, and it's still work all these years later. Fortunately, I am very blessed to have the full use of my triceps muscles, another of those "gifts of functional return" as the swelling receded.

The triceps is a relatively small player in your upper arm, but it means the world to me. It does the pushing and the lifting. Without it properly functioning, I would be in a power chair instead of a manual wheelchair. I wouldn't be able to drive a car nor would I be able to lift myself up; someone else would have to lift me. These muscles play a huge role in my independence.

There are lots of ways to transfer yourself from your wheelchair to your bed, vehicle, favorite chair, airline seat, etc. Some use a "slide board" to scooch from one surface to another. Others scooch without the board, using the assistance of handrails or another individual. With practice and strength, I was able to graduate from a slide board to the "modified stand and pivot" method of transfer. It's modified because I don't really stand, but I have enough muscle tone in my right leg to bear some weight on it, so that it can act as a stabilizer while I swing my hips to wherever I'm transferring. One note of caution: I have learned over a lifetime that a few drinks greatly reduces that right leg tone, so transferring under the influence can be risky!

Transferring is a fundamental part of my everyday life. As a matter of fact, I recently had a second shoulder surgery and was talking to my cousin Brad about transfers. He had never given much thought to the vital role my shoulders play in my ability to get out of my wheelchair, and hence why the shoulder repair was so dramatic for me. For 90-plus days I would lose the ability to transfer—and my independence—while my shoulder healed. Brad asked me how I would get my strength back in the shoulder and I said, "Just by doing it." He replied, "Yeah, but that's only twice a day. It will take you forever."

It's one of those things you wouldn't think about unless you had to do it, and I explained the math. On a typical day, I will transfer in and out of my chair 16 to 18 times. It's six before I even leave the house (out of bed, into the shower, out of the shower, onto the bed to dress, off of the bed after dressing, into the car). A trip to my former office and then out to lunch, plus a couple errands would get me near 20 transfers pretty quickly. When I was traveling a lot for business, including airplanes, taxis, rental cars, trains, etc., I easily transferred in and out of my chair 40 times a day. And remember: Each transfer involves lifting 175-200 pounds, depending on how my diet is going. Human shoulders really weren't designed for that level of abuse.

That simple transfer out of bed was truly the first step toward independence. I recall some struggle, but was able to complete the maneuver, at which point some gathered staff congratulated me and someone said, "Ok, now spin forward." Spin forward—those words stuck with me. It reflects my fundamental mindset, how I try to live my life, looking forward, anticipating, planning, succeeding. Thus, it became the title of this book and the name of my consulting company.

But spinning forward for the first time in a wheelchair was easier said than done. I first had to figure out how to move the chair. There's a fair amount of coordination that has to take place in order to move a wheelchair. It's kind of like rowing a boat, where you need to apply more pressure on one side to make it turn. So there was a good deal of overcorrection as I learned this skill. I remember being up against the wall more than once which, of course, teaches you how to back up!

I had to use every muscle at my disposal in order to move

the oversized, overweight hospital chair—shoulders, biceps, triceps, etc. Since I don't have strong core muscles, I have learned how to lean into the push without going too far. When I slip, I end up with my head in my lap and I have a very difficult time sitting back up.

A little bit about wheelchairs: If there was anything good about the timing of my accident, it was how it related to the evolution of wheelchair design. Throughout the first three quarters of the 20th century a company called Everest & Jennings had a virtual monopoly on design, manufacturing and sales of wheelchairs in the U.S. After being found liable for antitrust violations by the Department of Justice in the 1970s, other companies began to take market share. The E&J chairs were real tanks. Made of tubular steel, they were indestructible and therefore very, VERY heavy. This was inconvenient for user and companion alike.

In 1979, a company called Quadra developed the first lightweight aluminum wheelchair. It weighed in at 30 pounds compared to E&J's 50-plus pound models. My first chair in the hospital was an E&J. It was good training, but I was thrilled that the first chair I owned myself was a Quadra. By comparison, the chair I use today weighs just 23 pounds. One ironic note: Until 1992 Everest & Jennings was headquartered in Camarillo, California—the same town we lived in from 1969-70. More on California later.

Besides learning how to move and operate the chair, my physical therapy also consisted of a number of strength exercises with stretchy bands. It was all hard, and at times discouraging because I was so fit and active prior to the accident. At times during those first few frustrating days of physical therapy, I wanted to punch a hole through the wall. I had to work through the anguish, and recalibrate both mentally and physically, to get through each session. But like anything else, when you see progress you want to do more.

My first physical therapist was an athletic, very friendly young man named Dave. We had a lot to talk about during our sessions, especially sports. Unfortunately, Dave would also make a sport of our physical therapy sessions and would get a kick out of making me pass out. After lying in bed for six weeks "patiently" counting the holes in the ceiling or the specks on the tile floor just to pass the time, it was Dave's job to prepare me to become an active member of society once again. The way to do this, apparently, was for him to strap me to what's known as a standing table—an 8- x 4-foot piece of plywood with a foot pedal on the bottom. Once strapped in, he would "stand" me up and I would subsequently pass out, usually in a matter of seconds.

In layman's terms, the reason I lost consciousness was because my inner ear was all messed up, causing my equilibrium to be out of whack. This therapy apparently had some sort of therapeutic benefit—it's also good for the longer bones of the legs and for increasing circulation in the legs—although I'm sure my therapist benefited most by it. I'm convinced he wanted to see how fast he could get me to pass out. To him it was great fun. To me, it was just another part of the journey on this roller coaster ride.

My occupational therapist, Sue, wasn't nearly as sadistic. Quite the contrary: She became a friend. She would talk to me about her upcoming wedding plans while she was teaching me how to perform certain functions. When doing repetitious actions like putting food on a fork and eating, it's nice to have a conversation about something else.

The hardest thing I had to do in physical therapy was learn how to climb into my chair from the floor. This requires strength, balance and a bit of technique. This was taught to patients who were able so that they could independently recover from a fall. It took me a number of attempts over three or four days, but I finally mastered this skill and luckily have not had to use it all that often. After almost 40 years and two rotator cuff repairs, I could NOT do this now. In fact, I stopped being able to lift myself off the floor a long time ago. I was on a business trip a decade ago when I fell out of my chair. I was "chair napping" in my room and fell forward (I have since learned to chair nap with a table in front of me), and had to call two associates who were at the same hotel to come help me up. This required me to scooch on my butt over to the door to unlock it. Thankfully, I could reach the knob.

Had my associates not been there, I would have had to call hotel security, and I'd do just about anything to avoid having to make that call. Case in point: I was once on a hotel toilet in Seattle when the seat bolts came loose as I tried to transfer back to my wheelchair, causing me to fall into the toilet. I was able to lift myself out of the toilet but could not get into my chair so I ended up on the floor. I needed a stable surface high enough to allow me to transfer myself into the chair, so I scooched a good distance on the floor to the bed while dragging my chair behind me.

I tried to get up on the bed several times by "climbing" up the sheets, but all this did was bring the sheets and comforter down on my head. Undeterred, I squirmed my way on the floor to the head of the bed and tied a sheet to the headboard, from which I was able to pull myself up on to the bed. All of this took about an hour. I was completely exhausted, but I dug deep to find enough strength to get dressed and go down to the hotel bar, where I enjoyed a much-deserved martini.

Over the years I have shared this particular incident many times with family and friends. I love to tell stories about my travels and this one always gets a good laugh.

In addition to daily therapy sessions, there were other people and other unusual blessings that seemed to happen for no rhyme or reason that made my stay at the hospital bearable, and helped me get through my darkest hours. Things fell into a sort of routine, which was good for me.

There was my sister Priscilla's friend Kathy who gave these glorious foot massages. She said she was studying "reflexology," and needed the practice. I didn't care what she was studying and told her she could practice all she wanted. There was my friend Jeff from college who lived in nearby Lockport, N.Y. He would arrive weekly at my bedside to watch Monday Night Football with prime rib sandwiches and cold beers. And, of course, there was Priscilla there every night, heels clicking down the corridor, just like clockwork.

FIVE

My Battle for Independence Begins

*The future will present insurmountable problems
only when we consider them insurmountable.*

—Thomas S. Monson

I vividly remember my first day pass from the hospital. It was part of the therapy and recovery process to "let me out" now and then. It was important for me and my family to get used to managing things on our own, without the safety net of nurses and therapists nearby to solve problems. With combined excitement and trepidation, Pam and I rolled out of the hospital for the first time.

It was October 1983, less than two months after the accident, and I was in this big, heavy, clunky wheelchair. But I was outside the four walls of ECMC. There were two big events that day. First, Pam and I went to pick out her engagement ring at a local Kay Jewelers store. Pam drove us in the yellow Datsun B210 she had at the time. It was our first effort using a transfer board to get in and out of the car, which went pretty well. (Thankfully, I wouldn't need that board for long.) She picked out a narrow gold band with a microscopic diamond, but it meant the world to us.

That evening was our engagement party at Priscilla's apartment. Unfortunately, her apartment was on the third floor and had no elevator. The place was not even remotely wheelchair accessible. It wouldn't take me long to realize just how few places were wheelchair accessible. The church we would be married in the following year wasn't accessible. The office I would return to work at was inaccessible but for a homemade ramp. The Americans with Disabilities Act (ADA), after all, was still six years away.

My friends adapted almost immediately. Even in those early days after I was released from the hospital, our friends took us everywhere. We were all young enough and naive enough, I guess, to think that this whole "wheelchair experience" hadn't changed anything. Once I was stable and out of danger, I was back to being Doug. I used a wheelchair to get around, but I was still me. Even I started to believe it. There were things we did back then that seem crazy now, but we were determined to live life...to spin forward.

So on that night in October, Priscilla's boyfriend Jack, her roommate's boyfriend Donn, and Uncle Jim had to haul me up to the third floor. One step at a time, we planned and lifted, planned and lifted. We did that a lot back then. I didn't mind because I was safely in my chair and my friends were young and strong. I don't do it now, however, not even one step if I can help it. I've been dropped a few times over the years and, as I like to say, "My family and friends aren't getting any younger and I'm not getting any lighter."

I am always a little nervous in situations where I can't easily or independently get out, in case of a fire, for example. If there had been one in Priscilla's apartment that night, it would have been very difficult to get me and everyone else out safely. Ironically, very few hotels have accessible first floor rooms. Most accessible rooms are on upper levels, and I've stayed in thousands of them. To this day, I look with some curiosity at that little picture by the elevator that says "in case of fire, use the stairs."

The engagement party would not be the last time that I would be moved, physically and mentally, out of my comfort zone. I do not like being dependent on others. Independence is one of those things you don't think about until you don't have it. The root of the word "depend" is innocent enough. I can "depend" on my bank to keep my accounts accurate. Hopefully, I can depend on my car to start in the morning, and I'd really like to depend on the New York Mets to win this year. But to be "dependent" is much different. It is a burden to the dependent person and equally to those upon whom you are dependent.

There are degrees of dependency and I went through them all during my initial recovery, and I still struggle with some today. Initially, I was in shock and completely dependent on others for everything from feeding myself, relieving myself and moving in bed, just to name a few. All I could do was talk and begin the process of learning how to ask for help. In a matter of hours, I went from being a very active 23-year-old to someone who needed to be fed like a baby by his sister, mother and girlfriend. It was very sobering and humbling, to say the least.

I'm not alone in the quest for independence, but the wheelchair sort of forces the issue on me sometimes. For example: We have good friends who live in a split ranch house. The husband is a strong guy whom I completely trust to lift me from floor to floor, but I don't like that he has to do it. Not only am I dependent on him, I really don't want to be the cause of anyone's back injury.

Of course, there are times I've had to completely rely on the goodness—and muscles—of others to get me out of some serious jams. I have enough stories to fill a few chapters. One particular experience stands out. It happened in 2005, when I was traveling for my company, VersaTrans. We had an office in Missoula, Montana, that I visited quarterly. By this time, traveling had become pretty routine for me—book a flight, rent a car, book a hotel room, attend meetings and head home. In those days, I rented a large Chevy Monte Carlo—the same car I had at home—so lifting my chair in and out of the car was natural and I felt like any other business traveler.

I was heading home on this particular morning. At 4:30 a.m., as I was getting ready for a 6 a.m. flight back to Albany, high-pitched fire alarms began blaring. I would later learn that a 14-foot high truck had driven into the hotel's 12-foot high portico and ripped out the sprinkler system's main pipe. The elevators were shut down and I started to question how I was going to make my way down three flights of stairs and get to the airport in less than an hour.

"This is not good," I thought, so I called the front desk. "I've got a problem," I told the receptionist, sharing my predicament with her. She tried her best to put my concerns to rest. "We'll take care of it."

In a few minutes, there was a knock at my door. Four fairly sturdy looking guys were ready to take me downstairs. I was quite grateful and maybe a bit surprised by the prompt service. As we made our way to the stairwell, I instructed my escorts on the best way to do this, and we began the step-by-step bounce down the stairs. As we got into a rhythm making our way down, I mentioned (mostly just for something to say) that "I hoped not to miss my flight."

The guy in back, holding me upright with the push handles of my chair asked, "Are you on Delta to Salt Lake?"

"Yes," I said.

"Don't worry," he said, "I'm your pilot. You're not going to miss your flight."

He greeted me like an old friend 45 minutes later as I rolled into the cabin of his Boeing 737 to my favorite seat, 1A.

Interestingly, there are times when people are not aware that I use a wheelchair. This has led to a few awkward "teachable moments," like the time I needed to get new tires on my car. I drove to the local tire shop just to see if they had the tires I needed. It was the late 1980s, so there were no cell phones yet, and I didn't feel like getting my chair out and rolling into the store just to ask that question. So I drove around to the front of the store, rolled down my window and called out to a worker under a car on a lift. The guy stopped what he was doing, gave me a perturbed look and shouted at me from 50 feet away: "If you want something, come over here. Are your legs broken?"

I was underwhelmed with his customer relations and I had a choice to make: Do I just drive away, do I get angry and rip into this guy, or do I "teach" him something? I took the high road.

I waved him over and he grudgingly left his bay and walked toward my vehicle. As he approached, I answered his question: "No, my legs aren't broken, I'm a quadriplegic. That's my wheelchair in the back." He looked skyward out of embarrassment and wasn't sure what to say. I simply asked if he had tires the right size for my car. Sadly, he did not.

I suspect he remembered that exchange and maybe he's better for it. I have found that proactively educating people gets me better service and hopefully puts them more at ease in their next encounter with a person needing help.

There is one other place where my disability isn't immediately evident to others and can lead to some teachable moments, and that's on an airplane. I am typically the first person to get on the plane. When you hear the gate agent say the following words over the loudspeaker, "Those needing additional time or assistance may pre-board," that's me.

To board the plane, I roll down the jetway and out of view of the other passengers who will be joining me in a few minutes. I then transfer into an aisle (or "straight back") chair which fits down the narrow aisle of the plane. At this point, the ground crew takes my wheelchair and stores it in the belly of the plane for the flight. I then transfer into the airline seat and they take the aisle chair away. My disability is now invisible, which is why I ALWAYS reserve a window seat.

There are three good reasons for this: 1) I like it; 2) if I'm in an aisle seat, people boarding the plane will expect me to get up so that they can get to their window or middle seat, which requires me to repeatedly explain that "I can't stand" (people are typically understanding, but it becomes cumbersome for them to climb over me); and 3) if I'm in an aisle seat and one of my row-mates needs to use the bathroom, they have to climb over me again. Twice! And for some reason, that person is always in their 70s or 80s and has a gas problem. Not pleasant for Doug!

Another interesting phenomenon occurs in large gathering places, such as malls, theme parks, airports and sporting venues. I can be rolling along down a corridor or pathway and approaching from the other direction will be a mother and father with their two young kids. From as far as 50 yards away, they will start adjusting their direction and harnessing their kids so as to avoid me. They do this with panic in their eyes and fear for their safety, as if I'm determined to run their kids down with my wheelchair.

I know they are trying to be courteous, but it can be comical at times. I've gotten good at indicating from a distance which direction I will be going, and that I mean no harm to their family. There have been times when I'll hear the kids ask questions like, "Why does he use that chair?" or, "What's wrong with him?" I'm okay with that and am always happy to talk to them, but their parents usually want to skirt past my chair and move on as quickly as possible.

Adults can be funny. One time, Pam, Priscilla, my cousins David and Brad and their wives were in the Finger Lakes Region and we decided to go on a wine tasting tour. The front door to one winery was up four steps, so we asked if there was a handicap accessible entrance we could use. The owner said, "Sure, go over to that garage door and we can let you in that way." We went over to the door, as directed, and as it went up it revealed another step to get in. I indicated that this was still a problem, and one guy said (I kid you not), "Can't you walk, just a little?" I tried not to skip a beat and responded, "Nope, not even a little bit." Now, I try to be fair. There are a number of people who use wheelchairs that can stand a bit, but they don't look like me and their chairs don't look like mine. I wound up staying outside the winery while the others in my group went on the tour.

I wish I had a dollar for every time we asked if a restaurant was accessible and the response was, "Sure, it's only a step or two."

While many of these incidents were frustrating to me, I learned to accept them and use them as ways to educate others so that they'd be more respectful and understanding, and not just jump to conclusions. In terms of my own quest for independence, it was largely progressive. By that, I mean I had frequent successes and a few frustrating failures. I still do. It's a learning process. The last thing I ever want to do is ask for help. Something as simple as opening a door—especially inward, toward myself—was a skill to be mastered. So I worked at it, and when I got it, I did it over and over again.

It can get discouraging when you think you have it, then fail, and someone has to help you. I remember one night when Pam and I were getting ready to go out to a local bar to meet some friends. It was no more than nine months after the accident, and we were still getting used to simple things like going out to eat or going to the movies. We were leaving our apartment and something happened at the doorway. I still don't know how, but I ended up falling backward in my chair and onto the floor. Then, it took both of us seemingly forever as we struggled to get me situated and back in my chair.

The whole process threw me into a terrible mood. One minute I was excited and eager to go out and see our friends, and the next minute I was reminded that I had this terrible situation, and that I was totally dependent on Pam and others. I was embarrassed that I was no longer "that cool, athletic, put-together guy," but a disabled man, and I completely lost the mood to go out. Pam, on the other hand, was eager to get out of the apartment and enjoy a "normal" night. There had been so few of these normal nights in the nine months after my accident, and my change in mood angered and saddened her and the reality of everything kind of came crashing down on both of us. It was a terrible night. We wound up staying in and it was completely my fault.

I still hate to think about how much I disappointed Pam that night. In fact, we still talk about it now and then. It was clearly a low point in my struggle to regain my independence and adapt to my new life.

Of all the things that did help me feel somewhat independent again, especially in the early going while I was in the hospital, none was bigger than my graduation from my heavy, clunky, hospital-assigned wheelchair to the more slick, lightweight Quadra wheelchair. I know this sounds like a commercial, but the 50-pound Everest & Jennings behemoth I first had to learn how to drive was unfit for a person with a previous active lifestyle such as mine, and getting the Quadra proved to be a godsend. It was sleek, sporty and cool, and far easier to lift and transport than the horribly institutionalized hospital model.

Quadra was the first of the lightweight "sports" chairs. It was created by Jeff Minnebraker, a licensed pilot and actor best known for the films, Get It Together (1976) and Coming Home (1978). Minnebraker was also an L1 paraplegic with an engineering streak. He got his pilot's license after an automobile accident left him paralyzed below the waist. Rick Miner, who produced, wrote and edited Get It Together, a documentary film about Minnebraker's life, said Minnebraker started the era of wheelchair sports and taught himself and others how to play wheelchair rugby, basketball and tennis after becoming a recreational therapist.

I will always remember the first time I saw a new aluminum Quadra wheelchair. I was lying in my bed at ECMC and my PT

Dave rolled it into the room. It was a demo model on loan from the company. My immediate impression was that it looked more like a bicycle than a wheelchair. Honestly, that's just because it had an orange frame, not silvery steel like every wheelchair in the world at the time. "I could look cool in that," I thought.

But they didn't come cheap, even back then. The Quadra wheelchair I purchased back in 1983 cost roughly the same as one does today, around $2,600. (That would equate to about $6,800 in today's dollars.) I recall a bit of a struggle to get the insurance company to pay, as these models were brand new to the market. That chair brought me an emotional lift and gave me hope that there was life outside of the hospital. I had my first Quadra wheelchair for a decade.

Another lift came from my good friend Artie Banks. At a particularly low period while I was still in this hospital, I rolled down the hallway with Artie to the elevator. I was bummed that he was leaving and, frankly, just bummed in general. I had experienced a bad day, although I don't remember why. Then Artie asked me a pointed question. Artie was always direct.

"How long do you think it's going to take to get used to all this?" he asked, referring to my wheelchair and all that it represented.

How do you answer a question like that? It wasn't rhetorical and it touched upon the unknown: What did the future hold for me? I had no idea what was coming, even tomorrow. I was playing this whole disability thing by ear. In that moment, I figured it took me 23 years to get where I was before the accident, so it would probably take another 23 years to come to terms with this new identity. So, that's what I told Artie as he was about to leave. "Twenty-three years," I said.

In Artie's mind, my answer was wrong and his words still resonate with me.

"Nah!" he said emphatically. "You've got this," as the doors to the elevator closed.

This was Artie being Artie, thank God. He probably had no clue at the time just how those four words would penetrate my head and lift my heart. The things people say—how simple, yet how powerful, they can be. What may have seemed like an inconsequential and off-the-cuff comment before catching an elevator, elevated me.

I turned 180 degrees and began to roll myself back to my room, thinking: "Maybe I'm farther along than I think I am."

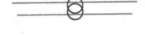

SIX

GROWING UP IBM

*No subject occupies more executive time at IBM than
the well-being of our employees and their families.*

—Thomas J. Watson (1958)

If there was ever an idyllic time and place to grow up, it was the 1960s and 70s in Crestview Heights, a neatly-cropped subdivision located just west of Endicott, New York.

Crestview's curvy streets were tucked into the rolling hills of New York's southern tier. There were 500 or so colonial- and ranch-style homes on quarter-acre lots. Like ours, almost every home housed an IBM family. Our neighbors were IBM families, and our schools and churches were filled with IBM families. Crestview Heights existed, almost exclusively, for executives, engineers, accountants and salesmen who worked at the International Business Machines corporation.

Although we didn't see it then, my sister and I now refer to Crestview Heights as "Stepford," after the satirical 1975 novel and movie, The Stepford Wives. It was very homogeneous— lots of families of four with two cars and dogs. And a lot of bikes. There were no highways nearby, so we kids rode our bikes everywhere from 7 a.m. till dark. I had a group of four or five guys I hung out with, and all of the moms had to be prepared to feed five growing boys on demand as we rotated from house to house for lunch. It was all very safe, very familiar and very IBM. Truly a company neighborhood and suburban heaven.

My parents, the former Mary Jane Fisher and Morris Douglas Hamlin, met as freshmen in 1953 while attending what was then known as the New York State College for Teachers. It is now known as the University at Albany. Dad was drafted into the Army the following year, where he "fought" the waning days of the Korean conflict at Fort Dix, New Jersey.

After being discharged from the Army, Dad landed a job at IBM, and started on May 6, 1956—which would be my birthday four years later. IBM was hiring every smart person they could find at the time. Even though my dad was neither an engineer nor scientist, he applied for and was hired into their procurement group, where he negotiated equipment and services contracts for the labs and computer rooms.

Dad worked at the Federal Systems Division (FSD) in Owego, New York, an eight-mile drive from our house in Crestview and about 15 minutes west of Endicott. FSD did all of the defense contract work including radar guidance for jets, ships and missiles. Eventually, they would do groundbreaking work on the computer systems for the space shuttle.

Dad never returned to college. Instead, he moved on, marrying my mom in July of 1956. (He had proposed to her in an Albany bar that would become one of my college hangouts 25 years later). In August of '57, my sister Priscilla was born. I arrived two-and-a-half years after that.

It was about this time that my mom and dad—Midge and Mo to their friends—bought their first home in an adjacent subdivision known as Pine Knoll. It was a white ranch-style home with red shutters that was all of 900 square feet. Pine Knoll was sort of like the minor leagues compared to Crestview Heights. Whoever coined the term "starter home" had a place like Pine Knoll in mind. It was a nice, safe neighborhood that was meant to be an early stop on the road to success for those rising through the ranks of IBM.

Pine Knoll was a place where parents could leave their young children at home to stroll next door for a visit with neighbors. In those days, your neighbors were your closest friends. When Mom went to the hospital to deliver me, Priscilla stayed at a neighbor's house. Once, when I was 1 or 2 years-old, Mom and Dad put us to bed in the bedroom that Priscilla and I shared and told us to go to sleep. Then, while I know this may sound strange by today's sensibilities, they headed across the street to visit with friends. I woke up and began whimpering and Priscilla gently chided me.

"You can't cry now," she whispered into my crib. "You have to go back to sleep."

So, I did. I've always respected my sister.

I'd be lying if I told you I had many memories of this first house. What I do remember is the big cement porch out front. On warm sunny days my mother would hand me a coffee can full of water and a paintbrush and have me "paint" the front porch. When the porch dried (almost immediately), she'd tell me I should paint it again.

My mom was brilliant. All this painting kept me busy for hours.

It was while living in this house that I attended kindergarten and took my first bus ride, which would prove prophetic. It was also here where Mom began her life as the quintessential IBM wife, a role she'd play to perfection for 16 years. When she was pregnant with Priscilla, she quit her job as a high school English teacher to join the legion of other housewives just like her, taking care of the kids and making our house a home.

It was a happy home. My sister and I got along famously. We had the typical squabbles and skirmishes siblings have but deep down we really liked each other. All my friends thought my parents were the coolest. They were reasonably strict but also understanding. I was never grounded and Priscilla was grounded only once. That was the biggest punishment ever! Don't misunderstand, it wasn't that I was the best behaved kid of all time, it's just that my parents weren't big on actions of discipline. A stern look from my mom or dad was all that was needed. If they expressed their "disappointment" in me, it would send me into a funk for a week.

My father frequently let my sister and me know how much he loved us. Family time was really important to him, and he looked forward to coming home from work and relaxing with us. To be sure, my dad was good at his job and was proud of the career he built as a mid-level executive at IBM, but he didn't talk much about work at the end of the day, and he rarely brought work home.

My parents were different from each other and had a healthy appreciation for those differences. My father, for instance, wasn't the life of the party that my mother was. But he loved to sing. He had a booming bass voice and he loved to use it, singing in various choruses and church choir for as long as I can remember. Sunday mornings at home were marked by him warming up his voice, rehearsing all of the hymns we'd be singing later that day in worship. To this day, Priscilla and

I honor my dad's memory by texting each other with "Jesus Christ is Risen Today" on Easter Sunday.

One of the sadnesses of my life was that I didn't get to know my father better as an adult. We had a great father-son relationship, but he died when I was only 24. (More on this later.) I never got to the friend zone with Dad. That said, he became my hero retroactively. I look back at what a devoted family man he was and wonder if I could have done the same had I been a father. He was obviously respected at work, and the way he handled his illness was a great inspiration to me during my recovery. He rarely complained—with us around anyway—and he worked up until six weeks before he died. He also continued to follow his passion for singing in choruses and choirs. He was a class act.

As for my mom, well, she was the best mom ever! Who doesn't say that? Again, you don't see these things at the time, but in hindsight, Midge Hamlin was a remarkable person. She was driven and very successful—a high school valedictorian who had multiple teaching offers right out of college. Then, she quit all that to be a stay-at-home IBM wife and raise her children. She was one of those moms that was always ready to feed the neighborhood kids. She went to ALL of my Little League games, swim meets, tennis matches and soccer games, and was always encouraging when I performed badly and thoughtful when I was good—meaning she didn't want me to get too cocky. Mom eventually went back to work when I was 16, first as co-president of the Binghamton YWCA and later as communications director at Binghamton General Hospital. She also served as communications director for the Red Cross, the Roberson Museum and Science Center and finally capped off her career as communications chief for the Broome County United Way. This put her side-by-side at fundraising events with all the IBM bigwigs that Dad had worked for over the years. She, too, handled her illness with grace, calm and class and also worked up until she passed, just 5 short years after my father.

Mom was the one who held the family together, keeping us on schedule and making the household run like an efficient business operation. Each day, she made us all breakfast, packed our lunches and then sent Priscilla and me off to school on the bus and Dad off to work. Then she'd meet up with some of the neighborhood ladies over a cup of coffee or tea, and do it all over again the next day.

I'm sure Dad's life had the same repetitive cadence as well. I visited his office several times and subconsciously made the connection that a successful man came dressed in a dark suit, a tie, a white shirt and black shoes. That's the way every dad in the neighborhood dressed. I focused on the tie. I knew from an early age that wearing a tie to work would mean I had made it. It wasn't until I was 12 that I came to understand that there were people in the world that worked for companies other than IBM. When I found out a neighborhood friend's dad was a vice president at the Endicott-Johnson Shoe Company, the other large employer in town, I thought, "What did he do wrong? For some reason he can't work at IBM, so he had to settle for vice president at a shoe company?"

The village of Endicott, located 15 miles from the Pennsylvania border, was named after Henry Bradford Endicott of Massachusetts. It was Henry who founded the Endicott Johnson Corporation and started the shoe company with his factory foreman, George F. Johnson in 1899.

Endicott is considered the birthplace of IBM. In 1924 IBM was formed out of the Computing Tabulating and Recording Company, and they built a huge factory on North Street to manufacture time clocks for schools and factories. As IBM shifted its focus from clocks to early card-based tabulating equipment and eventually to modern computers, the company grew exponentially. In the early 1960s, Thomas Watson Jr., son of the founder, bet the entire company on the development of the IBM System/360, billed as the most modern computer ever designed. The S/360 ushered in a new era of computer compatibility, and Endicott was the hub of it all with IBM's manufacturing, research and development and its legendary sales school. For the next 20 years, the Endicott plant would churn out S/360s and its descendants, destined for corporations, governments and universities all over the world. Employment swelled to more than 16,000 workers.

Endicott was truly a company town. IBM made life pretty easy for its workers and their families. They paid their employees well, with access to excellent benefits. They provided workers with inexpensive ($5.00 per year) memberships to their country club where family members could be entertained during the day while the mostly male workforce built the giant company. IBM was so accommodating to its workers, in fact, that if Big Blue wanted you to relocate, the company would buy your house if you were unable to sell it in 90 days. Of course, the downside was if IBM wanted you to move, you moved, prompting its other nickname, "I've Been Moved."

The Hamlins learned this firsthand when I was 8 years-old. Mom and Dad called a family meeting, where Priscilla and I learned that we were moving to Camarillo, California, about 50 miles northwest of Los Angeles. I don't know if my father had a choice in the matter, but he seemed excited. This wasn't a take-a-family-vote meeting, it was a we're-moving-to-California meeting. And we were told that it was to be a permanent move.

There were a lot of pluses to heading West. Our Spanish-style home was brand new, had stucco walls, a tiled roof and was much bigger than our previous house. More importantly, it had an in-ground pool in the backyard. One of my first memories in this house was watching Neil Armstrong and Buzz Aldrin walk on the moon on July 20, 1969.

Camarillo wasn't a company town like Endicott, but it had a familiar suburban vibe. I had the freedom to ride my bike from sunrise to sunset. I also took swimming lessons in the summer and one of my jobs at home was to vacuum the pool and check the chemical levels. It was Endicott only better—it never got cold! We did have some earthquakes, but apparently, I slept through them.

Being so warm, there was quite a bit to do in Southern California. A Brooklyn Dodgers fan as a kid, my dad was glad to be a Dodgers fan "out there," and took me to several ballgames at Dodger Stadium. And being only eight miles from the Pacific, we spent a good deal of time at the beach.

As the new house was being completed, we lived in a hotel, the Westlake Inn. Of course, we didn't know anybody. It's hard to think what life must've been like for my mom during these days, and how lonely it was for her while Priscilla and I were off at school and Dad was at work. But she never complained, at least not to Priscilla and me. My parents were great at presenting a "united front" to us kids and rarely fought.

Starting classes mid-year at a new school was tough, largely because we were outsiders. But it made Priscilla and me closer, even though we'd never admit it at the time. Near the hotel, Priscilla and I would walk past this pond that was home to a number of geese, including one particularly loud, annoying goose. She honked so much that she gave both of us a headache, so we called her Excedrin.

Decades later the memory of Excedrin surfaced again when I was in Buffalo visiting my sister. We passed by a pond complete with some geese on the way to the grocery store, a route my sister frequently takes.

"Doug, I always think of you when I drive by here," she said from the back seat.

"Oh yeah," I replied, "you mean Excedrin?" Funny how both of us remembered this goose so many years later, but I guess some memories are stronger when they're shared with someone else. No one else has or understands these memories.

As it turns out, we weren't destined to get to know Excedrin too well. Thirteen months after the big move we had another information-only family meeting. Apparently, this time, the Company gave Dad a choice between Austin, Texas or a return ticket to Endicott. Mom and Dad chose Endicott.

No one in the Hamlin household was too upset about the move back to New York, despite the loss of the pool. Dad would return to the same building, if not the same office, and we'd get a new house—in Crestview Heights. I returned home as kind of a big shot with my friends at school, having lived "all the way" out in California for more than a year. Not much had changed since we left, except for the new elementary school that had been built right in Crestview and named after Thomas J. Watson, Jr. It was a five-minute walk from our house.

I had a happy childhood. There was an order to things. Even when life threw some curveballs like moving to California... and back. We weathered them together as a family. I spent most of my childhood living a very IBM-centric, family-oriented lifestyle.

IBM relocated manufacturing operations in the early 1980's, leaving behind an environmental mess and hulking factory buildings that sit and rot to this day on North Street. The spirit of what IBM was in the 60's and 70's days really stuck with me. They cared about their employees, paid them well, and provided a family-oriented environment that made people want to spend their entire career there. This heavily informed my view years later when I had a chance to lead a company myself.

In terms of dealing with my accident and its realities, growing up in a positive, stable, nurturing house and town gave me a perpetually optimistic view. I learned how to find the bright spot even in the darkest of days, like when both of my parents were sick. It is integrated in who I am. I don't dwell on bad stuff too long, I try to chart a path forward and focus on what's important.

SEVEN

WELCOME TO THE REAL WORLD

*Nothing can stop the man with the right mental attitude from
achieving his goal; nothing on earth can help the man
with the wrong mental attitude.*

—Thomas Jefferson

After four years of a stellar social life, and a remarkably average academic life, to everyone's relief I graduated from The State University of New York at Albany in the spring of 1982 with a degree in geography. You may ask, "What does one do with a geography degree?"

As it turns out, quite a bit.

To look at my resume today, one could infer that there was a clear, well-thought-out plan designed to one day put me in charge of a software company that blends mapping and technology. But to be honest, in May of 1982 I didn't have a plan or a clue where I was headed or what I wanted to do with my life.

Entering UAlbany as an 18-year-old freshman, I had a vague notion that I might want to be a doctor, so in addition to the required classes, I loaded up on science classes as much as I could. I soon found out, however, that my party schedule and the 8:00 a.m. chemistry lab were entirely incompatible. I chose the former. Thus ended my career in medicine. I also took a Geography 101 course that year as part of a social science requirement. I clicked almost immediately with the mapping/cartography aspect and I found the coursework interesting as it involved both physical and social history.

As for a minor, I kind of fell into computer science, a relatively new academic discipline in 1978. I have learned countless times since then that the distance between brilliance and luck is not very far. Let's call this one luck.

As an undergrad at UAlbany, I gravitated toward the social sciences, which in addition to geography, included sociology, psychology and philosophy. For some reason, I also migrated toward statistics. I was good at it. I found probabilities and predictive statistics interesting because you could apply them to so many disciplines. Since I got good grades in my Introduction to Statistics class, I was reasonably sure I could do well in the statistics courses associated with psychology, business, economics and math. These all had basically the same elements of study, just applied to different subject matter, so I did pretty well. I took as many statistics courses as I could, regardless of the discipline. This provided a good foundation for my graduate work in urban and regional planning. My advisor began pushing me in that direction.

In the fall of 1982, I enrolled in graduate school at UAlbany, becoming the first student in the school's master's program in urban and regional planning. The program would one day become quite well respected (ranked #12 in the U.S. in 2019). This new world included courses in transportation planning, civil engineering and environmental and land-use planning. But what made this fledgling program most appealing to me was that it was taught by local practitioners in the field. They were living this stuff by day and teaching it in our classes at night.

Early in the program, I was researching the history of urban transportation planning in the United States. The textbook we used at that time was written in 1965 by Roger L. Creighton, titled appropriately enough, *Urban Transportation Planning*. It was widely considered the authoritative work on the transportation planning process throughout the 1970s and early 1980s. Creighton was a giant in this sector. He led research and helped draft the first Chicago Area Transportation Study (CATS 1955-1963), and was credited with pioneering many of the processes, methodologies and techniques that would cement his reputation in urban planning. His process is still in use today.

Luckily for me, he also lived not far from UAlbany, in the hamlet of Delmar, New York. Mr. Creighton was a big supporter of UAlbany's master's program. (Yes, Mr. Creighton, it would be nearly 30 years before I would call him Roger.) When I read that he would be attending a wine and cheese networking event the department was hosting, I jumped at the opportunity to meet him. I even called ahead to confirm that he would be there. Mr. Creighton, and my advisor, Paul Marr, were friends so it was easy for me to drop Paul's name and verify that Mr. Creighton was coming.

My good fortune continued the day before the event in January 1983 when I noticed a job posting in the graduate office. Creighton's firm, Roger Creighton Associates Incorporated (RCAI), was looking for part-time computer programmers. So I ripped the slip of paper off the bulletin board (in fact I took them all so no one else would see the opportunity). Rather than call Mr. Creighton, I decided I would approach him personally at the small gathering the next day. When he arrived, he surprised me. While larger than life in the urban planning world, he was very unassuming in person. At 5-feet-10 and a slender 150 pounds, he didn't command much attention in the room. And yet he had a presence. Mr. Creighton carried a confidence that was unmistakable. This was likely a combination of his quiet demeanor and my projection of the fact that he literally wrote the book about the studies that interested me most. It would be like Tom Brady entering a room and taking a seat or quietly introducing himself to others. He owned the room but didn't need to say it.

I anxiously approached him. I introduced myself and told him how much I enjoyed his book, although for the most part I fumbled through our brief conversation. I don't recall other details from that conversation, but I did muster the nerve to ask him about the job posting.

Mr. Creighton's company was looking for someone to flesh out a new team he was building for a product idea he and his senior partner, Chuck Manning, were working on. Keep in mind: This was just seven years after Microsoft was founded and three years before the first version of Windows was released. Mr. Creighton was building an early software company. I told him that I thought I could handle the duties of that job. He told me to come in and see him the next day.

And that was that.

I don't recall much about the interview the next day, except that I got the job, not knowing it would change the trajectory of my life. It was a small beginning. I'd be an independent contractor working 20 hours a week with a salary of $10,500 a year with no benefits.

I do remember wearing a tie to the office on my first day at RCAI. The tie symbolized so much more than a restrictive piece of neckwear. It was a sign that I had arrived, harkening back to my days as a kid and watching my father leave for work at IBM. It was a big deal, and I called my dad to tell him about my first "real job." He was a little happier compared to the time I called to let him know I was using my college degree at Friendly's doing dishes and scooping ice cream.

On that first day, it took me four hours to complete the amazing task of getting an Apple II computer to display my name on the screen. Sad, I know. Until that point, my programming experience had been completely mainframe based—mostly on a UNIVAC 1100 series using either punch cards or a DECwriter keyboard terminal. (Wow does that date me!) Apple introduced the Apple II in 1977, mostly as a personal computer for home use. It had not reached academia at all.

It was a new computing environment for me. I was completely unfamiliar with floppy disks, managing my own input/output routines, engaging compilers in the right order, etc. This was early in personal computing, so all of those things you find packaged and ready to go today were very much "do-it-yourself" back then.

You're probably thinking I should've been fired for taking so long to enter my name. Needless to say, I was a little anxious about telling Mr. Creighton about my "accomplishment," when he came by at the end of the day.

"He's going to ask me what I did and then he's going to think I'm an idiot," I thought to myself, mustering up all the confidence I could to overcome those insecurities one can have on that first day on the job.

Instead, Mr. Creighton appeared pleased.

"That's great," he told me. "Good progress."

I think he was just being encouraging and kind. He wanted me to be successful, for his sake and mine, so he called that a success for the day.

There was no new employee orientation in those days. Nor was there a three-ring binder outlining the various job duties for my role. I wasn't required to read anything about RCAI and its human resources policies, benefits or culture. I got to the end of the day and I don't think I even knew where the bathroom was.

Instead there was an assumption that I, and the other employees, already knew that stuff and would quickly figure out how to get into the flow of things. It would be years later, when I took over the company later known as VersaTrans Solutions Inc., that we added a new employee orientation program, HR policies, handbook, etc. It wasn't my idea, but some other, smarter employees who suggested creating a program for onboarding people. It even included a map to the bathroom.

I soon quit my job at Friendly's, which I had since my sophomore year in high school. Putting in hours at the restaurant, taking graduate classes and working at RCAI didn't mix well. At my new job, I was only making 25 cents more per hour than at Friendly's but more importantly, this was a career-oriented position, not a job. Within months, I would be working full-time on a project for the New York State Department of Transportation.

My life toggled between two worlds—grad school and RCAI. I was living the life of a faux academic. I'd show up at the graduate office around 8:30 in the morning with a newspaper in one hand and a hot coffee in the other. My fellow students and I would smoke cigarettes and think big thoughts—or so we thought. It was in grad school where I finally learned how to write and appreciate the importance of good writing. It's hard to believe that this lesson escaped me during four years of high school and another four years at college (AND having an English teacher mother). When I later became a boss, I realized my experience was not unusual. After hiring a number of people who didn't know how to string a few sentences together, we started requiring writing samples from candidates. (I probably wouldn't have been hired at RCAI if such a test existed then!)

Most of my education in graduate school occurred outside of the classroom at Roger Creighton Associates. The firm taught me one lesson after another—the first being that there is a corporate environment other than the IBM one I had seen growing up. I was both thrilled and intimidated to be there, in awe of the intelligence of my fellow programmers and the professionals around me. Neither my experience nor my education measured up to those of my co-workers. I had minored in computer science and took a few courses in programming. My colleagues either had master's or bachelor's degrees in math and computer science and were far more elegant software engineers than I was. I could play the notes, but I couldn't write the music.

I soon came to realize that there was a place for that guy, too, at RCAI—i.e., "the hard-working, 'non-nerd'-programmer type," as Chuck later described me. The picture would become clearer over time, how a person with my skills and personality would fit into the bigger vision of the company.

To be honest, I didn't completely understand the science

behind the first few projects that I worked on. They were borne out of traffic engineering theory regarding traffic signal timing and the volume of traffic generated by various land uses. This was well accepted "settled science" so there were countless resources to learn from. I learned a lot.

At a time when some people start thinking about retirement, Mr. Creighton, 60, was looking for the next big thing. He'd already made a name for himself but he was never content to rest. He's what I'd call a visionary and an early adopter. Those words are thrown around pretty freely these days, but early on they applied to Mr. Creighton.

Back then, computers were quite expensive—about $3,000 (roughly $9,000 today) for the Apple II. They were not a staple on every desk, even for software developers. There were just two of these computers for four programmers, so we had to sign up for computer time. I did much of my early coding on paper while waiting my turn. Chuck would bring his black and white television in from home to use as a monitor, then take it home every night to watch TV. It was a simpler time, but Mr. Creighton was always pushing the envelope on technology. Since RCAI was essentially a consulting firm churning out reports and documents for clients all day every day, Mr. Creighton invested in an expensive Wang word processor in the late 1970s that took up an entire room and probably set the firm back 10 grand. But that's how Mr. Creighton thought. He had a vision and didn't want to get hung up on how hard it was to do the job. He had been on the front lines of computer technology in the transportation field back in the mid-1950s, when he worked for the city of Chicago designing the system of freeways we all know so well there now. The hardware was expensive, but a fundamental requirement to doing the job well.

Mr. Creighton and Chuck's philosophy, if I could paraphrase, was straightforward: "Let's be smart and do it right, and if it costs us a bunch of money to buy the right tools, we'll figure it out." When the Apple II's arrived, they wanted the computers pushed to their limits. We would soon be feeding these new machines fairly significant scientific problems, traffic engineering and routing algorithms that would one day be the heart of the company.

I was moving out of the world of the hypothetical and theoretical work I did at grad school and into the real-world of problem-solving. We were working on commercially viable products that people would actually buy, with money. Up to that point, I worked on projects in school that might work once and never again, and that was fine. I learned what I needed to from the experience and then moved on to other projects. Not so in the real world. If people were spending money on our products, they expected them to be reliable and idiot proof. For the first time in my life, I had to start thinking about "the customer." That would shape the rest of my career.

My respect and admiration for Mr. Creighton grew as I worked for him, and eventually alongside him. It was always intimidating because he was so smart and well spoken. He was demanding in a quiet yet intense way. I always wanted to please him. I would take an "Atta boy!" or "Good job!" from Mr. Creighton over a raise because he didn't give them out very often. But when he did pat you on the back, it left a lasting impression.

While demanding, Mr. Creighton also understood that to

get the level of quality he wanted from his employees, he needed to give them freedom to work. He was especially patient with the programmers who were the pioneers in the organization.

We programmers also had each other's backs. We had what we called an "RLC ALERT," which (respectfully) meant that Roger L. Creighton was on the prowl. Mr. Creighton had mastered "management by walking around" described in Tom Peters' *In Search of Excellence*, but I suspect Mr. Creighton never read the book.

The team atmosphere was great. It felt more like a big research project we were all doing rather than developing software upon which to base a business. A lot of that came from Mr. Creighton. He wanted us to focus on the work. I don't recall lots of talk about "business models" and revenue and profit projections. This was a small hand-to-mouth consulting firm. Us newly minted programmers didn't care or have much insight into where the money was coming from. I did my best to learn from my co-workers and found parts of the software development effort that I was pretty good at.

Mr. Creighton had a vision of what he wanted that first software product to be. He'd often call us into his corner office, close the blinds and write—in yellow chalk—excruciatingly detailed flowcharts and diagrams depicting how this futuristic product would work.

Mr. Creighton had no idea how to pull off this vision technically. And, to be honest, we had no idea how to achieve the vision he'd set forth, either. But Mr. Creighton knew he'd assembled the right kinds of minds to make it happen, and he showed us some patience. He was a scientist at heart and he accepted our word when we said we'd need a day for this project or a year for that project. We didn't know for sure what we were talking about because we'd never done it before, and he wouldn't know because he never had anyone do it for him before.

This place would become a lifeline for me. Of course, I couldn't see around that corner at the time but Mr. Creighton, Chuck and my colleagues—not to mention the work—would all become essential to my survival.

At the moment, this was my job...where I got to wear a tie.

The Hamlins at the Cottage on Skaneateles Lake, 1978

High school diving team, competed from 8th grade to graduation

Spent most winters on the slopes, skiing Greek Peak near Cortland, NY, 1976

*My Mom,
Mary Jane "Midge" Hamlin,
early 1980s*

*My Dad,
Morris "Mo" Hamlin,
early 1980s*

Pam and I in her college apartment,
Summer 1980

Pam and I going to a friend's wedding,
Summer 1980

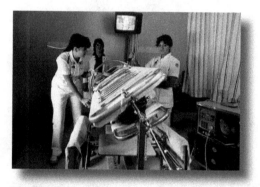

The Stryker Frame. I was sandwiched and turned over every two hours for ten days before surgery to stabilize my neck.

My first wheelchair, "The Tank," tubular steel, approximately 50 pounds

Current wheelchair, titanium and aluminum, approximately 23 pounds

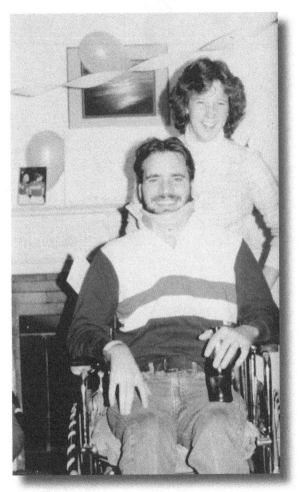

*Our engagement party in Priscilla's
third-floor apartment*

Dad, Mom, Jimmy, David,
Aunt Marilyn, Uncle Jim, Christmas 1983

Priscilla and me, 1984

Welcome back to work party,
April 2, 1984

Chuck Manning and Roger Creighton
making presentations at a company dinner

Our wedding,
September 15, 1984

Our First dance. "Not a dry eye in the room."

EIGHT

My New Normal

Being challenged in life is inevitable, being defeated is optional.
—Roger Crawford

There were times when I wondered if hospitals were always going to be a part of my life. That's a pretty sobering, depressing thought. For some people, it is a reality. As I prepared to leave the hospital for the very first time after my accident, I wasn't sure what the future had in store for me. I was both eager and nervous to find out.

Before the accident, I was an invincible 23-year-old who, besides my father's cancer diagnosis months earlier, had experienced very little devastating news in his life. I don't know if I thought I had control of my destiny, but I certainly thought the future was bright. The accident shook that foundation loose. My body had betrayed me and, at least for the immediate future, I was forced to take things one day at a time.

After 91 days, I was released from Erie County Medical Center on Saturday, November 19, 1983. I went to stay with my "Capital Region" parents, Aunt Marilyn and Uncle Jim Fisher, in Schenectady, N.Y. Their home was just 10 minutes from Sunnyview Rehabilitation Hospital, where I would continue my rehabilitation in two months' time. My mom's hands were full with my ailing father back in Binghamton.

Thankfully for all of us, the Fishers saw that their home would be the best place for me to recuperate and begin to adjust to my new life.

Uncle Jim is my mom's brother, and the two of them were very close. From as early as I can remember, we saw my aunt and uncle more than a half-dozen times a year for holidays and family vacations up and down the eastern seaboard. They had a camp in the Adirondacks, and I would go there in the summer to spend time with them and my cousins David and Brad. Uncle Jim was an active man, taking us hiking, fishing, skiing and occasionally horseback riding.

The trip home from ECMC was actually a series of planned events. Pam drove us in Uncle Jim's 1979 Volvo four-door sedan. It was an easy trip along the New York State Thruway. We decided to break it up halfway and stay in a hotel in Syracuse that Saturday night because, well, you know—it had been 91 days! We chose the Holiday Inn downtown and began learning what my new reality would be right away. It was my night to have a bowel movement (remember, these things are scheduled now), and ECMC had neglected to send me home with any suppositories. Pam immediately found herself in a sketchy neighborhood in an unfamiliar city looking for something she had never purchased before. Luckily she found them, and I was able to make do in a completely inaccessible hotel bathroom.

The next day we travelled to Pam's parents' house for a celebration with her family. I remember a crowded kitchen with many smiling faces and lots of champagne. We left Cherry Valley late that afternoon headed for Schenectady and another party with family and friends at the Fishers' house.

Almost immediately after we left Cherry Valley, I began to feel uncomfortable. I had a strong urge to urinate, but my body would not cooperate. If I had full sensation, I'm sure I would have been in pain, but I just felt "weird." Pam and I had both learned how to catheterize my bladder in the hospital—something I was then doing twice a day—so I suggested to Pam we do it right then to ease the discomfort. So, on the side of a rural road in upstate New York, Pam found the equipment in the trunk and catheterized me in the passenger seat of the Volvo.

The procedure went fine, but the results were not good. My urine was cloudy and full of blood, a sure sign of infection. We packed up and moved on, but my mood turned immediately sour as it dawned on me that this might require a trip to a hospital. We arrived in Schenectady to a house full of family and friends, but I was not in the mood to party. What should have been a real high point had turned quite dark for me.

Built in 1847, the Fishers' house was far from wheelchair friendly. It had five steps from the street level to the living area, and we struggled to navigate those steps when we arrived. The following morning my temperature soared to 105 degrees. It was time to go to the emergency room. Uncle Jim had already left for work, but without hesitation, Aunt Marilyn and Pam sprung into action. Like a NASCAR racing pit crew, they got me down the stairs and out of the house in about 60 seconds.

They rushed me to Ellis Hospital 10 minutes away, where I spent the next few days recovering from my infection. Sadly, those few days included Thanksgiving, so the holiday was dampened quite a bit while we "celebrated" in the hospital. I was released that Friday.

Back at the house on Thanksgiving Day, Dad tried to say grace and cried—they all cried.

Despite the infection, it was an exciting time for me. While I knew I had more rehabilitation in my future and wasn't leaving the hospital life totally behind, it felt as if I had been deinstitutionalized. To sleep in a normal bed on a schedule of my own making and eat home cooked meals was truly refreshing. To do so at the home of my aunt and uncle, with Pam around as well, was remarkable. That support was invaluable. I was by no means fully independent, but I started to feel like myself again. Each day gave me some additional confidence that the future would not be consumed with constant thoughts and worries about "my condition."

I began carving out a new normal the moment I left ECMC and Buffalo. What had been routine or normal prior to my accident didn't apply any longer. It was almost irrelevant. I was now challenged every day to figure out what kind of life I could have for myself.

At the Fishers, I started a semblance of a routine, wading in to work life and some form of independence in the safe confines of their spacious and very comfortable home. One day that stands out is the day my computer arrived. My father had purchased the computer for me just after my accident—an IBM PC, of course—for $3,200 after his company discount. It wasn't a symbolic gesture, as I had plenty of work to do to keep me busy on that machine.

Roger Creighton, the man who wrote the book on urban transportation planning and gave me my first career opportunity while in grad school, visited me one day at ECMC. He was on his way to Cleveland for business and decided to drive instead of fly so that he could stop in and see me. Mr. Creighton was a quiet, thoughtful man of few words, which were always well chosen. He spent about an hour at my bedside. I don't recall many details about our conversation, and yet it was one of the most important visits of my entire stay.

As Mr. Creighton prepared to leave, he looked at me sincerely and said, "Your job is waiting for you when you are able to return to it." Those fourteen words were instrumental in my recovery. In one sentence he had provided light at the end of a very long tunnel. Aside from his humanity, he had no real reason to make that offer. His was a small firm—12 people—and the unknowns about my timeline and future abilities were many. It was risky just to leave a spot open for me, but he did, and in doing so he gave me hope.

At the time of my accident, we had been working on a New York State contract to develop a fare system for transit buses in Ulster County, just south of Albany. Instead of flat fares, the system would charge varying rates based on distance. My role, along with another programmer, was to design the software to be used in the transit office to calculate the fares.

It was this project that Mr. Creighton asked me to continue to work on in the hospital. I didn't have a computer there, but could certainly contribute design and system comments to the work being done back in Albany. Mr. Creighton wasn't simply giving me work to do out of the kindness of his heart. He expected me to make real progress when I was up to it.

A few years ago, before Mr. Creighton died, Pam and I visited with him at an assisted living facility in Walnut Creek, California. And I asked him, "Why did you do it? Why did you keep me on?" He said that it occurred to him, after my accident, that I was going to be someone who really had to excel using his mind rather than his body, and he knew that he could offer me that opportunity and be part of my recovery. It just floors me to this day to think about it. He was a very special man.

He was right, too. While I was in the hospital, it dawned on me that my current occupation was ideal for me because it was more desk work than physical work. I even toyed with the possibility of getting a PhD because my brain was my ticket to my future, not my body. Clearly any kind of physical job was out. But when I looked around at some of my fellow spinal cord patients at ECMC, I really began to see how lucky I was. Many couldn't return to work or even return home.

We all have an impact on other people's lives, whether it be through a kind or harsh word, giving someone a ride somewhere, helping someone move, recommending someone for a position or some other "act of kindness." The magnitude of that impact is often unknown. Pam is a retired elementary school teacher who invested herself in hundreds of children's lives during her 23-year career. Yet, despite all of those lessons and all of those words of encouragement and guidance, it's likely she'll never know just how great her impact was on those kids.

Mr. Creighton's decision, about which he had consulted with his wife Martha and business partner Chuck Manning, made an indelible impact on my career both as an employee and eventually company owner. I would never forget his courageous decision to keep me onboard, train me and invest in my career. In turn, I did all that I could to never give them a reason to second-guess or regret that decision.

As Dave Gonino put it, "Doug wanted to not just meet expectations but give back in spades."

To my family and friends, Mr. Creighton was considered a Godsend for keeping me on. In fact, at the time of the accident my mom had just joined Toastmasters, an organization that helps people with public speaking and leadership. In one of her first talks, she toasted Roger: "When Doug's accident happened, there were two miracles," she said. "One was Pam, and the other was his boss. Because they never wavered, never flinched."

As I settled into Schenectady with my new PC, I continued work on the Ulster County project as I learned how to use the new machine. I even had a modem which I used to communicate with the office. This was the first opportunity to be somewhat on my own. Yes, I had my aunt, uncle and Pam for both physical and emotional support, but I wasn't surrounded by nurses, doctors and hospital chaos. They would all leave for work at their respective jobs in the morning and I would ease into a new schedule of my own design.

For several reasons, though, it was hard to settle into any kind of work rhythm. First and foremost, I'm not a good work-from-home guy. I need social and intellectual interaction. Secondly, I was still dealing with feelings of uncertainty and fear about my new life and future. This made it hard at times to concentrate on technical issues. There were more than a few "does this really matter" moments. Over time, however, I do remember gaining some semblance of satisfaction that I was contributing something to a larger project. The work provided a diversion from the accident and its intrusion into my life and gave me the confidence that I could, in fact, be a gainfully employed contributor to society. These were welcome glimpses.

Also living in the Fisher house at the time was a gentleman named Jimmy Starchinsky. He lived in the apartment downstairs. Born sometime around 1915, Jimmy had been labeled severely mentally retarded in 1940 and was about to become a ward of the state when Aunt Marilyn's grandparents took him in to live with them. He couldn't read or write, but Jimmy was very bright, and he was able to help out around the house. Today, Jimmy would be described as a person with a developmental disability.

When Marilyn's grandparents died, Jimmy went to live briefly with Marilyn's aunt before she moved to Ohio. He returned as a ward of the state and was put to work on a farm. Aunt Marilyn's father soon found out that Jimmy was being overworked and treated like a hired hand and decided to bring him home. They made a tiny makeshift bedroom for him in their home in Skaneateles, New York, and Jimmy spent most of his days doing various household chores for four or five other families nearby. Jimmy was never afraid of a hard day's work. A few years later Jimmy moved to Florida with Marilyn's parents when they retired.

After Marilyn's parents passed away, Jimmy came to live with Uncle Jim and Aunt Marilyn and soon became the caretaker of their home at 50 Washington Avenue. He would be seen about the house, doing gardening, cleaning the dishes and performing various other sundry jobs. He couldn't drive so Aunt Marilyn would take him shopping once a week. He cooked his own meals and rarely ate with my aunt and uncle.

Jimmy was in his 70s when he came to Schenectady, just a

few months before I arrived. Thinking back on the short time I was there, Jimmy and I forged a very special relationship. He was just a fun guy and he was always there for me. He would come up from his basement apartment every day, cook me lunch—usually a can of Beefaroni (my choice, my favorite)—join me in conversation, wash whatever dishes there were and then head onto the next task of the day. I would then go back to work or watch TV.

These new living quarters required some adjustments. The Stockade neighborhood in which my aunt and uncle lived was one of the oldest in the United States, and when the homes were built in the late 1700s, they really didn't have wheelchairs in mind. Uncle Jim turned to his oldest son, David, who's 18 months older than Brad, to build a serviceable ramp for me between the kitchen and the living area. David was the go-to guy for these kinds of projects. He's a computer analyst by trade but designs theater sets for a hobby. I think he built three or four ramps for me in various houses over the years.

After about two months at 50 Washington Avenue, I headed to nearby Sunnyview Rehabilitation Hospital, where I would spend the next three months. Sunnyview was a well-respected regional rehabilitation facility connected to Ellis Hospital, where I was treated a few months earlier for my urinary tract infection. Besides being near my aunt and uncle's home, it was also fairly close to Pam and the office.

During this time, I had to put work on hold because my main job was to learn how to live a fully independent life. My physical therapist at Sunnyview was Kathy Buccieri, and in the months and years to follow she became more than just my physical therapist; she and her husband Bob became part of my extended family. When I was later discharged and was living at my aunt and uncle's again, Kathy made sure to schedule her visits on Friday nights at 6 p.m., the cocktail hour. No matter what else was going on, at 6 p.m. we had this ritual of having a couple of drinks and I provided the entertainment of trying to do this "walking thing" around the backyard.

Kathy had a brace made for my left leg which forced it to remain straight. With crutches, I was able to ambulate down a hallway the length of a football field and that would become part of my therapy every day. It was good exercise, but I don't have the trunk muscles to keep myself balanced in a way that feels comfortable without close supervision. And, well, you already know how I feel about supervision and being dependent on others. It became quickly apparent to me while walking with this brace on that utilizing crutches was impractical for me. Thus I had no "false hope" that I would walk again.

At Sunnyview, Kathy worked me pretty hard to become independent during our one- to two-hour daily appointments. She made me perform a variety of range of motion exercises to keep my inactive muscles and tendons loose and also practice how to get in and out of a car. Sunnyview had this old Chevy Nova—well, half of one—in the gym for that purpose. There was also an accessible van where patients were taught how to drive with hand controls. The first time I did that was really a special day. I had studied how the controls worked and got pretty good, very quickly.

When Kathy wasn't working with me, it was up to me to create my own regimen to do the exercises she'd given me.

Sunnyview wasn't just about helping me regain the strength and motor skills necessary to be independent. It had a socialization aspect to it as well, whether they designed it this way or not. Unlike some hospitals, where the future is pretty uncertain, patients at Sunnyview (at least in my area) were generally healthy and working hard to achieve their highest and best skills for whatever malady they endured. There was a coaching environment, to which I responded like an athlete. There were hours of downtime though, which I filled by rolling the halls and visiting anyone who wanted to chat...another step toward "normal."

One of the patients I met at Sunnyview was a guy named Joe. He had grown up in Middleburgh, New York, a small town less than an hour away from Albany. Joe still lived there and worked repairing cars. At this point, as naïve as it may sound for a 23-year-old, I still had the mindset that pretty much everyone worked at IBM or at least in an office.

I don't remember how Joe got hurt, but he was now a paraplegic. His injury was lower than mine which meant he had full upper body strength on both sides and full use of his trunk muscles. This gave him the potential to stand comfortably in leg braces for a time. I envied this. But I remember the grieving process he went through, before my very own eyes, as he mourned the end of his "old life."

"What am I going to do now?" It's a question that we all were struggling with on some level. For Joe, I felt it was an even tougher question than for me because he was such a big, physical guy. He worked with his hands, standing hunched over the open hood of a car. He was an outdoorsman, a hunter and a fisherman. He realized his life was going to be significantly different. We were two guys with major, life-changing circumstances, headed on two different paths. I heard not long ago that Joe had passed away. I'm not sure he ever got over the loss of his pre-injury life.

When I looked at how different his life was going to be after his accident, I realized again how fortunate I was. I know that may sound strange. I'm still in a wheelchair just as Joe was, but he was likely looking at having to start a whole new career. This was going to be a struggle for him.

This all added to my confidence that my goals and plans were accomplishable, in time and with the right amount of effort.

In fact, they were. Sunnyview and Kathy had done their job. When I left on Friday, March 30, 1984, I was more than a few steps closer to independence. I reported back to work full-time at Roger Creighton Associates the following Monday, April 2. I never looked back.

NINE

BACK TO WORK!

*Be of good cheer. Do not think of today's failures, but of the success
that may come tomorrow. You have set yourself a difficult task,
but you will succeed if you persevere, and you will
find a joy in overcoming obstacles.*

—Helen Keller

My return to work was a little more than seven months after the accident. This was six years before the American with Disabilities Act (ADA) became law, and the converted two-story apartment building my firm rented at 274 Delaware Avenue in Delmar, New York, wasn't exactly wheelchair accessible. Not even close.

The building was split into two halves, each containing four two-bedroom apartments—two upstairs and two downstairs. There was no elevator, only a stairwell that ran down the center of the building. Roger Creighton Associates Incorporated (RCAI) occupied both floors of the left half of the building (facing from the street). The eight bedrooms were converted into offices, while the living room areas became common work spaces. One kitchen on each floor served as a break area, while the other two served as computer and supply rooms.

There was also a residential bathroom in each "apartment," including one just off the kitchen downstairs. It was big enough to get the job done, but not big enough to fit my entire wheelchair. I could roll the front end about halfway into the bathroom, but couldn't get the back wheels through the doorframe. The wheelchair just stopped. I'm sure that on more than one occasion, someone stopped in the break room to get coffee and had a chuckle at my wheelchair sitting halfway in and out of the bathroom, but it didn't bother me. I would've laughed, too. And, fortunately for me, the toilet was immediately on the left as you entered the bathroom. That made it easy for me to empty my catheter bag into the urinal container I kept on the floor and dump it into the toilet. It was about a 30-second process, one that I would repeat again and again for many years.

Prior to the accident, I worked in the communal work space on the second floor, but upon my return I shared a "bedroom" office on the first floor very close to the main entrance out back. The lone physical modification that was made to the building was the addition of a handmade 8-foot ramp serving the step out back. This allowed me to wheel my chair right into the building from the parking lot without much difficulty. It was a serviceable ramp, albeit not very comfortable. For whatever reason, the builder—whom I suspected was my immediate boss, Chuck Manning—put these 1 x ¼-inch slats across the ramp every 6 to 8 inches. This made for a very bumpy ride!

RCAI wasn't a very large firm. All told, there were about a dozen employees, some of whom worked as transportation planning or traffic engineering consultants, and some of whom, like me, worked on the computer programming side. On my first day back, there were only five or six people in the office, so it was a fairly reserved welcome back celebration. I remember a few of us, including Pam, enjoying some cake for about 10 minutes and then it was right back to work for everyone.

For me, that meant a completely different project than the bus transit fare system I had been working on in the hospital. This one had to do with writing software for the timing of traffic signals. There is a standard science behind the timing of signals to process traffic most efficiently, and it's largely based on approach volume. For example: Let's say you have a four-way intersection and you've got traffic coming from all directions. Typically, there's a dominant street with a higher approach volume, so you have to give that more green light time. You also have to account for how many people are turning left or right. If there's a pedestrian crossing button, that takes precedence over everything and shuts the intersection down. Then you have to start all over again.

There are six "Levels of Service" ranging from level A, which means the least amount of traffic (i.e., free flowing), to level F, which is failure or, essentially, gridlock. The higher the level of service—i.e., the closer you are to gridlock—the more difficult the timing challenge. My charge, along with several other programmers, was to take traffic volume inputs and manipulate the signal timing and intersection design to optimize the potential Level of Service. This would translate in the field to software and hardware to run the actual traffic signals. Many traffic lights today use actuated signal timing, relying on in-ground or overhead sensors at the intersection to detect the number of cars approaching, and adjust intersection performance in real time.

The name of the program was CAPCALC, which stood for "capacity calculations." I remember spending a lot of time in those early weeks back on the job in Mr. Creighton's office. He would stand at his chalkboard describing precisely what he wanted and how he wanted it to work. He and Chuck decided to write software for this task because, as traffic engineers, they were doing this all of the time for clients, and they were sick of doing it by hand. They decided that, not only should we write it for ourselves, but we should make it available to other private and public entities. This was our first foray into software licensing—a beautiful business model that would eventually be the foundation of the company. Unfortunately, not long after we released CAPCALC, the federal government came out with their own version available for $15 (versus ours at $295). Despite Mr. Creighton's forceful letters to congressmen and senators, this put an abrupt end to CAPCALC.

I worked for about a year on CAPCALC before it met its demise, but it would be wrong to suggest that those first 12 months back on the job were a complete waste of time. On the contrary, it helped return a sense of normalcy and purpose to my everyday life. Being back on the job gave me a routine. In the hospital, there is no set routine, no organization to your day. Now, I had one. Pam would drop me off at work (it would be another year before I would drive again) and then head to her job at Albany Medical College. I would work all day until she picked me up. I frequently brought my own lunch, but as luck would have it there was a Friendly's next door! So, on occasion, I'd wheel myself over there and order from the menu that I still had memorized. I had an everyday routine, like most everyone else, and it felt really good.

Most important of all, being back on the job gave me a purpose. In my time away, I grew up a lot. While I was doing the same kind of work as before, I understood the significance of the job in my life a whole lot differently. Prior to the accident, I might have taken it for granted and, who knows, maybe even lost my job due to a lack of respect for it. I felt quite differently about things upon my return. Knowing that I was a contributing member to the firm and of society, and that I could support Pam and myself, all became much more real to me than it was eight months prior.

I felt little anxiety about my first day back on the job. There really were no physical barriers to doing my job. I had everything I needed in the office. The operating system we were using at the time was transportable across hardware platforms so it was the same one that I worked on with my IBM PC at my aunt and uncle's house, as well as the Apple II before my accident. I now found myself using a Radio Shack TRS-80, but it was very familiar.

One magic pill for me was that I had regained full use of my right hand about six to eight weeks after the accident. Absent that, I would have had to use adaptive equipment to manipulate the keyboard (this was long before voice activated commands and speech recognition). While I'm sure I could have made this work, my fully functional hand made things that much more "normal." In a short amount of time, I became very good at typing one-handed. From a business standpoint this also gave me the ability to look someone in the eye and shake their hand—a vital function of being an executive. Yes, I could have adapted, but it would've been difficult for me emotionally.

From day one, it was pretty much business as usual. I remember working hard to learn the science behind the intersection capacity project. I hadn't learned this in school. There was a lot of math to it. It was an interesting challenge to catch up with the engineers that knew it so well. But they didn't know how to write the software to make it happen, so it was a good match.

If there was anything hindering my ability to do my job it was my stamina. I was so tired that first month back that I'd fall sound asleep in my chair for about an hour each day around lunchtime. I hadn't worked a full day in nearly eight months, and unless I was in rehab, I spent most of my time in the hospital in bed. Thus, I didn't have enough endurance built up yet. The chair nap was a skill worth learning. Even today, I'll nod off from time to time in my wheelchair. It's extremely comfortable. In fact, I can sleep in my wheelchair as well as I can in a bed.

During that first year back on the job, I went through another transformative event: I started driving again! For about a year after I got out of the hospital, Pam was driving me around. I couldn't wait to drive again. It represented a huge step on my road to independence. First, I had to taking driving lessons—at age 24! I needed to get certified by DMV to drive with hand controls. These controls can be fitted to almost any vehicle and are very simple mechanical devices that connect to the pedals. I contacted a driving school and mastered the skill in two short lessons, I was very motivated. Next I started shopping for a car. I had thought about this A LOT. I did not want to buy a van with a lift. All that machinery can break, and a car is just way cooler to drive, and would make me feel "less disabled." To do that, however, I needed to figure out how to manage my chair. I got the basics from a physical therapist. I would get a two-door car so I could fold my chair and stow it behind me. I thought through this for hours and remember practicing in the living room of our apartment. I would transfer into this old green chair, fold my wheelchair and lift it behind me as if I was putting it in the back seat. I was confident I could figure it out in a car. So, I picked out a maroon 1985 Oldsmobile Cutlass, convinced Uncle Jim to cosign a loan (I was 24 with zero credit history), and started driving the next day. The chair dance was more complicated than the living room. Turns out that after I transferred into the drivers seat I had to remove one wheel of my chair, set it aside, pull the seat cushion off the chair, set it aside, then fold the chair and lift it into the back seat, then put the stray wheel and seat cushion on top of the chair. I got so I could do all of this in about 60 seconds. Then I would lift my legs, one by one, into the car and DRIVE. It was true independence. Given my routine both at home and on business trips, I have calculated that I did that transfer and chair lift nearly 100,000 times. (Thus the torn rotator cuff you'll hear about later).

A work colleague of mine, John Deer, was also a big reason why I was able to keep pace during my first few months back on the job. John and I started at RCAI at roughly the same time in 1983. He was a paid intern and I was a contract worker. Then, sometime when I was in the hospital, he became a full-time software engineer. The two of us worked side by side on CAPCALC and, later, the school bus routing project for many years.

John was a thousand times the programmer and mathematician that I was. He was brilliant. He held a bachelor's degree in Computer Science and Math from Hartwick College and a

Masters in Computer Science from Rensselaer Polytechnic Institute (RPI). I learned a lot from John. I would do things in my own measured way and he'd show me how I could do it more efficiently. He was the brains behind a lot of the programming material. I was able to write a fair amount of the software for CAPCALC, but I looked to him for a lot of guidance.

John and I also worked together on RCAI's next project, which conveniently enough was called CARS—the Comprehensive Assignment and Routing System. (We were heavy into acronyms.) What CARS did was attempt to computerize the gravity model, which holds that the interaction between two places can be determined by the product of the population of both places, divided by the square of their distance from one another. We then translated that interaction into traffic, both automobile and transit. Refined enough, the model can help determine the traffic impact to changes in land use. The addition of a shopping mall, for example. We computerized all this information so that a county or municipality could better model the traffic flow in that area and in surrounding towns.

Why would you do that? Let's say a big grocery store chain wants to build a warehouse somewhere in town. Well, it's going to generate a lot of truck and automobile traffic for employees and so forth, so you can plant that into your model and see where the impacts are on the road system and ultimately at each intersection. That was the CARS system. I probably worked on CARS for another year before getting involved with the School Bus Routing System (SBRS) project that would largely change the trajectory of our company, and my career. Unfortunately, CARS met a similar fate as CAPCALC, and didn't become a product we marketed to anyone. However, it did have some applications to SBRS.

The School Bus Routing System project was Mr. Creighton's brainchild. The firm was contracted by the New York State Department of Education to conduct a study on whether it would be possible to save money if computers were used to help route school buses. Chuck wrote most of that report. While doing the research, it occurred to Mr. Creighton and Chuck that our small firm could write the software to route the buses, if we hired the right programmers. And so, in 1982, SBRS was born.

Mr. Creighton was the driving force behind the design of the system. He spent countless hours at his chalkboard (always with the blinds drawn for security) with flow charts figuring out how the whole thing was going to work. He hired one programmer, Theresa Mikol, to work on the project, and she would be the sole programmer on SBRS for the next three years. Theresa wrote the guts of the software on how to route school buses and, much like John, she was brilliant at her job.

I didn't get fully involved in SBRS from the programming side until Theresa left, although I did play a small business role in the summer of 1985 when Mr. Creighton asked me to attend a school bus related meeting in Boston. This would be my very first business trip since the accident. The state of Massachusetts was developing a contract to basically do what we were doing and automate school bus routing. The Massachusetts Department of Education was holding a meeting to better understand how this was going to work, and neither Mr. Creighton nor Chuck could attend, so they chose me for whatever reason. I had just purchased a new car in

May—the aforementioned large, two-door 1985 Oldsmobile Cutlass Supreme—and this would be a great opportunity to stretch it out.

Before I left, Mr. Creighton called me into his office and said, "I want you to do two things: 1) Write down everything you hear, including the names of everyone who is there, and 2) don't say a word!" So that's what I did. I took A LOT of notes. The meeting lasted all of about 90 minutes, and that was that. I was back in my car and in Delmar by 3 p.m. in the afternoon. Nothing to it. When I got home, I couldn't wait to call my mom and tell her that I successfully executed this business trip to Boston. It seems trivial now, but at the time it was a tremendous achievement for me.

I recall being met in the parking lot by the leader of the Massachusetts work group. He appeared out of nowhere as I was getting my chair out of my car. He asked if I needed help and I declined, but he stuck with me and escorted me into the building. Turns out, Mr. Creighton had given him a heads up, and asked him to look out for me. As I said, Mr. Creighton was a special man.

Before Theresa left, she had already programmed the science on how to produce efficient routes from a laboratory sense. What John and I did was modify it to represent the real world. We developed databases that held the names of the students, their home addresses, the locations of the schools and their bell times, the number of buses available and so forth. And because there were only three programmers working on the project at the time it went to market in 1987, we also had to man the phones and provide tech support. The very first software system we sold was to the school district in Delmar.

We set up an office in the transportation department of the school district to help run the program for the entire school year and found all kinds of "opportunities for improvement." It was great, real work experience with a forgiving client. We came away with a thousand ideas on how to make the system work easier and faster.

The biggest contribution that John and I made to the SBRS project, however, was the development of a graphical street map that we could incorporate into the software. This was pre-Google Maps, and we were working on a text-based system. It was a two-person operation with one person at the computer literally calling out numbers to another stationed at a paper wall map. It was not an efficient way of doing things, that's for sure, but Mr. Creighton was sure it was sufficient and rebuffed our proposal to write a mapping application.

John and I were convinced we could do it so we spent a weekend at it. We got far enough that we could show Mr. Creighton a computerized image of New York State by Monday morning. A picture is worth a thousand words, and he greenlighted our idea, including the purchase of a $10,000 digitizing table to turn paper maps into language the computer could understand. We digitized the New York Department of Transportation's road maps by laying them on the giant tablet and then tracing them into the computer. I recall Mr. Creighton being impressed with our weekend effort, but also commented that we did not have the boundary of the state quite geographically correct. He wanted to be sure we knew he had his eye on the project.

I continued to work as a programmer on the SBRS project until 1991. That's when an interesting job opportunity arose with a company in nearby Troy, New York called MapInfo Corporation. MapInfo was the great, great, granddaddy of the modern maps we all have on our cellphones. They were a technology darling of the Capital District. The company had not yet gone public—that would happen a few years later—but it was a company on the move.

MapInfo's headquarters was located in the Hendrick Hudson building on the Hudson River in Troy. I met with the company's CEO, Mike Marvin, on a Friday afternoon, which was a smart recruiting tactic on his part as MapInfo closed shop early on Fridays for one of my favorite things—Happy Hour. As I watched the beer roll in, I couldn't help but think, "Wow, would this be a cool place to work."

MapInfo was creating a data products division and offered me the director's position. It was less money than I was making at RCAI, but it wasn't programming. By 1991, I was burning out on writing code. I had been at RCAI for more than eight years. I had been grieving my mom, who passed away two years earlier and still thought often of my dad. As a result, I started to re-evaluate my life, and it became increasingly evident to me that I needed to do something more with my career.

This was one of many times I wished my father was still around. I wanted to ask him if he had ever felt the itch to leave IBM. The company was so big and had so many divisions, that you could move from one department to another or from one region of the country to another and never lose your seniority or perks. I also wanted to know if he dealt with any mundane feelings about his job, and how he kept himself on top of his game during those periods. Did he just do his job to support his family or did he ever want more?

It wasn't just the company I worked for, but my very position that I was re-evaluating. I concluded that I did not want to be a computer programmer all my life. I wasn't a strict techy. I needed more contact with people. So to settle that grass-is-always-greener itch, I went on the job interview with MapInfo.

I was really torn on whether to leave the firm or not. By that time, SBRS was the only software product we had, and was clearly on its way to becoming its own company. And I continued to feel indebted to Mr. Creighton and Chuck for taking such a huge gamble on me and allowing me to make a living. It was a debt I could never fully repay. Yet MapInfo was an exciting up-and-coming company and represented a new opportunity.

So I told Chuck about MapInfo's offer. "Chuck," I said, "I love this company. And you've been great to me. You gave me an opportunity. But I'm kinda done with programming. I need to see if there's a way I can move to the consulting side of the business." I told him that I didn't want to take it, but that I needed a change. He said that he would noodle on it for 24 hours and came back the next day with an offer that would allow me to do both. He said that he would create a role for me on the consulting side, and I would continue to do some programming at the same time. I told him "that works for me," and I had responsibilities in both roles until 1995.

I also remember a conversation with Artie and Dave about needing this change. Dave was well aware of the opportunity MapInfo presented. He was currently the Treasurer at Rensselaer Polytechnic Institute, where MapInfo was born. Artie took a practical approach and said, "At this point in your career, why would you take a pay cut?" This helped my decision.

One of the projects that drew a lot of attention in the consulting business was the repurposing of Plattsburgh Air Force Base as an industrial park. I spent hours driving to and from Plattsburgh (just south of the New York/Canada border) working on a traffic model for the area. I remember one night going to a meeting at 7:00 pm to present some information to the local Town Board. It was cold, upstate New York winter cold. When I went into the meeting the parking lot was dry and there were just a few flurries in the air. Two and a half hours later, there was 14 inches of snow on the ground and visibility was about a foot. The Town Board supervisor watched as I struggled to push my chair through the snow toward my car for the three-hour drive home. He said, "You're not driving home tonight, go check in to that hotel across the street, it's on me." I said, "Really? How?" He said, "I own the hotel, I've already called." He had reserved their wheelchair accessible room for me already. It was quite comfortable, and way better than driving home.

I was also part of the team that created the transportation plan for Woodstock '94, a music festival commemorating the 25th anniversary of the original Woodstock festival in 1969. This one would be held at Winston Farm in Saugerties, New York, about 70 miles northeast of the original festival site near Bethel, New York.

We started the project in the fall of '93. What followed was nine months of bedlam and craziness as we figured out how to transport a half-million people on and off this tiny farm served by three country roads. We wound up developing 11 remote parking areas and utilizing 700 school buses 24/7 for four days to shuttle concert-goers to and from the site. On the bright side, we did get to meet and work with the promoters from the famous '69 concert.

A few weeks after the festival, Michael Lang (the original Woodstock visionary) invited some of the consultants to his house just outside the village of Woodstock for a celebratory dinner. In 1969, after the first Woodstock, Michael had purchased a large rambling farmhouse with a number of outbuildings. There were a couple of recording studios on the site. Michael was a record producer and that night there were various aspiring musicians wandering about. Dinner was in a large timber framed dining room. At one point, I must have looked a bit distracted and Chuck leaned over and said, "What are you thinking about?" I replied, "I just want to know who else has had dinner in this room." I was a little star struck, and I knew from my music interests that his neighbors in the area had names like Dylan, Danko, Helm, Fagan, Raitt and Rundgren among others.

Three things took place in the summer of '69 that have always fascinated me: The moon landing, the Manson murders (about 50 miles from Camarillo, California) and Woodstock (about 90 miles from Crestview Heights). It's astonishing to think that these three iconic events took place within four weeks of each other. So to meet Michael Lang, the artistic visionary behind Woodstock, was a real treat. (Thankfully, I never met Manson or any of his "family," though while on business trips I did drive—twice—to the location in Beverly Hills where it happened.)

For Woodstock '94, we modeled the potential traffic as best we could. During the permitting process, I was required to present complex material to the town boards and the public. I began to realize that I liked speaking in public and henceforward gravitated toward any opportunity that would allow me to get in front of people, whether it was planning boards, town boards or public assemblies.

Besides learning and improving my public speaking skills, I was also getting a business education. I started learning about revenue generation, gross margins and the value of time. None of this was relevant to me when I was writing computer programs and was simply taking home a steady paycheck. But now I was understanding the value of a $10,000 project, and how $9,500 of that money went to pay employees to do the work. In my own little microcosm, I learned how we analyzed the business at the end of the year, how each unit was performing and which units were a drain to the company.

It would be great training for what was yet to come.

TEN

OUR WEDDING

*When you realize you want to spend the rest of your life with
somebody, you want the rest of your life to start as soon as possible.*
— "When Harry Met Sally"

Everyone loves a wedding. Ours was no exception. It was
a very special day with no lack of uniquely poignant
moments stemming from various circumstances.

You'll recall our highly romantic engagement story. In my
hospital room at Erie County Medical Center we "mutually
agreed" to get married leaving both of us to conclude that we
were officially betrothed.

We would be married approximately a year after our engagement, on September 15, 1984, at the First Presbyterian
Church of Cherry Valley, New York, Pam's hometown. A
beautiful old stone building, the church wasn't at all accessible. I had to be carried up the stairs in my wheelchair before
the ceremony and down the front stairs after the receiving line
had dissipated. Again, we didn't think much of it at that time.
It was just part of my life now.

During the months leading up to the wedding, I had been
intent on using the leg brace and crutches that had been created
for me while in rehab to stand for the ceremony. As the day got
closer, I was increasingly anxious about this to the point where
I was more focused on standing than I was the wedding and
what it meant. It became so much of a distraction that a few

days before, I decided not to do it. I felt a bit like I was "giving up" and I was apprehensive about telling Pam. She was very supportive and just wanted me to do what was right for me. The relief was immediate and I am certain that I enjoyed the entire event more than I would have with that pressure on myself.

The entire weekend was a well-planned series of events. It was all quite traditional and "do-it-yourself." This was long before wedding planners and intricately staged and choreographed productions, certainly in rural upstate New York. Pam had a vision of how it would go and she, her family and her bridal party did the bulk of the planning.

My parents arranged the rehearsal dinner at The Otesaga Resort Hotel in nearby Cooperstown. The Otesaga was a five-diamond hotel and restaurant venue located right on Otsego Lake, just a couple blocks from the Baseball Hall of Fame. Mom and Dad really wanted to make it special. They really loved Pam and the group of friends we had. They had also invited a number of their own friends to the wedding who were staying at the hotel so it was a chance to party with them as well. Ultimately, and very sadly, my father couldn't make it, which added a layer of emotion to the evening. His cancer had made traveling to the wedding impossible. Like my graduation from the University at Albany in 1982, the man who meant the world to me, taught me a strong work ethic and how to be a great husband, could not join us. Mom was in her element as hostess and we all followed her lead in recognizing the sadness of Dad's absence but also enjoying the evening and the celebration that it was.

That night before the wedding Dave, Artie and I stayed

in a cheap, non-wheelchair accessible motel not far from Cooperstown, all in one room, as college wasn't that far behind us. The rest of my groomsmen were at the same motel. We stayed up a bit, drank some drinks and smoked some cigars. Some things just don't change.

I recall getting up the next morning and putting on my tux at 7 a.m.—even though the wedding wasn't until 1 p.m.—and being pretty annoyed that Dave and Artie were still sleeping. Eventually, they awakened. Dave was my best man and we needed to get to the church earlier than the rest, so we got in his car, had a long breakfast at a local diner and then drove the 20 minutes to the church. Along the way, we listened to a cassette tape of Prince's 1980 album, Dirty Mind, and shouted the words to the song, "When You Were Mine," a constant party tune throughout our senior year at UAlbany.

The friendship between Dave and me is long, strong and deep. Our connection began in October of 1978 when the rest of the guys had gone out, but Dave and I were both nearly penniless in our dorm rooms. He said, "I have a bottle of vodka," I said, "I have two quarters for the vending machine." So, we shared vodka and Sprite throughout that evening and started a lifelong bond.

I relied on Dave that wedding day, as I do now, as a guide, mentor and friend in every sense of the word. Recently we were having a discussion about health insurance costs. Since Pam worked at a school district, our rates are comparatively low for very good coverage. I boasted that, "The smartest thing I ever did was marry a teacher." Dave corrected me and said, "The smartest thing you ever did was marry Pam." He, as always, was right.

The ceremony itself was fairly traditional but punctuated with some very special elements. I had asked Drew, the pastor from the Endicott church, to officiate. He worked out the service with the resident pastor and delivered a special and meaningful message that day, noting again that sadness and happiness of the moment. I had also asked two longtime high school friends if they would sing at the wedding. The Wilcox sisters, Kathy and Karen, were both members of the same youth group in Endicott. Each had a musical talent and sang beautifully. Together their harmonies were incredible. They not only sang at the wedding, Karen wrote a song for us, "A Special Time" which generated the first of many tears that day. This one verse captures its theme:

> *Time will help you to grow closer*
> *You'll share the happiness and the sorrow*
> *You'll have a home where love is flowing*
> *You'll always reach out for tomorrow*

Others have told us that swimming peacefully under the surface of the traditional pieces and parts of a wedding was the joy and celebration that transcended all of those things. More than any wedding any of us had attended up to that point, ours was truly about the love of two people who had been through hell together—and emerged stronger. We were meant to be together forever. This was made more poignant by Dad's absence which somehow made the joy and love that much more important and real. All of this combined to allow tears to flow more easily and for more reasons than many weddings.

We had about 120 people at the wedding. It was a pretty eclectic group, including many of our college friends, some camp counselor friends of mine, some high school friends of Pam's and a few of my parents' closest friends. Then, of course, there was Pam's extended family, who made up a good portion of the population of Cherry Valley.

Our photographer that day was Mr. Toles. Mr. Toles was an old man. He had been a professional photographer from Cobleskill, NY for as long as anyone could remember. He was kind of a traditional part of many weddings in the area. It was all we could do sometimes to suppress our chuckles as he tottered about with his ancient tripod trying to get the best shots. But he did, and we are grateful for it.

Our reception was at The Elm Tree Restaurant on Route 5 in Fort Plain, NY. It was a casual buffet-style affair perfectly befitting our personalities and stage of our lives. Unlike most weddings today, we had a live band. The Milton Deane Cooper Band was a local '70's and '80's cover band with a flair for country music as well. This was important for a number of reasons. First, Pam's dad Norm just loved to dance. I can't remember a party we went to with him where he didn't go through at least three towels as he sweated on the dance floor. In fact, we all loved to dance. We were only a year or two out of college and dancing at parties still flowed pretty strongly in our veins. Thankfully, the band also ran the reception for us. We don't recall too much planning around the first dance, dollar dance, cake cutting, etc., but they guided us through each element while we enjoyed ourselves.

I was determined to uphold the tradition of the first dance between the bride and groom. Just two weeks prior to my accident, Pam and I had danced intimately together at the wedding of two college friends in Dutchess County. Our first dance would not be like that one, but it would still be special. Our guests circled the floor and Pam and I entered the circle, she in her wedding dress and me in my wheelchair. She then sat on my lap, and we rolled around the dance floor to the Eddie Rabbitt/Crystal Gayle song, "You and I." The lyrics have proved to be prophetic:

Just you and I
Sharing our love together
And I know in time
We'll build the dreams we treasure
We'll be all right, just you and I

The dance lasted four or five minutes, and I don't recall feeling nervous beforehand or relieved afterwards. Pam said that not dancing "normally" with me at the wedding was one of the hardest things for her about that day which is hard for me to hear, but I think it was moving for a lot of people given my ongoing recovery. There were people at the wedding who had not yet seen me in my chair so it was all new to them. As Drew recalled later, "There wasn't a dry eye in the room."

There was one additional highlight—it was Pam's brother's birthday. Jim turned twelve years-old that day and not only was he in the wedding party, he got a cake at the reception! Pam is the oldest and Jim the youngest and they have a special relationship. I think Jim was saddened to see his sister being "taken away" by this other man, but she made sure he had a special time that day as well.

We made quite the scene as we left the reception. It would be nine more months before I could drive again so Pam took the wheel of my Uncle Jim's Pontiac that we were borrowing (Pam's wedding dress alone would have filled the passenger compartment of our Datsun B210). As she and I drove past the assembled crowd, bits and pieces of her dress started to flap in the wind outside the window. The dress had this "big, puffy petticoat-type thing on it," recalls Pam, and "I had to tamp it down just to get it under the steering wheel."

The looks that dress got from the tollbooth ticket takers on our way to Albany were priceless, and I'm sure they thought "poor bride—husband was too drunk to drive to the hotel." Just recalling this moment makes us both laugh hysterically now, but at the time all it did was underscore how different our wedding day, and our lives, really were. Yet, as I look back on it today, I can honestly say that I wouldn't have it any other way. Sure, I would've liked to have carried my bride over the threshold and driven her off into the sunset, but sometimes you have just push forward, not wallowing in regret and instead looking ahead to the future. That's what we chose to do.

We honeymooned on Nantucket, following in my parents' footsteps. As it turns out, Nantucket is far from wheelchair friendly. This was evident the minute we stepped off the ferry from Hyannis. When we showed up at restaurants billed to be handicap accessible, we found stairs or an extremely steep ramp leading to the entrance. Cobblestone streets were everywhere—not exactly a wheelchair user's best friend. One particular highlight was the "walking" tour we took via car. What should've taken an hour or more lasted maybe 10 minutes as we zipped from location to location, quickly checking off each notable spot. We did it twice. We still laugh about this.

What wasn't funny were the stares we got. This was the first time that Pam and I were exposed to people blatantly staring at us, and we were confused as to why they would stare. It's normal for us now, but back then it felt very uncomfortable.

"It wasn't like we were in a circus sideshow. This was our life," recalls Pam.

As Pam and I experienced more and more of these types of reactions, we learned to become more sympathetic to other people and how they felt about something that is different. Sometimes you can't help but look.

"There were a lot of experiences we went through together," said Pam. "Situations like that can come between you, but it brought us together, trying to see the humor in it. We could laugh about it, roll our eyes."

While 1984 doesn't seem like that long ago, society was struggling with how to handle individuals with disabilities in public places. There was no wheelchair seating at ballgames or restaurants, and The Americans with Disabilities Act (ADA) didn't become law until six years later.

One of my deepest regrets in life is that we did not visit my father at home in Binghamton before heading off to Nantucket. It would've been easy enough, but our plans had been made and we were in our own newlywed world. When you're young, you do things—or don't do things—that you regret later. Like other regrets, I can't linger there for long because it does no good for anyone. But for the record, if I had one do-over, we would have celebrated that night with my dad in person.

The good news is that Dad did get to see and celebrate our

wedding. Thanks to what at the time was modern technology, my cousin David had taken it upon himself to videotape the wedding. It was his idea after he heard a couple weeks earlier that my father wouldn't be able to make it. He put down a deposit of something like $1,000 to rent a Betamax recorder, and recorded the entire wedding. My sister Priscilla and her boyfriend at the time stuck around long enough for David to get a feel of the reception, then rushed to Dad's side in Binghamton with the tape in hand.

"It was the most wonderful, wonderful thing to do," Priscilla said. "About halfway through watching the tape, my dad said, 'I feel like I got to be there. I feel like I was there.'"

They would watch the tape several times before the night was over. Priscilla would later say that my wedding made my father feel more at ease and at rest—that I had made it through this horrible time and was not only moving forward with my life, but also with the love of my life. I think that it gave my dad some peace of mind.

A month later, he died.

ELEVEN

MY DAD'S ILLNESS

*Most of us have far more courage than
we ever dreamed we possessed.*

—Dale Carnegie

"Your father is sick," said the voice on the line. It was my mom.

Those words didn't go together—"father" and "sick." My father never got sick. As far as I can remember, he never took a sick day. He may have stayed home from work once, and I think that was to take care of my mom or one of us.

It was late in the afternoon on a warm day in May 1982, 15 months before my accident. I was alone in my apartment in Albany, my college career fast approaching its end, when Mom called. My father had been experiencing some abdominal pain, which the doctors presumed had something to do with his gallbladder. That's before they went in and found a growth in his colon.

Growth. The word just hangs there, like a euphemism for some word or phrase that no one wants to hear, like when your girlfriend says, "I think we should see other people," or your boss says, "Layoffs are coming." But this was far more serious. Everyone knows what the word growth means. It means cancer. It was 1982, the MRI had yet to be invented and CT scans were primitive by today's standards. So the doctors conducted rather invasive exploratory surgery on my father.

120

They closed him back up almost immediately after realizing removal was not an option and they needed to develop a different game plan.

"We don't know how bad it is," my mother said.

At that time, colon cancer was far more of a death sentence than it is today.

Up until that day I'd never received any really bad, life-altering news. Yes, I had experienced death in my family—my grandfather and one great uncle, both who'd lived full lives. That was to be expected. You're born, you grow old and then you die.

But my dad was just days away from turning forty-nine years old—49.

I got off the phone with my mom, and Artie walked through the door. I wept on his shoulder for an hour.

I didn't take the news well. I had no frame of reference for it, no pegs to hang my emotions on. I wasn't really processing this news. I was in a suspended state of reality. My whole world just changed, I just didn't know what it looked like, my dad was a rock...impenetrable. A great husband, father and worker, and a tremendous friend. He was reliable, even tempered and kind. I could depend on him even if I didn't talk to him for weeks. Just knowing he was there gave me a sense of security I didn't realize I depended on.

That was all about to change.

As Artie said later, it was a defining moment in our lives because, until that point, we'd all lived a happy-go-lucky existence. None of us had experienced this "cold slap of reality," although Artie did learn a few months earlier that his parents were splitting up after 20 years of marriage. Yet even that seemed to pale in comparison to the awful news about my father. From that point forward, the two of us agreed that our families needed us to be strong and take on more responsibility. No matter what.

Next, I called cousin Brad. We were very close—and not just because we had gotten drunk together as teens in his parents' basement in Schenectady. We were both the same age, and had many mutual interests growing up, including swimming, diving, skiing, breaking things just to fix them and making stuff out of wood. When we were together, our parents could count on us entertaining each other all day long. Brad went to nearby Union College in Schenectady and would come to UAlbany often for weekend parties because, well, they were better.

I shared what I knew with Brad. He said, "Let me grab mom's car and I'll be right over, we're going there tonight." I hadn't even thought about my next move (and had no car at the time), but thanks to Brad, thirty minutes later the two of us sped off for Binghamton to see my dad.

You don't forget moments like that. Artie just being there for me and Brad making my dad and me his top priority. These were selfless acts of kindness that are burned into my memory.

Brad and I arrived at Lourdes Hospital, a Regional Cancer Center in Binghamton around 11 p.m. that night. We found an unlocked back door to avoid being denied access by any rules-driven nurse seeking to enforce "visiting hours." Priscilla had arrived earlier in the day from Buffalo. The family was now together around my father's bed and we began weeping, including Dad. This lasted about 20 or 30 seconds until my dad stated, "Ok, that's enough. We're not crying anymore.

Let's just move forward." Of course we would cry more but in that moment, we did start to move forward.

That was Dad, not overly emotional and not in love with being the center of attention. His reaction to his family provided me with some insight on how he was going to manage this "thing," and that was with elegance. He was going to do his best to control it rather than let "it" control us.

Still, it was hard to see my father this way. He stood about 5 feet 10 inches tall, and never weighed more than 160 pounds despite a routine of a beer and a sandwich every night at 9:30—something he learned from his mother. Now here he was in bed, weak and looking a little small, defenseless and vulnerable.

The doctor came in at some point and confirmed what we all knew, dad had colon cancer. "It's pretty bad," the doctor said.

Lourdes was a well respected cancer center and we were confident he was getting the best care available. IBM, as you might expect, provided top notch health coverage. In fact, they covered all his medical costs. We never saw one bill.

I should point out that at the time of my dad's illness, there were other cases of colon cancer in Crestview Heights. Our neighborhood was located only five miles from IBM's main plant in downtown Endicott. Just a few years earlier, in 1979, there had been a large spill of toxic chemicals prompting a massive cleanup of the groundwater and soil in the vicinity. (In fact, remediation efforts continue to this day.) The dangerous compound was purported to pollute the ground and the groundwater in a fair amount of downtown Endicott forcing people to move out of their homes or get their drinking water from elsewhere. IBM took responsibility for the spill and spent millions and millions of dollars to help clean up the contamination, but the town was and is not the same. The once vibrant factories that employed nearly 20,000 IBMers lie desolate and decaying today. Endicott is a shell of what it once was, and it makes me sad to go back.

My father worked 20 miles away in Owego, not at the Endicott factory that put the pollutants in the ground so there's actually no direct link to his cancer. It was also well before regular preventive screening for the colon (i.e., a colonoscopy) was routine. There's no telling if these tests would've caught his cancer in time and to be able to treat it. The outlook was grim.

More tests would reveal that there would not be a simple fix. Dad received a colostomy, a procedure which creates an opening in the abdominal wall and allows the colon, or large intestine, to pass stool into a collection bag. We were learning so many new medical terms and procedures so we could understand just what Dad was facing and know what questions to ask.

In as little as one month, my dad went from being seemingly healthy to very ill and recovering from major abdominal surgery. He was sick enough that he wouldn't be able to attend my college graduation later that month. Of course, we were both disappointed. His voice cracked when we talked about it on the phone. I was saddened and remained confused by this intrusion into our lives. As it turned out, Dad didn't miss very much. The ceremony on the old football field lasted a grand total of 15 minutes thanks to a downpour. To move things along, UAlbany officials breezed through the ceremony, having entire schools of study stand up as they announced each group had completed the necessary coursework to graduate. The keynote speaker never spoke.

It was fine with me—kind of exciting and fun in its own way. I had other things on my mind, like moving into my summer apartment, starting grad school, and my father.

There would be multiple trips to visit Dad in the next few weeks. And typical Dad, just as soon as he was able to recover from the surgeries, he was back to work at IBM. When we pressed the doctors for a timeframe, they gave him about eight months. With that, he was determined to work and live as normal a life as possible. It was what he did. He was still the primary breadwinner of the family and hadn't even turned 50 yet. It was supposed to be the heyday of his career. His goal, like mine, was always "to get back to work."

My father took his role as provider seriously and had worked hard to advance his career. That being said, he was ALWAYS home by 5:30, when Mom would have dinner on the table. He'd eat, watch Walter Cronkite on the evening news and then head out for the evening activity, which back then was either a Little League game I was playing in or a baton twirling performance for Priscilla. Or it was choir practice for himself. He was also a Deacon at the church for as long as I can remember. In the Presbyterian church, the Deacons are the "do-gooders." They take care of the shut-ins—those people who are confined to their homes due to age or a physical or mental disability. Deacons also manage the service on Sundays.

I remember one of these shut-ins, Mr. Hager, whom Dad visited once a week. Mr. Hager was very old and couldn't walk very well. He lived in a small walk-up apartment in Endicott. When I was about 10 years-old Dad would frequently take me along on these visits. We would take him food and sit and talk with him for a bit, even though his apartment smelled like "old man." Mr. Hager always gave me a quarter, which Dad let me keep. One day he was so sick that Dad decided we should take him to the hospital. We helped Mr. Hager as he shuffled down the stairs on his bottom. Once he was admitted to the hospital, Dad and I went home. Later, Dad had to gently tell me that Mr. Hager passed away. I cried, maybe because I thought I was supposed to, and Dad held me.

Dad continued to sing in the choir for as long as he could. I'm guessing he continued to perform up to six months before he died. Work, along with rehearsal, had to be too much at some point. Dad also liked to garden and tend to flowers and plants around the house and the cottage. African violets were a favorite of his indoors and geraniums outdoors. He had a room in one of our houses with growing lights and all sorts of plant foods. Had he been a different kind of person, one might think he was growing something else! I have pictures of him working with plants at the cottage when he was clearly very thin from his disease, likely the summer before he died

My father also liked to drive. We traveled a lot by car when Priscilla and I were kids, and Dad always drove. We played all the typical car games. One trip was very special. In the summer of 1972, when I was 12 and Priscilla was 15, we did a trip across the country. Dad took six weeks off of work and we drove to California to visit friends that we had made when we lived there. Two weeks out, two weeks there, and two weeks back.

Priscilla and I still talk about that trip. We each got to pick a site to see. I picked the Football Hall of Fame in Canton, Ohio. Mom picked Nashville. These many years later, we can't remember what Priscilla and Dad picked. It was a budget-minded trip, and we took great pride in that. We stayed primarily at Motel 6, then $19/night for a family. Mom went grocery shopping and made sandwiches for us each day. In the hot, dry desert Dad refused to run the air conditioner because it would "kill the gas mileage."

Dad had a great, sometimes irreverent, sense of humor, too. I remember sitting next to him at church in my newly minted wheelchair on Easter Sunday 1984. The preacher was going on about how lucky we all were. It went on and on. At one point, Dad leaned over toward me, touched my chair and said, "I'm not feeling too lucky, are you?" We had one of those church moments where the harder you try not to laugh, the more you do.

Later that summer, I spent quite a bit of time with my father at the cottage in Skaneateles. He and I had our traditions there. We had built the dock together, which required frequent repair, and took the boat out together. He would drive while I waterskied. Then we'd end the day with some beers. My father was always proud that he could find the best deal on beer so we drank a lot of Piels Light. It was awful (he liked it), but at $0.99 a six pack it was "a deal." I brought a case of Michelob with me one weekend, but he said he didn't want to try it because he was afraid he might like it.

After Dad took ill and I got hurt, our traditions became less physical. Gone were the boat trips, replaced by quiet family time. We'd sit, talk, read and drink (gin for him, vodka for me). There's a dinner cruise boat on the lake and we all did that together that final summer. I have a picture from that night as well. What breaks my heart now is to know that he was in far more pain than he let on. But he always wanted to remain strong for us. He also knew his days were numbered, but we never talked about that. I don't know if he was scared, sad or worried. He just kept being Dad.

My father died on October 19, 1984, at home with my mom by his side. Doctors had given him just eight months to a year, but he lived almost 2-1/2 years after his initial diagnosis. Still, he was just 51. It breaks my heart to this day.

Mom said his passing was peaceful. He had been under hospice care for a time so I'm confident he was comfortable. My heart breaks as well for my mom being there with him, all alone, at just 50 years-old. But she would have wanted it no other way. She held it all inside to protect Priscilla and me as much as she could. She called the funeral director, Billy McCormack, that night to begin arrangements—the same guy I would call five years later after my mom passed away from the very same disease.

My dad worked for IBM for 28 years. On his 25th anniversary with the company, he joined the "Quarter Century Club." He was awarded a Rolex watch with the date and Club insignia engraved on the back. Dad got that watch on May 6, 1981, my 21st birthday. I have worn that watch proudly since the day he died.

I still miss my dad. So many times throughout my career as well as my personal life, I would have loved the ability to pick up the phone and get his thoughts on a given situation or share a triumph. I would have enjoyed being better friends with him, too. As I have watched other father/son pairs get older, especially Dave Gonino and his dad, they have formed deep friendships. They reflect on the days growing up in a different way, especially now that Dave's a dad himself. I'm sad that I never had that adult father/son relationship with my own dad.

It hurts me when I think of the void left by my father's death. What I wouldn't do to have one more chance to sit out on the deck with my father, look out at the lake and reminisce with him about the good old days...even if that means drinking another Piels Light.

TWELVE

THE OTHER TWO WOMEN IN MY LIFE

Be a strong woman. So your daughter will have a role model and your son will know what to look for in a woman when he's a man.
—from the *Boss Lady Motivational Notebook*

As I detailed in Chapter 3, my wife Pam played an instrumental role in my recovery and so much more. She not only stood by me during the most difficult time in my life, but she gave me genuine optimism about the future at a time when I really needed it. She afforded me a life that I could never have imagined staring at the floor from my Stryker frame in the days after my accident. She has been my best friend and soulmate for almost four decades now, and I'm simply blessed to have her by my side.

I've been equally blessed to have two other co-female MVPs in my corner for much of my life, and that's my late mother Mary Jane Hamlin and my sister Priscilla Hamlin Maddock. Both have been tremendously influential in my success, personally and professionally, and in shaping the kind of person I am today. I am greatly indebted to them both for their amazing support and for always lending an ear when I needed it most.

My mother was someone who always put her children, husband, friends and loved ones first, right until the very end. She was a woman of great energy, passion, integrity and empathy, and possessed an incalculable inner strength that would be greatly tested throughout the 1980s—from my accident to my father's illness and then her own.

She was born in Skaneateles, New York, on May 1, 1934, the daughter of a lifelong postal worker, Joseph Fisher, and housewife and schoolteacher, Olive Fisher. Much like my grandmother, my mom would go on to become a schoolteacher, teaching English at a local junior high school in Endwell, N.Y., where she and my father rented an apartment after getting married in 1956. I would be reminded throughout my life that my mother was an English teacher, as she corrected my papers, my grammar and even the letters I sent home during college. I'm sure if she was still alive today, she'd be editing all of my texts, emails and this book.

My mom's teaching career was short-lived, however. Not long after my sister was born in 1957, my parents bought their first house just minutes from the IBM plant in Owego, N.Y., where my father worked. Mom did what most other IBM wives and mothers did at that time, she became a full-time stay-at-home mom. And she was good at it. Mom would eventually settle into a routine of cooking, cleaning, doing laundry and caring for Priscilla and me, which later gravitated into shuttling us around to baton and swimming lessons and other sporting events as we got older.

My mom was a great mother, but she naturally cherished having some time to herself once we headed off to school. My sister and I still joke about it to this day: Any time we said we didn't feel well and could back it up with a fever or vomiting, my mom would say, "Oh shit!", since we just interrupted the flow of her day. But then she would recover quickly and be the best sick-day mom ever by showing great sympathy and letting us just lie on the couch and "be sick." Mom was a very social person who was active in the church and hosted countless bridge club sessions at our home. She liked to go out and have coffee or lunch with her friends. She also enjoyed writing.

While my mom was good at it and played the role well, she was not a "natural" housewife. She was a professional woman who shined in the workplace. So, not surprisingly, as soon as Priscilla went off to college and I was a reasonably responsible teenager, she took a job with the local YWCA as co-president. Like me, she was very career driven. She would move on to hold senior communications positions at the Red Cross, Binghamton General Hospital, Roberson Museum and Broome County United Way. Many of these positions required significant fundraising skills and she was very well respected in a professional community still dominated by the IBM good ol' boys club.

In addition to these paid positions, Mom also taught English as a second language through Literacy Volunteers of America. At some point, she also joined Toastmasters, an organization that empowers individuals to become more effective public speakers and leaders. She just loved it! My mother was always a prolific writer, and this gave her an outlet for that. As an example, there's a chair that's been in our family for four generations now that once belonged to my great-grandmother on my mother's side. It's known in the family as "Grandmother's Chair," and my mom once wrote a Toastmasters speech about the chair and the special place it has in my family's history. The speech was very personal and full of description and brought to life the meaning of the chair to my family and what a larger-than-life person my great-grandmother was. The chair now has a place of honor in my own home with my mom's framed speech on the wall above it.

To this day, I think about my mom when I speak in public. I think about how she would say it, and I always make sure to include something very personal in my speeches. I'm not the writer or speaker she was, but I enjoy both, thanks largely to her. It was with this in mind that I first signed up for The Dale Carnegie Course in 1993. Dale Carnegie Training was started by Dale Carnegie himself over 100 years ago. The organization offers a wide variety of business and human relations training designed to build professional confidence and skills. It is a 12-week course, and each week students must give a two- to three-minute talk about a specific topic completely from memory. This not only builds skill in speaking but in organizing concepts and thoughts. I truly enjoyed that experience and went on to be a graduate assistant for five more years. We made it a practice for years to send our management and executive level professionals to Dale Carnegie classes.

Besides being an excellent writer and public speaker, as well as a professional businesswoman, my mom was emotionally stronger than any woman I've ever known. She had to be because what she went through for almost an entire decade beginning with my father's cancer diagnosis in 1982 was something that would've broken most people. When my father got sick, Mom maintained all her activities and yet somehow spent every moment with him. She advocated for Dad in the hospital and at home to be sure he got the very best medical care possible. She also protected us kids. We were not denied information, but I'm sure we were shielded from the profound struggle they were both going through.

Even after I had my accident 15 months following Dad's diagnosis, she still managed to keep it together and be strong for the both of us. She had an endless well of empathy for my father and me. If my dad wasn't well enough to make the five-hour trek to Buffalo to visit me in the hospital, she would go it alone, but not before making arrangements with one or more of her friends to make sure that my dad was well taken care of. Mom advocated just as hard for me as she did for my dad, making sure that I got the best care possible and understanding the implications and risks of each decision we had to make.

My mother had a loud, infectious laugh. You could hear it distinctly in any room or from the other end of the hallway in the hospital. It didn't matter what she was laughing at, you just wanted to join her. It is a laugh that I remember distinctly from my initial three-month stay in the hospital. It helped me more than she'll ever know. For years we had this old videotape from a family get together, and there were a handful of moments on the tape where you could hear my mom's fantastic laugh. The tape is gone now. I miss that laugh.

On the day my father died, at the age of 51, she was home alone with him. She called us afterwards to tell us that it was a peaceful and private moment—a moment, sadly, that we would have with her just five years later.

I remember vividly the day my mom called to tell me that she was diagnosed with the exact same disease that had taken my father two years earlier: colon cancer. I was in the bathroom when she initially called, and as soon as I came out Pam said, "You need to call your mother right away." So I did. I said, "What's up?" And she said, "Well, you know," fully suspecting that Pam had already given me the grim news. Naturally, I was

134

devastated. I couldn't believe this was happening again! I cried a bit, but then I remember having one of our Hamlin family "Let's meet this head on" discussions and saying, "All right, what's next?" We had been through this before with Dad, and we knew there was a process. Unfortunately, that process turned out to be eerily similar to my dad's. First there was the exploratory surgery. Then there was an attempt to treat it with chemotherapy and radiation, followed by a colostomy procedure.

The progression was frankly almost identical to my father's as well. Priscilla and I knew what was coming, but my mother did a very good job of shielding us from her bad days and what she was going through, just as she did with Dad. I'm sure she was in a lot more pain than she let on, and like my father, she lost a lot of weight, but she always put up a good front.

It really bothered me that Mom was essentially living with this disease all by herself. Yes, she had a deep network of friends who would drop anything they were doing to help her, and Priscilla and/or me along with our spouses would visit almost every weekend, but Mom had no soulmate to share it all with in the darkness of each evening and the darkness of the disease itself. It was never really practical for Priscilla or me to move to Binghamton to care for her nor would she have permitted it. And it would have been nuts to move her away from her home. She wanted us to pursue our careers and the lives we had begun. That was Mom—even at her sickest, she was worried that we not focus too much on her.

My mom was a big-time worrier. She worried about being a good mother, a good wife and a good professional, and that drove her to be good at all of those things. It's a deep commonality that the two of us share. Priscilla as well. She worried about EVERYTHING, and it only got worse after my father got sick, and I had my accident.

Case in point: In the summer of 1988, about a year before she died, she hired a contractor to make the living space and entrance to the cottage more accessible for me. She was worried that I would not be able to spend time alone there as it was previously configured. There had been a step into the house and the bathroom door was a scant 24 inches wide. We worked around this by having others lift me to get in, and I would transfer to a smaller kitchen chair at the bathroom door and scoot my way to the toilet that way. Mom fixed all of that. She had the contractor replace the entrance with a ramp and put in a new bathroom. He even put on a new deck. She had him build a separate area off the porch that overhangs the main deck and seats about six people. We still call it Doug's Deck.

My mom did all that for me, just so I could enjoy the place independently, which I do. I'm sure I never thanked her properly, if at all, but it's just one of countless examples of my mom putting her loved ones first.

Mom, like Dad, worked nearly to the end, serving as the communications director for the Broome County United Way up until eight weeks before she died. It was important for her to work because it kept her vital and occupied. When it came time for her to take advantage of hospice care, she did it her way, not theirs. The normal hospice routine is that a primary caregiver lives with the patient and hospice volunteers or nurses spend a portion of each day there. Mom had no live-in primary caregiver, so she rallied her network of friends and convinced hospice that they would cycle through her apartment and function as a collective primary caregiver. If they had to stay overnight, bring her food or take her to a doctor's appointment, they could.

This primary caregiver by committee featured both professional associates that she had become very close with, like Judy Peckham and Bonnie Donovan, and her bridge club friends including Barbara Work, Pat Stuempfle, Jane Park and Fran Ebbers. I'm probably leaving out several names, but they all made it work. It worked because they cared so deeply for my mom and we all knew that if she could do this her way, she would be far more at peace with the whole situation.

On the day she died, nearly three years after her initial diagnosis, we were all there—Priscilla and her husband John and Pam and me. It was a Thursday. We had all visited the previous weekend and gone back to Albany and Buffalo for the work week. But on Tuesday, the nurses called and said, "You guys better come back." We hung out in the hospice room (as Mom was an inpatient by then). She was pretty well sedated but awake enough to say some occasional morphine-induced nonsense which we all laughed at, including her.

The hospice nurses had nailed it. She slowly faded but rallied enough to have some private moments with each of us. Thursday night at about 10:30, she began to repeat that she loved us. Over and over she said, "I love you," until her last breath at 11 p.m. She was just 55 years-old.

I grew up a lot in the 30 minutes that followed. I called the funeral director, did the paperwork with the hospital and made sure that everyone had a place to stay that night. I also insisted on some final private moments with my mom's body before they took her. I'll never forget that, and I'm glad I did it. I told her I loved her, that I was honored to be her son and that I would try to make her and Dad proud. I knew they were together then, and that comforted all of us.

Priscilla and I may not have talked about it out loud then, but we shared the same sad sentiment: "It's just us now."

I said earlier how my family was my "rock" during my recovery, and it's safe to say that Priscilla stood atop that rock. Not only was she there every single night of my 91-day hospitalization at Erie County Medical Center, but she spent a lot more time on the phone with my parents than I did, providing them with updates on how I was doing both emotionally and physically. She was also the one who had to make the initial call to my parents and Pam when I was hurt and prepare them for what they were going to see in the hospital. In addition, her apartment had become Command Central in the days after the accident. Whenever anyone came to town to visit me, they first called Priscilla to see if they could stay at her place or if she could recommend a hotel nearby. It was an awful lot for a 26-year-old to handle, but she never wavered and assumed the role of communications and hospitality director, therapist and "best sister ever" all in one.

Priscilla being there for me every single day meant the world to me. First, this gave me a regular event to look forward to. I knew at the end of the day she'd be there and we'd eat together, watch the baseball playoffs on TV or just read our books in silence. Other times, we talked the whole time or cried about my father. It wasn't a big production, but it was a routine that became very important to me throughout my stay as I really had no other set schedule in the hospital. Secondly, she provided a connection to my family and the outside world every day. My parents did their best to come up as often as possible, and Pam could only see me on the weekends because of her job. I had a number of friends come visit me, especially early on, but Priscilla was the one consistent presence.

My sister and I were very close prior to the accident, so I don't think all that time we spent together in the hospital made us any closer. But it certainly strengthened what we already had. It was a bond that would become unbreakable after what we still had to go through with our dad's illness and death and then Mom's.

As kids, Priscilla, who is three years older, and I got along better than many brothers and sisters did. Sure, we had our share of sibling differences, but at the end of the day we were always there for each other and we never had a time where we were so angry at each other that we couldn't talk with one another. We were different in many ways: I was an athlete who was always out and about in the neighborhood, riding bikes or playing sports with my network of friends, and she was a bookworm who spent much of her free time reading. Sometimes during the summer months, her friends would join her in the backyard and they'd read for hours. Mom tried to get her involved in ballet at the IBM Country Club, but every time Mom went to pick her up to come home Priscilla was engrossed watching the baton twirlers practice. Mom adapted and ballet turned into baton pretty quickly.

I still find it funny every time we go back to Endicott to visit our parents' graves. Priscilla will be driving, and she'll be asking me for directions. And I'm like, "How is it you don't know your way around here?" And she'll reply, "Because I always had my nose in a book and wasn't paying attention." She doesn't know where anything is!

She did have a good sense of direction when it came to her career, though. At the time of my accident, Priscilla was working at the Fisher-Price toy company in the Buffalo suburb of East Aurora, where she ultimately became a senior toy researcher of the play lab. As part of her job, she would care for the employees' kids in the morning (as well as some select local kids in the area), and then in the afternoons work with toy engineers and designers on how to make the products even better for the kids. You see, the toys that the children would be playing with in the mornings were the ones slated to be released the following Christmas or the Christmas after that. Essentially, she was a crucial part of the design and testing process. I am always so proud when I get to describe to others what she did there.

Priscilla spent 17 years at Fisher-Price before working briefly for another product testing lab and eventually settling into a job as co-director of the Westminster Early Childhood Programs, the largest childcare facility in the Buffalo area. The center, which had a staff of more than 40 employees and cared for approximately 200 children, was affiliated with the Westminster Presbyterian Church. My sister retired from that position a few years ago and now works as a receptionist at the University at Buffalo Child Care Center, where she is THRILLED to have much less responsibility, and still greatly enjoys being part of an early childhood education community.

Priscilla is a lot like Mom, in that she's tall, loves to swim (especially in Skaneateles Lake) and is a big worrier. Her friendships and career are important to her as well. She and I have spent hours talking with each other about how to handle various situations at work. It was so important to get the people-part of the business just right.

Priscilla and her husband, John Maddock, the senior associate athletic director at Canisius College, were married in 1987. They have two adult daughters, Mackenzie and Mikaela. Mackenzie looks to be following a similar career path as her grandmother and works as a Peer to Peer Fundraising Manager at the Roswell Park Comprehensive Cancer Center in Buffalo. Mikaela's career choice, on the other hand, may have been inspired by me. She got her Doctor of Physical Therapy (DPT) in Physical Therapy & Rehabilitation Sciences from Drexel University and now works as a Pediatric Physical Therapist in the Charlotte, N.C., suburb of Concord.

Mikaela, for some reason, bonded with me at a young age. She was very interested about how my wheelchair worked and would crawl around it until she could eventually climb up on my lap. She loved to sit there, and I like to think that her fascination with my wheelchair and her special bond with me had something to do with her getting into physical therapy.

Priscilla is every bit as good a parent as she is a sister. I think that's something else she inherited from Mom and Dad. One of Priscilla's biggest sorrows is that she never had her mother to call in the middle of the night for advice when one of her girls was sick. Mackenzie was just a year old when Mom died. However, I'm sure that had Mom been around to take those calls, she would've told Priscilla that everything would be just fine and to take everything one day at a time. Then she probably would've hung up the phone and stayed up all night worrying about her granddaughter.

Priscilla and I remain as close as ever. We talk a couple times a week and text more than that. We are blessed to still have the cottage, just four miles from my house, where we see a lot of each other in the summer. We've each had our share of medical issues in recent years—a cancer scare for her; kidney, shoulder, stomach ulcer and atrial fibrillation (AFib) issues for me—but we are there immediately for each other. We advocate, do research and ask the right questions. We take care of each other, just like Mom and Dad.

THIRTEEN

THE IMPORTANCE OF FAITH

Sometimes life hits you in the head with a brick. Don't lose faith.

—Steve Jobs

Summers as a kid were magical. No homework. No schedules to keep. Everything was just about having fun. From the moment that final school bell rang in June until that dreary post-Labor Day morning when the yellow buses rolled again, my world shifted from home in Endicott to camp.

There were two important camps for me in the 1970s. One was Uncle Jim and Aunt Marilyn's family camp, a 600-square-foot cabin with a big hearthstone fireplace on a lake in the Adirondacks. Here, the four cousins (Priscilla, David, Brad and Doug) lived a very Huck Finn type existence, enjoying outdoor activities from fishing, boating, kayaking and swimming to hiking and biking. Oh, and Priscilla read books. Lots of them.

Then there was Watson Homestead, a church camp located at the site of IBM founder and former CEO Thomas Watson Sr.'s childhood home. Set on hundreds of acres of woods and fields, and located about 45 minutes west of Endicott, I spent many summers there as both a camper and counselor.

As a camper, I had come to look up to the counselors, and one group in particular dubbed the "High Nine" by my youth pastor Drew Mann. In his first year as director of the camp, Drew inherited a group of nine counselors who had been together for at least two summers. They were a tight-knit group and exceptional in their roles as counselors.

By 1975 the High Nine was breaking up, aging out of the church camp life. A couple had gone on to become camp directors for a week or two, but most were either seniors or out of college entirely. I was two or three years removed from this elite group. To me, they were the pinnacle of coolness to which I aspired. Three of the High Nine attended the First Presbyterian Church in Endicott—an IBM church through and through—and I had the privilege to watch them, study them in their coolness and take mental notes.

As the High Nine moved on they were replaced by the next generation, which included Priscilla. Also in that class of counselors was, in my estimation, the coolest of them all, Armand Cianciosi. We called him Armie. He was just "that guy." He was a soccer star, had the right girlfriends and a wicked sense of humor.

I tried to copy his sense of humor, and my jokes fell flat more often than not. But one time I got to share the stage with Armie. I'm sure it isn't even a blip in his memory, but to me it was a monumental moment. Armie and I performed the entertainment at camp one evening as mock sportscasters. My fellow campers in the audience were eating it up, laughing at Armie and me. They were looking at the two of us like we were best friends. I think I remember that night so vividly because it gave me a real boost in self-confidence.

A few years later, I would become a counselor-in-training and then a counselor for two summers (1978 and 1979). I would become that role model. Funny, I had no idea how big a role camp would play in life, both in my development as a person and my growth as a leader, until I started this journey of reflection to tell my story in these pages. It was here at Watson's Homestead that I got my first taste of meaningful leadership.

To get everyone on the same page as camp counselors, Drew conducted staff training for a week at the start of each summer. He was very good at telling stories and getting young minds to look inward at their own strengths and weaknesses. I swear it was his goal to get one, if not all of us, to cry at some point that week. It might be a story about someone's hardship or some heartbreaking story that would evoke some deep inner feeling, but he usually succeeded.

Being that there were several very attractive girls around, I was doing my best to appear tough and in control. I would not shed tears. "Keep talking, Drew. You're not going to get me to cry," I kept telling myself as one by one my fellow counselors spilled tears around the campfire.

Of course, Drew would succeed, and I would cry. It was all about learning empathy for each other and the campers who would be in our care for the summer. We learned how to understand and manage our emotions. We were young ourselves (17 or 18) and responsible for hundreds of kids each summer.

I remember my first week as a camp counselor. I had nine kids in my charge, ages 8 to 10. Each day a counselor and their group of campers were responsible for that night's campfire and entertainment. On my chosen night, I decided I was going to build the biggest, baddest fire in Watson Homestead church camp history. This was going to be the campfire that these kids would remember for the rest of their lives.

It was a very rainy night. My nine little charges gathered around in their colorful plastic ponchos, bibles clutched in their hands underneath, and watched while I stacked the wood high and doused it with lighter fluid. This downpour was not going to interfere with my awesome blaze.

Only it wasn't lighter fluid, it was white gas—the kind you put in a Coleman lantern. With the flick of a match, Watson Homestead experienced an explosion I'll never forget. I dove away from the airborne logs and ended up on the ground behind a tree. I was afraid to even peek at my little campers, fearing that their ponchos had flash-melted to their bodies. But by the grace of God, they were fine and had really enjoyed my "fireworks" show. Priscilla told me later that I had a stunned look of fear on my face the rest of the night. I hadn't realized until that moment that I really was responsible for the well-being of these youngsters—for the entire summer!

The counselors would alternate between three different venues. Some weeks I would be with campers in permanent tents on platforms in the woods, or we'd be in cabins. There would also be a series of hiking/canoeing "wilderness" trips in the Adirondacks that lasted seven to ten days. Counselors worked in pairs and were assigned "units" of campers ranging from five or six to as many as ten kids—even more on the wilderness trips. Weeks were arranged around age groups—grades 3 through 5, 6 to 9 and 10 to 12. Each day counselors were responsible for teaching (both bible study and nature skills), feeding (helping campers prepare and cook their own meals in the woods or waiting on tables in the dining hall) and entertaining (sports, games, hikes, etc.) the campers. This meant a lot of prep with your "co-counselor" the night before. And yes, "prep" frequently turned into camp romance.

In my first year as camp counselor, I got a little more than I bargained for with regard to the 10-day wilderness excursion. For many of the campers, it was their first true exposure to "roughing it" in the wild. It was a real wakeup call, especially for some of the girls. Before heading out, we would inspect the kids' backpacks to make sure they had the right gear critical for the journey.

Bug spray? Check.

Vinyl poncho? Check.

Flashlight? Check.

Hair dryer? Check.

Wait. What?! Yes, one by one some of the girls started pulling curling irons and blow driers out of their backpacks, even makeup mirrors. Apparently, they thought they were going to plug these items into a tree. Needless to say, their bags were much lighter and expectations much different after we repacked them.

Typically, these wilderness trips were led by a director, usually a minister, and two counselors—one male, one female. The directors were the adult supervision and spiritual guidance on the trip. We counselors were only a year or two older than the oldest campers. On this particular trip, however, the Director pulled me aside just before we shoved off to share some rather important information. "I don't know anything about canoeing or backpacking," she confessed. "You're going to have to take the lead to get us from here to where we need to be 10 days from now because I don't get it. I can't read a map."

For some reason, I didn't flinch. I didn't feel overwhelmed or look for an exit. Maybe it was because of the four-stanza

"Invictus" poem by Victorian poet William Ernest Henley I had memorized in high school that I could readily accept such a challenge.

> Out of the night that covers me
> Black as the pit from pole to pole
> I thank whatever Gods may be
> For my unconquerable soul.
>
> In the fell clutch of circumstance
> I have not flinched nor cried aloud
> Under the bludgeonings of chance
> My head is bloody but unbowed.
>
> Beyond this place of wrath and tears
> Looms but the horror of the shade,
> And yet the menace of the years
> Finds and shall find me unafraid.
>
> It matters not how strait the gate,
> How charged with punishments the scroll,
> I am the master of my fate,
> I am the captain of my soul.

When I was in ninth grade, I had an English teacher named Mr. Hines. Priscilla had him also. He was famous for his first-day assignment, in which he required all of his classes to memorize "Invictus." We had one week to do it. From that point on, he reserved the right to call on you anytime to recite the poem with as much emotion and drama as you could muster. The more drama, the better your grade. He could call on you anywhere, too, not just in the classroom, but in the hallway, cafeteria or even at a football game. He even caught one student in a department store while he was shopping with his mom. He jumped up on a display of clothes, screamed out the poem and got an "A." Mr. Hines got me in the hallway. I was embarrassed and henceforth very reserved, which led to a "C"—my typical grade in English (much to my mom's chagrin). I still remember the poem verbatim, so does Priscilla. There are parts of it I can reflect on that help me through the challenges that I even face today.

Leading that group of 20 kids (and the Director) through the wilderness was a big challenge, but I was undaunted. "I can do this," I thought. It was exhilarating and, yes, a bit intimidating, to realize I was responsible for marshaling 20 junior/senior high kids along a mountainside and actually getting them to perform certain life-building skills every day. And yet I lived to tell about it. The good news is that all 20 campers did as well. That trip was another real confidence builder and growth experience for me. I was thrust into a very real role of responsibility and leadership and I embraced the challenge, almost naturally.

Drew got a good chuckle out of my wilderness adventure. He was a somewhat counter-culture youth pastor who didn't fit the conservative mold created by the IBM church community. Instead, he had a tinge of rebel that endeared him to those in his charge. Our church was Drew's first job out of seminary, and it was my first year in youth group. I was 12 years-old. In some ways, Drew and I grew up together—he in his ministry, and me in my adolescence.

Under Drew's leadership, the youth program became more popular. That's because Drew got us. He understood us because he could still remember what it was like to be a kid. It was hard to picture the Elders—the name given to the church's board of directors, most of whom worked at IBM—as kids, dunking their friends in the pool, trading baseball cards or being anything less than mature.

Drew and I clicked pretty quickly. I was a quick-witted, respectfully irreverent kid with lots of questions. Drew tells people in those days I was viewed as a "cut" (i.e., "ripped," in today's parlance) jock and the girls watched me as I entered youth group. I was clueless about this at the time, which was probably a good thing. In my mind, I was an insecure teenager finding my way.

What I wasn't clueless about is who was winning and who was losing the various games Drew planned for us each week. I didn't like to lose, still don't. I didn't care if it was team sports, individual sports or my favorite baseball team, the New York Mets. I had a running tally of wins and losses. It's how I was wired.

Drew and I shared that competitive spirit. Once a week or so we played tennis together at one of the local parks. One day I was playing particularly well and in response to one of my lightning serves, Drew did something not very pastor-like. He had a John McEnroe-like tantrum and threw his racket, then turned his head in anger and, I think, swore! That just made me like the guy all the more.

Despite having this competitive streak, I still looked out for the less-than-athletic among us—i.e., those guys who'd be picked last when setting up teams in gym class. It's just in my nature that I like to see everyone included (which can have a negative side as you'll read later).

Drew more than tolerated adolescence. Because he was still fairly young himself (he was in his mid-20s at the time), he seemed to have the patience to weather whatever phases we were going through. He also endured more than one controversy, going to bat for his group. For example, at a leadership meeting in the winter of 1978 some church leaders voiced their displeasure about the 15 teenagers (myself included) who would sit in the front row on Sundays in their brightly colored ski outfits. When the last note of the final hymn sounded, we would storm to the area behind the choir section, grab our skis and rush to our cars to drive to Greek Peak, where we'd ski for four hours and then be back at the church for youth group at 6 p.m.

Parishioners and church leaders spoke one by one at this meeting (we were not there) about their concerns for us teens and our stampede out to Greek Peak. They felt it showed some disrespect. Then Drew spoke. "Yeah," he said, "maybe they're rushing off to the slopes right after church. But they're staying till the end of the service every Sunday, and they're paying attention."

Like I said, he got us, and we got him. Drew was able to convince the adults that church had become the fabric of our Sunday routine, and that this was a good thing. We had at least made church a priority. Drew told me later that, as a teen, I had a keen sense of seeing hypocrisy in others when words didn't match deeds and vice versa. I was still working on that on my end as well, and Drew was there to help us all. Frankly, I don't know if I would have been there if it hadn't been for Drew.

Drew helped me build the foundation of my spirituality and taught me that it was okay that my relationship with God was complicated. He even said it was okay to get mad at God, even though I loved Him. When Drew spoke from the pulpit, he made Jesus real to me. The struggles He had, tempted in every way yet sinless. Drew spoke as if he was talking just to me. He focused on helping me form my own opinions rather than spoon-feeding me what he thought I should think.

The Endicott church and its youth ministry led by Drew was a lightning-in-a-bottle period in my life. I've spoken to others from that time who say the same thing. It was just the right time and place for us. The few churches I've belonged to since fill different roles in my life and faith but are not the center of my universe like it was in Endicott. It was about the people, and I am extraordinarily blessed to have had that experience.

It would be years before I became a member of another church. When I was in college, I was convinced no church could be like the one I grew up in and my lifestyle didn't really support getting up on a schedule Sunday morning. That said, I am not a person who needs a "church" to have a strong relationship with God. It was there. I leaned on it when I needed to, especially during the most difficult times.

After my accident, I went through a "What did I do to deserve this" phase. I needed time and help understanding that it doesn't really work that way. It's not necessarily God's job to keep you safe and happy, but to stand by and with you as you manage and endure challenges as they present themselves. Over time, Pam and I have reached an "Everything happens for a reason" method of dealing with life's difficulties. Even this gets tested pretty hard, as we've had to deal with the early passing of my parents from colon cancer, Pam's father died young from lung cancer, we were unable to have kids naturally, and most recently we suffered the loss of Pam's sister in a fatal car accident.

I've come to understand that my accident was part of God's plan for me. Once I embraced that, I was able to adopt an "I've got to be the best quadriplegic ever" attitude. I wasn't going to be able to change my body, so I decided to do the best with what I had. I still had a good heart (actually and figuratively) and a functioning brain. I put both to good use.

A whole lot of good fortune has allowed me to be my best version of myself. I am generally healthy and not burdened with some of the devastating medical issues that can accompany a spinal cord injury. I am adaptable to changing situations. I have unparalleled support from family and friends. I hope this all has allowed me to be an example and maybe even an inspiration to some. I think that's all part of His plan.

My faith is my faith. Pam and I did not go to church for the first 18 years of our marriage, but my faith was still very strong. If it grew, it grew because I got older and maybe a little wiser. In 2002, Pam decided she needed church again. Our inability to conceive had led us through a series of painful, emotional and eventually unsuccessful IVF treatments. We were very sad. We had poured ourselves and most of our savings into the dream of having children and had to accept that it just wasn't in the plan for us. We needed to move ahead. Pam had attended church with her mother and grandmother growing up. We church-shopped for a year or so and eventually found a warm and welcoming congregation at Delmar Presbyterian Church, about a mile from our house. We were members there until we moved to Skaneateles.

When we started going to church again, I found ways to use my business strengths as part of church leadership. This connected me to the church and God a bit more frequently, but I think I've always spoken to Him the same way. Today we are active members of the church my mom and uncle attended growing up and where my parents were married in 1956.

My faith is just as real as it ever was, and is a big part of who I am today. I don't argue with people over their views or preach. I just know what I believe.

And I got that in Endicott.

*I presented an "Accessible Concert Award"
to Michael Lang at Woodstock 1994*

*Just one of hundreds of trade shows
with the VersaTrans sales crew*

Dave and I at my retirement party.
He flew in from a business trip
to Shanghai.

Last visit with Roger,
Walnut Creek, CA 2015

Boys weekend 2018, Artie, Dave and I
at Dave's lake house, Lake Lure, NC

My retirement party at Woolfert's Roost Country Club,
Albany, NY, November 2010

John Robinson and I,
Journey Along the Erie Canal,
July 4, 2017

First bike, another "Tank"
Upright, very heavy, very hard to pedal

New bike!
Aerodynamic, very light, 30 gears!

Pam and Andrea
"The Our Ability Wives"

John the cabbie in Scotland
Check out the "ramp" into his car!

My high school friend Terri and I
with the table I made for her.

Pam and me

Priscilla and Me

Our Skaneateles dream house,
just four miles north of the cottage

FOURTEEN

MY BIG BREAK

Great moments are born from great opportunity.

—Herb Brooks, Lake Placid 1980

By 1995, the School Bus Routing System (SBRS) software product was reliably producing its own revenue and profits. We began to realize that both parts of the company (software and traffic engineering) were growing and were very different. The work product and culture of each division were very unique, and so we formed another company called Creighton Manning Engineering (CME) to house the traffic engineering business.

With this separation, I would eventually have a choice to make. In 1992, I had started acquiring stock in the company. I liked owing a piece of the pie, and I knew there was more on the horizon. CME was formed as a professional corporation. Among other things, this meant that owners had to be licensed engineers, which I was not. And I had no real interest in going back to school. While I still enjoyed the transportation consulting work, I knew I would never own part of that company. This led me to focus a bit more time on the software side, although I would continue to work on "both sides." I even drew separate paychecks.

At this point in the mid-to-late 1990s, we had most of the suburban school districts in New York State on SBRS, plus a strong presence in Massachusetts and New Jersey. Even Illinois had become a big market for us. We were growing substantially in our little niche and had about 300 clients nationwide.

Then in February 1998, I caught my big break. I was driving home from Ithaca, New York, where I had done some training on traffic modeling, when I received a call from the vice president of Creighton Manning Associates (CMA), Brant Gardner. Brant said that he was leaving the company to work for a competitor that had "a clearer vision of what a school software company could be." They were closer to where he lived in Albuquerque, New Mexico, and also offered more money. I'm sure that helped with his decision.

Brant, who took over as VP of the software company in the late 1980s, had grown increasingly frustrated about the direction of the company. Like most of us at CMA, he had evolved into his role. Neither Roger Creighton nor Chuck Manning spent a lot of time on organization charts and corporate strategy and planning so things just morphed sometimes without much guidance. Roger had retired from the day-to-day in 1982 and Chuck was a consulting engineer at heart.

Chuck was the president of both companies—CMA and CME—and Brant reported to Chuck but at the end of the day, Brant was the person in charge of product development and sales for the software company. At his level, Chuck was never deeply immersed in the school bus product, and it was Brant's job to drive it in a forward direction.

Brant planned to tell Chuck his decision in the morning but first wanted to give me a heads up. I think he was also seeking my support. Quite honestly, before I was even off the phone with Brant, I was thinking about what a huge opportunity this could be for me. With Roger retired and Chuck largely focused on engineering, this presented a gaping hole that I knew I could fill.

The next morning, after Brant's call, Chuck called me into his office, and we discussed my filling that role. While I knew it was a great opportunity, I asked if I could have 24 hours to think about it and talk to Pam. I also wanted to talk to Dave. When I told him what this all represented, he simply said, "You're going to say yes to this." This was classic Dave Gonino advice. He didn't say this as an assumption that I had thought it through and decided to say yes myself. This was a directive from Dave. He was telling me that I was going to say yes because it was the best career move I could make.

I knew I would, but I took the day anyway. The next morning, I met with Chuck again and told him what I was thinking. He said, "Good, you're it. You're the new VP. Figure it out."

It was immediate. I cleared my desk that morning of all the traffic work I was doing, and Chuck either reassigned it to others or did it himself. I was finished on that side of the business and fully invested in the software company. It was also the beginning of my rise to senior leadership, and eventually CEO of VersaTrans.

Brant's departure proved to be fortuitous in a number of ways. In addition to creating a new career for me, it might have stopped me from seeking another growth opportunity elsewhere. When I was getting bored with my programming job back in 1991, Chuck found a way for me to work on both sides of the company. I may well have become restless again had Brant not left.

Before he moved on, I was straddling two roles. I was a project manager on the software side and a senior transportation planner on the engineering consulting side. Suddenly, I was the boss of approximately 30 people. I was about as ready to lead CMA as I was to lead a group of campers through the woods. But, just like the camping experience decades earlier, I had the full faith of Chuck and Roger. With that support, I could confidently jump into the new job.

Looking back, Brant had faith in me as well, despite the fact that we had some battles in the previous years. Brant was a very interesting person. He had a PhD in Anthropology, wrote prolifically about the Mormon Church and somehow became the first sales person and long-term product visionary for CMA. Brant, his wife Val and their five kids lived near Pam and me in our first house, outside Albany. On occasion, he and I would ride to work together when one or the other's car was in the shop. Brant and I spent a lot of that time talking about how we could run the company better than Roger or Chuck. Of course, in our minds, they were paying us far too little for our value and they weren't investing in the growth of the software business quickly enough. In hindsight, I would come to learn how naïve I was about running a business.

As I dug deeper into the operations of the company, I read and learned a lot about labor rates, overhead, billable hours, accrual-based accounting, profit, loss and so much more. With the exception of a statistics course, I had not stepped foot into the business school at UAlbany, so these concepts and their real-world application fascinated me.

This is where Brant and I began to see the world differently before he left. We would argue tooth and nail over the feature set that ought to go into the next product release. As a product visionary and perfectionist, Brant always wanted "just one more" feature added to the product before any given release date. On the other hand, I was always pushing to put it into the field so we could charge more in support fees and sell more products. In the end, there came a point where we finally just said, "This is it. We've got to put a staple in this and sell it the way it is, and push all of the other stuff to the next version." It was always a day too late for me and one feature short for Brant.

Brant's departure turned out to be short lived. His other opportunity wasn't what he thought it would be, and he asked if he could come back to VersaTrans. It was a little awkward in that I now was the one to hire him, but it worked out really well. I brought him back as a salesperson and, more importantly, he resumed his role as product visionary which served us well long term. Years later, I would often say that I hoped Brant was never truly happy with a product. That way, it just kept getting better.

Brant and I were trying to take the company to the same place, but I didn't think Brant's strategy to get there was doable. Brant was not a businessman. He was a product person. He wasn't interested in labor costs or how much we were going to charge for customer support nor did he care how much profit we made, just so long as we beat the competition. Conversely, since I had spent a lot of time doing consulting on the traffic engineering side, and each project had to make a profit, I looked very closely into the labor we were putting into it and how much we were promising to deliver in terms of support. Therefore, I was looking at the software company in a way a business or operations guy might look at it.

Since I still had much to learn about business, I started studying some of the young software companies in the Capital Region and what they were doing to be successful, and how we were different from them. We differed because we were born out of a consulting company, and we approached each project as a consulting engagement. We didn't look at ourselves as a commercial off-the-shelf software company. We were selling a software product and a pack of services to our clients, which included building maps and student databases as well as providing customer support. That would make us grow much more slowly.

Ours was not a volume business. There are 15,000 school districts in North America. That was basically our entire potential market. There was a lot of labor involved in making each client happy and successful. The software license price was less than all of the labor required to make the system functional for each client. We were spending hundreds of thousands of dollars on development and that was outpacing the dollars we were getting back from selling software licenses, so some of the labor had to go to fund the development efforts. It was not a clean revenue picture, and Brant never looked at any of those metrics.

When I stepped into Brant's job, I changed the role of VP significantly. Since Brant was the very first salesperson Roger hired, his sales background put him in a leadership role in many ways. Brant had his hands in the marketing, management and development process of the software product. I assumed the title and some of the same roles as Brant, except I was not a sales guy. I learned this fairly quickly when I went out and tried to sell the product during my first 10 months on the job.

I didn't have the depth of knowledge about how the product worked nor did I know how to present it like Brant did, even though I had watched him do it a hundred times. I couldn't stand up there for two hours and demonstrate the product like he did. I needed a person to do that, and that person came in the form of a gentleman named Michael Lowenstein. Michael worked for our biggest competitor in the school bus routing software industry, Education Logistics, based out of Missoula, Montana. Michael and Brant had traveled to many of the same conferences and trade shows, and thus had become good friends. After Brant left, Michael called me and said that he'd like to come work for us, so I flew out to Montana to meet him and decided that he might be that guy to demonstrate the product and lead our sales efforts.

By that time, we also had one other salesperson, Merle Winn, a friend of Roger's. Then I hired two more salespeople in pretty quick succession so that by 2000, we had four salespeople on board. Michael stayed in Missoula and identified three other people inside Education Logistics that expressed a desire to come to work for us, and so I hired them. They were mostly trainers and implementation people. I leased some office space in Missoula and they all stayed out there. Michael was on the road most of the time, just as Brant was. He even served as a marketing guy and product visionary.

It was around the same time I hired Michael that I realized I had too many people reporting directly to me. For example: I had half the product development team reporting to me rather than a software development leader or project manager. I began to recognize that there was value in having a leadership position that oversaw each department. I saw that my role was to manage people and manage the process and to be the face of the company in the field rather than filling so many needs behind a desk.

Thus, I started to put in place a management team to help oversee each department within the company. Michael was part of this first group, as were Chuck and Barb Manning and Terri Fallon, whom I hired in 2000 to serve as our marketing director. Terri had worked at MapInfo in the company's early days, just before it went public, and would serve a valuable role with our company for the next decade. The management team would eventually grow to around a dozen department leaders before I decided it would function much better with half as many people, and that's when I consolidated it further into an executive team and an operations group.

By 2000, Chuck had enough confidence in my leadership skills to promote me to president of the software company, which had been renamed VersaTrans a year earlier. The traffic engineering company remained Creighton Manning Engineering but now operated in another building entirely. Chuck was CEO of both companies, and so I still reported to him.

While Chuck spent the lion's share of his time on the engineering side, he did teach me a lot about the business side. I had known Chuck for 15 years, so I did things much the same way he taught me. Chuck helped me understand how to present complex, very technical information in a simple way. In fact, some of the basic spreadsheets we used to track performance numbers were his. From Day 1, he made me prepare the budget for the software company.

He and I also had frequent discussions about what we were

doing and what our plans were. I don't recall asking him for advice or what he'd do in "such and such a situation." It was more like, "Chuck, I think it's time we hire two more software developers, and here's why." And I would have numbers and projections to back it up. At this time, Chuck and Barb still owned the majority shares in the company. It was their name on any credit or loans that we had, so ultimately all financial decisions were theirs to make.

With the management team in place, I stayed out of the weeds as best I could and focused more of my time on company strategy and developing partnerships within the industry. That meant traveling much more than ever before, which was very exciting to me. Since the accident, I had only flown a few times (on vacation trips with Pam). I had been fascinated with flying since I was a little kid and thought that it would be great to fly as part of my job. And now I had that opportunity.

Brant had traveled extensively when he was VP, which I envied. The company was at a point where it needed a consistent "face" of executive leadership in the field and at trade shows and industry conferences. So wheelchair and all, in my first 10 months on the job, I flew 10 times, meeting with various school officials and transportation personnel all around the country.

I remember vividly the first trip I took as VP. I called our company travel agent and told her I needed to fly to Florence, Alabama, and that "I use a wheelchair and I really don't know what the rules are." She did a fair amount of research and was able to educate me on how the airlines managed people in wheelchairs. It turns out the airlines were way ahead of the Americans with Disabilities Act. I had to work on my fear of having to go to the bathroom, which I described earlier in Chapter 4, but the rest of it was quite natural and exciting. I always enjoyed the travel part of my job. I loved boarding an airplane and going somewhere. As I was earning my Delta frequent flyer privileges, I swore I was never going to be one of those snooty first-class passengers with an attitude. Well, once I got there, I found myself saying, "Here's my jacket, and yes, I'd love a cocktail," just like all the rest. I was flying first class most of the time, and when I wasn't, back then it was easy to find a coach seat with an empty seat next to it. Happily, I could rent basically the same car model I drove at home (GM 2-door body style) and AVIS would install hand controls for me. I got to the point where the rental car personnel in most major cities knew me. I even recognized (by certain blemishes or dents) that I drove the same rental cars over and over again. This made me completely independent on trips. Ironically, I can't do that anymore. Those big two door cars are no longer in production and four-door cars don't accommodate the same wheelchair stowage routine I have. If I were still traveling for business, it would be a much more difficult and complicated experience today.

By 2000, I was on an airplane about three times per month. I know this because I kept a notebook with the destination, the date and the purpose of each trip. I would take 541 such trips over the next decade.

As I alluded to earlier, my purpose wasn't to sell the software, it was to "sell" the company and make our clients understand that they were valued customers and that we were always there for them. I attended many of the same conferences Brant used to go to, except I brought a salesperson along with me to run the booth as I worked the crowd. I always viewed trade shows as customer service events. We looked our clients in the eye, shook their hands, bought them dinner and, most importantly, asked them to come to our booth and talk to potential customers about how great our services were.

I met with many of the big school bus companies and their senior leadership people, as well as representatives from the school districts. This gave us a certain amount of respect in the industry and also put us in a place to form several new partnerships over the years. I would also roll around the floor and introduce myself to our competitors and try to understand their view of the world. Frequently, we'd go to school administrative and superintendent shows as well because at the end of the day, that's where the check gets cut. It was important for us to share our vision of the company and how we were different from our competitors. This way, when that contract got to his or her desk, they would immediately recognize the company and, of course, that guy in the wheelchair who represented the company.

I think my disability helped me in this regard. It made me easily recognizable and memorable—I was always the bald guy in the wheelchair. I was also the VP and President and, later, CEO of VersaTrans, and those things mashed together created a certain level of respect.

My disability never impeded my ability to advance within the company nor inside the industry. For one thing, I could travel independently. I also didn't have any medical issues that prevented me from working 15- to 18-hour days if necessary. Some people with disabilities are not as fortunate. That being said, I truly believe that I would have ended up in the same position as VP/President and CEO regardless of my disability because I was never content with simply having a job. I wanted a career, and eventually I realized I wanted a company. I was grateful for every opportunity and I knew I wanted to be more than a computer programmer.

In the musical Hamilton, there's a song titled, "The Room Where It Happens," that describes how Alexander Hamilton, James Madison and Thomas Jefferson privately strike a deal to locate the new nation's capital along the Potomac in the South. From early in my career, I realized that I wanted to be in the room where it happened with Roger Creighton Associates and later CMA and VersaTrans. If there was change going on or a growth opportunity within the company, I found a way to be in that room. Disability or not, if someone has passion about what they're doing, they can find a way to be in that room. Once Brant left, I seized that opportunity and before I knew it, I was CEO of a multi-million dollar company.

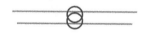

FIFTEEN

CEO

Leadership and learning are indispensable to each other.
—John F. Kennedy

Several years before I officially became CEO of VersaTrans, I sat and listened to my friend Amy Johnson tell me things about my leadership style that I really didn't want to hear.

"You know, Doug," she said, staring me right in the eyes, "you're not really an entrepreneurial software guy or even a traditional business guy."

"What?!" I thought to myself initially. I wasn't some college kid or intern. I was the president of a growing tech company, and she had the audacity to tell me that I wasn't a "business guy?"

I had entered into a new phase of my career and was ready to project a more business-aware, professional persona. Business was good. I didn't need her to tell me her opinion. And yet, that's why I wanted to see Amy. Her assessment of me and my leadership skills cut a little close to the bone—and they were dead-on accurate.

Amy wasn't just a friend, she was one of VersaTrans' primary headhunters and would recruit many of our senior leaders and salespeople. With a degree in engineering from Union College, Amy cut her teeth in the technology world, reporting to Steve Jobs at Apple for seven years. She eventually settled in Albany where she became an executive search professional and business coach. She had done all of the recruiting for MapInfo for years, and if we needed a senior executive, Amy was the one we turned to. I valued her ability to size things up and be brutally honest, but fair.

Deep down I knew she was right. At this point in time, I was reading business books voraciously. These included *In Search of Excellence* (by Thomas Peters and Robert Waterman), *Built to Last* (by Jim Collins and Jerry Porras), *Good to Great* (also Collins and Porras) and virtually all of the Jack Welch books. (This was in the heyday of Welch's run at General Electric.) Each of these books concentrated on what made businesses succeed and fail and how to build a strategy for success. I wanted to picture myself as one of these seasoned, bottom-line oriented executives getting the most out of every employee and transaction. I knew that to take VersaTrans to the next level, we needed to be more disciplined about our approach to business. Building that bridge to the future was my responsibility.

As I wrestled with Amy's assessment, I came to understand that I was not cut from the same cloth as bottom-line-driven leaders like Welch. I also realized that this was a good thing.

Welch is an extreme case. His path to shareholder value and company growth was disciplined, logical and brutal. He had an A, B, C approach to assessment and performance. The top 20 percent of employees were A players, the middle 70 percent B players and the bottom 10 percent C players. The C's had to be fired every year. That's how he believed an organization would continually improve itself.

I understood the logic behind his system, but I hated the brutality of it. Nor did it fit my empathetic personality. This method would not have been a good fit culturally at VersaTrans. But reading his books, it was apparent we needed to implement an organized way of evaluating and compensating people for their performance. That much I learned from Jack Welch.

In the early 2000s, there were a few high-profile, risk-taking CEOs also making a name for themselves in the Capital Region. Headlining this group were Craig Skevington and Bob Godgart. While not household names outside of Albany, these guys were held in high regard in the community for their ability to land venture-capital money and build an organization to the point where it was acquired or taken public. They had each grown and sold several companies by the time I officially began to run VersaTrans in 2000.

These were the Mark Zuckerbergs, Steve Jobs and Bill Gates of our region. And apparently, I didn't measure up. It was a hard assessment for me initially because I desperately wanted to be held in the same high esteem as these guys, my heroes in the business community. But the words from Amy rang true deep down. I wasn't an entrepreneur of that type. That's not to say I didn't feel some risk, like the time early on when Pam and I had to personally guarantee a $1 million line of credit with the bank (when our entire net worth was about $250,000!).

Always a glutton for punishment, I asked Amy to go deeper. If I wasn't a business guy, then what was I? She didn't pull any punches.

"In some ways, you're a politician," she said. "You're a person worried about culture, about values, about everybody— probably to a fault—having their say. You're a consensus builder."

Now, if she'd been wrong about any of those things, I would have stopped her. I wouldn't have cared about her opinion and probably wouldn't have been seeking her advice in the first place. But she was right. I wasn't the business guy I'd imagined. My dad going to work every day in a white shirt, tie and dark suit had formed one image of what the business world was like in my impressionable early years. Roger Creighton and, to some extent, Chuck Manning, had largely shaped my evolving view of the other. My mental image didn't match my actual persona.

Roger probably had the biggest professional influence on me, both as a person and a leader. He had the ability to be demanding without being a jerk about it. For some reason, I always wanted to please Roger, not only because he was signing my paycheck, but because he had high expectations. He made these expectations very clear, and it was important to me to meet them.

That said, Roger was also the man who gave me my first job and held it for me during all those months I was laid up in the hospital with an uncertain future. That gratitude never left me. I owed him for his faith in me and empathy for my situation. That was the kind of company I wanted to run.

In reality, while I strove to be more like Roger in those early days of leading VersaTrans, I was actually more like Chuck. He was a consensus builder, almost to a fault, just like me. As a result, I had a hard time making decisions without having ALL the information. Thankfully, I got better with time.

Amy also helped me to understand the kind of business we had. At the end of the day, I could never be Skevington or Godgart because in terms of market and culture we just didn't have that kind of company. We were in a finite business-to-business market (15,000 school districts) that would never support a $100 million company. Our growth would be largely organic and our trajectory fairly linear. This was not a model that would allow a venture capitalist to quadruple his money over five years.

The right culture was vital to our success as a business. In the school software business, the customer goes shopping for two things: 1) a product and 2) a relationship. This is the way I viewed it anyway. Once we signed a school district as a client, our goal was to keep them as a client forever (and we were very successful at it). This way, in addition to charging them an initial software license fee, we continued to collect support fees from them every year. These were the profitable dollars. It was on us to make both the product and the relationship work. We needed to make sure that our culture would reflect something that the client would be proud to be associated with—not only the performance of the product, but the relationship with the organization.

We therefore built a culture matching that of our clients. Trust me, school transportation professionals don't do it for the fame or the money. Rather, they are relationship builders. They are soft-hearted and empathetic. Their primary mission is the safe transportation of students to and from school each day, and secondarily the district's bottom line.

My leadership style helped build and grow our culture. It's what I knew. I grew up in a nurturing IBM culture and then observed Roger and Chuck run a demanding yet family-oriented organization, one that looked at employee's needs and tried to meet them as best they could in the context of the success of the business. So there was a softer side to it.

Quite frankly, there was not a lot of focus on the bottom line before I took over as president and then CEO. Chuck was never laser-focused on how much money we were making, just that we were making enough money to pay our bills, keep our employees gainfully employed and keep our clients happy.

If I was to succeed as CEO, I needed to develop a leadership style that was as much business director as it was camp counselor. I needed to be more attentive to our bottom line. That meant developing budgets and establishing quarterly and annual targets and goals, all those things that go with growing a company. And I needed to be able to objectively hold people accountable for their performance.

But I couldn't do this alone. I had to make some crucial hires. I needed experienced leaders who could fill in my gaps. I was going to have to be okay with the idea of working with more type-A individuals and not feel threatened by their more forceful—or, say less democratic—approach to leadership.

The first of these hires was a new marketing director, Terri Fallon. I was introduced to Terri through a consultant we were using for marketing at the time. Our profile was becoming national in scope (actually, all of North America) and we needed to significantly boost our image. Enter Terri, who had worked for MapInfo during their fast-growth years.

Neither Terri nor I knew what a disruptor she would be to the company. She was the first "outsider" from a big company that I hired. Her position was also a new one. She didn't fit into one of our established "departments." Terri represented change, which I knew we needed, but not everybody agreed with Terri's ideas or her approach. She was direct, at times unwavering, and not "VersaTrans-like" in the eyes of many.

This was my first, rather uncomfortable lesson in real leadership through growth. To build that bridge from our "old school" image and ways, we needed some of Terri's ideas. At the same time, we needed the skills and culture that had brought us to where we were. I found myself alone in the middle of that bridge more than once, wanting simultaneously to hold on to the comfortable past and lean into the exciting, if somewhat unknown, future. Bringing people along with me, especially long-timers, was not always easy.

The next crucial addition to the team was Jim Guzewich, who I brought on as Chief Financial Officer in 2003. (He carried the additional title of Chief Operating Officer starting in 2006.) Jim had a long history in the Capital Region, having been part of the mergers and acquisitions team at KeyBank. He also served as CFO at several insurance and technology companies and had a wealth of financial management and leadership experience on the executive level. He was also involved in an angel investment group which he personally brought me into as well. We'd listen to pitches Shark Tank style from countless technology companies and decide to invest in them or not. Jim had the ability, because he was a numbers guy, to evaluate businesses very quickly, including ours. In his first week on the job, he looked at our tax position for the previous three years and discovered a strategy that got us a $200,000 refund in 2003. In other words, Jim covered his salary on Day 1. I liked that.

I found Jim through a CEO network I belonged to. He was looking for a new challenge at the time we hired him and was a great match for VersaTrans and me in particular. Jim was a rare breed—someone who knew he was more experienced and, in some areas, smarter than the top guy, yet also knew he wasn't No. 1. That's what made him the perfect wingman for me. Regardless of how strongly he may have wanted to tell me I was wrong or that I should go in a different direction, he always posed his ideas as suggestions or recommendations. They were extremely well thought-out with detailed costs and benefits. And when he left my office, usually with his idea intact, he didn't give the impression that he'd "won." That's pretty special. He got it.

Jim also came on at a pivotal time when I needed a right-hand associate that I could trust. In a relatively short time, VersaTrans had nearly doubled its employees from 35 to 60. We were not a huge company by any means, but we certainly were getting more complex. We had been hiring from some of the top tech companies in the region like MapInfo and CommSoft. Jim was a brilliant financial guy, but he was so much more. He was also a really good operator—he understood how organizations worked in terms of people and numbers. For instance, when he started, he took the opportunity to sit down and have a half-hour discussion with nearly every employee. After that series of meetings, he came to me and said, "Doug, almost nobody here knows how the company makes money."

This was astounding to me because I assumed everyone understood the business model. I'd been living it for 20 years by that time and it was just so natural to me. Those conversations completely changed the way we did our staff meetings and other internal communications moving forward. We would go over our performance for each month, what went up, what went down, where we needed to improve and so forth. Lo and behold, people began to own their part of it, which was very cool.

The culture of the company was beginning to change. When I took the helm of VersaTrans, the employees must have thought it was going to be a picnic since I was so soft-hearted and family-oriented. I was a familiar entity. I'm sure most thought that things wouldn't change very much.

But we were growing. I was adding quality individuals to my senior team who came from successful companies and I needed to meet their expectations. High performers need systems and tools, some of which we didn't have or were outdated and inefficient. They also needed strong leadership that could set direction and make decisions. I had to redefine myself more like that fictional CEO I'd imagined. They didn't know the Doug who had started here as a programmer and was getting his shot at the top. They saw, I'm assuming, CEO Doug Hamlin, the leader of this well-run business that was on the move.

I began to grow, with their help, into the leader I needed to be. This was not always easy or comfortable, but I was confident in my position and my ability to adapt and perform at a higher level. In retrospect, I think my disability helped me in this growth. I never talked about it with clients, employees or job prospects, but it was there—very visible. It helped create an image or opinion along the lines of, "This guy has obviously overcome some stuff and look where he is. I think I might want to be part of that."

As we brought on more and more new employees, word got back to me that our onboarding process stunk. In fact, it barely existed at all. Our new employees let me know that the initial orientation process at VersaTrans wasn't much fun at all and lacked any real process or content.

I asked my new executives to develop an orientation and education process for new hires. Part of my growth at this point was realizing how much I took for granted simply because I had been there for so many years already—basically from the beginning. Having these new folks teach me about my own company was both enlightening and humbling.

The next big hire we made was a gentleman by the name of Ted Thien, who came on as our VP of Sales in January 2007. Ted came highly recommended by Amy, largely because she felt he could cover my flank and be that person I wasn't. He was someone that had a little bit of that swash-buckling air to him. He was very driven. He had worked for all kinds of organizations, big and small, including Oracle, and had started his own software business. After three years, he sold it to another company and was working inside that company when Amy and I met with him.

Amy told me how lucky I was that Ted was available, and she was right. Ted was the best VP of Sales I ever had. He was fantastic. Ted took over the sales organization and ran the heck out of it, utilizing all of that entrepreneurial spirit. At the same time, he understood the culture of the company and was able to adapt to that fairly quickly. He was good at the numbers, good at making deals and just a really, really smart guy.

How good were the hires of both Jim and Ted? After we were acquired by Tyler Technologies, Jim replaced me as president of the VersaTrans division when I left in December 2010. Ted then took over for Jim in January 2013 and still heads Tyler's VersaTrans Division as a VP and General Manager. VersaTrans is now a $30 million division of Tyler, more than double what it was at the acquisition in 2008.

While I was good at hiring people—well, mostly—I struggled with the firing part, especially early on. It just didn't fit with my empathetic leadership style. I had never been fired or laid off so I had no idea what it was like to be shown the door, to be told to pack your belongings into a box and leave. That had to be very difficult. One day you're necessary to the overall operation of the company and the next day you're not.

Unfortunately, I was the one holding the trigger, and it was very stressful. I didn't like it. I agonized over firing people. I also wasn't very good at it. I remember having to fire one of our senior salespeople and botching it big time. I knew I needed to fire this person, but I didn't want to do it over the phone. It would only be fair to meet with this individual face to face, I thought. So I flew to San Francisco and met with this individual over lunch. Then I made a critical and unforgettable error—I fired them right there after we put our orders in. Thus, we had to sit there, wait for our food and then eat lunch, which was wildly uncomfortable. It was a painful lesson and one I'd never forget.

Business leaders roundly agree that when you know it's time to let someone go, you just do it. It doesn't help anyone to prolong the agony by moving someone around or giving them a million chances. When it comes time to fire someone, it shouldn't be a surprise to them. They ought to know that they're about to be let go. Still, early on in my role as president and later CEO of the software company, I would try just a little too hard to give someone a third or fourth shot.

The person who taught me how to manage someone out of a company rather than just fire them was Tom McBride. Tom was a gentle giant of a man from near St. Louis, Missouri, and had been vice president for a large school bus company. His boss called me one day and said, "Doug, I need to lay off Tom, but I want you to hire him as your sales leader." So I did, and it worked out great. In his role, Tom had to fire two or three salespeople, and he was so thoughtful and optimistic in his approach. He was one of the few people in the world that could fire someone, make them feel good about it and then take them out to dinner. He would help people understand that maybe their current role didn't suit them, but that there would be better fits out there for them.

The fact is, if you don't act decisively when you know you need to, you lose your credibility as a leader. Usually, co-workers know who the underperformers are. When you give these people a second and third chance, the whole staff suffers and they begin to wonder: "Does Doug see the incompetence around him?" In the end, I got pretty good at making decisions and moving on and managing people out of the company. And I think those who left were freed to find a place where they were indeed a better fit.

Besides learning how to hire and fire people the right way, I also had to change the way I thought about work. When I started working for Roger Creighton Associates, the 8 a.m. to 5 p.m. work day was devoted to the client. Period. Both Roger and Chuck had this mindset. Anything you did internally on the company side, even accounting and HR, you did after hours. During the day you were only on the clock working with clients.

So, as CEO, much of my time was spent working with department leaders, human resources or talking with my right-hand man, Jim. I began to feel like I was neglecting my responsibilities, and what had been drilled into me since Day

1 in 1983—that is, if you're not working with clients, you're not really working.

Thankfully, I had some key advisers who helped me off the ledge. One of these was Mike Marvin, the former co-founder and CEO of MapInfo, one of the darling software companies in the Capital Region. As CEO, Mike had taken MapInfo from four employees to more than 500 before they went public. The company was later acquired by Pitney Bowes in 2007 for nearly a half-billion dollars in one of the largest deals ever in the Capital Region.

I first met Mike back in the late 1980s and again in 1991 when I interviewed for a position at MapInfo. From that point on, as I grew into a leadership position with our little software company, Mike was always someone I knew I could call if I had any questions. He was considered a mentor to many young executives in the Albany area and would give freely of his time, helping me understand that it was okay and even necessary to "work on the business."

I remember one particular call I had with Mike back in 2001, when I was president of VersaTrans. Our business model just wasn't working anymore. We had grown to the point where the positions we had just didn't make sense anymore. Employees were angry because their roles weren't clear enough, and the people we brought in from elsewhere had certain expectations about how things ought to work.

Mike loved to talk business and share some of the lessons he'd learned, including those he learned the hard way. He told me that as CEO, the only constant was change, and that I'd begin seeing more and more transitions at VersaTrans. MapInfo was seemingly always in "growth mode," and he didn't have to look far for examples of what we, too, would be facing in the near future.

"Your company is going to 'break' at least four times," he said. "Right now, because you're at $1.5 million, it's going to break at $3 million and $5 million and $10 million. It just is. And you've got to embrace that change and understand that there's going to be a period around each one of these revenue marks where things just aren't going to feel right. Don't worry, it will again."

What Mike meant by the word "break" was that things were going to get screwed up, and it was the CEO's job to unscrew them. He said that once you become a $1 million company, you had to act like one. You had to hire more people, have a middle layer of management and have some rules and policies and regulations in place. He helped me understand that part of the leader's responsibility was to anticipate what that growth was going to do to the organization, and how to build and maintain a culture whether it's 40, 80 or 100-plus employees. I had to constantly pay attention to that culture being right.

Mike was absolutely accurate. You can't put a price tag on the right kind of mentors.

From the time I took over as president in 2000 until 2008, when we sold the company to Tyler Technologies, we experienced a 163% annual growth rate. We weren't a huge company, but I believe that the issues, pains and successes associated with any rate of growth are similar regardless of the raw numbers. I know my personal and professional growth never stopped. I read as much business literature as I could both inside and outside our industry. I also made it a point to befriend others in similar positions, and I even asked a few to join my Board of Directors so I could force myself to report to them.

What I learned about myself was that I was good at growing VersaTrans to our current size. Eighty-five employees was the limit of what my "camp counselor turned CEO" personality was going to support. To go to the next level, which I thought would be an organization that could reach $50 million and maybe 200 employees, we needed an infusion of cash, business expansion and risk-taking that were likely beyond my ability to lead.

At the end of the day, I remained a people pleaser and a consensus builder. My adviser was right. But I definitely developed more confidence and trust in myself and in my decisions as a leader. As time went on and we became more successful, I started to understand my role better and better. I don't think that understanding ever ends, what the leadership role is in the organization. I got comfortable with the fact that I didn't have to be the one who had every new bright idea. That's what I wanted to be in the beginning, the guy with the ingenious idea that spurred a billion-dollar corporation. What I found to be more important was to understand what needed to be done and know how to find the right people to do it. That's what I got good at. I was a relationship builder, both internally and externally.

SIXTEEN

SELLING THE COMPANY

All progress takes place outside the comfort zone.

—Michael John Bobak

When I took over as vice president of the software company in 1998, our bottom line or net profit hovered somewhere in the low single-digits. While far below what most off-the-shelf software companies strive for, we were primarily a consulting company and were plowing most of our income into growing the business.

Encouraged by our continued growth, I decided that year to have our revenue numbers published in the local business paper, the Capital District Business Review. I did this as a benchmark to see how we stacked up among similar local companies. At the time, it was a way to promote ourselves to potential employees, but it turned out to be an important first step in the eventual sale of the company, which would not happen for another decade.

The Business Review would rank the top 20 software companies in the Capital Region every July, and very slowly over the next decade we worked our way up from No. 11 to No. 3. We were experiencing steady, solid growth in both revenue and profit. We weren't a huge business nor would we ever be in our niche market. That said, we were leading our market in many ways.

Once we began making our numbers public, the phones began to ring from prospective buyers. At first, it was only a few calls per year, evenly split among financial buyers (mostly boutique private equity firms) and strategic buyers (those in complementary businesses). But as our revenue grew and our standing in the Capital District improved, outside interest increased. By the time I took over as Chief Executive Officer, we were hearing from more and more interested parties with specific ideas about how we could partner.

As these discussions became more frequent, I wanted to put together some parameters and guidelines to help evaluate the promise of each opportunity. I knew a few things: 1) To get to $30 or $50 million in revenue was going to take a massive infusion of capital; 2) I was only interested in a good strategic fit with organizations of similar culture and values; and 3) this would stretch me. A big investment or all-out acquisition would mean loss of some or possibly all control of the business, something I was quite used to having by now. That was a high bar. As one financial buyer put it to me, "Doug, there's a number at which all your principles and parameters go away." This was probably true, but that number would have to be very, very high.

I also could not do this alone. I brought my Chief Financial Officer Jim Guzewich into the conversation fairly early. I trusted him implicitly, as he had plenty of experience in mergers and acquisitions and, most importantly, he wasn't as emotionally tied to the business as I was and could offer objective advice.

Jim and I had a policy where we always said yes to the first meeting. There was nothing to lose and probably a few things to learn about how we were viewed by potential investors.

Ninety-nine percent of the time, it'd be a nice conversation and we agreed "to talk again in a year." We probably had a dozen of these meetings in 2006-07. When Tyler Technologies called us in September of 2007, the call lasted more than an hour (a lot longer than most). Jim and I were on the speakerphone in my office, and I recall us glancing at each other more than once during the call with looks of surprise and interest. When we hung up, we each sat there for a moment and finally said almost simultaneously, "That was different." It was, very different.

The call was from Brian Miller, who at the time was Tyler's vice president of finance and treasurer. (He's now their executive VP and CFO.) His job was to seek out potential companies for purchase that would fit well into Tyler's increasing portfolio of businesses. Tyler Technologies was a fast-growing technology company. It was originally an industrial goods company after purchasing Tyler Pipe, a manufacturer of iron pipe, in 1968. In the late 1990s, its board of governors decided they wanted to become a tech company, so they sold off all of their hard goods and entered the government software market. (Thus the name Tyler Technologies.)

By the time they called us, they had already acquired more than a dozen smaller public sector software companies to fit into their growing collection of government technology solutions. What piqued our interest was that they were looking to expand their offerings to school districts. They were talking to software companies that had built viable student databases, grade reporting, school lunch systems, business office systems and district management systems. They were looking at the entire school district environment, including transportation.

Jim and I were the only two people on these calls. We needed to keep it very close to the vest until there was really something to talk about. Acquisition rumors can grind a business to a halt as they fly around the building. Jim was incredibly valuable to me throughout the entire process. He was more than just a CFO and COO. In any other world where you don't have titles, we would've been straight up business partners. I learned more from him in seven years than anyone about the machinery of running a business. He was a very important part of the acquisition with Tyler because in his prior life, he had been on the other side of the table, figuring out how to buy companies.

After several phone conversations with Brian, Jim and I were invited up to Portland, Maine, as that's where Tyler President and CEO John Marr was located. Tyler's headquarters were in the Dallas suburb of Plano, Texas, but only about 10 percent of the employees worked there. The nexus of the company was in Portland, which was home to one of the first software companies that Tyler had purchased.

Besides Brian and John, we also met with Tyler Vice President and Legal Counsel Lynn Moore Jr. It was another good conversation. I must admit I was a little intimidated by John. He was about my age and we actually had similar backgrounds in early personal computing technology. He and his dad built the company that became Tyler's first software acquisition. John was now CEO of a $400 million publicly-traded company and interested in buying our company.

While the talks to that point had been encouraging, I remained skeptical. Could any other company really "get" how special VersaTrans was? That being said, the culture of the Portland office, while much larger, felt a lot like ours. I was able to observe their teams working and understand a little more about how Tyler went about their business and, more specifically, how they integrated all of the companies they acquired. They purported to have no interest in moving our company from Albany. Thus, they appeared to meet two of my non-negotiable criteria: 1) That they were a good culture fit; and 2) that they would not uproot us. Now I wondered if we could make a deal that would be good enough for our shareholders, our employees and our clients.

From the time I became VP in 1998 to the end of 2007, our revenue had grown by a factor of seven. We had 1,500 clients across North America and were approaching 100 employees. Like MapInfo nearly two decades earlier, we had become one of the most desirable places to work in the Capital Region. This was not going to be a colossal deal like Facebook buying Instagram for a billion dollars but everything is relative. It did involve several million dollars and the livelihoods of scores of people.

When I became President in 2000 and especially when I became primary shareholder, I began to look at the business as it affected the employees. As I wandered the halls and cubicles, I would see staff in the context of their lives: Some had new mortgages, new car payments, children with special needs, aging parents and other financial strains. They relied on a stable business and work environment to support their lives. I took that as my personal responsibility.

I also thought about our clients. I had personal relationships with hundreds of transportation directors and school superintendents. I needed to be sure that the service and products we continued to provide them would maintain the level of quality VersaTrans had promised.

In the world of acquisitions, this all happened fairly quickly. Our initial call with Brian occurred in August 2007, and less than five months later we had a deal. Tyler's first offer came in around Thanksgiving. We negotiated back and forth in December and by early January, we had a deal that both Jim and I thought was good. That's when I brought the executive team into the loop. I had said to Tyler: I need to do one test before we close on the deal. I need to bring my executive team to Portland and have them meet with their counterparts. I needed my director of marketing and my vice president of production to meet with theirs, and so on.

I realized that this meeting could be a bit dicey, since two of the people on my executive team had gone through difficult acquisitions with other companies. So I knew they would be wary. I said to the team, "Look, we're going to go up to Portland and meet with their people, and if any one of you comes back tomorrow and tells me this is a horrible idea, I'm going to listen to you." It looked good to me, but it needed to work for everybody.

When the team returned from Maine, nobody could give me a reason not to do the deal. They weren't overwhelmed with excitement, but they could also see it working, which was the best response I was going to get. And the aforementioned two people I was most worried about said they could get on board with it, which made me feel very comfortable about the deal. Now I just had to run it by the other 15 minority shareholders.

The night before we were scheduled to close the deal with Tyler, Jim and I met with these shareholders. I was really nervous about the meeting because these were people who trusted me, and I had been keeping them in the dark for five months. It was difficult for me to inform them that this negotiation had been going on for a while, and that we had a deal in place. We needed 67 percent of the outstanding shares to agree to the sale. Together, Jim and I owned more than 70 percent. The deal was going to happen.

That I owned well over half of the company at the time of the sale was a bit of luck and good foresight. I'd always been someone who embraced change every chance I could. Whenever there was an opportunity to advance my career or be part of something big within the company, I found a way to involve myself in it, such as making sure I had a role in the 1994 Woodstock music festival, stepping up when the previous VP, Brant Gardner, left the company, or buying company stock. There were opportunities along the way that for whatever reason, I was confident to put myself in a leadership position.

In 1992, Roger Creighton had decided to retire, although he still wanted to retain majority ownership in what was then Roger Creighton Associates. Fortunately for myself and a few others, including Chuck and Barb Manning and Brant, he was willing to make available some shares in the company. So I paid roughly $10,000 for 10 percent of the company at that time. Then in 1998, Roger decided to sell all but a very small percentage of the company to roughly the same group of people, and I borrowed some money against my house to purchase another 20 percent. Finally, in 2004, Chuck and Barb chose to reduce their ownership stake to less than 20 percent. I borrowed $100,000 and bought the majority of what they were selling, after which I owned roughly 55 percent of the company. My holdings grew further through various smaller transactions.

By January 2008, Jim owned another 15 percent through direct purchase from the Mannings and our employee stock purchase program. In 1998, we had developed a stock ownership program where if you had been with the company for three years or more, you were allowed to buy a certain percentage of shares each year. That's where our minority shareholder group came from.

On the night I spoke to the shareholders, I brought our company lawyer to the meeting so that he could explain the intricacies of the deal to everyone. I also brought along a financial adviser so that he could answer any questions the shareholders might have about Tyler's employee stock option plan and other tax implications of the transaction. The deal was good. Tyler was offering approximately 75 times what the average VersaTrans shareholder had paid for their shares. I saw everyone put their heads down and do the math. After that no one had questions for the attorney or the financial advisor. People did very well. Several people became very wealthy that night. The shareholders were comfortable with the deal.

As I explained to the executive team and the shareholders, and the employees at a company meeting the next day, another reason why we did the deal was because VersaTrans needed a path to double in size to stay on top. We didn't have the wherewithal to do it on our own. We needed to invest in new production and technology, and we didn't have the means to write checks big enough for such things. We needed a cash infusion, a merger or an acquisition in order to grow our business exponentially. Tyler Technologies provided us with that. Yes, we'd lose control from our end, but we still would remain our own division and I was confident that Tyler would live up to their end of the deal and let us run our business.

As part of the deal, I stayed on as president of what was now the VersaTrans Division of Tyler Technologies. And the business continued to operate out of the British American office park in Latham, N.Y., which was near Albany International Airport. Jim remained in the positions of CFO and COO.

Timing is everything. Remember, this was 2008, the year of the financial crisis that devastated Wall Street and the banking industry. Things were already on fire in January, although I don't think anyone had any idea how big a blaze it was going to be. We were the last acquisition Tyler made for another four years!

After the transaction, there was one person remaining that I needed to speak with, and that was Roger. Quite frankly, I was more nervous talking to Roger than I was the executive team or the shareholders. I was worried he might say, "You ingrate. I gave you this great opportunity and now here you are selling it!" While he no longer had any financial interest in the company, he was still a very trusted adviser and mentor, and I felt I owed it to him to tell him face to face. I took him to lunch, filled him in on the whole story and then stopped talking. After a few anxious seconds of silence, he looked me in the eyes and said, "I hope you got a good price...and I'm proud of you." I nearly wept.

I continued on as president of the VersaTrans division for nearly three more years before stepping away in late 2010. While our company had made significant gains in the short time I was CEO, we were just a small fish in the Tyler acquisition pool. To put it in context, our company represented only 4 percent of all of Tyler's revenue. But we were also one of their most successful acquisition stories because we didn't leave anything for them to fix. They bought us and left us in place, just like they said they would. They didn't have to fire anyone, and there wasn't a lot of overlap with any of their other businesses.

Sure, there were some bumps in the road. At the executive level, the culture was much more corporate, and the accounting and human resources systems changed. And, being a publicly traded company, we became beholden to quarterly financial reporting. We suddenly had numbers to hit, for real. Jim and I had to sign Sarbanes/Oxley compliance statements every quarter, and I had to present our numbers (good and bad) to John Marr and the Tyler brass. It was all very "grown up."

Tyler took it pretty easy on us at the beginning, but then they started making our numbers harder and harder to hit. For the guys who were running the $100 million divisions, I'm sure my little report seemed very insignificant, but for me it was all part of a fantastic education. I learned a lot about how public companies run and how different they are from small, family-oriented private businesses. I also learned that however insignificant your numbers might seem in the grand scheme of things, they're not. I was always under the microscope.

Case in point: The first time I encountered John Marr after the acquisition was at the quarterly meeting of divisional heads in Portland in March 2008. I was in the hallway prior to the start of the meeting when I bumped into John. We exchanged 10 seconds of pleasantries, and then he proceeded to grill me on my numbers for about five minutes. He knew my numbers better than I did, and he could tell when I was trying to BS him. I felt as if I were being interrogated in a courtroom (and remember, VersaTrans was 4% of his portfolio). That wasn't fun. I prepared harder the next time.

In the first month, I received an email from John's No. 2 guy, Dick Peterson, the president of Tyler's School Division. Dick, whom I reported to, was basically trying to refocus me on my numbers and help me understand how he was going to interpret them. Essentially, he was laying out to me what his expectations were in terms of my quarterly goals. I did not take it very well. I responded with a three-page rant that said he didn't understand our business model and what makes it successful. Now, had I been in his position on the receiving end of such an email, I might have fired my ass. Fortunately, he'd been through it before and let me have my moment, then he kept my feet to the fire for the next three years.

When I agreed to stay on for three more years, I was pretty sure I would call it quits at that time, and by December of 2010 the timing never felt more right. I could've stayed on longer as division president but the company had grown beyond me. I was really good at getting it to this point, but I wasn't the one to take it any farther. Both Jim and Ted had worked for bigger companies with much more financial stress and were much better at dealing with upward politics than I was. Jim would replace me as president, and was later followed by Ted.

I had gotten really used to being the No. 1 guy. I hadn't reported to anyone in over 10 years. I was financially secure and while I could have embraced the challenge of being a part of Tyler's team long-term (they said I could stay as long as I wanted), I knew I was never going to be "in the room where it happened" at Tyler. The other thing I always knew was this: Mom and Dad had never been able to enjoy any kind of retirement. I had vowed to myself years earlier that if I could do that for them, I would. I was in a position, at age 50, to do that now.

The fact that I needed surgery for a torn rotator cuff in my right shoulder made the decision to leave even easier for me. I had first started experiencing discomfort in the shoulder two years prior, and the throbbing, aching pain had become so bad that I couldn't sleep at night. I also had a very difficult time getting in and out of my car and transferring myself from my wheelchair in general. My arms simply couldn't do it anymore. It was beyond time to get the surgery done, so I used up all of my banked vacation days so that I could finish before the holidays and had the surgery the Tuesday following Thanksgiving 2010.

It all worked out for everyone involved. The VersaTrans division now employs nearly 150 people and revenue has nearly tripled since 2011. Tyler's market cap is almost $14 billion and they joined the S&P 500 in 2020. As for me, I'm enjoying a fourth career as a part-time consultant for young executives and businesses, working from my lakeside home in Skaneateles, N.Y. There are no executives to grill me every quarter about my numbers, and no one I have to report to but myself. I have even discovered a couple new passions. What a deal!

SEVENTEEN

JOURNEY ALONG THE ERIE CANAL

*The future rewards those who press on. I don't have time to feel sorry
for myself. I don't have time to complain. I'm going to press on.*

—Barack Obama

The morning sky was blue on Day 1 of the inaugural
"Journey Along the Erie Canal," interrupted occasionally
by small cotton ball-like cumulus clouds that did not block the
sun. It was hot. To my left, the Niagara River flowed powerfully
northward in its never-ending quest to empty Lake Erie into
Lake Ontario, a mission it has been on since the recession of
the Wisconsin glacial episode approximately 11,000 years
ago. In fact, the water passing me at that moment would soon
drop 167 feet over Niagara Falls.

The Niagara Escarpment, the reason Niagara Falls exists,
presented one of the largest challenges to the original engineers
of the Erie Canal, a man-made waterway that connects the
Great Lakes to the Hudson River in Albany. At its completion
in 1825, the Erie Canal was the second largest canal in the
world (363 miles long). Boats laden with goods ranging from
flour to lumber could now float unimpeded from New York
City to Buffalo rather than in wagons fighting rutted, muddy
paths. The cost of moving goods inland was reduced by 90
percent.

The Erie Canal project didn't start out so pretty, however.
New York Governor DeWitt Clinton was met with nearly

20 years of rejection, frustration, jeers and sideways glances. Thomas Jefferson himself called his plan "nothing short of madness." Eventually, Clinton's persistence paid off.

Speaking of "nothing short of madness," in January of 2013, 196 years after the opening of the Erie Canal, my friend John Robinson told me of his intentions to ride his modified bike the length of the canal trail sometime in June of that year. John is a quadruple amputee and the goal was to use the ride to raise awareness about his company, Our Ability, Inc. His bike was a gift from an adaptive sports organization, and his wife Andrea had been prodding him to go on a bike ride for some time. She wasn't talking about a Sunday afternoon ride in the park but a monumental journey across New York State.

John said if he was going to make such a trip, he'd make a big deal out of it, raising awareness for his organization, which strives to create more employment opportunities for people with disabilities. But a several-hundred-mile journey across the Eric Canal? Frankly, I thought he was nuts. So did the Canal Corporation. When John and I respectively waddled and rolled into its headquarters in Albany and announced our intention to ride our bikes across the state, we drew some strange looks. Months later, we found out that they thought our plan too was "nothing short of madness."

John and I met in the summer of 2010 in the Southwest Airlines boarding area at Albany International Airport. John is a congenital amputee, born without the full extension of his arms and legs. His arms end at his elbows, and his legs end where his kneecaps would be. He stands just 3-feet-9 inches tall.

At the time we first met, I was still CEO of VersaTrans. My time with the company was winding down, and I was generally on a tour of North American client sites telling the Tyler story and turning things over to my successor. I had only about a half-dozen more trips to go on before wrapping things up. On our initial encounter, John was on his cell phone. I was close enough to eavesdrop, and I learned that he was headed to Sacramento for a speaking engagement, filling in for a keynote speaker who'd bailed just six hours earlier.

"This guy's a public speaker," I thought to myself. "That's something I might want to do."

After John got off the phone, I went over to introduce myself. We hit it off, talking all the way to Chicago. He told me all about Our Ability, an organization with a two-pronged focus: 1) To educate and inspire people with disabilities to enter the job market or start their own businesses; and 2) urge businesses to understand and tap into this overlooked labor pool.

When John returned from Sacramento, we reconnected and quickly became good friends. Most of our conversations took place over bacon and eggs at Mancuso's Luncheonette in Delmar. It was here that I first learned of John's drive and ambition. John had recently been invited to an event at the White House for President Barack Obama's announcement of "Startup America," a small business initiative which, among other things, was intended to "inspire and empower an ever-greater diversity of communities and individuals to build great American companies."

At the time, Our Ability was a non-profit organization running primarily on donations and small grants. John did not want to go to this event as the Executive Director of a non-profit. He wanted to go as the CEO of a corporation. Problem was, he wasn't. He said to me over coffee, "I want to develop the business plan, differentiate it from the non-profit, and incorporate it before I go." We had 30 days. I worked on the budget and the legal stuff while John fully developed the vision. In March of 2011, John was able to sit side by side with other corporate leaders in the East Room of the White House to hear the announcement. His business card said, "Our Ability Incorporated, CEO."

It was at Mancuso's nearly two years later that I first learned of the bike trip John was planning. He was in search of a project manager for the trip. I don't know if he was trying to lure me to the bait, but I took it nonetheless and during a weak moment over bacon, I piped up and said that I would like to join him on this Journey Along the Erie Canal.

Fast forward about six months and there I was, undertrained and riding the wrong piece of equipment, wondering just how I got myself into this predicament.

John and I began training for this journey during the chilly days of March. Even then it was apparent that John was in better shape than I was. He was also better equipped—his bike was sleek and suited him well. Mine was a tank that had been collecting dust for eight years.

By the time the ride began, I had resigned myself to just riding a third to maybe half of each day's itinerary. I would handle the logistics, setting up speaking engagements and other activities for John at stops along the way. It was exciting to have Congressman Brian Higgins join us at our sendoff in North Tonawanda, near Buffalo, along with Steve Goodwin from Disabled Sports USA, who was promoting the rise in adaptive sports.

I was frustrated that my participation in the physical part of the initial ride was limited both by my lack of conditioning and inferior equipment. This trip was a challenge. It opened my eyes that for the better part of almost 20 years, I had sort of coasted. Sure, I had become CEO of a tech company, traveling as much as two weeks per month crisscrossing the country. I was in and out of airports, hotels and rental cars, and navigated all types of climates the country had to offer. For some people with disabilities, this kind of lifestyle would've been considered a stretch. But I had grown accustomed to it. It was no big deal, and I enjoyed it.

I realized along the canal as I struggled with my heavy bike from town to town that I had stopped pushing the edge of my abilities and had built a box where I was completely comfortable, completely independent.

Now, I was not. And I hated it.

I was struck by how my friend, with no arms and no legs, could jump off his bike and walk to a tree and eat his lunch in the shade, yet I was stranded until someone brought me my wheelchair. That is not independence.

At the end of our journey in Albany the entire welcoming committee and dignitaries had to hold up their closing ceremony speeches because my wheelchair was in my van, a quarter of a mile away. I was frustrated, being at the mercy of others. And I was upset that others were being delayed by me, the people pleaser.

Additionally, it became clear to all that I'm really not much of a details guy (something I already knew). On Day 4 of the Journey, I had double-booked John to be speaking in two different locations, Brockport and Spencerport, at the same time. These were canal towns about nine miles apart. John's an amazing guy, but even he couldn't pull that off. It upset me that I'd dropped the ball and let him down, despite his graciousness.

Both events were important. One featured 160 children with various disabilities that I knew would be encouraged by hearing John's story. In Spencerport, the mayor had arranged a local jazz band to greet us and hold a benefit concert.

So here I am, realizing I can't ride the full distance each day, and failing to hold up my end of the bargain with planning. My job for more than a decade was to get the big picture. My support team was critical (and very good!) in nailing down the details. Now I WAS the support staff and it wasn't my strength.

I didn't realize being No. 2 would be so hard for me. There's a certain mindset that comes with being a CEO that one can't just turn off. Sure, I knew how to work with others, build consensus, rally the troops, be a team player, etc. etc. etc. But at the end of the day, I also knew that I had the final say and we either prospered or sunk on based my decisions. I liked getting the 30,000-foot view and setting visions, not getting lost in the weeds. During the planning of this trip, I told myself that it was nice not to be the top dog for a change. It would be refreshing to not have the weight of this trip on my shoulders. I was wrong.

John was the lead in this play, and he deserved to be. That was never clearer than when we rolled into Albion. I arrived early to prepare for John's arrival. Already, 50 people had gathered under a tent to hear John speak. Not a small crowd. Then even more people started arriving by buses and vans. I sort of slid into town to get things ready, and no one knew who I was.

To be honest, it was humbling.

At VersaTrans, when I was out on the road, meeting with clients or speaking at events, I was an industry thought leader, and the bald guy in the wheelchair. I stood out in most crowds, whether big or small. Not many CEOs are in wheelchairs. It added to the way people viewed me, and I was well aware of that. It made me memorable.

Now, in this Our Ability environment, that juju was gone. I was not an industry expert and wheelchairs were everywhere—many occupied by bald guys! At one point I called Jim Guzewich and told him, "Nobody recognizes me anymore!"

In Albion, I had that similar feeling. There was nothing to distinguish me. When John and his entourage began to roll in, two Albion police cars escorted him and his team, along with the mayor and an assemblyman. It was like royalty had arrived. This was the person they had waited to see and hear.

John spoke for about 10 minutes at that event. Everyone from 5 years-old to 50 waited in line after to shake his hand. I sat back and took it all in. "This is what this trip is all about," I thought. "It's not about me. It's about making sure this happens." It was a very special night.

It would happen again and again during this trip. People were inspired by our visit, but we, too, were inspired by them and their stories.

In Utica, we met about 100 people who make up a company called Human Technologies Corp. It's a diverse company with several business units that work primarily on defense contracts.

Its stated mission was "to enhance the quality of life for people with disabilities and others who have barriers to employment."

This company was a complete surprise to us. We had never heard of them and yet they personified what the entire ride was about—employment opportunities for those with disabilities. As we toured the facility, we met people from station to station with a wide variety of physical and developmental challenges, some far greater than ours. Yet, this was not their focus. They were extraordinarily proud of their work, which consisted largely of manufacturing military clothing. One gentleman's entire job was to trim excess rubber from helmet nets. He explained its importance to the process and took great pride as he demonstrated his technique.

We also joined Ryan Chalmers for his "Welcome Home" event at Frontier Field in Rochester after he completed a 71-day cross-country trip. Chalmers, who was 24 at the time, was a paraplegic with spina bifida who clocked 65 miles a day in his wheelchair. Ryan delivered an emotional, moving talk.

I was also inspired by John that night, who'd been asked to pinch-hit as emcee moments before the start of the event when the scheduled master of ceremonies, a TV anchor, had to rush off to cover a shooting downtown. John just lit up, delivering a speech like he'd been working on it for months. This was no canned speech, it was fresh and tailored for Ryan's big day.

I was next to John's wife and whispered to her, "Wow, he's really good at this."

"Yeah," she said. "Just don't tell him."

I also was inspired by the people who worked with severely disabled individuals. I saw passion in their eyes. They had a mission and a purpose, like the woman who ran a program for 16 elderly people with developmental disabilities and at various stages of Alzheimer's disease. Her entire focus was making their lives special.

The kids at the Wayne County facility hosted a lunch for us. They had made some 20-plus signs that circled the board room, each highlighting an ability rather than focusing on a disability. "I can…"

"I can sing."

"I can paint."

"I can play piano."

These were messages I needed to hear, because sometimes on this trip I focused too much on what I didn't do very well. This journey wasn't about what I couldn't do or what other people can't do. Just the opposite, it was about celebrating what we can do, what we are capable of doing when we allow ourselves to be stretched and pulled out of our comfort zones.

As it turns out, I was an unwitting inspiration to someone on our journey. During the planning of the trip, John and I realized there would be some rough patches along the trail. It's known as being relatively flat, but we would joke with each other, "Yeah, it's flat, except where it's not!"

There were three main surfaces along the path: pavement, packed stone or dirt. The pavement was great, the stone was okay and the dirt was simply awful. And there were also some hills to negotiate when crossing roadways. We just didn't know what to expect.

So, I reached out for volunteers familiar with the path who would like to join us, probably at a much slower pace than they were accustomed to. Trish Zdep wanted the job and was persistent about getting it. For months we exchanged emails, but we didn't meet until we kicked off the trip. A physical therapist with Orleans ARC, Trish got me right away. She knew when I needed help—big, heavy bike and all—and stepped in without making a big deal out of it. She also knew when to be invisible, when I needed to work through something. That's a gift. Most importantly, she immediately became part of our Erie Canal family, and even though we didn't need her support the way we thought we might, she has joined us on every ride since.

Trish is an elite athlete, much like John's wife Andrea, and at one point she left our group to compete in a triathlon in Buffalo. Trish said that during the running portion of the triathlon, she really wanted to quit.

"And I thought of you," she told me.

I inspired a triathlete to complete her race. And she inspired me to continue the journey.

That I needed help at all really bothered me. I decided before the end of Journey 2013 that Journey 2014 needed to be a completely different experience for me.

And it was.

In the year following the inaugural bike ride a lot happened. Pam and I finished packing up our house in Delmar and moved into our now completed lake house in Skaneateles. We said farewell to old friends and began to build a network of new ones. Most importantly, as it relates to the Journey, I bought a new bike!

I had begun researching high-performance hand cycles in the evenings during the first Journey. I landed on the one I wanted and called the company almost as soon as we got home. The salesman on the other end was ready to take my order right on the spot. But as anyone who knows me well can tell you, I am NOT an impulse buyer, especially when it comes to spending $8,000 for a hand cycle I haven't even seen yet. I asked if there was a chance I could demo a model somewhere. He said, "Sure, you can try mine at my house." I said, "Great, where's that?" He said, "Akron, Ohio." It's roughly 350 miles from Skaneateles to Akron, but I said, "Okay," and Pam and I planned an impromptu "vacation" to Akron that included a very cool stop at the Rock and Roll Hall of Fame in Cleveland.

The salesman, who also happened to be named John, was very helpful and I was convinced this was the machine for me. So I ordered it. The bike arrived at my house a month or so later and I also bought an indoor training frame for it. My new, sleeker ride was black and had red lettering that said, "Top-End—Force RX." I still ride it today.

When I'm on the bike, I'm lying almost flat on my back. The pedals are above my chest and I have to use the force of my shoulders and back to push the bike forward. And it has 30 gears! Over the winter of 2013, I rode it on the trainer enough to learn how to pedal it efficiently and use all of those gears. Once spring arrived, Pam and I got out on the Erie Canal trail (which is only 15 miles from our house) and rode—a lot.

This bike is a dream compared to my previous one. Not only was I sure I could ride the entire length of the canal in 2014 and beyond, but it provided Pam and me with an outdoor activity we could do together. I need her help to manhandle the bike on and off the rack, but after that we're "equals." She doesn't need to adapt her riding style and I can ride alongside her for hours at a comfortable cruising speed. This was really special for us.

The weather on the Day 1 of "Journey 2" was identical to the year before. The sun was bright, there were few clouds and it was HOT. My outlook, however, was entirely different. On my new bike I was confident and excited to ride the entire length of the Canal with the others. And I did. Was it easy? No. Did I lead the pack? Rarely. But I did it, and it felt great to begin and end every day with the group.

I rode the whole length for three more Journeys, through 2017, and it got better each year. We gained public recognition of the effort; and raised a lot of money and recognition for John's company. We fought rain and mosquitoes just like the builders of the Canal 200 years before. We also learned a lot from Canal historians who rode with us. The Canal Corporation was inspired by our use of the Canal trail as an accessible recreation asset, and began plans to make it more adaptable.

Most of all, we made great friends. We became one of those "magic in a bottle" groups that fought adversity and achieved success together.

Of course, none of it would've been able to happen without the "Our Ability wives." Pam and Andrea had never even been introduced prior to the morning of the first "Journey Along the Erie Canal." I think John and I just assumed they would get along. The naivety of that assumption aside, they did. Both have shared common experiences as the spouses of individuals with disabilities. They have supported, encouraged, endured frustration and risen again, just like John and I. It's not lost on either of us that there is a great deal of physical effort on our wives' part to pull off the Journey, and we are eternally grateful for that. But we are most grateful for their undying belief that we can do what we put our minds to and be part of it with us.

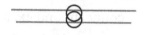

EIGHTEEN

SPINNING FORWARD

It's my life. It's now or never. But I ain't gonna live forever.
I just want to live while I'm alive.

—Jon Bon Jovi

Retirement felt like anything but in the early going. Pam continued to teach in nearby Voorheesville, New York, a small village outside Albany, and I spent my time at home recuperating from rotator cuff surgery on my right shoulder. We were also closing on a property we had just purchased on Skaneateles Lake, four miles north of our family cottage.

The surgery took place on the Tuesday after Thanksgiving in November 2010, less than two weeks after I had my retirement party from VersaTrans and Tyler Technologies. There were more than 125 guests at the party, including just about every employee and spouse from VersaTrans. Friends and family including Priscilla and John, Brad and David and Uncle Jim and Aunt Marilyn were there, as well and Pam's mom and brother. Even Drew and his wife made it. Dave Gonino received the long-distance travel award, having flown in from Shanghai to attend the festivities. My mentors Roger Creighton and Chuck Manning were also in attendance, as was my right-hand man, Jim Guzewich, who would be taking over for me as president of VersaTrans. One highlight of the evening had to be when all four VersaTrans' presidents past and future—Roger, Chuck, myself and Jim—posed for a picture together.

Rotator cuff surgery for someone who uses a wheelchair is profoundly debilitating. My shoulders are my source of mobility, from pushing my chair to transferring from my chair to the toilet, shower, bed, car, etc. If I'm down even one shoulder, I am completely dependent. In preparation, I had to rent a power wheelchair, a hospital bed, a private nurse (for personal care every other day) and a mechanical Hoyer lift for transfers.

It was not a pleasant first two months of retirement, as I hated being completely dependent on others. I couldn't drive. I couldn't even empty my catheter bag in the toilet. I was completely idle. All I could do was sit in my chair and read or watch TV. Fortunately, I was able to sneak my right hand far enough out of the sling to feed myself and also sign any papers that needed signing. This was important because in January 2011, from my power chair, we were able to close on a property on Skaneateles Lake that in 2-1/2 years' time would become our dream home.

During the 30-plus years we visited the cottage in the summer, Pam and I said that if the stars ever aligned, we would build a house on the lake. In 2009, they did. Shortly after I sold the company to Tyler Technologies, we began looking at property along the lake. We wanted a house that would be 110 percent ADA accessible. That meant either a major renovation or finding a vacant lot on the flattest piece of property possible. Level lakefront was hard to find on Skaneateles Lake, which has a very steep watershed surrounded by cliffs and bluffs. After about two years with a VERY patient real estate agent named Wendy, we were able to locate the perfect lot.

We wanted to build a house that was not only our dream lakefront home but a place where friends and family could visit comfortably and often. Because of the nature of the lot, we would need a multi-level home requiring an elevator. This, combined with rather strict and varied zoning regulations in Skaneateles, required us to get approval from the town planning board—a board, ironically, to which I would be appointed just three years later.

Picking a builder was easy. Way back in 1987, when my mother was upgrading the cottage before she died, we got to know Scott McClurg. He had done all that work to make it more accessible and maintained it in-between. I had said to him for years that if I ever built a house, he would build it. He had grown from a one-man shop to a 50-person design-build firm, but it was like calling an old friend when I reached out to tell him of our plans.

Over the next year, I spent a lot of time driving back and forth between Albany and Skaneateles to meet with the architect as we were going through the planning process. Once we got approval and construction began in June 2012, it took about a year to build the house. Every Monday morning, for 52 consecutive weeks, I got in my Chrysler Minivan (I had graduated to a van to help save my shoulder) and drove to the lake property to meet with the architect and contractor to see how everything was taking shape. Finally, in August 2013, just weeks after the first "Journey Along the Erie Canal" bike ride, we settled into our new house.

As tired as I was of driving back and forth, the move itself fell all on Pam. At the time, she was 53 and two years away from retiring, but as luck would have it, the school district was offering an early retirement incentive, which she happily took. Her last day of teaching was the day before the bike ride, which she participated in as well. Between the ride, the move itself and cleaning up of the old house, it was a very trying time and rough summer for Pam. It all happened way too fast, for both of us. We never even had time to bid our old friends and neighbors in Delmar a proper, emotional goodbye.

Not long after my shoulder healed enough for me to drive again, I had a chance to take a swing at some consulting. I had established my own company, Spinforward, LLC, in January of 2011. As you may recall from Chapter 4, the name Spinforward was inspired by one of my therapy sessions while I was in the hospital recovering from my spinal cord injury. After successfully transferring myself from my bed to my wheelchair for the very first time, the therapist said, "Okay, now spin forward." In other words, use the wheels to move the chair. That phrase just stuck with me. It also reflects my outlook—I generally look forward and don't spend a lot of time dwelling on the past.

This first consulting opportunity brought me together with a fellow quadriplegic named Dave Whalen, whom I had met for the first time almost 30 years before at Sunnyview Rehabilitation Hospital in Schenectady. Dave and his friend Mike had invented a device called "Jamboxx." Jamboxx is a Musical Instrument Digital Interface (MIDI) harmonica that connects to a computer, tablet or phone and through some very cool technology translates your breath into the sounds of virtually any instrument you want to play. That includes the guitar, drums, trumpet and saxophone, among others. You play the notes by sliding the mouthpiece just like a harmonica. Dave's skiing accident left him with very little mobility below his shoulders and he saw Jamboxx as a way to continue his passion as a musician. He and Mike had tinkered for years with the idea to create a hands-free, adaptive musical instrument that anyone could play.

When I came onboard to assist them Dave and Mike had been working on the technology for years, but hadn't really formed a business around it, which is what I thought I could help with. After about six months we really hadn't gotten much farther and they struggled with what direction they wanted to go. I also knew that to be truly successful in the venture I really needed to be personally passionate about it. I just wasn't the right fit for them at the time, nor was I adding any value. A humbling but valuable lesson. I am happy to say that these many years later Dave and Mike are on the road to success and Jamboxx is being marketed as a respiratory therapy device in hospitals and rehab centers.

Over the ensuing years, I've done three or four consulting jobs for young software companies in an effort to help them organize for the next level of growth. I'm proud of that work, but I've discovered that consulting doesn't scratch the business itch for me. I miss doing the "mental gymnastics" of running a business with a team. I miss being part of a collaborative problem-solving effort, whether it be with the executive team or just Jim and myself. I even miss the productive tension between the sales and operations teams or between myself and leadership and the employees. All of that I found a great challenge to manage.

The VersaTrans experience was so rewarding because of our collective passion about what we were doing. We had created the product and the business model. It was our baby, and we were helping it grow and mature. I could never find that level of passion in my consulting work. The environment just wasn't the same. And, to be honest, I didn't want to work full time. I had retired for a reason. I simply don't have a part-time personality so that conflict was never going to resolve itself. It's very flattering and exciting to start a consulting engagement, but then it becomes a job and then I don't want to be doing it. Pam and I are incredibly fortunate in that we don't have to do anything we don't want to. We can focus on things we're passionate about and that make a difference. Or, we can focus on doing nothing at all! We do a little bit of both.

This brings us back to the "Journey Along the Erie Canal" bike event (see previous chapter). In 2014, I got a much better bike and was proudly able to ride the entire 363 miles on each Journey from 2014 to 2017. Not only was I excited about riding the full distance across New York State, but I grew excited about the Erie Canal itself and meeting with a few of the non-profit boards that supported the canal and the bike ride. As Vice President of Operations for Our Ability, Inc., and the bike event, I was heavily involved from a planning and logistics standpoint for the ride and spent a lot of time working with the Canal Corporation, which was a lot of fun. Today I'm chairman of the board for Our Ability Alliance on the non-profit side. John and I also talk on the phone every other week. He has a way of picking my brain and I find that very valuable.

Since retiring and moving into our new house, I've also been able to devote more time to my woodworking addiction. For as long as I can remember, I have appreciated fine woodwork. I didn't know much about how things were made, I just liked the look of richly stained wood furniture and crafts, especially oak. I had had fits and starts at workshops in previous houses, but never really had the room or the time. Here, I have both. I have spent an inordinate amount of money on tools and have watched hundreds of hours of YouTube videos to train myself on various techniques.

I build small projects mostly. I caught the reclaimed wood bug by watching Joanna Gaines, co-star of HGTV's "Fixer Upper." I like to make meaningful projects, things like personally laser-etched cutting boards and beer flight holders (made from old barrel staves) for my beer-loving friends. I also like to make clock cases. A few years ago, I was able to "harvest" some early 19th century floorboards from our favorite bar in Skaneateles, The Sherwood Inn, when they did a major renovation. I have since made cocktail and end tables from that wood for friends who also like the Sherwood.

One of my favorite projects so far is one I made for a very good friend from high school named Terri Butler-Stivarius. Terri and her husband John were renovating their house near Atlanta. I secretly asked the contractor if he could harvest some wood from the demolition so I could make them a meaningful gift from parts of their "old" house. He said, "Sure, how about you make Terri's writing table?" I was picturing a small desk. I said, "Ok, about how big?" Well, it turns out Terri wanted a 9 foot by 3-1/2 foot table! He FedEx'ed one-thousand pounds of wood (yes, FedEx). Over the next six months I was able to make a nine-foot trestle table in ten separate parts so I could fit it in my van. Pam and I delivered it together. It meant a lot for me to be able to do that for an old friend.

For the first two springs in Skaneateles, we also continued our spring tradition of taking a Caribbean cruise with two of

Pam's teacher friends and their husbands. The six of us started doing this back in 2008. They are very close friends, and we always looked forward to this relaxing time together.

Sadly, in 2015, we had a family tragedy during our cruise. We had been on the boat for only one day and were just leaving Nassau in the Bahamas when my phone rang. It was Pam's brother, Jim. Pam's youngest sister Kristine, only 49, had been killed that Easter Sunday morning in a car accident along Interstate 81 in Pennsylvania, just a few miles north of the Pennsylvania-Maryland border. Kristine and her husband, Steve, had been driving south on I-81 to their home in Roanoke, Virginia after visiting Pam's family for Easter weekend when a northbound car lost control somehow, crossed the median and hit their car head-on. Kristine, who was in the passenger seat, was killed instantly. Both passengers in the northbound car were also killed. Steve, whose left ankle and knee were crushed in the accident, was the only survivor.

Had I received the phone call just one hour earlier we could've hopped on a plane in Nassau and flown home, but we were stuck out at sea for two more days before we docked again in St. Thomas. It was a very difficult 48 hours for Pam and the rest of us. We spent the entire first evening in our cabin being profoundly sad and talking to Pam's family on the phone, periodically checking in on how Steve was doing. It was just brutal. Pam spent the whole night scrolling through pictures of Kristine on her phone, which was how she chose to grieve at the moment. But Pam, being the unselfish person she was and always putting others first, rallied the next day. She knew there was little she could do for the next 36 hours, so she managed to disassociate herself from the tragic events and actually encouraged us to go to dinner and a show. The next morning, we were on a flight back to John F. Kennedy International Airport, where our car was, and we drove home to Skaneateles from there. It was a very long day, as we pulled into our driveway sometime around midnight.

Steve needed some time to recover and heal, so the services for Kristine in Pam's hometown of Cherry Valley, N.Y. were delayed a bit. Kristine's body was flown up from Harrisburg, PA to Albany, where Pam and I met up with the casket and followed the hearse to the funeral home. This was one of the saddest experiences of my life. Kristine was a cheerful, funny person who took great pride in her work as an accountant at a factory in Roanoke and also lived a bit like a pioneer in their house in the woods. She even raised her own chickens. She was kind and rarely thought of herself. As she was Pam's younger sister, we always tried to find ways to "take care of her." I was honored to build two large crosses in my shop with her name on them. One sits at mile marker 5 on I-81 south near Greencastle, PA where the accident took place. The other is on the side of Steve's shop in Smith Mountain Lake, VA. We miss Kristine to this day.

Two years later one of my all-time favorite experiences happened when we tagged along with Pam's brother on a business trip he had to Australia in 2017. We spent three wonderful weeks Down Under, visiting Sydney, the Great Barrier Reef up north and Melbourne. We were surprised by the terrain For some reason I had always pictured Australia as flat. It is not! We huffed and puffed up hills around three or four cities. Jim and Pam both pushed on the way up and held me back on the way down.

A year after that, Our Ability was proud to be invited to do a canal trail ride in Scotland from Glasgow to Edinburgh in 2018. This put my logistics skills into overdrive getting us and all of our equipment over there for a week, but it was well worth it. Most of the Erie Canal family came along and even Jim Guzewich and his wife, Nora, were able to join us.

It was a wonderful trip. The people and the country were both beautiful. On this trip, Pam and I met the most delightful and persistent taxi driver in the world. Scotland (and Australia for that matter) are a bit ahead of the U.S. when it comes to service for the disabled. In both countries, ALL public transportation including taxis are required to be wheelchair accessible. However, "accessible" isn't necessarily clearly defined. That's where taxi driver John comes in. We were in Edinburgh and really wanted to visit the castle there. We hailed a cab and John pulled over. John's version of "accessible" was two 3-foot 2x4's that he lined up with my wheels and he pushed me into the taxi at a 45-degree angle. I thought for sure I was going off one edge or the other, but John had clearly done this a million times, and suddenly I was comfortably inside. The road to the castle is VERY steep, not something I could negotiate even with Pam's help so John was to drive us all the way to the top. Unfortunately, the local roads were closed for, of all things, a bike race! John tried at three checkpoints to get through, but the race officials were persistent. Well, so was John. He insisted that his disabled passenger had the right to get to the castle and he was going to get me there! At the fourth checkpoint, upon denial, he threatened to call the cops. They said, "Go ahead," so HE DID. Two police officers showed up and John pled his (my) case. They actually opened the door to see that I was in a wheelchair and eventually let us through. John won the day and we paid him a fare four times the usual rate. We will never forget him.

With my blessing, Pam has replaced the Caribbean cruises with several Viking River Cruises, traveling with her brother and her mom. The European ports are all 2,000 years-old and aren't very accessible to someone in a wheelchair, so I'll have to find another way to see Europe.

I had a second rotator cuff repair (same shoulder) in August 2019, which again forced me to be dependent for a few months, but that turned out to be nothing compared to my next great health hurdle. Not more than a week before Christmas 2019, I came down with a urinary tract infection (UTI) which, if you'll recall from earlier, seems to happen quite a bit around the holidays. My doctor prescribed me the same broad-spectrum antibiotic, Cipro, that I always take to stop the infection, and I waited.

Normally I feel better and my urine looks clearer within 24 hours. But by Saturday night, I felt worse and come Sunday afternoon, my fever stood at 104 degrees. Pam drove me to the emergency room and as it turned out, I had a bacterial infection that could only be treated with IV antibiotics. "Uh oh," I thought. I certainly didn't want to spend the holidays in the hospital. The doctors did everything they could to get my fever down and I was home in time for Christmas.

I was on the antibiotics for 10 days and as soon as I went off them, my fever spiked again and we were right back in the hospital. This time, the doctors determined I had two stones in my left ureter, which was causing a blockage. They decided at some point to take me to the O.R. and put a stent in my kidney to bypass these two stones, and deal with them later. I was back on the IV antibiotics again, although this time I stayed in the hospital for six days before coming home. Once home, it wasn't long before I was feeling ill again. I went to lie down one day, but when I tried to get up, I nearly passed out. This happened twice as I attempted to transfer myself from my bed to my chair, so it was back to the ER yet again. This time by ambulance.

It turns out I had a life-threatening bleeding ulcer in my small intestine totally unrelated to the UTIs. I underwent endoscopic surgery to cauterize the bleeding (they had to give me eight units of blood to replace what I'd lost), and then spent the next four days in the intensive care unit. Then they 'scoped me once more and I had to stay a few additional days in ICU to make sure that I was healed and could tolerate real food again.

The bleeding ulcer probably should have come as no surprise to me or the doctors, given all of the aspirin I've had to take for my AFib and the tons of Aleve and Advil tablets I've swallowed for the pain of my two rotator cuff surgeries. All of these drugs are very hard on the stomach, as is the drug I've also been taking for my ongoing osteoporosis. It's a good thing I can't feel the kidney stones, otherwise I'd probably be taking some ulcer-inducing drugs for that as well.

All of these health issues have been challenging emotionally. As I have said a few times, I have been blessed to avoid many of the medical maladies that tag along with spinal cord injuries. Now, it seems they are catching up with me a bit. I am not a good patient. I am having to work harder this time to maintain my optimism and find myself often fixated on what the future holds. I am terrified of being dependent on others, especially Pam. But she remains by my side and is a wonderful "nurse" and "coach." She'll take care of me when I need it, and similarly tell me to "Get over it!" when I need to hear it.

Illness and injury have kept me off the bike for two years. I currently have my sights set on another Erie Canal ride (all 363 miles) in 2021 as long as my orthopod will clear my shoulder!

What's next for me? I specifically remember saying to Pam back when we were 30 that given what my parents went through and my situation, I'd be happy to get to 60. Well, I'm 60. But I'm not going to set a new goal. I am determined simply to enjoy and embrace every day that's given to me. One thing that should keep us both busy in the immediate future is another house project. This time, Pam and I bought a place near her mom in Cherry Valley, so that she can spend more time with her family than just a couple of days or a weekend.

The idea came to me last summer when we were driving home from a funeral for the mom of a high school friend of Pam's in Cherry Valley. I said to her, "You know, there's going to come a time when you're going to want to spend more time in Cherry Valley than you do now. And there will also come a time when your mom may need a fully accessible house. Why don't we take a look and see what's for sale?" Well, driving around looking at houses is like going to the pound or puppy breeder—you know you're going to come home with something! Sure enough, we came across a 19th century Victorian house that we closed on in January 2020. We had a contractor friend of Pam's gut the inside and rebuild it so that it would be ADA accessible and hope to have it finished by the summer of 2021. This will become another family nexus for us over the years.

As far as what I want to do outside our two homes, I still haven't found the perfect avenue to give back and recognize all of the help that I received along the way. My hope is that this book is a start and will help people with or without disabilities succeed in both business and life and accomplish their dreams.

A good friend of ours' daughter teaches an inclusive recreation course at Paul Smith's College in Lake Placid and invited me to speak in front of her students after she learned about me participating in the "Journey Along the Erie Canal" bike ride. I've now spoken to her students on several occasions, and it's been a blast. The students have enjoyed it, and I like that they ask a lot of questions. Once this book is published, she'd like to use it for her class and have me speak again. That feels better to me than going to speak at a young executives' conference or at some corporate retreat. I've done that before, and the words don't seem to resonate for them as much as they do these young, hungry students. I'll look to do more of this.

I also plan to explore more volunteer opportunities that allow me to flex some business muscles. I continue to serve on the board of directors for Albany Medical Center and the planning board for the town of Skaneateles and was recently named president of the Skaneateles Historical Society's board. I'm also the Treasurer for the First Presbyterian Church of Skaneateles—the very same church where my mother and father were married and my grandparents and great-grandparents were members. In addition, I'm sitting on a Syracuse University committee that is working on an entrepreneurship program for people with disabilities.

And then there's the book. When I first started to write my memoir, I did so with the intention of telling my story. It wasn't intended to be an inspirational memoir or business memoir. If in telling my story, I end up inspiring even just one person to overcome their challenges and to never give up on their dreams, then that's awesome.

I wrote earlier that even if I had not broken my neck and was able-bodied, I believe I would've ended up on the exact same career path. I didn't let my disability stop me from having a "normal" life and a successful career. Yes, I've had the good fortune of having an incredible support team around me, led by my wife Pam. I have embraced my disability and incorporated it into my life. It does not define me. I found something I was still very good at, and I worked very hard to improve on that skillset each and every day to the point where I became CEO of a successful software company.

I will keep spinning forward, and I hope that everyone who reads this book will find something that drives them to be their very best. It is on that journey that you find true happiness in this life.

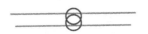

Printed book and eBook available at:

www.Amazon.com

To contact the author:

Doug Hamlin
Spinforward, LLC
doug.hamlin@spinforward.com

About the Author

Doug Hamlin was born in 1960 in upstate New York. Growing up he developed a clear vision of what success looked like. In his twenties, that view was severely challenged by personal and family tragedy. He found in himself an optimism and determination to move forward and achieve goal after goal. Having enjoyed careers as software engineer, transportation planner and software company CEO, Mr. Hamlin is now an occasional consultant, public speaker, woodworker and admitted vodka snob. *Spinning Forward* is his first book.

Rick D'Errico's journalism career spans more than three decades with stints at *The Boston Globe, Conde Nast, Dow Jones & Co.* and Gannett publications. Rick met Doug while covering him as a reporter at *The Capital District Business Review*. Rick now serves as Managing Director of the New York BizLab, a business accelerator for startups. www.nybizlab.net

Acknowledgments

Spinning Forward is designed in many ways as a "Thank you" to many of the people who have been by my side through my entire life's journey.

I would like to acknowledge all of those that helped in some way to make this book happen:

Pam Hamlin, my loving wife, got to see firsthand the fits and starts of this project which had various versions over nearly ten years. Always patient and supportive, she urged me to go at it when I was in writing mode, and also told me it was okay to take a break (which I did often!).

Rick D'Errico was instrumental in getting me started on this path by interviewing me like the good reporter that he is and diligently transcribing those interviews into the raw material that formed the foundation of the book.

David Allen served much the same role for me as I reached the end of the project. His "patient persistence" really allowed me to push it over the goal line. David co-authored John Robinson's inspirational memoir, *Get Off Your Knees*, and has co-authored or edited more than a dozen books, most notably *Golf Annika's Way* with LPGA Hall of Famer Annika Sorenstam. His edits and suggestions for "using my voice" are greatly appreciated.

Priscilla Maddock, my sister and hero in life, channeled my English-teacher mother during the final read-through and editing. We both commented often that we felt Mom right there as we word-smithed sentences.

John Robinson served as an inspiration on this book as he has in other ways in my life. His insistence that I have a story to tell gave me the confidence to press forward when I got blocked or discouraged.

As background for *Spinning Forward,* Rick conducted many interviews with family, friends and coworkers, many of whom you will meet throughout the book including:

Uncle Jim and Aunt Marilyn—My "Capital District parents," who turned into true friends.

Cousin Brad—The brother I never had.

David Gonino—My college roommate who remains my confidante, very best friend and mentor.

Artie Banks—My other college roommate and still great friend and honest adviser.

Terri Stivarius—A close friend since we were 15 and will remain a friend for life.

Drew Mann—Aside from my family, I've known Drew the longest of anyone mentioned in this book. As my spiritual guide and supportive friend, Drew helped me in the early years to grow into what I've become today.

Chuck Manning—Along with **Roger Creighton**, in many ways established the culture and set the tone for the kind of organization VersaTrans was to be. I reflected often that our approach to problem solving and growing pains were rooted in the supportive environment that Chuck espoused.

Jim Guzewich—Business partner, teacher and truth-teller. Jim knew the business in many ways better than I did. He filled my business gaps and educated me along the way.

Ted Thien—One of the best hires Jim and I ever made at VersaTrans. He was able to bring a strong business and sales acumen to our unique culture. I am thrilled that Ted is still at the helm of the business while their success is unquestionable.

Andrea Rutherford—One of the great VersaTrans "long haulers." Andrea watched me and the company grow and was always there doing the hard work for us.

Julie Smithson—Now a VersaTrans lifer, Julie brought insight and observations from "the outside" that helped us move forward more elegantly.

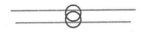

CPSIA information can be obtained
at www.ICGtesting.com
Printed in the USA
FSHW020109220521
81587FS

9 798749 929959

To Molly,
and the next
generation of the
earth's primates

Preface

Gorilla Behavior is the second volume in a series of reference books about the great apes. Like *Orang-utan Behavior* before it, this book integrates the findings of field and captive research but is decidedly oriented toward the problems of captive management, as it is our special objective to contribute to the welfare of great apes in captivity. Readers may initially wonder why we have chosen also to include so much historical material. This too is a result of a personal mission: to retrace the steps of our predecessors in search of still useful bits of wisdom. We have not been disappointed in this search and have taken every opportunity to illustrate the early insights of these pioneers of primatology. We trust that the reader will find these contributions to be as helpful as we have.

We are very grateful for the support of research grant RR00165 from the National Institutes of Health which provides for the animals and facilities of the Yerkes Regional Primate Research Center. For the opportunity to work there we thank Dr. G. H. Bourne and Dr. Fred King. While engaged in this work, we have been assisted and guided by many gifted colleagues. For their cooperation, support, and stimulating conversation over the past four years, we thank Dr. I. S. Bernstein, Dr. L. D. Byrd, and Dr. E. O. Smith. Our collaboration with Dr. R. D. Nadler has been a particularly valuable experience for which we are deeply indebted, and we are equally grateful to Dr. B. Swenson who has given so much insight into the applied problems of great ape management and medical care. Our further understanding in this dimension has been aided by our professional association with Jimmy Roberts who probably has a better intuitive understanding of apes than anyone that we know. Frank Kiernan supplied us with many of his excellent photographs and assisted in other technical aspects of the book; we thank him profusely. Other illustrative materials were kindly provided by the Houston Zoological Gardens, Philadelphia Zoological Gardens, San Diego Zoo Photolab, Woodland Park Zoo, Antwerp Zoo, J. Stephen Gartlan, J. P. Hess, Mary Keiter, Stephen Joines, Susan F. Wilson, W. Mager, Francine Patterson, Jorge Sabater Pí, and the Erwin Archives.

For their continued patience and valuable editorial assistance we thank Ashak Rawji, Alberta Gordon, and Susan Munger. On this and the other volumes of this series, they have steadfastly labored on behalf of the authors. We are deeply grateful for their efforts. Gary Mitchell originally reviewed the manuscript and we are most grateful for his participation in this and other aspects of our research. For research access to additional captive gorillas we thank William Meeker and the Staff of the Sacramento Zoo, and Ron Forman, David Anderson, Betsy O'Donohough, and the Staff of the Audubon Park Zoo, New Orleans.

For writing sanctuaries, where we have done our best work, we thank the Edward John Noble Foundation, New York Zoological Society, American Museum of Natural History, and the staff of St. Catherine's Island (John T. Woods, John Lukas, Jim Evans, and Royce Hayes), Yerkes librarian Nellie Johns, the library staff of the Georgia Institute of Technology, and the capable professionals at P. J. Haley's.

For permission to reproduce tables and figures we are grateful to the following publishers, journals, and organizations: A. S. Barnes and Co. (Table 1-1); S. Karger Co., publishers of *Folia Primatologica* (Tables 1-2, 1-8, 1-9) and *Bibliotheca Primatologica* (Table 1-7); *Journal of Zoology* (Table 1-3); *Nature* (Table 1-4); Academic Press, Inc. (Tables 1-5, 1-6, 4-1, 4-2); *Behavioral Ecology and Sociobiology* (Table 1-10); *Social Science Information* (Tables 1-11, 1-12); University of Chicago Press (Tables 2-1, 3-2, 3-3); Jersey Wildlife Preservation Trust (Tables 2-5, 2-6, 4-4, 5-3, 5-8, 5-9, 5-10, 6-2, 6-3, 6-4, 6-5); Indiana University Press (Tables 3-4, 3-7, 3-8); American Psychological Association, publisher of the *Journal of Comparative and Physiological Psychology* (Tables 5-6, 6-1); *Developmental Psychobiology* (Tables 5-4, 5-5, 5-6); Garland STPM Press (Tables 6-6, 6-7, 6-8); and the Zoological Society of London, publishers of *International Zoo Yearbook* (Table 7-3).

For photographs from the field we are also grateful to John Fowler and the National Geographic Society. We appreciate especially the opportunity to carry out collaborative research at the Karisoke Research Centre in Rwanda. For this special privilege we thank Dian Fossey. Ray Rhine coordinated the African field effort, and we are indebted to him for his kindness. Mary Elizabeth Wisdom has supported this field project with a generous research grant. We cannot begin to express our gratitude for her generosity and keen interest in our work. For information concerning the ecology of the western lowland gorilla, we are especially grateful to Dr. J. S. Gartlan.

As always, we remain solely responsible for any errors in this volume, having carefully attempted to avoid them. As we continue to monitor the growth of the literature, we trust that future editions of this book will increasingly add to our knowledge of gorilla behavior.

Terry L. Maple/Michael P. Hoff
Atlanta, Georgia

Contents

Gorilla Behavior

1
Gorilla in its Natural Habitat

. . . it is of more importance to judge the gorilla correctly than any other animal for he is unquestionably the nearest akin to man . . . In the whole doctrine of evolution there is no one subject more interesting or likely to be more fruitful to study than the gorilla.

C. E. Akeley, 1923

The vast majority of books concerning the gorilla—and there have been many—have emphasized the sensational features of this awesome creature. Since they have been written for a popular audience, they frequently gloss over the facts, oversimplify them, or downright distort or ignore them. Although we are hopeful that *Gorilla Behavior* will achieve some measure of popularity, we admit from the outset that we have a different audience in mind. It is our hope that this book will be a useful *reference* volume for those who seek an up-to-date source of information on the behavior of this ape. We have aimed for accuracy in detail, and an appropriate integration of the field and captive data. Like *Orang-utan Behavior* before it, this book is especially written for those who are concerned with the management, study, and appreciation of *captive* gorillas. We have taken this approach, in part, because we are better acquainted with captive conditions, and therefore better qualified to contribute to the welfare of captive apes. We could never hope to improve upon Schaller's excellent descriptions of the wild mountain gorilla, and we fully expect that Dian Fossey will soon publish an astonishing record of her landmark study. Our efforts are therefore meant to complement and compliment both the field and the laboratory worker, for it is our steadfast belief that a primatologist cannot succeed without a proper appreciation for the diversity of research approaches.

Excellent accounts of gorillas growing up in human households have been provided by Cunningham (1921), and Hoyt (1941). Reviews which contain a wealth of popular information and gorilla lore can be found in Reynolds (1967), Morris and Morris (1967), Willoughby (1979) and Bourne and Cohen (1975). We will not attempt to duplicate here what they have done so well. It is our aim instead to review the scientific literature concerning gorilla behavior and thereby contribute to an improved understanding and better treatment of these animals wherever they are to be found.

Our own interest in the gorilla stems from a life-long fascination with the creature. One of us (Maple) first encountered them as a child in his family visits to the San Diego Zoo. Vividly remembered are the old great ape cages which were succeeded by modern grottoes in the sixties. Like many California children before and since, it was the apes that captured our attention and fed our imaginations. We have been luckier than most folks in that watching gorillas has been part of our life's work. With this gratitude in mind, we are pleased to be able to share with the reader all that we have been able to discover about *Gorilla Behavior.*

Figure 1-1. *Massa,* the oldest-living captive gorilla at fifty years of age. (*Photo by Franklin Williamson, courtesy Zoological Society of Philadelphia*)

It should be stated at the outset that there is a lingering possibility of subspecies differences in the behavior of western lowland and eastern mountain gorillas respectively. Field studies continue to emphasize the latter, while captive* observations have been primarily focused on the former. Since there is currently no way to determine whether the taxonomic variable is contributing to the respective findings, we will not attempt to emphasize the point any further. It will suffice to state at the outset that we are inclined to believe that there are subspecies differences, and we will be anxious to examine the data from future field studies of the lowland taxon. Until then, we must remain cautious when we compare results from the field and captive setting. Whenever we speak of particular studies, we will be careful to identify the population from which the subjects derive. Some generalizations can safely be made, but we are painfully aware of the limitations that are imposed by the historical directions of the literature.

TAXONOMY

There is considerable disagreement regarding the appropriate taxonomic label for gorillas. We will refer to them here as *Gorilla*, but Goodall and Groves (1977), who must be regarded as authorities, have placed gorillas within the genus *Pan*. In this usage, they are in agreement with the findings of Tuttle (1967). Among the characteristics common to chimpanzee and gorilla, differentiating them from both *Homo* and *Pongo*, are: (1) the nature and hue of hair pigmentation; (2) the presence of a white pygal tuft in the young; (3) a drastic reduction of the thumb musculature; (4) terrestrial adaptations in the foot (more man-like than orang-like); (5) the form of the skull, including the lateral buttressing of the orbits, the low position of the braincase, and the common existence of a frontomaxillary suture in the orbit; (6) the relatively homomorphic incisors, the semisectorial nature of P_3 with only a small metaconid, the form of the wrist, features of blood protein chemistry and the chromosomes; (7) sociability relatively greater than *Pongo*.** Conversely, Goodall and Groves noted that differences in temperament, vocalizations, and social organization suggest retention of a separate *Gorilla* genus. The fossil record is apparently of little assistance in resolving the issue.

---

*In the United States, mountain gorillas are said to be exhibited at the Oklahoma City Zoo. One of these animals appears to be *grauri*; the other may well be a true *beringei*.

**This will be elaborated further within the text. As suggested elsewhere (Maple, 1980a), the sociability of *Pongo* has been greatly underestimated. This issue cannot be resolved without further careful study.

The historical nomenclature for gorillas is very confusing. In many accounts (e.g., Napier and Napier, 1967) the list of synonyms is incomplete. Elliot (1913) provided an early record as follows:

1. *Troglodytes gorilla*, Wyman 1847
2. *Gorilla gina*, J. Geoffroy 1852
3. *Pithecus gesilla*, Blainville 1839-64
4. *Troglodytes savagei*, Owen 1848
5. *Troglodytes gorilla*, Duvern 1855
6. *Satyrus adrotes*, Meyer 1856
7. *Gorilla gorilla*, Owen 1851, 1859
8. *Gorilla castaneiceps*, Slack 1862
9. *Anthropopithecus gorilla*, Anders 1881
10. *Gorilla mayema*, Alix et Bouvier 1877
11. *Gorilla beringeri* [sic], Matschie 1903
12. *Gorilla diehli*, Matschie 1904
13. *Gorilla gorilla matschie*, Rothschild 1904
14. *Gorilla gorilla diehli*, Rothschild 1904
15. *Gorilla gorilla jacobi*, Matschie 1905

Although Elliot did not list Thomas Savage as a collaborator, the original description of the gorilla has long been attributed to both Savage and Wyman (1847). In fact Owen (1848) recognized the participation of Savage in his suggestion of the name *Troglodytes savagei*.

The details of the gorilla's discovery were recently described by Kennedy and Whittaker (1978). Thomas S. Savage was an American missionary who paid a visit to the Reverend J. L. Wilson in West Africa. They met in the vicinity of the Gabon River in 1844. Wilson had in his possession a skull of a large ape which the local people referred to as *enge-ena*. Thereafter Savage employed a local hunter to assist in collecting more skeletal material. In addition, Savage gathered information on the animal's nesting habits, social interactions, and other behaviors. This material was subsequently given to Professor Jeffries Wyman who coauthored the paper based on Savage's material. The curious title of the paper was "*Troglodytes gorilla*, a New Species of Orang from the Gaboon River." The name "gorilla" was selected in view of its use by Hanno of Carthage who encountered a large primate during his West African travels of 470 B. C.

The first live gorilla was brought to England in 1855. Subsequently live specimens were briefly exhibited in Berlin during the next 30 years. In all of these instances, the apes' lives in captivity were short. The first live gorilla to reach the United States arrived in 1897, an infant between one and two years of age, judging from its photograph. This animal died within five days, and the body was subsequently purchased by Cornell University on behalf of Professor Burt Green

Wilder, an anatomist. His study of the brain and organs of this animal mark the beginning of gorilla research in America (Kennedy and Whittaker, 1978).

The various names* in use were due to variability in the specimens described. In 1903, Matschie described the mountain gorilla for the first time, and despite some further dispute at the turn of the century, the major subdivision into lowland and mountain types has been retained. In addition, the modern nomenclature has been further differentiated into the three categories, *gorilla, beringei,* and *graueri.*

In an impressive early monograph by Coolidge (1929) gorillas were subsumed under a single species with two subspecies *gorilla* and *beringei.* This nomenclature was subsequently adopted by Schaller (1963) in his monumental study of the mountain gorilla. However, as Goodall and Groves have pointed out, a study of the mandible of gorillas by Vogel (1961) revealed that *beringei* could be divided into two geographically distinct populations. Vogel therefore elevated *beringei* to the species level, and recognized the subspecies *beringei* (from the Virunga volcanoes) and *graueri* (from the eastern lowlands and nearby mountains). The two-subspecies system of Coolidge and Schaller was labeled by Goodall and Groves as a "fallacy." According to Goodall and Groves, based on Groves' 1970 revision, the acceptable taxonomy is as follows:

1. *Pan gorilla gorilla.* Western lowland, or coast gorilla; broad face, small jaws and teeth, short palate, single mental foramen under the premolars; straight vertebral border of scapula; long humerus; short, divergent hallux; short fur; gray with lighter "saddle" in adult males extending to the thighs; presence of a "lip" at upper end of nasal septum.

2. *Pan gorilla graueri.* Eastern lowland gorilla; narrow face, larger jaws and teeth, longer palate; mental foramen often multiple and further forward; straight vertebral border of scapula; long humerus; short, divergent hallux; fairly short fur, black with whitish "saddle" in adult males restricted to back and sharply defined; no "lip" on nasal septum.

3. *Pan gorilla beringei.* Mountain gorilla; low broad face; very large jaws and teeth, very long palate; multiple mental foramen, often under canine; sinuous vertebral border of scapula; long hallux, parallel to other toes; long, silky, black fur, with whitish sharply defined saddle restricted to back in adult males; no "lip" on nasal septum.

In a paper by Cousins (1974), subspecies *gorilla* is additionally distinguished from the other two races by a more pronounced, less hairy supraorbital ridge,

---

*Elliot (1913) elected to put *G. mayema* into a separate genus which he labeled *Pseudogorilla* in view of the fact that specimens of this type seemed to share characteristics of both gorillas and chimpanzees (see also Chapter 1 of *Chimpanzee Behavior* for a discussion of the taxonomic status of the gorillalike *Koolokamba* chimpanzee).

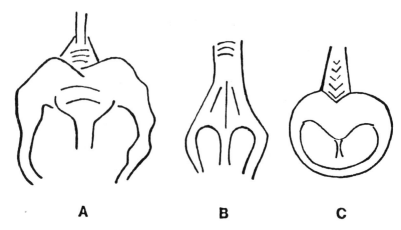

A   **B**   **C**

Figure 1-2. Nasal identification in three races of gorillas: A. *gorilla;* B. *graueri;* C. *beringei.*
(After Cousins, 1974)

and the nose characteristics of side-splaying and padding. The two eastern sub-species are characterized by narrower nostrils and a supraorbital ridge with a hairy padding. The noses of the subspecies are depicted in Figure 1-2 after the drawings provided by Cousins.* *Graueri* is apparently morphologically inter-mediate between *gorilla* and *beringei* and, according to Cousins, is often erron-eously represented in zoos as the mountain gorilla. Only the Cologne Zoo cur-rently exhibits *G. g. beringei,* the true mountain subspecies. As Goodall and Groves have shown, there are many intermediate forms which make labeling difficult, leading them to describe one population, from Mt. Kahuzi, as "*P. g. beringei* with a touch of *graueri*."

In a special report to the *International Union for the Conservation of Nature (IUCN),* Gartlan subscribed to Groves' use of the genus name *Pan.* However, Gartlan further suggested that recognition of the additional western highland race, *P. gorilla diehli,* was worthy of support. According to recent surveys, this taxon is an isolated deme which currently inhabits an area of hills which rise to over 5000 feet. Coolidge (1929) found *P. g. diehli* to be as distinctive as *P. g. graueri,* whereas Rothschild (1923) placed the former in a position intermediate between the eastern and western races. Gartlan suggested the differentiation of four groups of western gorillas, organized in such a fashion to facilate their con-servation rather than to further clarify the taxonomy. We will take up this matter in Chapter 8.

----

*However, see Schaller (1963) for examples of the considerable variability in individuals of the *beringei* subspecies.

Figure 1-3. Physical characteristics of *graueri* subspecies. (*Photo courtesy V. Six and Zoo Antwerp*)

Table 1-1. Characteristics which differentiate the mountain from the lowland gorilla. (After Schultz, 1–20; Coolidge, 21–25, and Willoughby, 26–29)

1. Greater length of trunk
2. Higher-situated nipples
3. Narrower hips
4. Lesser length of neck
5. Shorter lower limbs in relation to height of trunk
5a. Longer lower limbs in relation to length of upper limbs
6. Much shorter upper limbs
7. Broader and shorter hand
8. Great toe reaching farther distally
9. Great toe branching from sole more distally
10. Less convex joint at base of hallux
11. Relatively shorter outer lateral toes
12. Usually webbed toes
13. Higher face
14. Narrower width between eyes
15. Smaller average number of thoracolumbar vertebrae
16. Absolutely and relatively shorter humerus
17. Absolutely and relatively longer clavicle
18. Absolutely and relatively longer ilium
19. Relatively longer radius
20. Peculiarly curved vertebral border of scapula

Table 1-1. Characteristics which differentiate the mountain from
the lowland gorilla. (After Schultz, 1–20; Coolidge, 21–25, and
Willoughby, 26–29) Continued

21. Longer palate
22. Generally narrower skull
23. Thicker pelage
24. Large amount of black hair
25. Fleshy callosity on the crest (of the head)
26. Relatively shorter arm-spread or span
27. Broader shoulders (due to longer clavicles)
28. Thicker neck
29. Greater height and weight

INFLUENCES ON *GRAUERI*

In a recent revision of gorilla taxonomy, Groves and Stott (1979) argued that previous classifications of Mt. Kahuzi, Mt. Tshiaberimu, and Kayonza Forest gorillas were oversimplified. In their view, both Kahuzi and Tshiaberimu specimens are close to *graueri* and should be included in that category. However, in different ways, each of these populations also approach *beringei*.

These researchers have noted further that the Utu and Itombwe populations of *graueri* are very similar, despite their different ranges of altitude. Living at high altitudes (approaching that of *beringei*), the Itombwe gorillas exhibit *beringei*-like adaptations; e.g., more flared jaw angles, slightly higher frequency of multiple mental foramen, and forward-placed mental foramen. At much lower altitudes, the Utu gorillas also exhibit some *beringei* features; e.g., sinuous vertebral border of scapula, and higher frequency of the bifid mandibular condyle.

Groves (1970, 1971) had previously considered the Tshiaberimu population as the *graueri* subspecies, despite some *beringei* characteristics. Tshiaberimu gorillas are intermediate between *beringei* and *gorilla* with respect to the form of the foot.

Regarding the Mt. Kahuzi gorillas, Groves and Stott offered the following curious remark:

> The Kahuzi gorilla has never been awarded subspecies rank; Goodall and Groves (1977) comment that there is some irony in this, as it seems a fairly distinctive population morphologically—a comment which should not be read as a hint that it be given a subspecific name! (p. 173).

Groves (1970) had placed the Kahuzi gorillas in *beringei* but Casimir (1975a) asserted that these gorillas should be considered as *graueri*. Complications in the

Figure 1-4. Head of an adult male of the *graueri* subspecies. *(Photo courtesy V. Six and Zoo Antwerp)*

measurements employed by both authors account for their earlier difference of opinion. However, as Groves and Stott explained:

> Were it just for the cranial morphology . . . the Kahuzi gorilla would be frankly *graueri*. But . . . the data of the postcranial skeleton have until now seemed to be just as frankly *beringei*. (p. 174).

Moreover, Groves and Stott compared the Kahuzi and Tshiaberimu populations and determined that both are intermediate between *graueri* and *beringei* (although nearer the former than the latter.) In the characteristics of its skull, the Tshiaberimu population is more *beringei*-like. The more *beringei*-like skel-

Table 1-2. Characteristics of *beringei* and *graueri* according to the classification of Groves and Stott (1979).

Characteristics	G. g. beringei	G. g. graueri
Skull	Larger than *graueri*; palate larger in males; jaw angles enormously flared; ascending ramus high, muscularly molded, more differentiated in females	Smaller than *beringei*; palate shorter in males; jaw angles don't flare; ascending ramus low
Humerus	Short; great toe long, stout, springing from sole 75% of the distance from heel to tip of second toe	Long; great toe short, heel-to-hallux tip only 84% of heel-to-second tip
Mental foramen	Multiple in over 90% of specimens; infra-orbital foramen less often multiple; mental foramen in forward position in one-third of specimens; "rocking-jaws" common	Multiple in two-thirds to three-quarters of cases; infraorbital foramen multiple in 90–100%; mental foramen in forward position (ant. to post.) in under 20%; "rocking-jaws" uncommon
Vertebral border of scapula	Sinuous	Straight
Hair	Long, shaggy, noticeably on scalp, and forms a long beard with cheek whiskers which partially obscure the face; supraorbital torus covered with shaggy hair	Relatively short, especially on scalp and around face
Nose	Angular nostrils, less padded alae, well outlined above and below; upper lip clearly padded only a little below nose, extending only 1/2 down the lip	Rounded nostrils, well-padded alae, tending not to be strongly outlined above; upper lip diffusely padded below nose, padding extending 2/3 down the lip

etons, however, are those of the Kahuzi specimens. In both populations, the foot is more like *beringei* than *graueri*. As the authors suggested:

Presumably, at some distant time in the past, both were in contact with the Virunga population; when the contact was broken, gene-flow from one direction only (*Utu*) gradually influenced them, but in somewhat different ways, though why this should be is mysterious. (p. 175).

Reservations notwithstanding, Groves and Stott willingly accepted Casimir's classification of Kahuzi gorillas as representatives of *graueri*.

Although the evidence is scarce, it appears that gorillas from the Kayonza Forest have been most influenced by the Virunga populations; e.g., *beringei*. Supporting this position is the observation that the Kayonza Forest was once joined to the Virunga Volcanoes. On the contrary, there is no evidence that forest ever connected the Kayonza region with the nearest *graueri* area (Tshiaberimu). As Groves and Stott stated:

> It seems most likely, in any case, the Virunga Volcanoes and Kayonza Forest are a last refuge for gorillas to the east of the Albertine Rift, rather than outposts. (p. 176).

Groves and Stott extended their observations to include a hypothesis on the historical dispersal of gorillas across the Rift Valley. As the argument suggests, faulting in the Albertine Rift began in the Miocene and was renewed in the early Pleistocene or possibly the Pliocene, the time at which the Virunga Volcanoes were most likely formed. Calculations of the motion of the African plate indicate that 1.2 million B. P.* is the most likely time at which the three most eastern volcanoes were habitable. The whole of the eastern volcanoes could have been inhabited by gorillas about 800,000 B. P., according to these calculations.

Groves and Stott hypothesized that the Virunga Volcanoes must have been invaded by gorillas from east to west. They further suggested that the central cluster (Visoke, Karissimbi, and Mikeno) is a youthful habitat. Moreover, the most recent migration across the Albertine Rift probably occurred during the last interglacial period. Given the much earlier date of the first dispersal across the rift, Groves and Stott believe that gorillas on the northern end of the Mitumba range (e. g., Tshiaberimu) have experienced gene-flow from the Utu lowlands for about 100,000 years. Thus, despite high altitude adaptations (e. g., flared nostrils, longer hair), the morphology of these gorillas was influenced in the various ways that were previously described.

In this book, we have taken the position that the genus name *Gorilla* is to be preferred over the name *Pan*. The former is by far the most frequently used. However, we recognize that there are some good reasons to seriously consider *Pan*.** To clarify the issue and to put it into current perspective, we recently

---

Before Present; referring to geologic time before the appearance of humankind; i.e., the pleistocene epoch.
**In a recent text, Szalay and Delson (1980) also relegate *Gorilla* to the genus *Pan*.

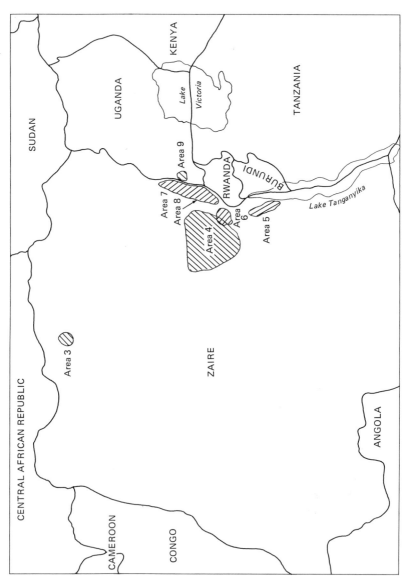

Figure 1-5. Approximate geographic locations of *graueri* and *beringei* in areas 3-9 as described by Goodall and Groves (1977)

Figure 1-6. Head of an adult female of the *graueri* subspecies. *(Photo courtesy V. Six and Zoo Antwerp)*

corresponded with Groves on the matter. With his permission, we quote his personal communication as follows:

> The category of Genus lacks the objectivity of that of species. Van Gelder (1977, Mammalian hybrids and generic limits, *Amer. Mus. Novit.*, no. 2635, pp. 1–25) proposes to erect an objective standard, but his suggested criterion —whether two species can hybridize or not, even in capacity—has problems associated with it and, in any case, could not in the present state of knowledge be applied to the question of the generic status of the gorilla vis-à-vis the chimpanzee.

> We are left with the sliding scale of phylogeny. Is the gorilla really the chimpanzee's closest relative? I have believed so; but Sarich and his colleagues have insisted for fifteen years that the gorilla/chimpanzee/human separation

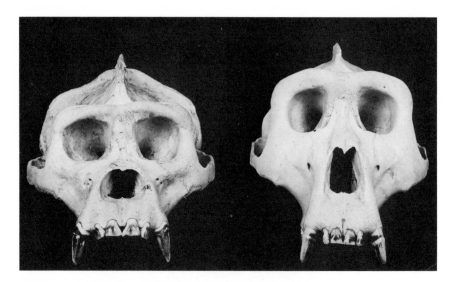

Figure 1-7. Two adult male skulls of *G. g. beringei* (left) from Mt. Mikeno, and *G. g. gorilla* (right) from between Youkadouma and Pandou, Cameroon, respectively. *(Photographs courtesy C. P. Groves)*

was most likely that rare phenomenon, a trichotomy. If this is correct, then of course the gorilla cannot be congeneric with the chimpanzee unless the human, too, goes into the same genus! In the present climate of uncertainty the wisest course would seem to be the conservative one, i. e., leave the gorilla in a genus of its own.

INTERNAL CHARACTERISTICS

Detailed anatomical studies have appeared in Keith (1896), Duckworth (1915), Sonntag (1924), Schultz (1927), Raven (1950), and Steiner (1954), and are reviewed in Napier and Napier (1967). Cranial capacity is in the range of 340-685 cubic centimeters in adult males; the largest recorded cranial capacity is 752 cubic centimeters. Calvarium is surmounted by large bony flanges, with a sagittal crest in adult males and a nuchal crest in all specimens, with females showing cresting in about 30% of the specimens. Though sometimes absent, the mastoid process is variable, and continues to grow throughout life. The face is markedly prognathic, the orbits are rectangular, and widely separated by fused nasal bones which form a sharp medial crest. There is a strongly developed supra-orbital ridge, deeply excavated by the frontal air sinus. The long hard palate extends well beyond the third molar, particularly in *beringei*. The mandible is stout and lacks a chin.

The right and left halves are braced by a shelf of bone (simian shelf). The third to seventh cervical spines are long, stout, and nonbifid. There are thirteen thoracic vertebrae, three to four lumbar vertebrae (seventeen total in lowland, sixteen in mountain forms) and five to six sacral vertebrae. The sternum is broad with separate elements, and there is a sinous vertebral scapula border in *beringei*, a straight border in the others. The os centrale is fused with the scaphoid. Phalanges are stout, heavily buttressed, and slightly curved. The skin on the back of the middle phalanges forms knuckle pads. The tarsus and heel length is the longest of all nonhuman primates. Dental features are: $= \frac{2}{2} \frac{1}{1} \frac{2}{2} \frac{3}{3} = 32$ with supernumerary molars occasionally present (4%) but supernumerary premolars are very rare. The caecum and colon are very large, an appendix is present, and liver lobes are variable up to six. There are coronary vessels and laryngeal air sacs (for details on thoracic viscera and genitourinary system see Washburn, 1950, and Steiner, 1954, respectively).

Schaller (1963) noted that wild mountain gorillas rarely attain a weight of more than 350 pounds for adult males. However, a wild specimen from Mt. Kahuzi was alleged to weigh 460 pounds (cf. Goodall and Groves, 1977). One zoo specimen, described by Cousins, attained the incredible weight of 776 pounds, and 500-pound captive males are not uncommon. Average heights and weights for the three subspecies were calculated by Groves (1970) as noted in Table 1-3.

Asymmetry in mammalian skulls is generally rare. Nevertheless, there has been considerable recent interest in human asymmetry and the concomitant lateralization in brain function. Among the nonhuman primates, only the gorilla exhibits marked asymmetry. As Coolidge (1929) noted, lowland gorilla skulls are usually longer on the right side, whereas mountain gorillas are usually longer on the left. In a re-examination of Coolidge's data supplemented by additional specimens, Groves and Humphrey (1973) found that lowland gorillas did not exhibit a significant asymmetry, whereas the two other subspecies (*beringei* and *graueri*) did exhibit highly significant left-sided asymmetry. This difference is somewhat greater in *beringei* than in *graueri.*

According to Groves and Humphrey, the form of the brain has little direct effect on the shape of the skull, and they were therefore unable to determine whether there was asymmetry in the cerebral hemispheres of these gorillas. As they further argued, however, the observed skull asymmetry may reflect asymmetry in chewing, although this chewing preference is merely inferred and has not been directly observed.

As Schaller (1963) determined, an analysis of the chest-beating display of mountain gorillas revealed evidence of handedness. In these displays, all eight gorillas exhibited a right-hand preference, using the right hand first in fifty-nine of the seventy-two recorded chest-beating sequences.

Handedness was also discussed by Robert and Ada Yerkes in 1929, wherein they noted that Mollison (1908) had inferred from skeletal measurements that

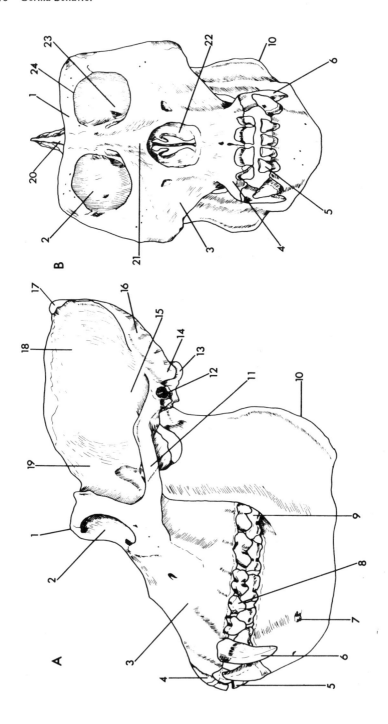

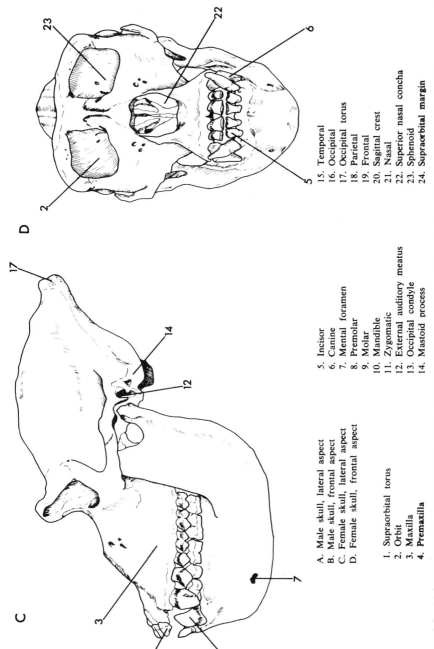

A. Male skull, lateral aspect
B. Male skull, frontal aspect
C. Female skull, lateral aspect
D. Female skull, frontal aspect

1. Supraorbital torus
2. Orbit
3. Maxilla
4. Premaxilla

5. Incisor
6. Canine
7. Mental foramen
8. Premolar
9. Molar
10. Mandible
11. Zygomatic
12. External auditory meatus
13. Occipital condyle
14. Mastoid process

15. Temporal
16. Occipital
17. Occipital torus
18. Parietal
19. Frontal
20. Sagittal crest
21. Nasal
22. Superior nasal concha
23. Sphenoid
24. Supraorbital margin

Figure 1-8. Major components of the gorilla skull. *(Courtesy Carolina Biological Supply Co., Lehrmittelverlag Wilhelm Hagemann, and Denoyer-Geppert Co.)*

Figure 1-9. *Mbongo* at the San Diego Zoo. *(Photo courtesy Zoological Society of San Diego)*

Table 1-3. Mean heights and weights as calculated for adult male gorillas.
(After Groves, 1970)

Subspecies	Height (cm)	Weight (lb)	Sample
gorilla	166.6	307.3	37
graueri	175.0	360.3	4
beringei	172.5	342.9	6

gorillas (and chimpanzees) were predominately left-handed. By contrast, other reports (cf. Fick, 1926) came to an opposite conclusion or suggested that the ape might in fact be essentially ambidextrous. Robert Yerkes himself (1927a) found that the mountain gorilla *Congo* was right-handed, but left-footed. Testing for maximal arm- and leg-reach, preference for one side in reaching, and in the manipulation of objects, Yerkes described this preference as follows:

I set the problem in six different locations and despite the variations of conditions Congo consistently reached with her right arm and hand, if the object

Figure 1-10. Closeup of *Ngagi's* facial features during his tenure at the San Diego Zoo. *(Photo courtesy Zoological Society of San Diego)*

Table 1-4. Gross asymmetry in *G. g. gorilla, G. g. graueri* and *G. g. beringei*. (After Groves and Humphrey, 1973)

	Right side longer	Left side longer	No difference
G. g. gorilla	8	8	122
G. g. graueri	–	2	15
G. g. beringei	–	17	21

20   Gorilla Behavior

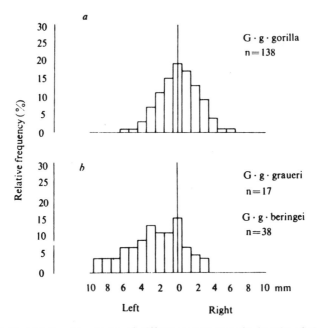

Figure 1-11. Relative frequencies of differences between the lengths of the two sides of skulls of the *gorilla, beringei* and *graueri* subspecies. Lengths were measured from the anteriormost point of the temporal fossa to the gnathion. Histogram *a: gorilla,* n = 138; Histogram *b: graueri,* n = 17; *beringei,* n = 38 (adapted from Groves and Humphrey, 1973).

was near, and with her left leg and foot, if the object was beyond arm reach. These confirmatory observations are mentioned because of the unexpectedness of the marked preference and its possible significance . . . (pp. 71-72).

It is most interesting to note that lateralization of brain *function* has been confirmed only in humankind, and is assumed to be associated with language potential. If the gorilla is found to be similarly blessed, its intellectual functioning may take on an even greater significance (cf. Chapter 6).

GENETICS

Chromosomes are 2n = 48, and serum precipitation data demonstrates a close phyletic affinity to *Pan* and *Homo*. There is an insignificant difference in human and gorilla Hbs with respect to amino-acid composition, and the P.T.C.* tasters to nontasters ratio is 14:4. ABO polymorphism is characteristic of gorillas but

---

Phenylthiocarbamide; a compound in which the ability to taste it is inherited as a dominant trait. In human beings, the compound is intensely bitter to about 70% of the population, and nearly tasteless to the remainder.

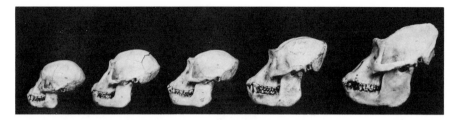

Figure 1-12. Growth of the skull of *G. g. beringei* (Mt. Mikeno) as indicated by specimens (left to right) of an infant, juvenile I, juvenile II, young adult, adult. All skulls are from males except juvenile I. *(Photograph courtesy C. P. Groves)*

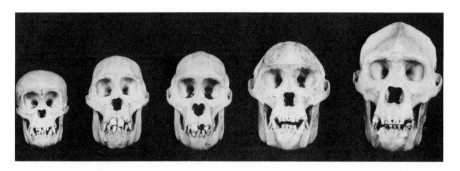

Figure 1-12a. Frontal view of above illustration.

they lack the "O" phenotype (cf. Napier and Napier, 1967; Goodman, 1964; Williams, 1964; Franks, 1963; Wiener, et al., 1966).

A white lowland gorilla was captured in 1966 by representatives of the Barcelona Zoo. The location of the capture was the equatorial forest of Nko near the River Campo in Spanish Guinea. At the time of its acquisition, the animal was about two years of age. A male, it had skin and hair that was completly devoid of pigmentation. The eyes of this unique ape had a bluish sclera normal cornea, and light blue iris which was transparent to transillumination. Accommodation and refraction were normal, the media were transparent, and the fundus of the eye was normal and without pigmentation. Of particular interest was the evidence of photophobia, such that its eyes repeatedly blinked when exposed to bright light. In diffuse light, such as that encountered in its natural habitat, the white gorilla was found to blink about 20 times per minute (Jonch, 1968).

The Spanish authorities originally named the animal *Nfumu* which means "white" in the local *Pamué* language. More recently he has been referred to as *Capito de Nieve*, Spanish for "snowflake." Although complete albinism had not previously been observed in gorillas, the Spanish field station has records of partial albinism in this species. In these cases, the absence of pigmentation always occurred on the hands or the feet. However, Jonch noted that there had been one previous unconfirmed report of a young gorilla which was unpigmented on portions of the head and neck. As the author pointed out, albinism is extremely rare in nonhuman primates. Nevertheless, a clan of the local *Fang* tribe revere a white chimpanzee as a totem figure, suggesting that such an animal may have once existed in that region. This totem figure is also called *Nfumu*.

Snowflake currently resides in the Barcelona Zoo where he lives in an enclosure with several normally pigmented females (cf. Figures 1-13 to 1-15). Several reports of this gorilla's behavior in captivity have been published by Jorge Sabater Pi (cf. 1967). The Spanish authorities are very hopeful that the union of *Snowflake* and his consorts will eventually produce albino offspring, a distant possibility since albinism is a recessive trait, transmitted exclusively through the father.

Figure 1-13. Albino gorilla *Snowflake* at age fifteen in the Barcelona Zoo, Spain. *(Photo courtesy J. Sabater Pi)*

Figure 1-14. *Snowflake* in 1966 at the Barcelona Zoo, approximately three years of age. *(Photo courtesy J. Sabater Pi)*

It is interesting to note that *Snowflake* adjusted to captivity better than any previous gorilla in the possession of the Spanish authorities. As Jonch explained it:

> It is possible that, because of its appearance, the young albino gorilla was not fully accepted by other members of the family group in the wild; and it is also possible that a visual deficiency decreased its optical powers, which could have also made it less acceptable to the group. These circumstances could have made it especially sensitive to demonstrations of affection and attention (p. 197).

Of course, it could also have been the case that its unique appearance drew an unusual amount of attention and affection. The resultant attachment between *Snowflake* and his captors may have therefore determined his unusually smooth adaptation to captivity.

That there may have been other instances of white pigmentation in gorillas is also suggested by Yerkes and Yerkes (1929) who reported that both Ford (1852-

Figure 1-15. *Snowflake's* preferred female consort at the Barcelona Zoo. *(Photo courtesy J. Sabater Pí)*

53, p. 31) and Garner (1896) had remarked on the phenomenon, the latter as follows:

> A white trader living on this lake claims to have seen a gorilla which was per-fectly white. It was seen in the plain near the lake. It was in company with three or four others. It was thought to be an albino, but in my opinion it was only a very aged specimen turned grey. A few of them have been secured that were almost white. It is not, however, such a shade of white as would be found in an animal whose normal color is white. I cannot vouch for the colour of this ape seen on the plain, but there must have been something peculiar in it to attract so much attention among the natives (pp. 208-211).

STRENGTH OF GORILLAS

The strength of gorillas is a subject of considerable public interest. It was once claimed, for example, that the famous Ringling Brothers' gorilla *Gargantua* had the strength of 27 men! The only *objective* data that we possess on the subject, however, are the dynomometer measurements made on chimpanzees by Bauman and Finch in the thirties and forties (cf. Maple, 1980a). These efforts have determined that chimps are certainly not much stronger, if at all, than a well-conditioned human male. Professional football players and amateur power-lifters must certainly be stronger than a chimpanzee. However, as the gorilla is much larger than a chimpanzee it is presumably also much stronger. It remains to be demonstrated whether the gorilla is as strong as it looks. We trust that an enterprising young scientist will soon answer the question by the employment of a suitable test of strength.

One rather subjective indication of strength is to pull against a gorilla in a tug-of-war contest. *Gargantua* was an early student of tug-of-war.* John Ringling North has been quoted as saying "he could always win if he wanted to, but each time the gorilla threw the end of the rope out, he would shorten it, hoping thus to lure the human player closer so he could grab or bite." (Plowden, 1972). In 1978, we arranged for the local zoo gorilla, *Willie B.*, to receive a tug-of-war rope. The first rope was donated by the NROTC unit at Georgia Tech, and an even longer rope was donated by the Coast Guard after *Willie* destroyed the first. Our original plan was to provide the public with periodic opportunities to pull the rope against *Willie.* However, after a careful consideration of the potential legal ramifications of inevitable human injury, we elected to keep the rope on hand for publicity tug-of-wars only. So far, *Willie* has pulled only against crowds of local celebrities and staff. Like *Gargantua*, he always wins when he wants to, pulling when he perceives relaxation in his opponent. His objectives are somewhat less diabolical than *Gargantua's*, as he tries only to get the rope into his cage where he can play with all of it.

As for his strength,** there are plans to pair him off against large local athletes to see how he fares in a genuine contest. So far, local professional wrestlers have declined to pull against him, but it is expected that other courageous strongmen will foresake their egos and soon step forward to accept the challenge. In much the same way that the tourist industry contributes to a country's conservation efforts, public interest in a famous animal can greatly contribute to the success of a zoological park, as it strives to improve its facilities and its performance. We

---

*The strength of the gorilla Cameroun was subjectively conveyed to us in a personal communication by Jack Throp who, in describing his tug-of-war apparatus, wrote:

We had to find a material durable enough to use for a pull. The first material was a 1,000-pound test nylon chain. Cameroun just laid it across his chest and "Samson-like," popped it into pieces. A steel chain was tried, but was too noisy and it kinked. A cotton rope was quickly turned into a frayed rag and hemp rope untwisted. Success was finally achieved with braid-woven nylon rope.

**The *Guiness Book of Records* has proclaimed as follows: " . . . a 100-pound chimpanzee achieving a two-handed dead lift of 600 pounds with ease suggests that a male gorilla could, with training, raise 1,800 pounds!" (p. 67).

are convinced that the zoo that succeeds in installing some strength-measuring device for their apes will reap dividends from the initial investment.

DISTRIBUTION

Goodall and Groves (1977) reported that the genus *Gorilla* has been known to occur in the following regions: 1. from the Sanaga river (Cameroon) south to the mouth of the lower Zaire river, east nearly to the Oubangui river where there is forest. The geographic limits of record are northwest at Edea (3.47°N, 10.10°E), northeast at Barundi, 22 miles northeast of Nola (3.40°N, 16.15°E), north at Touki near Bertoua (4.35°N, 13.30°E), south at Tshela in Mayombe district (5.05°S, 12.50°E). All of these locations are within the boundaries of Cameroon, Equatorial Guinea, Gabon, Central African Republic, Congo, Angola (Cabinda enclave), and Zaire. 2. A small region by the upper Cross River from Tingo (5.33°N, 9.35°E) northwest to the edge of the Obudu plateau (6.38°N, 9.06°E), on both sides of the Cameroon and Nigerian borders. 3. An isolated patch of forest near Djabbir, Bondo district, Zaire (3.55°N, 23.53°E). 4. Eastern Zaire lowlands, from the Ulindi river north to the equator. Geographical limits have been reported northwest at Lubutu (0.40°S, 26.55°E), north at Kilimanensa (0.35°S, 28.30°E), east at Pinga (1.00°S, 28.40°E), southeast at Bibugwa (2.30°S, 28.20°E), and south at Shabunda (2.45°S, 27.34°E). 5. The Itombwe Mountains, Zaire, between Mwenga (3.00°S, 28.28°E), and Fizi, (4.18°S, 28.56°E). 6. The mountains centered on Mt. Kahuzi, Zaire (2.10-2.25°S, 28.40-28.50°E). 7. The massif of Mt. Tshiaberimu, Zaire (0.05°N to 0.40°S, 29.00-29.20°E). 8. The six extinct volcanoes in the Virunga mountain range, straddling the Zaire-Rwanda-Uganda border (1.20-1.30°S, 29.24-29.42°E). 9. The Kayanza or Impenetrable forest, Uganda (1.00°S, 29.40°E). As Goodall

Table 1-5. Vegetation zones of the mountain gorilla range (after Goodall and Groves, 1977).

	South-western cluster	North-eastern cluster
Mountain woodland	5,000– 7,300 ft	5,000– 9,000 ft
Bamboo forest	7,300– 9,200 ft	8,500–10,000 ft
Hagenia forest	9,200–11,000 ft	non-existent
Hypericum and tree-heath forest	11,000–11,400 ft	10,000–11,000 ft
Alpine moorland with giant senecio and lobelia	11,300–peak	11,000–peak
Above 14,000 ft, vegetation very sparse		

and Groves pointed out, gorillas have not been reported in area 3 since 1908 and are presumed extinct. In area 2, the presence of gorillas was confirmed in 1957 but their current status is unknown. Gorillas are no longer found in the Mayombe district of Zaire (area 1), north of the mouth of the Zaire river. In the remaining regions they remain, although apparently in fewer numbers than originally reported.

The correct distribution of western gorillas is the subject of some dispute. To accurately reflect another point of view, we will directly quote from Gartlan's *IUCN* report:

> Within this broad geographical area, western gorillas are absent from closed canopy rain forest, a biome that covers much of the area; they are rare in forest of under 500 meters altitude. There is no evidence, for example, that gorillas have ever inhabited the stretch of lowland coastal forest, some 160 kilometers in extent, between the Cross river in Nigeria and the Nyong in Cameroon. A common error, perpetuated by Groves (1967, 1970), places *P. g. diehli* in the rain forest on the left bank of the headwaters of the Cross River, whereas in fact the right bank of this river is the southern limit of this deme. Western gorillas are found on forest edges, montane forests, secondary forest in all stages of ecological succession, light gaps, riverine forest, old logging roads and abandoned native fields (p. 1).

Gartlan noted that most museum specimens of western gorillas were likely obtained in either the hilly periphery of the rain forest or the riverine vegetation intertwined with the lowland forest. It was, therefore, naturally assumed that these regions were merely the outer limits of an evenly distributed forest population. However, Gartlan reported that he had never observed signs of gorillas in the closed canopy forest of Cameroon or Rio Muni. More importantly, by erroneously equating their distribution to the extant lowland forest, overestimates of the amount of remaining appropriate habitat have resulted. Thus, the status of these animals must now be questioned. We will return to this issue in greater detail in Chapter 8.

According to Gartlan, the current distribution of western gorillas suggests that they occupied highland or montane forests during a recent, cooler period. Their earlier niche subsequently regressed when the climate changed, isolating populations in the highlands. Gartlan has argued that this same process initially isolated the eastern and western populations.

HOME RANGE

Estimates of home range for gorillas are subject to great variation. Schaller (1963) observed home ranges of *10-15 square miles* for mountain gorillas at Kabara. Jones and Sabater Pí (1971) estimated *5.6 to 6.75 Km²* for western gorillas, whereas Goodall and Groves (1977) observed larger ranges in the Kahuzi region, up to *30 Km²* for eastern gorillas. Movement is apparently influenced by the

Figure 1-16. Interior of the equatorial rain forest in the *Mobumuom* region, near the *Lana* river in Rio Muni. *(Photo courtesy J. Sabater Pi)*

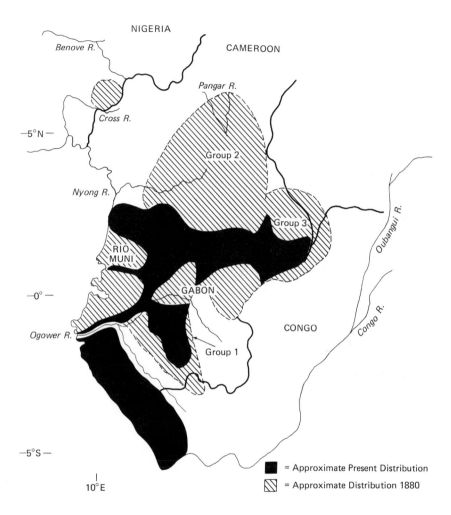

Figure 1-17. Distribution of western gorillas. (After Gartlan's IUCN report, 1980)

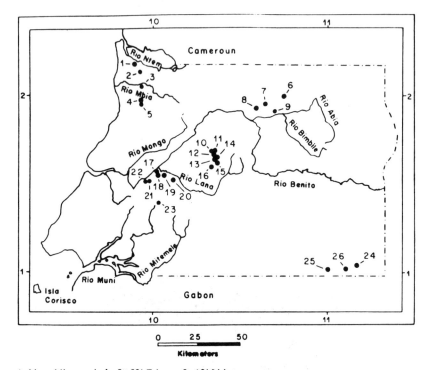

Figure 1-18. Known localities of western lowland gorillas in Rio Muni. (After Jones and Sabater Pi, 1971)

1. Near Nkgomakak, 9° 53′ E long, 2° 12′ N lat
2. Mangmeni, 9 56′ E long, 2° 8′ N lat
3. Rio Mbia, 9° 55′ E long, 2 5′ N lat
4. 2 km W Ndjiakom, 9° 55′ E long, 2 2′ N lat
5. 2 km S Ndjiakom, 9 55′ E long, 2 1′ N lat
6. Monung, 10 47′ E long, 1 59′ N lat
7. Obidng-Nkin, 10 39′ E long, 1 58′ N lat
8. Mokom, 10 36′ E long, 1 56′ N lat
9. Bisobinam, 10 42′ E long, 1 54′ N lat
10. Mbengui, 10 17′ E long, 1 41′ N lat
11. Ayene, 10 18′ E long, 1 41′ N lat
12. Mt. Alen, 10 18′ E long, 1 40′ N lat
13. Moka, 10 18′ E long, 1 39′ N lat
14. Etom, 10 19′ E long, 1 39′ N lat
15. Mt. Ndubu, 10 18′ E long, 1 38′ N lat
16. Mt. Bong, near Engong, 10 18′ E long, 1 37′ N lat
17. Old Abuminzok, 10 2′ E long, 1 37′ N lat
18. Abuminzok, 10 1′ E long, 1 36′ N lat
19. Aninzok, 10 4′ E long, 1 36′ N lat
20. 9 km E Aninzok, 10 8′ E long, 1 36′ N lat
21. Mt. Matama, 9 57′ E long, 1 32′ N lat

availability of food, but migration routes are remarkably stable over periods of years.

A landmark study of the home range of a group of mountain gorillas was published by Dian Fossey in 1974. The group (group 4) numbered from ten to seventeen individuals over the sixty-month period of study, living contiguous to three other groups, and sharing their home range with one of them. Within the various vegetation types as previously described, Fossey detected four types of travel as follows:

1. *Static*: The group remained either within one grid square* or between the mid-point of one square and the mid-point of the next.
2. *Regular*: The group occupied more than one but not more than four grid squares between the initial contacts and successive days.
3. *Rapid*: The group moved more than four squares between the initial contact on day one and the next contact.

Figure 1-19. Trail made by western gorilla in the forest of Cameroon. *(Photo courtesy J. Stephen Gartlan)*

---

*Each of the grid squares equaled 1/16 Km^2.

4. *Sudden change*: The group had been traveling in a constant direction for several days and suddenly reversed their general direction or altered altitude on the slopes markedly between one initial contact and the next. Travel was assessed as "sudden change" whether more or less than four squares had been covered (p. 579).

As the data indicated, group 4 moved daily about portions of their range. Fossey's observations led up to the following question: "Why, since substantial food appears to be available in all parts of their range, did they not steadily eat their way across it, instead of using energy and time in what would have appeared to the observer to be unnecessary locomotion? (p. 580)." The answers to the question are complex and we have paraphrased them from Fossey's discussion as follows:

1. Although food of some variety and quality is available in all zones, the digestive problems posed by certain foods place a premium on the most nutritious items. The gorilla also requires a greater variety of food than is found in any one zone.
2. In the long run, overall food availability is increased if each area is not cropped too severely at any one time.

Table 1-6. Food items consumed by feral mountain gorillas (After Fossey and Harcourt, 1977).

1. *Main food items*	Plants with a wide and plentiful distribution, eaten throughout the year but with some seasonal variation in amount, e. g. *Urera hypselodendron, Basella alba, Taccaza floribunda.*
2. *"Preferred" food items*	Plants with a very patchy distribution, often rare; these are almost always eaten when they are encountered, usually in great quantities, e. g. *Achyrospermum omicranthum, Galineria coffeoides, Coffea* sp., and species of semiparasitic *Loranthus.*
3. *Occasional food items*	Plants which may have either a wide or a patchy distribution but may or may not be eaten when encountered, e. g. *Hypoestes* sp., *Piper capense, Hagenia abyssinica.*
4. *Rarely eaten food items*	Plants with varied distribution but only seen to be eaten on one or two occasions, e. g. *Albizzia gummifera, Sericostachys scandens, Begonia* sp., *Dombeya goetzenii.*
5. *Seasonal food items*	Plants which are eaten in large quantities when they become seasonally abundant, e. g. fruits of *Myrianthus Holstii* and *Syzygium guinense*, bamboo shoots (*Arundinaria alpina*).

3. By moving about in their home area, predators may be avoided (especially the human variety).

4. Knowledge of total home-range conditions may be essential, requiring mobility, since food availability, and the presence of hazards and other groups can all be detected by movement.

All of the above are benefits of mobility, but the immediate determinants of the mountain gorilla's ranging behavior is probably not dictated by immediate food needs. Of greater importance, according to Fossey's analysis, may be the presence or absence of other groups. Thus a social rather than ecological variable provides the proximate stimulation for movement. As Fossey concluded:

> Ascribing the movement to an adaptive "tendency to move" does not of course explain it, but it does shift the emphasis from the frequently held view that the movements of groups of gorillas (or other animals) are always responses to immediate nutritional factors (p. 581).

ECOLOGY

The diverse biotopes inhabited by gorillas have also been described in detail in the important paper of Goodall and Groves. For the western gorillas, the major habitat type is equatorial rain forest from sea level altitudes to 2500 feet at the Cameroon plateau. The range of maximum temperature in this area is from $90°F$ at the coast to $99°F$ at Ouesso in the Sangha river valley. Minimum temperatures in this region range from $56°-68°F$. Rainfall is similarly variable from 59.7–122.3 inches. During the rainy season, humidity is universally 94–98%, but in the drier months it can drop to 45–50% in some areas. In the second region described by Goodall and Groves, the Cross River zone, the altitude at which gorillas are found ranges from 2000–5000 feet. Here they are most commonly found in a montane forest. While the temperatures generally equal those in the Cameroon plateau and rainfall is high, humidity is relatively low, in the range of 55–89%. Goodall and Groves' area 3 is assumed by them to be similar in its characteristics to area 1, despite a lack of any quantitative support for that assumption. In the eastern Zaire lowlands, where Schaller observed gorilla in the Utu region, the mean altitude is 2,000 feet. Here, gorillas live in a tropical rain forest with a narrower temperature range than in area 1. In the Itombwe region, *graueri* are common at 7,200–8,500 feet. The vegetation there is montane forest with bamboo above 8,000 feet, but beyond this fact, little is known. There is considerable information available about Mt. Kahuzi and Mt. Biega, montane forests where gorillas are found between 6,900–7,900 feet (cf. Goodall, 1974; Casimir, 1975a; Goodall and Groves, 1977). Maximum temperatures there are $64°F$ and minimum temperatures are $52°F$, each showing little variation from the norm.

Figure 1-20. Equatorial rain forest habitat of the western lowland gorilla, *Matama* region of Rio Muni. *(Photo courtesy J. Sabater Pi)*

Rainfall and humidity are highly variable, however, the former averaging 72 inches and the latter ranging from 50-85%. On Mt. Tshiaberimu, gorillas have been found at 8,600 feet, while at nearby Lubero, they are known to occur at 7,380 feet. In these locations, the average maximum temperatures are about 68°F with a minimum of around 52°F. Average yearly rainfall is 70 inches whereas the average humidity is 71% (cf. Goodall and Groves, 1978; citing Schaller's 1963 figures and a geographical handbook). This area differs little from Mt. Kahuzi. Finally, in the Virunga volcanoes, gorillas occur from 8,000-13,000 feet. However, it is believed that they typically frequent a narrower range of elevation from 9,500-11,000 feet. There are considerable differences in the characteristic ecology of the eastern and western volcano regions, as Schaller (1963) has shown. In the eastern group the bamboo zone is higher, extending up to 10,000 feet, followed by 1,000 feet of tree-heath and Hypericum. In the western group, the bamboo zone stretches from 7,300-9,200 feet, followed by a *Hagenia* forest up to 11,000 feet. The tree-heath and *Hypericum* region in the west covers only a span of some 400 feet above the 11,000-foot level. The *Hagenia* and bamboo are a temperate zone where the average maximum temperature is around 60°F with a minimum of 40°F. Average rainfall and humidity are 72 inches and 67–

Figure 1-21. Secondary rain forest growth of *Aframomum giganteum*, a favorite food of lowland gorillas in Rio Muni. *(Photo courtesy J. Sabater Pi)*

76%, respectively. Virunga is the coldest of all known gorilla habitats, and as Goodall and Groves (1977) suggested " . . . perhaps the most constantly damp, the most misty and sunless, the most marshy, and also the most open." (p. 607).

FEEDING HABITS

The feeding habits of gorillas have been studied by Schaller (1963), Casimir (1975a) and Goodall (1974). Schaller was not able to directly observe much feeding, relying instead on trail signs of discarded vegetation, stool samples,* etc. As Goodall and Groves concluded, however, direct visual observation of feeding is a more accurate technique for gathering reliable data. Schaller made this same point in his 1963 book. The Mt. Kahuzi food list of Goodall and a list compiled by Sabater Pi on the western Mt. Alen group contained 104 and 91 species of vegetation consumed by gorillas, considerably more varied than the lists of either

---

*In Rio Muni, lowland gorillas are apparently mutualistic with the plant *Aframomum*. Used by gorillas as food and for nesting, its viable seeds pass through the gastrointestinal tract and are thereby dispersed in their feces (Jones and Sabater Pi, 1971).

Figure 1-22. Bodily postures of a young lowland gorilla while feeding and resting in a tree in the *Abuminzok-Aninzok* area of Rio Muni. (After Jones and Sabater Pí, 1971)

Casimir or Schaller. Considering all plant food identified by the several observers, over 200 different items have been recorded. The mountain gorillas of the Virunga Volcanoes differ from all other gorillas in that their range of food items is narrower, half of their diet consists of herbaceous items, flowers are eaten, more roots and bulbs are eaten, and they consume far more stems and far fewer leaves. Gorillas which inhabit "intermediate montane" areas commonly differ from Virunga and true lowland gorillas in their food habits, eating more vines, bark and leaves, and fewer herbs. The common dietary preferences of lowland gorillas are fruit, shoots, and bulbs, but little bark. The feeding differences observed in gorilla populations are not wholly attributable to availability or energy requirements, as both individual differences and "cultural" differences appear to account for some of the variability. Categories of food items eaten have been derived by Goodall and Groves as follows: staples, specially preferred, seasonal, occasional, and very rarely. The small amounts of animal matter eaten are probably consumed for their vitamin B_{12} rather than their protein value. Adequate water is apparently supplied in the foodstuffs, but feral gorillas have been known to consume freestanding water.

Gorillas also form food preferences in captivity. Carpenter (1937) noted that the mountain gorillas *Ngagi* and *Mbongo* preferred foods in the following order: peaches, watermelons, grapes, bananas, oranges, and corn. When they were fed peaches and watermelons they became very excited to the point of emitting vocalizations. The gorilla *Congo*, studied by Robert Yerkes in the late twenties (cf. Chapter 2), was consistently fed baked sweet potatoes or yams, baked bananas, oranges, other raw fruits and berries, milk, egg, dry cereal, and raisins. Yerkes (1928) did not consider this diet to be completely adequate, as the following passage will illustrate:

> One may question the adequacy for anthropoid ape or man of a diet of sweet potatoes, bananas, sweet fruits, and milk. Possibly, cereals and raisins remedied certain deficiencies, but assuredly green vegetables and other plant products would have supplemented the diet importantly and probably also safeguarded the animal's health (p. 4).

The food selection of free-ranging mountain gorillas is not likely to be a matter of instinct. Goodall (1974) has carefully considered the factors which might influence their selection, and we therefore list these as follows:

1. *Abundance and availability* of the various plant species—including the influences of seasonality and interspecific competition.
2. *Nutritive value* in terms of energy, protein, vitamins, trace elements, minerals and water.
3. *Taste.*
4. *Smell or odor.*
5. *Size, shape and texture.*
6. *Preparation* necessary to render it ready for ingestion.
7. Physical action in the *digestive system* of the feeder.
8. Local or group *"tradition."*
9. *Individual (personal) preference.*

Goodall (1974) observed differences in foraging modes when Virunga and Kahuzi gorillas were compared. While the former were found to be exclusively terrestrial feeders, the latter exhibited evidence of arboreal feeding habits. These differences were attributed to the divergent vegetation types found in each respective region. The Kahuzi region, for example, was found to be a more three-dimensional habitat.

Wolfe (1974) recently surveyed the literature to compare the behavioral ecology of chimpanzees and gorillas. He sought to determine the relationship between diet, niche breadth, population dynamics, and the degree of territoriality and stability. His cautious conclusion was that population dynamics and group movement correlate with diet. For example, because of the gorilla's relatively stable habitat, Wolfe found that the populations were characterized by even adult sex-ratios, geographically consistent population densities, very low territorial responses, and no marked seasonal migrations. Chimpanzees, however, occupying diverse habitats with variable resources, exhibit disparate adult sex-ratios, population densities, and migration patterns.

According to Fossey (personal communication), feral mountain gorillas eat their own dung, but not the dung of others. This behavior occurs when there is inclement weather, when the animals remain in their nests.* Feral gorilla dung is trilobed and extremely fibrous. According to Fossey, it is also "good smelling" and the gorillas appear to relish it under the conditions as stated above. It would seem that the conditions that favor coprophagy in the wild are similar to those that prevail in captivity; namely, that confinement (e. g., to nest or enclosure) and reduced food availability are conducive to coprophagy. Relevent to these observations is a statement by Hladik (1978) as follows:

> The diet of *Gorilla* involves a large amount of bulk (lignin, cellulose, etc.) and some correlative differentiations of the digestive tract. The wild specimens examined have a relatively larger hindgut than all the species of primates that feed on fruits and leaves . . . As a consequence of this adaptation, a large volume of fodder is required for a normal behavior. Coprophagy may be practiced under conditions of low food availability. For example, some reintroduced gorillas, living on too small an island near Makokou, destroyed most of the lianas and edible trees. As a result they were not able to find enough leaves to feed on. Every day, they ate their feces which contain much fiber and perhaps some protein . . . (p. 385).

Recently, Harcourt and Stewart (1978a) published an interesting paper on the subject of coprophagy. In thousands of animal-hours of observing some 25 to 30 mountain gorillas, they observed only 25 instances of coprophagy. In two instances, the animal consumed two whole segments of dung ($\sim$200 g.), but many of the other records noted only "nibbling" by the animals. As the authors concluded, dung probably makes up only a minute proportion of the diet. This statement assumed, of course, that gorillas were not eating dung at dawn or dusk when observers were usually absent. Although Harcourt and Stewart found that, in most coprophagy cases, the producer ate its own dung, they also recorded four instances of young animals (less than eight years) eating the dung of an adult. Dung was generally consumed when it was less than five minutes old, and it was frequently deposited directly into the hand for immediate consumption. Coprophagy was most likely to be observed during or soon after rain, especially heavy rain. The significant climatic factor was therefore designated as precipitation. In addition, Harcourt and Stewart related coprophagy to activity. As they suggested, it was likely to occur within five minutes of the end of a rest-period, al-

---

*This observation has also been attributed to D'Arcy (cf. Hladik, 1978).

though this may have been an artifact of the defecation schedule. With respect to its causation, Harcourt and Stewart argued as follows:

> . . . Three explanations of the phenomenon of coprophagy by the Virunga gorillas seem possible. Besides it being of nutritional importance, two less significant, although in this case more likely, interpretations suggest themselves: either it is a reflection of boredom, or could it be that the animals want something warm to nibble on at the end of a long, cold, wet period without food? (p. 224).

Deborah Schildkraut and Jean Akers (personal communication) are currently engaged in a study of coprophagy and regurgitation/reingestion (R and R) in captive gorillas. The latter has apparently never been observed in the wild. In their survey of North American zoos, the two investigators found that both behaviors were common in zoo apes. In their work at the Stone Zoo in Boston, Akers and Schildkraut are systematically varying diet, feeding schedules, bulk and fiber intake, boredom and environmental/demographic factors in an effort to gain control over coprophagy and R and R. Their preliminary results suggest that both behaviors are influenced by multiple factors, and cannot be attributed to a single cause. This research is timely and important, and is clearly worthy of encouragement and further support.

ACTIVITY CYCLES

In the wild, mountain and western gorillas tend to be maximally active during early morning and later afternoon (Schaller, 1963; Jones and Sabater Pí, 1971). Schaller found that gorilla groups began to stir and then rise from the nest during the first two hours after sunrise (Figure 1-20). Early morning, until about 0900, is spent in intensive feeding. Between 0900 and 1000 the group begins to settle down for the midday rest period, with some animals resting while others continue to forage.

Table 1-7. Utilization of habitat by western lowland gorillas in Rio Muni (After Jones and Sabater Pí, (1971).

	Mature Forest	Regenerating Forest	Montane Forest
Feeding	X	X	X
Resting	X	X	X
Sleeping		X	

Between approximately 1000 and 1200 hours, the group rests, with sleeping, dozing, and sitting as the main activities. Both grooming and play among younger animals were sometimes observed. The rest period gradually ends as animals again begin to feed. Schaller concluded that a rest period was over when the silverbacked male began to feed.

After the rest period, activity varied considerably. Feeding was less intensive, and the group generally traveled greater distances than in the morning. Group activity generally decreased after 1700 with the gorillas constructing their nests and activity usually ceasing by 1800 hours.

Harcourt (1977) reported the same general cycle of group activity as Schaller. However, with his more precise measurement, Harcourt was able to investigate social behaviors that changed not only in frequency but in *pattern* throughout the daily activity cycle. Females were found to be more responsible for, and to spend more time near, the silverbacked male during the rest period than when feeding and traveling. Another interesting finding was that immature animals spent more time near their respective mothers during the rest period, but tended to congregate around the silverbacked male* when feeding and traveling. Har-

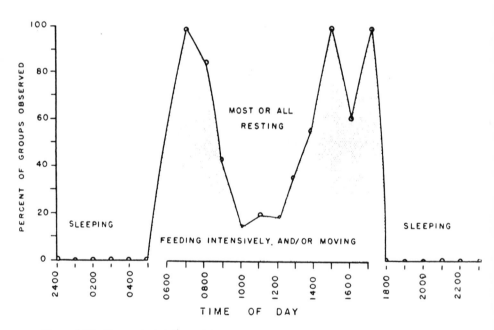

Figure 1-23. The typical daily activity cycle of mountain gorilla groups. (After Schaller, 1963) Copyright 1963 University of Chicago Press

---

*These data are for animals over one year of age. For infants younger than this, the mother was preferred both during rest and feeding periods.

court suggested that this was due to young animals using the silverbacked male as a convenient and safe gathering point for interactions during feeding periods.

NEST-BUILDING

About the origins of the nest-building habits of gorillas, the Yerkes' (1929) wrote the following:

> Nest building behavior, by some observers considered instinctive, may be partially so, as far as available evidence goes, or it may be imitational, traditional, or a result of definite parental or adult tuition. No observer has eliminated the possibility of social influence. (p. 420).

Schaller (1963) argued that the general pattern of gorilla nest building was innate, while specific adaptations were learned.* A superb early description of the nest-

Figure 1-24. Detail of a western gorilla's sleeping nest in Cameroon. *(Photo courtesy J. Stephen Gartlan)*

*As Schaller further pointed out, the literature contains a number of references to nests, as they remain visible for months and often are the only evidence of gorillas which observers encountered. We will review only the major works.

building habits of gorillas has been attributed to Reichenow (1920) and was quoted at length in Yerkes and Yerkes (1929) as follows:

The gorilla builds his resting place in this manner: he bends over in a circular area of two to three meters diameter, all the standing plants toward the middle of the place, or in a sidewise direction, and arranges this tangle of leafy stems, knitting them together so that the round bowl-like nest has a diameter of one to one and a half meters. Torn parts of plants brought from other places I have never observed. If one tears apart such a nest one finds that all the plants are still rooted in the earth. In spite of a large number of thorny plants which are mixed in the undergrowth, the animals are skillful in finding places which are free from thorns. On the other hand, large-leaved plants and high standing grasses are preferred for the nests. These nests which are built somewhat higher above the earth in a low strong bush are completed in a corresponding way to those on the earth. The separate branches of the bush are partly bent outward, partly bent in toward the middle, and woven together. These higher nests are distinguished in that they form an extraordinarily soft and flexible foundation. One can compare them with a spring feather mattress . . .

The gorilla builds his nest in forests and in treeless regions. He lays value only upon the thickest possible undergrowth. I have found nests equally in the thick primeval forest and in the old deserted negro farms on which no strong stand of trees had yet grown up. That no particular shelter is used against the rain I can establish with certainty . . . (pp. 6–7).

Osborn* (1963), in a report on the behavior of the Virunga Volcano mountain gorillas, provided interesting information concerning nesting habits, and we will review these findings as completely as possible. Osborn noted that nests were basin-shaped when constructed on the ground, or in bushes or trees. The nests were flatter if located in bamboo. Branches were used to frame the nests, with leaves or herbs apparently used as an inner lining. Osborn classified nests into day and night types, the latter type being more commonly found. Except for the nests of young, Osborn reported that night nests were invariably fouled with squashed dung, indicating that gorillas defecate in their nests. Contrariwise, day nests contained no dung and were less carefully constructed.

---

*Research on the behavior of the Virunga Volcano mountain gorilla actually began with the two-month study of Bingham as carried out in 1929 and published in 1932. In 1956 Walter Baumgartel began his informal observations (cf. 1959), and in collaboration with L. S. B. Leakey, enlisted two research assistants, Osborn (1963) and Donisthorpe (1958) to continue the observations. This work was the prelude to Schaller's study which began in 1959 and was published in 1963. Baumgartel should therefore be given proper credit for sparking the recent interest in the behavior and welfare of gorillas.

Osborn believed that nests were not built every night, so gorillas may occasionally use old nests or not build them at all.* While Donisthorpe (1958) reported that 54% of gorilla nests were close to the ground. Osborn reported a somewhat higher figure of 67%. Where groups of nests were located, there was usually found more than one type. Apparently, the location of nests reflects the predominant substrate, since ground nests were rarely found in areas of bamboo. Relative to females and young, silverback male nests were found closer to the ground. This is probably due to his weight rather than any conscious defensive strategy as has been suggested in popular accounts. However, smaller gorillas may indeed select higher nests for purposes of greater security from disturbance.**

Schaller's (1963) landmark study included a great deal of information on nesting taken from inspection of more than 3000 nests. Schaller, like Osborn, distinguished day and night nests; neither researcher found night nests to be used more than once. Schaller reported day nests to range from simple, crude masses of vegetation on the ground to elaborate tree platforms. Unlike Osborn, he occasionally found dung in day nests.

Nests were constructed with varying degrees of care; ground nests were often composed of a few handfuls of vegetation pushed down to form a partial rim. Schaller did find, however, complex and sophisticated ground nests, including a single instance of an apparent excavation of considerable soil at a nest site. Nests above ground were generally constructed with more detail paid to the bottom of the nest than in ground nests. Often they were relatively flat, with little deep cupping.

Schaller found individual nest size to vary with the size of the animal building the nest, from approximately two feet in diameter for juveniles to five feet in diameter for silverbacked males. The main body of the nest was typically constructed of whatever vegetation was easily available. He reported that only rarely did gorillas line their nests with any special materials.

The group pattern of individual nest locations was found to vary considerably both across groups and day-to-day within groups, as the total group nest site diameter was found to range from about 30 to 100 feet or more. Additionally, Schaller found great variability in locations of nests in the trees or on the ground, with ground nests accounting for approximately 21 to 97% of all night nests in his various study sites. He accounted for these differences as due to both differential availability of suitable vegetation for above-ground nests, and to regional differences among the gorillas themselves.

Subspecies differences in nest-building habits were also suggested by Reichenow (1920) who noted that the gorillas of the Cameroons and Gabon respectively

---

*Osborn, however, suggested that gorillas use each nest for one night only, despite her report that Akeley (1951, in Osborn, 1963) found fresh vegetation placed over soiled bedding, this suggesting their use over multiple nights. Sabater Pí (1960, reported in Schaller, 1963) also found that gorillas use the same nests over successive nights.

**Emlen and Schaller (1960) reported that some gorilla nests were found at heights of forty-five feet above the ground.

exhibited differences in the locations and height of their nests. Whether such differences exist must be verified, and further, it is unclear whether these presumed differences are inherent, acquired, or a bit of both. The Yerkes' cogently summarized the issue in the following passage:

> From the varied supplementary and partially contradictory information we reach the tentative conclusion that there probably are marked variations in nest building which are correlated with species and variety, with local environmental conditions, or with season. Possibly the factors of each of these categories may be contradictory. Suggested is the existence of three principal types of nest building habit, referable regionally to (1) the Cameroons, (2) the Gaboon, and (3) the Mountains of East Equatorial Africa (p. 415).

As Bernstein (1969) stated, given the adult gorilla's great weight, it is not surprising that nests are usually found on the ground instead of in trees. The heavy adult males, especially, would be unable to build nests in the higher and more fragile branches of trees. As Maxwell (1928) noted:

> Whereas the adult male gorilla seems to prefer ground seats, it not infrequently happens that the younger members of a flock occupy small platforms, from four to six feet above ground level . . . (p. 446).

However, Bolwig (1959b) discovered that if there was suitable vegetation available to construct stronger nests, fewer nests were found on the ground. Thus, the nature of the nesting material, rather than any particular preferences, may actually determine the location of nests. Bolwig further suggested that gorillas constructed *neater* nests than chimpanzees, owing to their tendency to twist the materials together.

A very recent analysis of nesting sites has been conducted by Casimir (1979). Working in the Mt. Kahuzi region of Zaire, the investigator observed a group of gorillas for fifteen months and closely examined 63 group nesting sites during this time. At these 63 sites, a total of 724 individual nests were examined. From Casimir's original list of 51 species of vegetation, we have listed herein the top ten in frequency (cf. Table 1-8). Casimir determined that the most frequently utilized species were those in greatest abundance. Thus, vegetation at hand is that which is used.

The diameters of 643 nests were measured and assigned to their appropriate age/sex class. The latter was accomplished by applying Schaller's (1963) technique of calculating the diameter of the dung lobes within or nearest the nest itself. The measurement of nests was accomplished at the maximum outer diameter. The largest nests were constructed by silverback males, ranging from about 110–140 centimeters. Mothers with infants built nests slightly larger than other adults. The former were from 95–125 centimeters in diameter, whereas

Table 1-8. Ten primary plant species utilized in the construction of 716 gorilla nests (Adapted from Casimir, 1979).

Genus	Species	Family	Vernacular name	n
Brillantaisia	nyanzarum (h)	Acanthaceae	Tshinononono	266
Dombeya	goetzenii (t)	Sterculinaceae	Musakule	73
Neobourtonia	macrocalyx (t)	Euphorbiaceae	Tshibirabira	38
Mimulopsis	arborescens (s)	Acanthaceae	Mbobwe	33
Chasalia	subochreata (t, +)	Rubiaceae	Kalampui	25
Vernonia	ampla (s, +)	Compositae	Keshushula	24
Arundinaria	alpina (bamboo, o)	Graminaceae	Mulonge	21
Triumfetta	rhomboidea (t)	Tiliaceae	Tshahunga	18
Allophylus	griseo-tomentosa (?)	Sapindaceae	Kashushumuhanda	17
Hagenia	abyssinica (t, +)	Rosaceae	Muisusi	15

t = Tree: h = herb: s = shrub: v = vine: o = plant of primary forest; + = species which is also eaten.

other adults built nests from about 90-120 centimeters. Juvenile gorillas constructed nests which ranged from about 60-100 centimeters in size. In general, the bigger the animal, the bigger the nest.

For 964 nests, Casimir determined that most were inadequately or not at all protected from the rain. Moreover, only a few nests were in a position to receive direct sunlight. In agreement with Bingham (1932) and Kawai and Mizuhara (1959), Casimir found that, at sundown, the prevailing conditions are accepted by the gorillas with no compensatory action.

The overall percentage of nests for Mt. Kahuzi and other gorillas is indicated in Table 1-9. As Casimir pointed out, the variation in ground-nesting frequency has not yet been adequately explained. However, a contributing factor might be the number of suitable trees in the vicinity. In calculating the range of nest heights, Casimir found that most raised nests (200/228) were 1-10 meters (3-33 feet) above the ground, and half of these were above 5 meters. Only twenty-eight nests were found at the height of 10-15 meters (33-50 feet). Thus, all gorillas appear to be inclined to construct nests at or slightly above ground level.*

Apparently, gorillas are the only great apes that defecate in their own nest. However, there appears to be some variation in the frequency of this habit. Gorillas from the Virunga Volcanoes were found to have defecated in 73% of the nests investigated (Schaller, 1963). However, gorillas in the Utu region appear to rarely soil their nests. Similarly, in the Kayonza Forest, Schaller found relatively few instances of defecation in nests. In Rio Muni, Jones and Sabater Pí (1971) found that 43.2% of the examined nests were soiled. Casimir determined that

*A growing number of corporate entities are contributing to ecology and conservation-related research. Casimir's study was supported by the Volkswagen Foundation.

Table 1-9. Percentages of ground nests discovered for individual populations of gorillas as summarized by Casimir (1979).

Population	Region	Nests on ground %	Reference
Eastern gorilla	Virunga Volcanoes	53.7	Donisthorpe [1958]
	Uganda side of the		
	Virunga Volcanoes	43.5	Kawai and Mizuhara [1959]
	Kisoro	45.3	Schaller [1963]
	Kabara	97.1	Schaller [1963]
	Mt. Muhavura	44.0	Osborn [1957]
?	Kayonza	53.4	Schaller [1963]
Eastern lowland gorilla	Utu	21.8	Schaller [1963]
?	Mt. Kahuzi	68.8	Casimir [1979]
Western gorilla	Rio Muni	84.0	Jones and Sabater Pi [1971]

dependent infants were more likely to deposit dung in the nest and subsequently lay in it (73.9%). Juveniles (36.2%) were more prone to this behavior than were adults, the latter defecating in the nest hollow only about 15% of the time. Thus, Mt. Kahuzi gorillas at least, learn to defecate outside the nest as they mature.

Corroborating the findings of Schaller (1963), Casimir similarly found no organization in the relative distances of nests according to age/sex class. In relation to each other, nests appear to be randomly distributed in space.

In his studies of the nest-building habits of captive apes, Bernstein (1969) first provided opportunities for eight young gorillas (2 1/2-3 1/2 years of age) to construct nests. These animals moved broken branches together on the ground, but recognizable nests were not found and the gorillas were observed to sleep in pairs on the ground. By contrast, the two orang-utans in the study bent the tops of trees together and bent others over them, tangling them all together to make a sturdy nesting platform.

To investigate the age of the animal as a factor in the construction of nests (cf. Schaller, 1963), Bernstein provided six juvenile gorillas with nesting material (hay, lengths of rubber and plastic hoses). These animals were tested in this manner on a number of occasions. Only three of the oldest juveniles made appropriate nests, and the oldest of these produced the best example. As Bernstein explained:

This female, about age seven, worked consistently and intently, starting her nesting patterns promptly when given access to materials, whereas the other gorillas often used the hay and hose in wild play sessions or explored their possible use for other purposes. (p. 396).

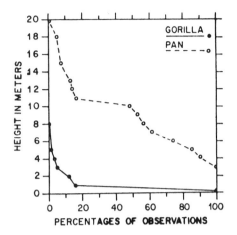

Figure 1-25. Height above the ground of western lowland gorilla and chimpanzee night nests ("beds") in Rio Muni. (After Jones and Sabater Pí, 1971)

With time, most of the younger juveniles exhibited some improvement in nest building. As Bernstein concluded, maturation is a necessary condition for sophisticated nest-building. In addition, it is likely that apes must learn nest building early in life, perhaps by observing the procedure as it is carried out by their mothers. Bernstein's data tell us a great deal about the acquisition of this complex behavior, but as he himself suggested, more research will be required before nest building can be completely understood. In the eleven years since his report was published, the necessary research has not yet been carried out.

INTERSPECIFIC INTERACTIONS

In Rio Muni, Jones and Sabater Pí (1971) observed or heard five primate taxa in association with gorillas. The most commonly associated primates were *cercopithecus nictitans*. Less frequently in association were *C. cephus, C. pogonias, Colobus polykomos*, and *Pan troglodytes* respectively. The response of lowland gorillas to their close kin *P. troglodytes* was appropriately summarized in the following passage:

> The presence of chimpanzees near to gorillas was detected rarely during this study. On one occasion, a group of chimpanzees passed close to a group of gorillas that were feeding . . . in the Mt. Alen area. Each group of apes moved in separate directions from this site. Although the chimpanzees were making vocal sounds at the time, no vocalizations or displays were made by gorillas. On other occasions, gorillas seemingly did not respond when vocalizations were given by chimpanzees that were in nearby areas. (p. 82).

According to the observations of Jones and Sabater Pí, the different habitat strata utilized by the various primates prevented close ecological associations among gorillas and other taxa. With respect to chimpanzees, ecological overlap did not occur because of incomplete overlap in the diets of *Pan* and *Gorilla*, and temporal differences in the utilization and occupancy of habitat by the respective taxa.

In Rio Muni, no direct interactions were clearly observed between gorillas and other large mammals. However, Jones and Sabater Pí noted that elephants (*Loxodonta africana*) occasionally damaged food plants utilized by gorillas (e.g., banana plants and *Aframomum* spp.). In those areas where recent signs of elephants were detected, there were no signs of gorillas. Apparently, leopards (*Felis pardus*) do not regularly prey upon gorillas in Rio Muni.

Schaller (1963) also described several instances of gorilla interactions with other animals. Generally, however, he found that mountain gorillas did not interact to a great extent with other species. Interactions with birds were largely confined to watching them and avoiding them (e.g., startle reactions). Similarly, these gorillas did not typically interact with mammals. Moreover, Schaller found no evidence for the common belief that leopards stalked and preyed upon mountain gorillas. Finally, he observed few interactions between gorillas and other nonhuman primates.

AGGRESSION TOWARD HUMAN BEINGS

As Sabater Pí (1966) has noted, gorillas* are, for the most part, timid and peaceful creatures. In fact, they generally shun contact with humans by hiding in the dense bush. However, when a gorilla has been wounded, it can be very dangerous. For example, in Rio Muni, sudden and unexpected intrusions have been known to precipitate attacks by dominant males, especially in groups containing very young animals. Seven proven cases of lowland gorillas attacking human beings in Rio Muni were recorded by Sabater Pí and described in his 1966 paper. We have extracted a portion of one description for the reader's consideration as follows:

> Manuel, amazed by the proximity of the group (3–4m) attempted a prudent retreat, facing the animals (it is a very strong belief among the natives that the gorillas will not attack if one always keeps his face toward them) but it availed him nothing. The dominant male, recovering from the fright, gave a loud shout and charged furiously, knocking Manuel down and biting him in the legs. (p. 124)

From this and his further descriptions, Sabater Pí was able to draw a number of conclusions about gorilla attacks on humans.

---

*Sabater Pí here refers to lowland gorillas. Schaller (1963) has also noted instances of mountain gorilla aggression toward human beings.

1. Considering the high density of anthropoids in the Rio Muni Zones that he described and the length of time over which the attacks occurred, the number of proven cases was minimal.
2. Nearly all gorilla attacks were found to be a response to an injury, generally inflicted by the victim.
3. The one case where the attacker was not injured, was precipitated by a sudden human intrusion into a gorilla family's area of security.
4. The adult male and females are especially aggressive in the presence of young.
5. The threshold and intensity of an attack greatly varies among animals.
6. The typical mode of attack is the employment of mouth and hands to cause lacerations in the victims legs, thighs, buttocks, and when resisting —hands.
7. Attacks are usually short in duration.
8. In no case was there a barrier to the victim's escape.

Schaller's descriptions of mountain gorilla attacks on humans are generally consistent with these conclusions. From both Sabater Pí and Schaller's observations, it is clear that gorillas are not by nature aggressive toward humankind. However, when provoked, a gorilla is a formidable adversary. Anyone who has worked with gorillas in captivity is well aware of their great strength. Even the most trusted captive gorillas may on occasion be frightened into a vicious and damaging attack.

SOCIAL ORGANIZATION

Mean group size estimates for gorillas as determined by Schaller (1963), Fossey (1972), Casimir (1975b), Goodall (1974), and Jones and Sabater Pí (1971) are 17 (Kabara, Visoke), 7 (Kisoro), 9 (Kayonza, Tshiaberimu), 11 (Mt. Kahuzi), 13 (Itombwe), 12 (Utu lowlands), 7 (Mt. Alen, Rio Muni), 6 (Abuminzole-Aminzok, Rio Muni), and 8 (Schaller's West African composite). From these data it is clear that the western volcanoes are inhabited by the larger groups, with somewhat smaller groups found in the intermediate mountains, and the much smaller groups inhabiting the West African lowlands. Similarly, group composition data suggest that 1-1.5 and 2 silverbacked males are represented in the lowland-intermediate areas and the volcano areas respectively. While silverbacks represent a smaller percentage of the group in the latter populations, blackbacked males are relatively more common in the western mountain gorillas surveyed. All of the data indicate that gorilla groups are fundamentally one-male groups, with younger adult males living a seminomadic, loosely group-attached existence. A ratio estimate of likely reliability for adult females to young is 1:1.2-1.5 (cf. Goodall and Groves, 1977).

Although gorillas are generally thought to be organized at a level no higher than the family group, Goodall and Groves have suggested that there may be larger local communities which contain the smaller families. These larger communities, extrapolated from Schaller's original data, were composed of 68 and 77 members for the two respective communities. Interestingly, if further research confirms this supposition, the argument that *gorilla* should be considered a species within the genus *Pan* would be greatly enhanced.

Mountain gorilla social structure is unique among the apes, since the highly cohesive gorilla groups are composed of more adult females than males. Moreover, among mountain gorillas, a majority of females leave their natal group at maturity (Harcourt, Stewart, and Fossey, 1976). Thus, gorilla groups are composed of females that are largely unrelated, and those that probably have not grown up together. Since there is evidence that bonds between these adult females are weak or even nonexistent, group cohesion must be due to the relationship between the silverbacked male and these resident females.

In Harcourt's (1979b) report on these relationships, spacing, proximity, grooming, and agonistic behaviors were recorded during a two-year study period. As Harcourt (1979a) previously determined, activity periods were divided into morning and afternoon travel-feed periods punctuated by a midday rest period. During rest periods, the gorillas were more tightly bunched than was the case during travel-feeding periods (cf. Table 1-10). Thus, the predominant activity of the group influenced measures of social interaction. In examining the propensity of females to interact with the silverbacked male,* Harcourt found that nearly all anestrous females spent more time near the silverbacked than the blackbacked male. Moreover, most of the time that females did spend near the immature male can be accounted for by the attracting presence of the silverbacked male. Thus, as Harcourt concluded, for these two mountain gorilla groups, the younger blackbacked male did not influence the behavior of females.

The factor which most affected female proximity to the silverback was the presence of offspring. Thus, females with dependents (less than five years of

Table 1-10. Records by percentage of different numbers of adults within 10 meters of each other during rest periods and travel-feed periods. The distribution between the two periods was statistically significant at the .001 level (after Harcourt, 1979b).

| | Nos. of adults within 10-m diam. | | | | | |
	1	2	3	4	5	*n*
Rest period	33.9	40.3	19.3	4.8	1.6%	62
Travel-feed period	64.1	30.1	2.9	1.9	1.0%	103

*Harcourt has referred to the dominant, silverbacked male as the *leading male*.

age) spent more time with the silverback than did those without dependent off-spring. Furthermore, Harcourt determined that as the offspring *increased* in age, mother's time near the silverback *decreased*. An interesting effect of this relationship is that as the offspring matured, and mother's time near the male decreased, the offspring's time near the male increased in relation to its time near mother. Thus, the general attractivity of the silverbacked male extended to the younger animals as well. Although data were available for only one female, Harcourt also discovered that after a birth she spent three times as much time near the silverback as before.

The death of an infant also led to behavioral changes in the relationship of one female to the silverback. As Harcourt explained:

To analyse the change, the mean time that each female in the group spent near the male after the death was compared to her time before it. Only two days were available for analysis after the infant was killed. Most of the data then were taken while the group members were clumped during a long rest period. Therefore, only similar days from before the birth were chosen for comparison (p. 331).

As Harcourt surmised, if the mother had not lost her infant she would have increased her time near the silverbacked male. However, an opposite trend was detected; relative to the male, she dramatically changed from being the most proximate to the least proximate female.

Harcourt also determined that behavioral indices of hormonal changes in adult females (e.g., courtship behaviors) influenced the temporal relations of the females and the resident silverback. Thus, when mating and nonmating days were compared, most of the females were found to significantly differ according to inferred hormonal status (see also Chapter 4).

An important question which Harcourt attempted to answer was: Which animal was more responsible for the maintenance of proximity? We (cf. Hoff et al., 1981; and Chapter 5) have similarly struggled with this question with respect to mother-infant relations. Harcourt determined that it was the adult females who were most responsible for maintaining proximity to the male. In his own words:

The greater responsibility of the females could have been due to them seeking the male more, his avoiding them more, or both. That the females sought proximity is indicated by comparison of the frequency with which males and females followed each others' departures . . . all females followed the departing male more often than he followed them. In fact, the male hardly ever moved after a female when she left (p. 332).

Agonistic behavior between the silverback and resident adult females was re-vealed in several measures (see also Chapter 3). First, while the silverback was observed to supplant females, they never supplanted him. Similarly, females sometimes avoided the male but he never avoided them. Second, the silverbacked male often emitted aggressive displays towards the females, but they never did so toward him. These displays (e.g., chest-beating and strut-walking) were more fre-quent than were his other aggressive responses, whereas females emitted primarily pig-grunts (cf. Chapter 3) when expressing "hostility" in the direction of the silverback.

Despite the fact that aggressive displays do occur within the group, they are most often emitted toward human intruders or other gorillas. However, an an-alysis of the group 5 male's displays indicated that they occurred most frequently at the end of rest periods. As Harcourt further suggested:

> It was shown that a common response of the group 5 females to displays by the leading male was to follow him if he left. Ninety percent of the 20 of these observed follows occurred at the end-of-rest-periods. These observa-tions suggest that the function of the male's displays then was to alert the females to his imminent departure, and so ensure that they did not remain behind when he left (p. 336).

While Schaller (1963) reported that a stiff-legged walk by the silverback in-duced following in the other group members, Harcourt found that running and occasionally attacking were also functional in this context. Another function of male aggression was its utility in the cessation of fighting by other group mem-bers (see also Hoff, Nadler, and Maple, 1978a; Chapter 5).

So what are the potential benefits to be derived from these observed relation-ships? Harcourt proposed the following benefits of close relationships between adult females and the dominant male:

1. Proximity to the male bestows protection to the mothers and the offspring.
2. Proximity to the male may increasingly free the female for unen-cumbered foraging, due to the offspring's growing attraction to the male.
3. The male's tolerance of proximity protects his genetic investment and increases the probability that his harem will remain intact.

Relations Among Females in the Wild*

In a number of primate taxa (e.g., *T. gelada, M. mulatta, P. cynocephalus*) females have been characterized as the more stable elements of the population.

---

*See also Chapter 2.

This has also been said to apply to gorillas (Crook, 1970; Harcourt, 1979b). The reasons behind this generalization, as Harcourt has stated, may be listed as follows:

1. In many primates, fewer females than males leave their natal group.
2. Those females that remain form strong social bonds to their relatives.
3. In general, female dominance hierarchies appear to be more stable than male hierarchies.

However, the mountain gorilla differs in the first category in that it appears that females move more between groups than do males. Harcourt has suggested that a consequence of the propensity is that most adult females in a breeding unit are probably unrelated and hence have not grown up together.

Harcourt's report on the social relations of mountain gorillas concerned the Virunga Volcanoes' populations. Data were primarily derived from two groups (designated groups 4 and 5), each of which was comprised of a mature male, an immature male, and a number of females and offspring. Harcourt specifically examined the behavior of nine adult females over eight years of age, and three subadults from six to eight years old.

In his records of proximity to others, Harcourt discovered that adult females spent significantly more time near the adult male of their group than they did with each other. Moreover, it appeared that when two adult females were together and near the male, it was the male's presence which accounted for proximity between the females.

An especially interesting finding was that related females and those familiar from immaturity spent more time together than unrelated or unfamiliar females. Unlike many other primates, the relationships of these female mountain gorillas were not greatly affected by changes of events. One change observed during eight of fifty-eight estrous events was the onset of female homosexual behavior, observed but not described by Harcourt.

The birth of a gorilla also affected the social relationships of females, but the greatest interest in the newborn was exhibited by a nulliparous female.* In general, as with other primates, a birth attracts other group members, but it also tends to increase the avoidance behavior of the mother.

Among unrelated females, Harcourt found that grooming was rare. However, a mother and daughter did exhibit a high degree of grooming, as did two gorillas which had been familiar since immaturity. Thus, grooming rates among gorillas in captivity may reflect their degree of familiarity rather than some species-typical behavior pattern (cf. Chapter 2).

---

*The immature group members were also greatly attracted to the mother and its newborn infant.

Regarding dominance, Harcourt examined the avoidance reactions of females and found that no female avoided one that avoided her. As Harcourt stated:

> This indicates the possibility of stable differences in status between females, but not necessarily of a hierarchy. In fact, the results provided very little evidence of the existence of an agonistic hierarchy, largely because of the paucity of records of avoidance reactions (p. 259).

Despite this result, Harcourt noted that all of the observers of these animals were able to agree on a linear ranking of females. This illustrates, we think, the subtle dimensions of social communication which characterizes gorilla behavior (cf. Chapter 3). It is exceedingly difficult to record these subtleties, but reasonably easy to recognize them.

Aggression was most reliably exhibited in the form of pig-grunt vocalizations. In eight of eleven, and nine of fifteen female combinations in the two groups, the pig-grunt was the most common mode of threat in the two respective years of recording. In 69% of these aggressive interactions, the pig-grunt was the only behavioral element recorded. Pig-grunting erupted into screaming interactions in 8.5% of the aggressive bouts, while stereotyped displays (chest-beating, strut-running) were characteristic of 15.5% of the interactions. Only 7% of all aggressive exchanges included attacks. Thus, aggression among females must be considered to be of relatively low intensity.*

Harcourt also determined that strange females entering a group for the first time are not generally treated any differently than residents. Among the female members of a group, aggression between them and the silverback male were more frequent than aggression among themselves. Needless to say, silverback-female aggression was almost exclusively unidirectional. Finally, Harcourt determined that the related females and those familiar from maturity engaged in less aggression than most combinations of unrelated and less familiar gorillas.

In general, female relationships within gorilla groups are characterized by mutual tolerance and little social contact. As Harcourt suggested, "if bonds between females are not established in immaturity, they are unlikely to be formed at all (p. 260)."

Our forthcoming discussion of the adult male removal in the Yerkes group (cf. Chapter 5) is relevant here. The *control role* of the adult male was revealed in many of the aggressive and affiliative behaviors that were recorded. Among the adult females, aggressive interactions increased dramatically when the male was removed. When he was reintroduced, aggression returned to preremoval levels. Infant behavior was similarly affected. Social play declined, and mother-

---

*This is consistent with our observations of female aggressive interactions in a group of captive lowland gorillas.

infant contact increased dramatically. These findings indicate that the adult male assumes the role of mediating intragroup aggression and maintaining the stability in the group. Presumably, silverbacked males are similarly inclined in feral populations of gorillas.

Relations Between Males in the Wild

Harcourt (1979) recently described the interactions of males living in groups 4 and 5 in the Virunga Volcanoes. In the two years of data examined, the males of group 5 spent more time within two and five meters of each other than did the males of group 4. In addition to this difference in the males of the two groups, Harcourt found that group 5 males were closer together during rest periods than they were during travel-free periods. However, group 4 males maintained a considerable distance in both periods. As is the case with females, it is clear from these data that there is sufficient tension during feeding to result in a greater spatial dispersion. Presumably, this reflects feeding competition.

Harcourt also attempted to determine which of the males was responsible for maintaining proximity. Using Hinde's (1969) responsibility index, whereby the percentage of approaches by one partner minus the percentage of the same partner's departures is calculated, Harcourt found that the group 5 males were just about equally responsible for maintaining proximity. However, when data for following were tabulated, it was discovered that the younger blackbacked male followed the leader in 27% of the leader's thirty departures, while the leader was never observed to follow the younger male. An index for group 4 males could not be calculated due to a paucity of scores in this dimension.

When the data for body contact were examined, Harcourt discovered that male body contact was rare in both groups. However, by comparison, group 5 males were more often in contact than were group 4 males which were never observed to touch. The group 5 males also groomed more frequently, 12 bouts to zero over two years. In group 5, the younger male accounted for virtually all of the grooming.

Furthermore, neither of the leading males ever avoided the nonaggressive approaches of younger males, but the younger animals occassionally avoided such approaches by the older males. A greater percentage of avoidance was found in the young group 4 male. Aggression between the males of each group was rare, occurring at a rate of less than one incident per eight hours of observation. In group 4, only the leading male aggressed, whereas the group 5 males were about equally aggressive. When only directed aggression was counted, however, the silverback of group 5 was twice as aggressive as his younger counterpart. The group 5 silverback never avoided the younger male's aggression; instead he generally ignored it. However, in both groups, the younger males commonly avoided aggressive outbursts by their older rivals. Consistent with the previous findings, it was the young group 4 male which exhibited this to the greater degree.

An especially interesting finding of Harcourt's was that, in the two groups studied, the young males were permitted to freely copulate with juvenile and subadult females only. Fertile females could not be so utilized. In this respect, Harcourt's own words are especially instructive:

> The young male of group 5 did, in fact, mate with two adult females, but in one instance the female was pregnant (as was the case for one, possibly both, of Schaller's . . . observations of a subordinate male mating in full view of the dominant male) and in the other the female was a nullipara in her first oestrus and so almost certainly still sterile (p. 45).

While aggression over females was not observed in group 4, there were many instances of competitive aggression in group 5, whereby the silverback interrupted friendly relations between the younger male and females.

As Harcourt pointed out, the only similarity in the relationships of the respective group's males was that, in both groups, the silverback dominated the younger animal. However, the way in which these dominance interactions were exhibited differed considerably. In view of the identical habitats of the two groups, Harcourt suggested that only their developmental histories, degree of competition, and consanguinity could successfully account for their respective relationships.

With respect to the first factor, the group 5 male was already an established leader during the infancy of the younger male. In contrast, the group 4 silverback replaced an old male which had been a kind of surrogate parent to the younger male during his infancy. An orphan, he was ignored by the silverback which took over the group. Thus, in group 5 the younger male had a friendly history of contact with the silverback, whereas no such interactions occurred during the maturation of the group 4 male. Moreover, it is possible that the younger group 5 male was, in fact, the offspring of that group's silverback.

From these studies, Harcourt concluded that where there were no "drawbacks or payoffs" in the group 4 relationships; there was a stable relationship between the males. Thus, in the face of stability, little or no interaction was evident. In group 5, however, where the silverback and the blackback competed at each other's expense, both affinitive and agonistic behavior were observed. The relationship of the group 5 males was, in fact, slightly unstable. The friendly behavior of the younger group 5 male was interpreted by Harcourt as efforts to further stabilize this relationship.

Solitary Males

Lone males are often found wandering over great distances. Vernon Reynolds (cited in Groves, 1970) believes that by their wandering they open up new habitats for the entire population. As Groves mentioned in his 1970 book, a lone male was once found some 200 kilometers from the nearest gorilla population. These lone males often attach themselves to a group, but generally occupy a peripheral position. It is interesting to note that some wandering males are not completely mature, that is they may be solitary at the blackbacked stage of development. Some of them have even been known to travel in the company of an infant or juvenile. Thus, there may be some previously unrecognized capacity for paternal* behavior in wild gorillas (see also Chapter 5).

As Caro (1976) has correctly pointed out, the vast majority of gorilla studies have emphasized the group. Thus, Caro set out to study solitary males. Schaller (1963) had earlier inferred that lone males eventually re-entered groups but he did not ever witness it. Caro intended to determine how solitary animals join and leave existing groups and/or form new groups by outlining the size and use of home range, and maintenance activities of two solitary silverbacks in the Virunga Volcanoes.

The study was carried out during a thirteen-week period which began in January of 1974. The two subjects of the study, *Samson* and *Brahms*, were followed by Caro for ninety-one and thirty-five days respectively. These two animals may have voluntarily left their natal group or else were actively expelled from same (Groups 8 and 5 respectively; cf. Fossey, 1974).

Caro determined that in certain parts of the lone males' range their trails frequently doubled back on themselves, as indicated by large areas of crushed and flattened vegetation. As Caro noted, Fossey (1974) considered this to be evidence of a defensive strategy. If this is true, Caro's findings also indicated that *Brahms* defended his area more vigorously than did *Samson*. With respect to their natal groups, 83% of *Samson's* range was found to be within the range of group 8, while *Brahms'* range was comprised of 96% of the range of group 5. This finding is clearly in opposition to Fossey's earlier contention that the lone male's core area was always *outside* the range of its former group.

The activities of these two males indicate that they are not fundamentally different in their habits than groups. Caro found that they spent 80.5% of their time resting, 14.7% feeding, and 4.8% moving. This compares favorably to Schaller's activity data for the mountain gorilla.

In explaining the circuitous movements of the two solitary silverbacks, Caro suggested that it may simply be a consequence of the lone male's long residence in a small area (both had been away from their natal group for several years at the time of the study). On the other hand, *Brahms'* circuitous behavior seemed to Caro to be effective as a deterrent to other gorillas, as group 5 entered his core area only once during the study period. *Samson* was intruded upon fifteen times

---

*In the wild, mountain gorillas assist in the rearing of offspring by tolerating their proximity when the mother is absent. In fact, Fossey (1979) has observed an extension of this propensity in males which have essentially *adopted* orphaned offspring.

by group 8. This difference is in part due to the contiguity and overlap of the respective core areas and group home ranges. Clearly, there is as yet insufficient evidence to determine whether the ranging behaviors of these solitary silverbacks are a defensive strategy.

The advantage of staying near the natal group is clear. The nearby male can effectively utilize his knowledge of the area, and will be able to come into frequent contact with those females with which he may eventually form a new group. However, the two males studied by Caro did not seem to be actively seeking such females. As Caro concluded:

> On present evidence ranging behaviour seems most likely to be related to food dispersion, apart from circuitous ranging behaviours possibly related to social factors. The gorilla's habitat of montane forest gives the impression of a superabundance of food, but nutritionally important food is likely to be localized and to vary seasonally (p. 896).

Thus the benefits of a lifetime of knowledge about seasonal food distribution may function to keep male gorillas in the same general area as their natal groups.

Emigration and Transfer

Harcourt, Stewart, and Fossey (1976) have discussed the way that mountain gorillas leave their natal group and acquire membership in another. In many nonhuman primates, it is the males which more commonly transfer membership, but there is evidence that in chimpanzees (*P. troglodytes*) it is the female which more commonly transfers (cf. Pusey, 1979). The research conducted in the Virunga Volcanoes of Zaire and Rwanda provided information about the emigration and transfer behavior of the wild gorillas in this region. In their report, both groups and lone gorillas were referred to as *units,* and a distinction was made between short *visits* and longer *transfers* (a stay of more than one day).

The first recorded emigrations of males occurred when they were about eleven years of age. Males that did not emigrate were the leading males or perhaps their sons. As the investigators noted, leader males inhibited the mating of young males* suggesting that competition for available females was a cause of emigration. Those males that stay are likely to be the sons of aging leaders, since there seems to be less conflict among father and son. Harcourt, Stewart, and Fossey suggested that this was the case, and that "inheritance of leadership may be a pattern common to most groups (p. 226)."

---

*Of course, as we have seen, silverbacked males frequently tolerate blackbacked mating attempts with *immature* females.

In addition to these findings, Harcourt, Stewart, and Fossey discovered that males usually do not join other groups but tend to remain alone. Their apparent strategy is to *attract* more than one female in order to form a new breeding group. According to these data, mountain gorilla males probably do not depose other leader males. As the investigators noted, a pair of gorillas does not seem to be a viable breeding unit.

When females reached maturity, at eight years of age, they too tended to leave the natal group, usually before they had given birth. Nearly all females, unlike males, eventually leave their group, according to Harcourt and his colleagues.

When females transfer, they almost immediately join another unit, exhibiting a tendency to transfer more than once. The length of a stay prior to transfer ranged from three days to three years, five months (md = 3 months; N = 13). Females initially transferred into a group with an overlapping range. Later transfers often took them out of contact with their natal group. Females transferred to lone males eleven times, and to groups nine times. Some of these movements were labeled as returns to previous groups, two of which were to the presumed natal group. As Harcourt et al., further determined:

> If returns are omitted, more females (6 compared with 4) transferred more frequently (9 transfers compared with 4) to more lone males (n = 4, possibly 5) than to groups (n = 2).

Another interesting finding was the observation that resident males prevented female emigration more by deterring proximity by other males than by herding the resident females. As Harcourt, Stewart, and Fossey observed, ten of the twelve transfer interactions were marked by aggressive displays or fights between the competitors, but males rarely coerced females into leaving a group. Rather females tended to transfer on "their own volition."

In attempting to explain why females selected a particular male, and why they remained or subsequently transferred, Harcourt and his coworkers suggested that it may be the quality of the male's range that determines the first decision. Whether they stayed was most likely due to success in raising offspring in a given unit. As the study revealed, two mothers which successfully raised offspring remained in their new unit. However, three mothers which did not succeed left the unit. Two of these offspring were actually killed during intergroup altercations.

Several explanations were offered for the finding that gorilla females transfer more frequently than do males. We have paraphrased them as follows:

1. If immature females assumed the rank of their mothers, as do macaques, it would confer no great advantage, since there is so little competition among feral gorilla females. There are therefore few advantages for a gorilla female to remain in her natal group.

2. The advantage which leads a male to stay in his natal group is the effective communal defense of their familiar surroundings and the potential for acquiring females.

In addition, young adults resist copulation with very familiar conspecifics, and since gorilla groups are small enough to guarantee familiarity, both sexes frequently emigrate.

The results of this study contribute to our understanding of breeding problems in captivity as well. Many young gorilla pairs were brought up together, and were so familiar that they interacted more on a sibling level. Harboring a propensity to emigrate, breeding (although not impossible) is certainly less likely between very familiar cagemates. The modern solution to this problem has been to permit females to "emigrate" to other zoos on breeding loans.

Evolution of Social Systems

In a valuable paper, Wrangham (1979) recently developed a framework for understanding the selection pressures which have influenced social evolution in the apes. As Wrangham asserted:

> It is no longer sufficient to argue . . . that social evolution occurs because the group gives safety from predators, the group enables individuals to find more food or a stable hierarchy brings peace to the group. Such statements assume that different individuals in the group have common interests, but this will rarely be the case. In particular, the sexes are likely to have very different interests in the consequences of social life (p. 336).

An assumption of Wrangham's analysis was that individuals maximize their inclusive fitness by maximizing their reproductive success. Thus, behaviors that contribute to individual reproductive success are favored by the process of natural selection. Furthermore, if resource access has different consequences for males and females, sex differences in competitive strategies are likely to evolve. Thus, males may compete for females, but females do not necessarily compete for males, especially in predominantly one-male groups such as the gorilla. Therefore, to the degree that resources differently affect each sex, their competitive strategies differ. Within the sexes, however, competitive strategies are likely to be more uniform. The principal determinant of these strategies is *intrasexual* competition, but it is necessary to determine how competition is resolved both between and within the sexes.

Wrangham's paper was concerned with both pongids and hylobatids, but we will consider only the former here, with understandable special emphasis on the gorilla. Because of the extensive ecological research in recent years, the apes are an ideal taxonomic group for the comparison of social systems. In Figure 1-26

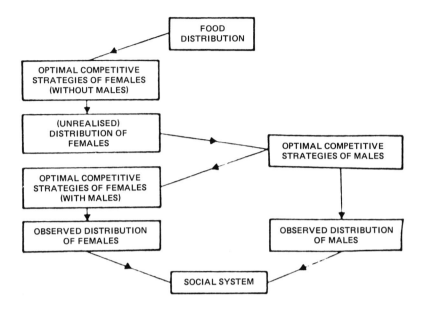

Figure 1-26. Framework for the analysis of ape social systems. The social system is viewed as determined by food distribution and ape morphology. Females compete to maximize food intake, and this leads to a given distribution of females. This determines how males compete for access to females, who prefer males whose interests coincide with their own. The strategies of these males may then in turn modify the behaviour of females. The entwined distributions of females and males yield the social system. (After Wrangham, 1977)

Wrangham's framework for analyzing ape social systems is presented. Table 1-11 is an adaptation of Wrangham's social system synopsis, while Table 1-12 provides data concerning the movements and foraging behavior of lactating female apes.

As Wrangham pointed out, *Pan troglodytes* is currently thought to be the most frugivorous of the great apes, but further studies of the smaller *Pan paniscus* may soon reveal that it consumes an even greater percentage of fruit. As theory currently suggests, smaller taxa need less food per day, but eat food items with greater nutritive content. Therefore, competition over individual food items is more important for the smaller taxa.

In both large and small taxa, the optimal foraging strategy may be to forage alone. As put forth by Wrangham, this argument goes as follows:

An individual accompanied by others suffers feeding competition whenever food sources are too small to satiate the whole party. The cost may be in extra travel time to satisfy the day's food requirement, in energy spent racing for the best feeding site . . . in too rapid, and hence inefficient, selection of food items, etc. (p. 346).

Table 1-11. Characteristics of great apes as derived from various field studies (After Wrangham, 1979).

	Gibbons and Siamang	Chimpanzee	Orang-utan	Gorilla
Frequency of affiliative interactions between males.	None	High, Frequent grooming, occasional touching, embracing etc.	None	Very low
Frequency of associations between males and females.	Continuous within groups.	Anoestrous females: low to moderate. Oestrous females: high.	Low, Oestrous females may form consortships with males.	Continuous within group.
Relationship of adults to natal group.	Males and females leave family as adolescents or young adults. Offspring may establish territories near parents.	All males remain in natal community. Most females move to new community at adolescence, some stay.	Males and females leave mother and travel independently at adolescence.	Males and females normally leave natal group at adolescence. Males travel alone and slowly attract females. Females transfer directly to new group.
Form of aggression between males	Displays and fights at territorial boundaries.	Within communities: frequent aggressive encounters with resultant dominance hierarchy. Direct fights over females rare. Between communities: parties of males from different communities display, chase and attack, leading to occasional serious injury.	Resident males chase wandering males from their area. Two severe fights seen, both over oestrous female.	Within group: one fully adult male (silverback) dominant over others, and aggression rare. Between groups: males attract females by attacking other groups.
Sexual dimorphism in weight	None	Male less than one-and-one-half times female.	Male about twice female.	Male about twice female.

Table 1-12. Ecological data on lactating ape mothers; data averaged or recalculated from original sources (after Wrangham, 1977).

	Weight (kg)	Percent feeding time spent eating fruit	Day-range (km)	Territory (sq km)	Core area (sq km)
Hylobatidae (Lesser apes)					
Gibbon *H. lar*	5	67	1.6	0.40	?
Gibbon *H. klossii*	5	?	?	0.07	?
Siamang	10	42	0.9	0.23	0.08
Pongidae (Great apes)					
Chimpanzee	30	65	2.7	—	2.1
Orang-utan	37	57	0.3	—	0.7
Gorilla	90	3	0.5	—	1.6

Field studies of gorillas have shown that they utilize dispersed but abundant food items of relatively low nutritive value.* Thus, by the argument previously employed, these apes should exhibit relatively low levels of competition. By comparison to *Pan* and *Pongo* this prediction is sustained, but even gorillas will fight over some types of food (e.g., bamboo shoots) and are known to maintain a greater social distance when feeding than when engaged in other activities (cf. Fossey and Harcourt, 1977).

Wrangham's data predict that females will forage alone to minimize competition. Among the great apes, orang-utan females do forage alone, and recent evidence indicates that chimpanzees travel more often alone than in the company of others (cf. Halperin, 1979). Females of both species tend to avoid other females when they are feeding. However, as Wrangham points out, gorilla females travel and feed in a group. Therefore, some strategy other than that related to intrasexual competition must be in operation. Another strategy to consider is territorial defense. Provided that the benefits of exclusive use outweigh the costs of defense, this strategy is likely to be so employed. However, in considering the data it is apparent that the great apes forage over daily distances that are too small to permit a sufficient defense of all parts of the home range. As Wrangham has shown, female chimpanzees, gorillas, and orang-utans travel similar distances daily.

Another dimension to the problem is competition between males. Males compete for food and available females. Because it may be as difficult for apes as it is for researchers to predict estrus, a useful strategy might be to travel for as long as possible with as many females as possible. This strategy is, of course, in conflict with the female's solitary feeding strategy.

It is this conflict which Wrangham recognizes as the fundamental determinant of the form of the social system. Wrangham further suggests that altering a female's optimal strategy** of solitary territoriality to nonterritorial polygyny requires that the male impose heavy costs or bestow large benefits on these strategies.

---

*The mountain gorillas of the Virunga Volcanoes must subsist on considerably less fruit than do their lowland counterparts.

**Theoretically, if males and females both maintain territories, males have at least three options as follows:

1) They can maintain a large territory which includes the territories of at least two females.
2) They can maintain a territory which includes another female's territory and parts of those of others.
3) They can confine themselves to traveling with a single female.

In theory, the first strategy is superior, but it does not occur in nature. The second option favors monogamy since females are likely to travel only with males whose territory entirely overlaps their own. Monogamy, of course, applies to the lesser apes but to none of the great apes.

The strategy of the male gorilla is easy to comprehend since he travels with many females without interruption. Thus, whenever they come into estrus he maintains exclusive access to them. But why does a female gorilla share her resources with other females in the company of one male only? Wrangham explained this as an example of benefits accruing from the dominant male's ability to repel other potential competitors and protect her (and his) resources. As Wrangham further explained:

> The costs which female orangs and chimps avoid by forming a consort partnership may thus be the same as those which have led female gorillas to live with a male: violent interactions involving females are rare within gorilla groups. This suggests that gorilla groups can be regarded as being permanent consortships which are accepted by females because of their uniquely low costs of feeding competition. This would explain why despite their long-term association the females of a group interact together little. If the presence of the male is the *raison d' être* of the group, social relationships among females may have little impact on reproductive success (p. 355).

The aggressiveness and dominance of the silverback male is therefore the regulator of food competition. The ultimate cause of female attraction to aggressive males is the advantage that his dominance bestows. The proximate cause may be the perceptual complexity that his behavior represents. Wrangham further developed this point in relation to female gorillas which leave their natal groups:

> This discussion is not meant to suggest that a female is expected to wait to be attacked before leaving her natal group and joining another. In the first place her father may be the only adult male in her group. Secondly, he should presumably prefer to protect her from other males throughout her life: the ideal would therefore be a young silverback. Thirdly, the argument suggests that other things being equal she should prefer a male who is traveling with as few other females as possible, thus minimizing feeding competition. Females could therefore be expected to choose males on the basis of simple characteristics which would enhance their probable reproductive success (p. 356).

As Wrangham concluded, animals compete with conspecifics of the opposite sex, and with other species as well, but the most important competition is with conspecific members of their own sex.

The natural habitats of gorillas are complex and variable. In this chapter we have described the salient features which characterize these places and some of the behavioral effects of ecological variables. Hopefully, the natural history and biology of gorillas is adequately outlined here, although we have not sought to provide an exhaustive account of it. In our opinion, the proper management, exhibition, and care of these anthropoids absolutely requires such information.

The gorilla is an organism that is well adapted to the demands of its natural habitat. It has not adapted so well to concrete and steel, but it is a gorilla regardless of where you find it, and the biological forces which have shaped its evolution are the only context in which its behavior can be fully understood.

2
General Behavior Patterns
of Gorilla

If I have used many terms which ordinarily designate forms or aspects of experience and have seemed to express myself anthropomorphically and with intent to humanize the life of my subject, I would not deny the fact. I could discover no better way of describing my observations . . . There are also times and circumstances . . . . in which the inadequacy of our present objective terminology is obvious and when we must either supplement it by use of subjective or mixed terms or fail of intelligibility.

Robert M. Yerkes, 1928

This chapter is concerned with some categories of behavior which are worthy of considerable detail. Since they are not necessarily *expressive, sexual,* or *developmental* phenomena, we have lumped them together here as *general* behavior patterns. This is a convention which was first followed in *Orang-utan Behavior* and will be further employed in *Chimpanzee Behavior.* The behavioral repertoire of gorillas in a more general sense will also be discussed in this chapter. We will first consider locomotor behavior, then play, and, finally, various aspects of grooming among gorillas. The reader should continue to be aware of the overlapping nature of these behaviors, several of which will also be taken up later in the text.

LOCOMOTION

An early description of locomotion in the gorillas *Mbongo* and *Ngagi* was provided by Carpenter (1937) as follows:

Characteristically the locomotion of gorillas is that of modified pronograde type. That is, the body is carried at an angle with the plane of support. That the head and shoulders are carried considerably higher than the hips is due to the fact that the arms are much longer than the legs . . . . The arms and hands

---

*According to Groves and Stott (1979) *Ngagi* and *Mbongo* were actually the *graueri* subspecies, not *beringei.*

are quite as important during locomotion as are the legs and feet. In the typical position of the hand during locomotion, the weight is placed on the knuckles and the first two joints of the fingers (p. 110).

As Carpenter further pointed out, gorillas exhibit several gaits which he characterized as "walking, trotting, and cantering." In the calculating manner of a well-trained experimental psychologist, Carpenter estimated that these captive gorillas typically moved about their enclosure at about 8 feet per second or 160 yards per minute. Additionally, as Schaller (1963) has pointed out, gorillas progress by moving diagonally opposite feet forward in a simultaneous fashion.

Gorillas are slow and cautious climbers, as revealed by Carpenter's (1937) observation that it took *Ngagi** in excess of two minutes to climb a tree in pursuit of a banana. As Carpenter further elaborated:

> That gorillas are somewhat reluctant to climb trees is indicated by the fact that they climb infrequently and that when one of the animals would seemingly escape the other during play, he would climb the tree and the other one would only infrequently follow him. These observations agree with those made in the wild, which indicate that gorillas are primarily terrestrial, ground-living animals. It is highly probable that their arboreal activity is restricted to occasional climbing during play, climbing for food and climbing for escape and protection (p. 111).

The arboreal potential of gorillas was also discussed by Yerkes and Yerkes in their 1929 masterpiece:

> There can be no doubt that the various races or species of gorilla are capable of tree climbing. Probably the lowland forms are more skillful in this, and naturally more given to it, than are the mountain varieties. It is commonly observed that captive specimens, if in good health, climb freely and with at least as much skill as the average boy or man . . . On occasion the gorilla may ascend to the very tops of tall trees, but in so doing it is said to proceed cautiously, testing limbs as it goes, to make sure that they will bear its weight (p. 408).

That these heavy anthropoids willingly ascend trees to great heights in captivity is well illustrated in Figure 2-2. The gorillas at *Apenheul,* which also climb trees, also constructed nests some 40-50 feet above the ground. Unfortunately,

---

*In Carpenter's original paper this animal is referred to as *Ingagi.* In all other reports with which we are familiar the spelling is the more appropriate *Ngagi.* Except when directly quoting Carpenter, we will use only the latter form.

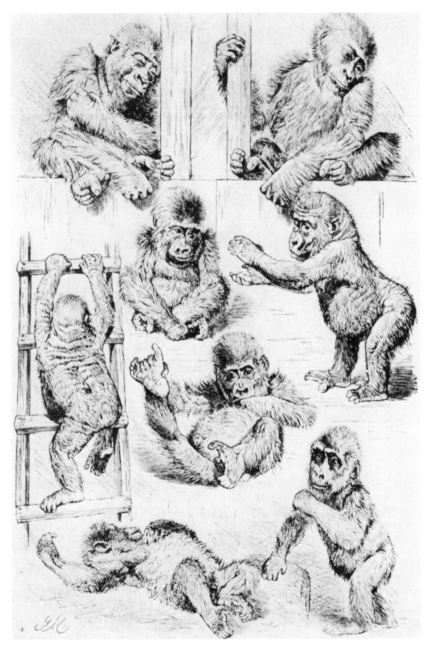

Figure 2-1. Bodily postures of a captive young gorilla as illustrated in Brehm's *Tierleben* (1922).

Figure 2-2. Adult male *Kiki* high in tree at Woodland Park Zoo, Seattle (*M. Keiter photo*).

the rapid demise of the trees ultimately led to the construction of barriers to prevent further tree climbing (Mager, personal communication).

Schaller (1963) has discussed arboreal locomotion as observed in his wild populations of gorillas. They climb cautiously in contrast to the chimpanzee, and remain largely quadrupedal. Although gorillas are anatomically capable of brachiation, Schaller never observed this in the wild. Neither blackbacked nor silverbacked males were observed to climb trees often. Females and infants were in the trees twice as often as adult males, and juveniles twice as often as females.

The Evolution of Locomotor Habits in Gorilla

Tuttle and Basmajian (1974) recently reported on their investigation of knuckle-walking, suspensory behavior, and facultative bipedalism in lowland gorillas. It was their aim to infer the phylogeny of these so called *positional behaviors* and hominid bipedalism. Although anthropologists generally agree upon the close similarity between humankind and African apes (cf. Washburn and Moore, 1974), there is little argeement about which positional behaviors preceded the terrestrial bipedalism which characterizes the hominids.

Several theorists (e. g. Keith, 1923; Gregory, 1927; Washburn, 1950; Tuttle, 1969) have suggested the existence of large-bodied brachiators as an antecedent stage in the evolution of humankind. Moreover, Washburn (1967) and others have discerned a stage of terrestrial knuckle-walking between the stages of brachiation and bipedalism. However, this position has been countered by Tuttle (1969), Simons (1972), and others who have argued that our hominid ancestors were bipedal from the virtual outset of their terrestrial period.

In examining the phylogeny of pongid positional behavior, some scientists (cf. Pilbeam, 1972; Simons, 1972; Conroy and Fleagle, 1972) have hypothesized that knuckle-walking may have first evolved in ground-dwelling apes, later radiating into part-time or full-time arboreality (e. g., chimpanzees and orang-utans). Because the technique of *electromyography* (EMG) permits the investigator to acquire information on the activity of muscles, it is possible to infer whether special bone/ligament structures are present in the joints. These structures may be associated with specific postural and locomotor modes and, in turn, may lead to inferences about the locomotor behavior of the ancestors of both apes and humans.

Tuttle and Basmajian (1974) conducted 120 experiments with apes as subjects, 60 of which were conducted with captive gorillas. In these tests, the subjects walked quadrupedally and bipedally on floors and incline surfaces, stood bipedally and reached overhead, jumped vertically, and climbed on a suspended trapeze (Figure 2-3). An EMG apparatus produced a record of the activity of shoulder, arm, forearm, hip, thigh, leg, and extrinsic pedal muscles.

Tuttle and Basmajian provided precise details of muscular activity which are beyond the scope of this book. We refer the reader to their paper for the entire argument. It will suffice to review here the major findings and conclusions in such a way as to reduce the jargon to a few lucid statements. First, the limited data suggest that gorillas are secondarily adapted for terrestrial locomotion, having evolved from ancestors that were considerably more arboreal in their habits. In the opinion of Tuttle and Basmajian, the wrists of the African apes were modified from those of their more arboreal ancestors to fit the special requirements of knuckle-walking. Other muscular adaptations for brachiation were detected in

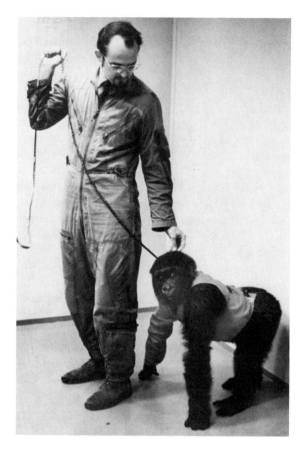

Figure 2-3. Anthropologist Russell Tuttle utilizing electromyographic apparatus to study the locomotion of *Inaki. (Photo courtesy Yerkes Regional Primate Research Center of Emory University).*

the gorilla, many of which underwent modification in the course of their recent evolution to terrestrial quadrupedalism. Apparently, many of the structural requirements for successful suspension were also conducive to the development of knuckle-walking.

Second, as we will see in Chapter 3, gorillas engage in bipedal postures in the natural course of social events. Bipedal locomotion in gorillas resembles that observed in chimpanzees, but both are generally different from that observed in human subjects. Ishida et al., (1974) have also highlighted the distinct differences in human and ape bipedalism. It is interesting to note that ape bipedalism is also considerably different from the bipedal locomotion of most monkeys. A phylogenetic continuum may be inferred on several dimensions, although evidence for convergent features also exists (e. g., between chimpanzee and spider monkey).

Finally, although there are few studies on knuckle-walking and suspensory locomotion in humankind, Tuttle and Basmajian cautiously rejected the notion of an intermediate stage of protohominid knuckle-walking. A heritage of arboreality, however, was confirmed. Relevant to this latter conclusion was the opinion that arboreal locomotion does *not* require that the ancestors be primarily characterized as brachiators. Rather, Tuttle and Basmajian suggested that specialized *flexible wrists* may have been an aid in suspensory feeding and arboreal climbing. This is consistent with Schaller's (1963) observations in which no brachiation was observed in the mountain gorilla.

It should be stated here that, despite the high degree of technical competence which accompanied these studies, the conclusions have been ultimately based on a logical scheme and, as the investigators themselves have admitted, must be exclaimed with caution. Nevertheless, the research of Tuttle and Basmajian did not prevent them from arguing that human evolution may derive from pongid or hylobatid (gibbon) patterns. Indeed, these investigators suggested that a hylobatid model of hominid evolution might better fit the relevant data than hypotheses which require a large-bodied brachiator, pristine ground ape, or knuckle-walking intermediary. As they concluded, "hominid bipedalism may indeed be rooted in bipedal reaching and branch-running behaviors of relatively small-bodied apes (p. 312)."

GROOMING AMONG GORILLAS

In many primate taxa grooming is a socially important behavior (cf. Hutchins and Barash, 1976). Considerable rest time is devoted to grooming, and it apparently contributes to socialization, affiliation, reproduction, and dominance. Grooming has been said to reduce tension (Terry, 1970), maintain the social group (Zuckerman, 1932), express social bonds (Washburn and DeVore, 1961), promote group cohesiveness (Lindburg, 1973) and allow for the development of interest, sympathy, and cooperation (Yerkes, 1943). As most studies of grooming have concerned monkeys, we know very little about grooming in the apes. In 1933, Robert Yerkes described grooming in apes as follows:

> Whereas grooming as social behavior is very frequent in chimpanzee and I have observed it hundreds of times, in orang-utan I have never seen other than casual scratching, mouthing or picking of a companion, and in gorilla not even this approach to social grooming. My tentative conclusion, from personal experience, checked against the almost negligible contribution of the scientific literature and the oral testimony of several other observers, is that this

behavior pattern probably is much more highly developed and more often exhibited as a social response in chimpanzee than in any other existing great ape (pp. 9–10).

Carpenter (1937) further noted that although gorillas groomed less than did chimpanzees, it was erroneous to say that the behavior was rare. (See also Schaller, 1963). He also observed that the mode or pattern of grooming was similar in gorillas and chimpanzees. A reliable difference, according to Carpenter, was that the gorillas that he observed were much slower in their grooming tempo and utilized their mouths to a considerably lesser degree than did chimpanzees.

Carpenter distinguished between self- and social grooming. Both forms were regularly observed in the two male gorillas that he studied, with *Ngagi* usually taking the active role in social grooming. Interestingly, the smaller *Mbongo* was dominant over *Ngagi* in play bouts,* and was also the recipient of the greater amount of social grooming. This is similar to findings in other species of primates in which dominant animals are more often the passive partner in grooming bouts (cf., Simpson, 1973). Thus, in many instances, social grooming may reveal underlying social relationships.

As Yerkes (1933) had earlier pointed out, adult social grooming may be considered a form of "mutually beneficial cooperation" in removing foreign matter from the skin. Grooming among Carpenter's San Diego gorillas was also directed toward the area of wounds. Both gorillas meticulously attended to their own wounds, and were attracted to wounds of the other. The attractiveness of wounds is also apparent among orang-utans as Maple (1980a) has suggested. Thus, grooming, as others have argued (cf. Zucker et al., 1977) has been found to serve both social and hygienic purposes.

Grooming Among Feral Mountain Gorillas

Schaller (1963) reported on both self- and social grooming among feral mountain gorillas. By far the most common participants in social grooming were mothers and infants, with mothers taking the active role. Adult females also engaged in grooming reciprocally, and with juveniles. Juveniles often groomed each other and infants. There were no recorded instances of adult males grooming reciprocally, and only a single observation of an adult female grooming an adult (black-backed) male.

---

*This is a complicated judgment since *Ngagi* was apparently dominant in feeding situations. It is especially difficult to discuss grooming in terms of dominance, although Carpenter stated that *Ngagi* was dominant in grooming while *Mbongo* was passive. Here it is necessary to determine whether dominance permits the animal to gain priority of access to groom or be groomed. We find this problem to be exceedingly difficult to resolve.

In a more recent study, Harcourt (1979b) observed divergent grooming patterns among two mountain gorilla groups living in the Virunga Volcano regions of Rwanda and Zaire. In his group 4, the dominant male was observed to groom the females, whereas in group 5 the females groomed the male. Harcourt's records further revealed that not all of the adult females engaged in grooming. However, all subadults groomed the respective silverback. In general, grooming between the silverback and the resident adult females was a rarely observed event. This finding supports the trend reported by Schaller (1963) who observed virtually no grooming between adult male and female mountain gorillas.

In Harcourt's group 5, all adult heterosexual grooming bouts were apparently initiated by the females, although in this group as we have seen, the male groomed females more than *vice versa*. In group 4, as Harcourt stated, the females often overtly solicited for grooming from the male, whereby they backed into him, or stood in front of him and presented their posteriors.* In most instances, the groomer terminated the bout.

An interesting finding of Harcourt's study was that the birth of an infant affected a mother's grooming behavior such that bout lengths and the total time spent grooming decreased. The rate of grooming, however, was not affected. As Harcourt reasoned, care of the infant doubtless took priority over other social interactions including grooming.

Harcourt extended Seyfarth's (1977) hypothesis to his gorilla data in order to provide a framework for understanding his findings. As Seyfarth argued, grooming among females improved the likelihood of such benefits as "aid in a dispute." His argument was predicated on the notion that, in any taxa, low-ranking animals groom higher-ranking group members. This direction is the more likely

Table 2-1. Parts of the body groomed by various age/sex classes (After Schaller, 1963).

	Arm and Shoulder	Legs	Chest and Abdominal Region	Not Recorded	Totals
Silverbacked male. .	9	0	0	0	9
Blackbacked male. .	3	0	0	1	4
Female	33	3	2	2	40
Juvenile	17	5	5	4	31
Infant.	4	0	0	0	4
Totals	66	8	7	7	88

Copyright 1963 University of Chicago Press

*The reader will note that these behaviors are typically associated with proceptivity (cf. Chapter 4). A common problem in primatological work is defining behaviors based on what follows. Thus, in this case, if the female backing into the male (grooming solicit) had resulted in the male copulating with her, the behavior of the female may well have been categorized as a sexual solicit on a post hoc basis.

because dominant animals are more capable of bestowing benefits. As Harcourt phrased it:

> . . . any less able partner, or the one that can benefit more from reciprocation of affinitive behavior with aid will either initiate or perform the majority of friendly behaviors within a dyad (p. 338).

This idea fits the data well. For example, Simpson (1973) and Carpenter (1937) found that dominant male chimpanzees and gorillas, respectively, were groomed longer than were subordinates. Harcourt's (1979) study demonstrated further that younger animals initiated more grooming bouts and groomed more frequently than did their older counterparts. As Harcourt suggested, an animal can sustain an affinitive relationship with another by either inviting grooming, or by performing it. According to Harcourt, the absence of grooming in older females can be explained by their already stable relationship to the male. By grooming the male, the younger females were therefore seen as working to establish similarly stable relationships. As Harcourt neatly put it: "In a long-standing relationship a pat might suffice for a greeting, while in one of shorter duration an embrace might be needed (p. 339)."

Fossey (1979) observed that, among feral mountain gorillas, grooming of an infant was initiated by the mother but was usually terminated by the infant. Younger infants were groomed on their genital areas, legs, arms, and backs in that order. They were often turned upside down or put into uncomfortable positions during these grooming bouts. Not surprisingly, the infants protested by wiggling, kicking, and "whacking" the mother. During the first six months, Fossey reported that the struggling of the infants were effective in terminating grooming. Later, the mothers began to rebuff the infants and persist in grooming them. The earliest episodes of self-grooming, and grooming of the mother was observed at one year of age. Peer grooming was first observed at 14 months. During the second year of life, the infants were more accepting of grooming by their mothers. The function of grooming was discussed by Fossey in the following passage:

> Because of the body areas involved as well as the concentration of the mother, grooming of the infant seemed to be primarily a functional rather than a social activity. This impression was reinforced when a 3-year-old infant lost her mother and was adopted by the silverback. Although he spent a considerable amount of time grooming the infant, she appeared conspicuously ill-kempt in comparison with other infants of the same age, indicating his lack of maternal experience. (p. 166).

Unfortunately, Fossey provided no quantitative data with respect to grooming of infants. As will be seen, in our studies of group living gorillas, mother-infant grooming was a relatively rare event.

Captive Studies of Grooming

In this context, we will now describe the grooming behavior of the captive low-land gorillas which we have studied in collaboration with R. D. Nadler. The subjects of the research are fully described in Tables 2-2 and 5-4. All of these animals were born in the wild or of wild-born parents. Both social grooming and self grooming will be described here. For a comparison to orang-utan grooming, we refer the reader to Maple (1980a).

For the purposes of this section, data from several different studies were combined, and several different data collection techniques* were employed. Data were obtained from both continuous-living dyads, and adult pairs brought together for timed-mating sessions. Grooming data on continuous-living animals were collected as part of a longitudinal study of a mixed-age group of seven lowland gorillas at the Yerkes Field Facility in Lawrenceville, Ga. Timed-mating studies were conducted at the Yerkes Primate Research Center by Nadler (1976). The latter studies employed a check-sheet data collecting system which provided frequency data, whereas the longitudinal studies used a focal animal activity record providing both durations and frequencies. In the present context, grooming is defined as a systematic examination of the skin, hair or nails, with both a visual and tactual component.

The basic gorilla motor pattern of grooming is the use of three to four bent fingers while the hair is held back with either the lower lip or the other hand. In some instances, fatty areas are lifted closer to the animal's face (e. g., stomach), or the area being groomed is held out so it can be seen better (e. g., lip). In self-grooming, the areas of the body attended are those that the animals can both see and reach, typically arms, legs, and chest. Social grooming is liable to occur anywhere on the other animal's body, particularly the upper body (e. g., shoulders, head, face, chest, neck and arms).

Table 2-2. Subjects from which grooming data were acquired at the Yerkes Primate Research Center (After Nadler, 1976).

Gorillas	Sex	Estimated Age (Yrs.)
Jini	Female	14
Oko	Female	14
Choomba	Female	14
Banga	Female	14
Katoomba	Female	15
Segou	Female	14
Rann	Male	14
Ozoum	Male	16
Calabar	Male	14

*These data were originally compiled by Zucker for a presentation to the membership of the Animal Behavior Society in 1977.

Table 2-3. Social grooming during timed-mating tests (Data courtesy R. D. Nadler).

Sex	# of Tests	Occurrences of Grooming	Freq., (Groom-ing/Test)	% of Total Social Grooming/Sex
M	188	9	.04	45
F	188	11	.06	55

During the timed-mating tests, as conducted by Nadler, both social and self-grooming data were collected for gorilla mixed-sex dyads. Tables 2-3 and 2-4 depict the social and self-grooming data respectively. The frequency of social grooming was characteristically low, and much lower than the frequency of self-grooming. Gorillas of both sexes displayed social grooming less often than they displayed self-grooming. There was no difference with respect to sex in the frequency of social grooming. However, male gorillas self-groomed more often than did females.

That both males and females seemed to groom equally often during the timed-mating tests is inconsistent with findings for many monkey taxa (Bernstein, 1970; Bolwig, 1959; Lindburg, 1973; Rosenblum, Kaufman, and Stynes, 1966; for a review of sex differences in grooming, see Mitchell and Tokunaga, 1976). As a variable, the duration of time a dyad spent together may be important. Alternately, and especially significant in light of Schaller's finding of virtually no grooming by adults, the timed-mating tests, with recurrent pairings and separations, may have altered the naturally occurring rates of social grooming. This latter possibility is supported by our studies of the captive, group-living lowland gorillas, in which we found a very low rate of social grooming among all age/sex classes. Unlike Schaller (1963), we found very little grooming of infants by mothers (Zucker, Wilson, Hoff, Nadler, Maple, and Dennon, 1977). Thus, the captive situation may alter grooming behaviors exhibited by gorillas in both timed-mating tests and in complex social groups.

Although the direct comparison of grooming data across several studies is difficult due to the different techniques employed, habitat, and population characteristics of the samples, these observations suggest some basic inferences about gorilla grooming patterns. First, as determined in other studies (cf. Schaller, 1963) social grooming occurs rather infrequently. Second, and particularly with respect to social grooming, there is considerable within-species variability.

Table 2-4. Self grooming during timed-mating tests (Data courtesy R. D. Nadler).

Sex	# of Tests	Occurrences of Grooming	Freq., (Groom-ing/Test)	% of Total Social Grooming/Sex
M	188	296	1.57	77
F	188	89	.47	23

With respect to the presumably low rates of gorilla social grooming when compared with *Pan troglodytes*, the following variables* may be relevant:

1. Size of the social group and its organization: Gorillas typically live in smaller groups led by a single silverbacked male, while chimpanzees live in large multimale groups.
2. Hair density or hair length: Gorillas possess dense short hair whereas chimps have a longer, less dense pelage (Napier and Napier, 1967).

It is possible that a single factor could account for grooming differences among the apes, but the identity of this variable is currently unknown. However, given the complexity and variability of other primate behaviors, it is highly likely that the determinants of grooming are likewise complex and variable. Additionally, it should be noted that we have not yet observed captive chimpanzees for direct comparison to the gorilla grooming data. The assumption of greater chimp grooming rates, however compelling, is not actually demonstrated here. It is even possible that the conditions of this research would suppress chimpanzee grooming to the level of the gorillas although this is unlikely. Horvat, Coe and Levine (1980) found regular grooming bouts among group living chimps living in an outdoor compound.

The gorillas which have been discussed here provide a basis for very tentative generalizations. We need much more data on this subject. Moreover, it should be noted that, as we have seen, wild gorillas do not live in pairs. For this reason, additional data are required from complex groups living in captivity. Much can be learned from the captive situation where closer observation is possible, but it will be necessary to verify these findings by continuing to observe gorillas in their natural state. Future research will determine the relative amounts of social grooming as exhibited by different age and sex classes and according to age and sex of available partners.

PLAY AMONG GORILLAS

Gorillas, like other primates, exhibit both self and social play. The former type includes both self-motion (called *peregration* by Mears and Harlow, 1975) and manipulative/exploratory play. Self-motion play is, in turn, composed of solitary swinging, twisting, rolling, running, and slapping. There are perhaps an infinite number of variations on this general theme. Manipulative play involves the self or inanimate objects. For example, an ape may "fiddle" with its fingers, toes, or genitalia in a playful fashion. It may also playfully manipulate rocks, vegetation, toys, or tools depending upon the setting in which it resides. We will here consider both self and social play, with object play considered in Chapter 6 (for further commentary on play, see Smith, 1978).

---

*These variables were first suggested by Evan L. Zucker.

Figure 2-4. Peer play in two infant gorillas at the Lawrenceville Field Station of the Yerkes Primate Center. *(T. Maple photo)*

Between the two gorillas observed by Carpenter (1937), play was the predominant activity. During the course of his observation of these two animals, Carpenter was able to break play down into the following categories:

1. Play with self such as manipulatory play, running, rolling or spinning and at times chest beating.
2. Play with objects such as ropes, balls, sticks, water, tires, decorative objects and occasionally small live animals which became accessible.
3. True social play such as wrestling, chasing, teasing, etc. (p. 112).

From these early observations, Carpenter further portrayed gorilla play as vigorous, persistent, and varied but "lacking in that quality intermediate between play and pugnacity, otherwise known as play fighting."

Under the category of self-play, Carpenter included a rather vague notion of "certain posturing which seemed to be enjoyed and was engaged in spontaneously." More specifically, the two gorillas often rolled over or turned somersaults, and were prone to manipulate their feet and toes in a repetitive manner. Carpenter also included the tactual exploration of teeth, mouth, ears, and genitals as examples of self-play. These behaviors are quite similar to those which have been attributed to young chimpanzees and orang-utans (cf. Maple and Zucker, 1978; Maple, 1980a).

These two gorillas also utilized objects in their play, and took advantage of certain environmental conditions for the same purpose. For example, Carpenter noted that they both utilized the suspended ropes and chains as a means of engaging in repetitive spinning. Not surprisingly, after a large number of turns, the animals often appeared slightly dizzy. Water was an especially preferred play substance, attracting their attention in the pool and from the cleaning hose. A type of skating or sliding play was also exhibited:

> After the floor had been flushed or after the apes dashed water on it from the pool, skating almost invariably occurred. Instead of skating with their legs and feet, they skated with their arms and hands. With their arms stiffened and held forward at an angle from their shoulders and with their knuckles in contact with the cement, while running with their feet, they would slide their hands from one end of the cage to the other and back again until they became fatigued (p. 113).

Although solitary play was frequently observed in this pair, Carpenter stated that social play was the more common mode of playful activity. Referring to one of the standard characteristics of mammalian social play, part of Carpenter's description is worth quoting in two passages as follows:

> At times the behavior was definitely regular and circuitous. During such times, definite patterns of activity were exhibited repeatedly (p. 113).

While the animals separated temporarily, they would beat their chests. This chest beating occurred typically just prior to an attack and seemed to signify a challenge for an engagement. While wrestling, each animal seemed to strive for that position of advantage which would allow him to bite at the nape of the other animal's neck. This seemed to be one of the main objectives toward which the behavior was directed (p. 114).

While *Ngagi* and *Mbongo* were known to intermittently wrestle for several hours, actual contact and vigorous struggle rarely exceeded a few minutes in duration. Carpenter estimated the mean time for such wrestling bouts to be 15–20 seconds.

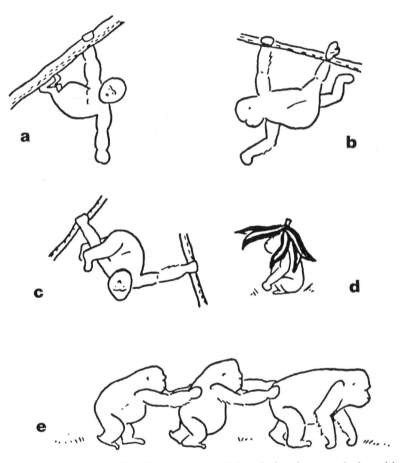

Figure 2-5. Body positions of gorilla youngsters at Kabara during play. *a–c:* body positions of infants during lone play in trees; *d:* an infant with a *lobelia* which it placed playfully on its head; *e:* three juveniles "snake dance" in play. (After Schaller, 1963) Copyright 1963 University of Chicago Press

Following these early observations, more information has accumulated, including important data from the field work of Schaller. In his 1963 volume, Schaller asserted that "on the whole, gorillas are not playful (p. 248)." As he further pointed out, it was not uncommon for days to pass without observing a single instance of play. However, when it did occur, it generally took place after the intensive morning feeding. Schaller accepted the following definition of play: *any relatively unstereotyped behavior in which an animal was involved in vigorous actions seemingly without definite purpose.* During the course of his field study, 91 play episodes were recorded for 156 animals. Schaller's observations suggested that after about 6 years of age, play behavior greatly diminished in frequency.

Recognizing two types of play, Schaller's solitary play category was labeled *lone* play. Slightly less than half of his observations were of solitary play, and almost 80% of these were of infants. Juveniles engaged in solitary play much less frequently, and adults were observed to do so only once. The majority of social play was also performed by infants, usually with other infants and less frequently with juveniles. Due to the delaying effects of maturation, infants generally did not engage in vigorous social play until the age of 4½-5 months. As Schaller himself described it:

Most play involved some form of running, climbing, and wrestling. Lone animals sometimes shredded leaves and slapped the vegetation, but inanimate objects were only twice the focal point of social play. Adults, even though some took the brunt of the youngster's exuberance, rarely entered actively into play, and I noted only one instance in which a female reciprocated with an infant. Nevertheless, adults, including the silverbacked males, were extremely tolerant of playing young . . . (p. 249).

Categories of lone play as suggested by Schaller's observations may be listed as follows:

1. climbing
2. swinging
3. jumping
4. sliding

5. waving arms/legs
6. batting vegetation
7. somersaulting
8. running back and forth with exaggerated gestures

In social play bouts, Schaller noted two characteristic behavior patterns:

1. Mock biting in the area of the angle made by shoulder and neck;
2. Sitting face-to-face or bipedal approaches while waving arms slowly and alternately overhead.

Schaller further described social play in the following manner:

Upon contact they grappled with a curious slow-motion effect, somewhat resembling the ritualized behavior of oriental human wrestlers (p. 252).

An examination of the play categories recorded for other species of great ape (cf. Maple and Zucker, 1978) reveals considerable similarity in the component play gestures and postures.

Adult Female Play in Captivity

Fischer and Nadler (1978) studied interactions among females in a group of four adults maintained in a large seminatural enclosure at the Yerkes Primate Center. The most frequent behavior during the course of this study was simple contact, but, somewhat surprisingly, the mean duration of play was much higher than any other type of interaction. There was also a relationship between homosexual interactions and the degree of labial tumescence. Thus, presumed cycling hormone

Figure 2-6. Two year-old gorillas engaged in play chase at the Lawrenceville Field Station of the Yerkes Primate Research Center. *(T. Maple photo).*

levels affected sexual behavior (see also Chapter 4). Individual differences in frequency of affiliative interactions was also reported. An additional interesting result was statistical support for the coincidental occurrence of play and the play-face expression. Maple and Zucker (1978) have previously questioned the predictive value of this expression in the playful interactions of apes.

Although Fischer and Nadler found that homosexual interactions were uncommon, when they did occur they exceeded in average duration sexual interactions between the sexes. For example:

> The initial approach was usually direct, with no observable sexual invitations. Once propinquity was achieved the dyad typically sat quietly for a time, in some cases performing mutual genital investigations either manually or through approximation of the face to the partner's perineum. The majority of pelvic thrusting episodes (73%) were performed in a ventral-ventral position with the animals recumbent (p. 660).

Since these contacts were related to inferred cycle phase, the authors argued that at midcycle female gorillas become more attractive to both males and other females.

Adult play resembed in form that described by Schaller (1963) for younger animals, and as Fischer and Nadler further demonstrated, when the playface was exhibited, play occurred. In nonplay situations, no playface was emitted. Although the authors stated this relationship in terms of a sequential case-and-effect, it appears to be a correlation. Thus, we cannot attribute to it a *metacommunicative* function in Altmann's sense. The playface may or may not tell another animal that "play is about to occur," but the Fischer/Nadler data cannot clarify this problem. With a correlation, we cannot know whether the playface *causes* play or play *causes* the playface.

Fischer and Nadler discovered a low rate of general interaction, and very few instances of grooming. Therefore, although playful and sexual relations occurred among these females, their overall sociability was as low as would be expected in this species. Field reports, as we have seen, consistently portray female gorillas as relatively antagonistic and unlikely to engage in sustained "friendly" contact. As Fischer and Nadler pointed out, unfriendly relations may contribute to a spacing strategy which, in the wild, promotes more efficient acquisition of food resources.

Acquisition of Social Skills

Redshaw and Locke (1976) have examined the acquisition of social skills in two infant lowland gorillas. In this research, they asked three basic questions:

1. What are the signals used in gorilla-gorilla encounters?
2. At what stage do these occur and does their use change over time?

3. Are these signals peculiar to the lowland gorilla or do they occur in other primate species? (p. 71)

The authors of this paper determined that the "bouncy extravagant gait" of these gorillas occurred in many other primates, including human beings. There are other expressions and postures which are similarly present in the repertoires of gorillas and other primates.

At the age of seven and five months respectively, *Assumbo* and *Mamfe* interacted socially. They engaged in reciprocal biting, and took toys from each other. When both individuals were attempting to simultaneously climb onto their caretaker, they emitted "cough" vocalizations, sounds which Redshaw and Locke compared to Fossey's (1972) "pig-grunt" category.

By the end of their first year, these two gorillas increased in the frequency and duration of their interactions. In the course of their study, Redshaw and Locke selected three time periods in which to collect their samples:

I. *Assumbo* at 34-54 weeks; *Mamfe* at 26-46.
II. *Assumbo* at 94-106 weeks; *Mamfe* at 102-114.
III. *Assumbo* at 154-166 weeks; *Mamfe* at 146-158 weeks.

In their system, the investigators always indicated the spatial relationship of the participants. This was accomplished by referring to the relevant code item for "contact behavior" as follows:

B   = major portion of the bodies are in contact.
T   = only limb contact.
R   = out of touch, but within arm's reach.
OR = out of touch, and out of arm's reach.
X   = cannot see the other.

A second analytical system provided for acquisition of sequential data from the video tape record. We have reprinted in Table 2-6 the manipulative behaviors which were engaged in by *Assumbo* and *Mamfe*. As the reader can see, the most common manipulative behaviors emitted by these gorillas were swiping, play-biting, and slapping. These are playful behaviors which also occur prominently in the repertoire of chimpanzees and orang-utans (cf. Maple and Zucker, 1978).

With respect to "contact behavior," as assessed by the first code system described previously, Redshaw and Locke found that during observation period I, the two gorillas were never out of sight of each other. In the later two sample periods they were rarely out of sight. Body contact increased over time, but the animals increasingly were observed out of reach of each other. As the investigators noted, these changes reflected the increasing mobility of the infants and the growing complexity of their play.* Wrestling gradually gives way to chasing, while games such as "King of the Castle" are possible by the age of three.

Mamfe exhibited the "bouncy gait" during period I, but later rapidly ran or climbed toward *Assumbo* to initiate play. *Assumbo* did not exhibit the "bouncy gait." Both animals developed in periods II and III a "floppy gallop" whereby the head was down, eyes often shut, and limb movements exaggerated.

Redshaw and Locke discovered that, in these two gorillas, the "playface" occurred in social play, and in solitary locomotor and manipulative play. There was no difference in the frequency of its exhibition in the two gorillas, but for both it declined in frequency over time. The behaviors most commonly associated with the playface are so-called "limb movements," e.g., touching, reaching, swiping, and pulling. The following quotation from Redshaw and Locke makes the context of the playface clear.

Not only is there a decline in the use of this particular expression over time, but its context seems to have changed: from being used in a wide variety of situations so that by period III it tends to be used only in close games for example when sitting or lying in close contact and mouthing or exploring each other's faces. It seems then, to be used in fairly slow-paced interactions with the gorillas in close proximity (p. 81).

In Table 2-5 we have presented the data from Redshaw and Locke which illustrates the gestures and behaviors which were directed at one animal by the other. As the reader can see, the visual category of "look" was the most commonly recorded for both animals. This is not so surprising in view of its economy relative to other behaviors. On the whole, gestural acts were more common than locomotor acts, or visual acts.

The auditory signal of slapping or beating (cf. Chapter 3) always led to the approach of the other animal. Thus its signal value has been demonstrated by Redshaw and Locke. It is especially interesting that, after eighteen months of age, these gorillas ceased chest-beating in a friendly social context. Thereafter, it was emitted in uncertain situations, indicating anxiety and excitement.

Freeman and Alcock (1973) also studied the play of young gorillas. Working at Seattle's Woodland Park Zoo, they observed two male and two female gorillas living in an enclosure with two young orang-utans. The oldest gorilla was forty-two months old at the time of the study, while the three younger gorillas were about 30–33 months of age. The investigators found that juvenile gorillas played differently than orang-utans. While the orangs leaped, swung around, and dangled, the gorillas ran about, climbed on the enclosure framework, and turned somersaults. As Freeman and Alcock suggested, these differences in behavior reflect

---

*We will discuss the development of play further in Chapter 5.

Table 2-5. Gestures and actions emitted by one animal toward the other for the gorillas *Assumbo* and *Mamfe* at the Jersey Zoological Park (after Redshaw and Locke, 1976).

	Assumbo	Mamfe
Look	114	109
Watch	20	10
Playface	66	28
Play-bite	67	15
Swipe	60	59
Slap	28	24
Grasp	11	7
Clasp	7	2
Push	3	0
Pull	3	2
Touch	4	12
Hit	2	2
Kick	0	1
Pat	9	3
Reach	14	18
TOTAL	408	294

the respective arboreal and terrestrial propensities of the two taxa. The gorillas were also substantially noisier than the orangs. In their social play, the Seattle researchers observed a considerable tendency for interspecific interaction (cf. Maple and Zucker, 1978). However, the gorillas preferred to engage in play with conspecifics of the opposite sex.

Concerning their interest in the physical environment, Freeman and Alcock found a high frequency of contact with water. This medium seemed to stimulate play (cf. Chapter 7). The most frequently used objects were the easily climbed

Table 2-6. Playful manipulations of objects and others (by individual components) for the infant gorillas *Assumbo* and *Mamfe* (After Redshaw and Locke, 1976).

Type of Activity	Time Period		
	I	II	III
Swipe	39.31	12.65	16.02
Reach	0.00	3.27	6.06
Touch	1.73	1.22	10.39
Pat	4.05	0.41	1.73
Slap	15.03	46.53	8.23
Clasp	1.73	4.08	8.23
Grasp	6.94	6.94	11.69
Let go	1.73	0.00	0.00
Push	0.58	0.00	5.19
Pull	0.00	1.63	1.73
Hit	2.31	0.00	0.43
Kick	0.58	0.00	0.00
Fiddle	0.00	1.63	0.87
Clap hands	0.58	0.41	0.43
Playbite	25.43	21.22	29.00

furniture: the metal framework, poles, ledges, wire walls, and free forms. The tire, wire cables, and heavily branched tree trunks were difficult to climb; hence, less utilized. As the investigators concluded, equipment will induce play if it can be easily climbed.

During the course of the study, many novel objects were introduced into the enclosure. These included hard rubber balls, thick strands of rope, an abstract painting, bamboo stalks, and gunny sacks. All of these objects were initially and thoroughly investigated, but their attractiveness waned with the passage of time.

A salient dimension in sustained attractiveness is *change*, as the investigators themselves contend:

> . . . persistently attractive objects from the gorilla's and orang's standpoint were those which could be manipulated and changed, such as the bamboo stalks and the gunny sacks. (p. 192)

Gunny sacks and bamboo stalks were especially effective in stimulating play, exploration, and manipulation. Moreover, when there were not enough gunny sacks for each animal, the animals were induced to greater social interaction.

Because loud noises or unfamiliar intruders inhibited play, Freeman and Alcock inferred that play may be dependent upon a stress-free environment. Thus, in their view, the quantity of play may be a useful criterion by which to judge the adequacy of captive environments.

The behavior systems which we have reviewed in this chapter will be reconsidered in several places later in the text. Our objective has been to provide some depth regarding some major components of gorilla behavior. With this information at hand, we can now examine in detail the expressive repertoire of gorillas, a topic deserving our careful consideration.

3
Expression and Emotion in Gorilla

They are exceedingly ferocious, and always offensive in their habits, never running away from man as does the chimpanzee.

T. S. Savage, 1847

I believe that the gorilla is normally a perfectly amiable and decent creature. I believe that if he attacks man, it is because he is being attacked or thinks that he is being attacked. I believe that he will fight in self-defense.

C. E. Akeley, 1923

In the course of his illustrious career, Charles Darwin was both naturalist and scholar. He made many insightful observations when young, but was unable to continue in the rigors of fieldwork when his health began to fail. Regardless of the source, Darwin collected volumes of information from his correspondence and the extant literature. He often made reference to the reliability of the reporter, as in "the accurate Rennger." In collecting this information, Darwin's scientific contributions appeared in lengthy volumes such as *The Origin of Species*. Two of his books are especially important for behavioral scientists, *Expression of the Emotions in Man and Animals* (1872), and *Descent of Man* (1871). Containing a wealth of information on behavior, these two books are especially well stocked with observations and notes on the behavior of non-human primates, including apes. From *Descent* and *Expression* we have here extracted and topically organized Darwin's few entries which refer to gorillas.* Darwin's knowledge of primates included both error and insight, but there can be no doubt that the monkeys and apes were a rich source of analogy and argument as Darwin developed his remarkable ideas. Our collection of "Darwiniana" is not exhaustive, as he wrote about primates in other sources both published and unpublished. For example, the unpublished and recently discussed "M"

---

*For assistance in this endeavor we are grateful to A. S. Clarke and J. Branch.

notebook was the source of one of his most interesting remarks (cf. Gruber and Barrett, 1974; Maple, 1979):

"He who understands baboon would do more toward metaphysics than Locke."

Most of the expressions attributed by Darwin to the gorilla were, understandably, aggressive expressions. Since the gorilla in Darwin's time was thought to be the epitome of brutality, it is no wonder that its mode of rage would attract some attention. For example:

> . . .The Gorilla, when enraged, is described by Mr. Ford as having his crest of hair "erect and projecting forward, his nostrils dilated, and his upper lip thrown down; at the same time uttering his characteristic yell, designed it would seem, to terrorize his antagonists." (*Expressions*, pp. 95–96).

Later, in the same volume, Darwin further elaborated on this mode of expressivity of the gorilla:

> The gorilla, when enraged, is described as erecting its crest of hair, throwing down its upper lip, dilating its nostrils, and uttering terrific yells. Messrs. Savage and Wyman state that the scalp can be freely moved backwards and forwards and that when the animal is excited it is strongly contracted; but I presume that they mean by this latter expression that the scalp is lowered; for they likewise speak of the young chimpanzee, when crying out, "as having the eyebrows strongly contracted." The great power of movement in the scalp of the gorilla, of many baboons and other monkeys, deserves notice in relation to the power possessed by some few men, either through reversion or persistence, of voluntarily moving their scalps. (p. 142).

An expression common to all apes, according to Darwin, was the yawn which we today recognize as containing elements of threat. Darwin extended this observation of the yawn-threat into the realm of human evolution in the following paragraph:

> We may readily believe from our affinity to the anthropomorphous apes that our male semi-human progenitors possessed great canine teeth, and men are now occasionally born having them of unusually large size, with interspaces in the opposite jaw for their reception. We may further suspect, notwithstanding that we have no support from analogy, that our semi-human progenitors uncovered their canine teeth when prepared for battle, as we still do when feeling ferocious, or when merely sneering at or defying someone without any intention of making a real attack with our teeth (*Expressions*, pp. 251–252).

Figure 3-1. Play face emitted by infant gorilla as it approaches a young spider monkey. *(Photo courtesy Zoological Society of San Diego)*

In addition to these responses, Darwin also recognized an expression which accompanied an upsetting state of affairs. This expression was inferred by Darwin and compared to that emitted by human children when pouting:

> . . .with the gorilla, the lower lip is said to be capable of great elongation.* If then our semi-human progenitors protruded their lips when sulky or a little angered, in the same manner as do the existing anthropoid apes, it is not an anomalous, though a curious fact, that our children should exhibit, when similarly affected, a trace of the same expression, together with some tendency to utter a noise. (*Expressions*, p. 232).

---

*Although the lip of the gorilla is capable of elongation, we know of no expression which is employed in the manner described by Darwin here.

The information which Darwin provided was readily incorporated into the works of others. For example, Forbes (1894) commented on the expressive potential of the gorilla as follows:

> The Gorilla has the power of moving the scalp freely forward and backward—as Man in many instances has the power of doing—and when enraged, of corrugating his brows and erecting the hair over the central bony crest . . . (p. 000).

The above quotes pretty well exhaust the early references to gorilla expression. For further information from earlier periods we must turn to the publications of Yerkes.

YERKES' OBSERVATIONS ON "AFFECTIVE PHENOMENA"

In his 1928 monograph, Yerkes objectively rated emotionality as relatively low in the female mountain gorilla *Congo*.* Nevertheless, he "remained in doubt as

Figure 3-2. Infant gorilla exhibiting alarm at the introduction of a novel organism. *(San Diego Zoo photo)*

---

*As *Congo* was captured on Mt. Mikeno, Virunga Volcanoes, and judging by photographs taken during her youth, it is very likely that she was indeed a true mountain gorilla. Pictures taken during her adulthood show an extreme loss of hair, making her taxonomic identity less clear.

to the correctness of this judgment (p. 54)." While he found expressivity to be obscure and difficult to evaluate in this ape, he suspected that a more intense and highly developed emotionality would ultimately be discovered. Comparatively, Yerkes suggested that both emotionality and expressivity were somewhat greater in gorillas than orang-utans, but distinctly lower than in chimpanzees. Cautiously, he argued that:

> Possibly my impressions and conclusions were determined rather by conditions of observations, especially my own increased familiarity with my subject and the radically different observational situation, rather than by psychobiological changes in the gorilla (p. 55).

Yerkes' growing familiarity with *Congo* was an important dimension of his observations. As he discussed it in 1928, he at first believed that *Congo* was "aloof and shut-in" suggesting an air of "superiority" toward people and other animals. With the passage of time, however, Yerkes determined that timidity was an important element in her alleged aloofness. He further suggested that her change in behavior was due to an increased familiarity, trust, and self-confidence, and a concomitant diminution of timidity. In his own words:

> At first, as I now see it, I misinterpreted the behavior of Congo precisely as we often misinterpret and misunderstand that of bashful or diffident persons. We mistake their timidity and shrinking from us for superiority, pride, aloofness, and when we should be sympathetic and aggressively friendly are critical and condemnatory. Probably bashfulness or aggressiveness, timidity or confidence and trustfulness can be induced in any anthropoid ape or any person by appropriate treatment (p. 55).

The contrast between *Congo's* behavior and that of chimpanzees that Yerkes had observed was striking. *Congo* was judged to be especially unusual in view of her restraint in the face of aversive situations. As Yerkes noted, Congo never exhibited pronounced or violent emotional expressions of terror. He believed that this was not a condition unique to *Congo* but instead was characteristic of the gorilla as contrasted with many other primates. As Yerkes put it:

> Even under the most disturbing of conditions Congo never in my presence cried out, trembled, or exhibited pronounced erection of hair as if in terror. Yet there were times when if capable of this emotion, she certainly should have experienced it (p. 59).

In the 1928 monograph, Yerkes asked the question "Why . . . this extraordinary contrast in affective behavior between gorilla and chimpanzee?" The following paragraph illustrates these differences as Yerkes had perceived them:

> Congo may be characterized as moody, whereas the chimpanzee tends to be mercurially emotional, almost kaledioscopic in its affective transformations

and pronouncedly impulsive in response. The gorilla's affective moodiness obviously enough is correlated with psycho-physical slowness and stability. These statements indicate the importance of the temporal relations of psycho-physical processes and the desirability that they be observed, measured with increasing accuracy, and used as basis for comparative study of the various type of primate (pp. 62–63).

The major difference in affect between gorillas and chimpanzees, according to Yerkes, was their inherent *slowness*. This attribute was furthermore seen to extend into other aspects of the respective apes' behavior. As Yerkes wrote:

. . .the slowness instead of being limited to simple sensory reaction extends to affective expression, general activity, and behavioral adaptation. This of course suggests the possibility that investigation may reveal fundamentally important differences with respect to the temporal relations of phenomena in the anthropoids, and that these differences may be of corresponding order of magnitude for sensory reactions and those associated with and involving discrimination, choice, judgment, varied ideational processes, and memory (p. 63).

Slowness notwithstanding, Carpenter (1937) considered the face* of the gorillas to be very expressive. The movement of the eyebrows and the degree of eye-opening determined the expression of the eyes, according to Carpenter. Even more expressive, however, were their lips:

The lips are the most expressive part of the face. The protruding lips and the degree of which the mouth is opened indicate in a general way the mood or emotional set for action. There is no doubt but that these finer changes of facial expression become conditioned stimuli for the associated animal and serve to indicate incipient gross behavior (pp. 116–117).

As part of his studies, Yerkes embarked upon an experiment to test *Congo's* threshold for fear. Assuming that large carnivores were natural enemies of anthropoids, he led her to within 100 yards of the home cages of some bears, lions, tigers, leopards, and hyenas. Moving forward, Yerkes found that at a distance of 20–25 yards, she was uneasy but perfectly willing to continue in the company of her human companions. We will now give way to Yerkes' own description of the events that followed:

When about seven yards from two large lions which were moving about in their cage and growling occasionally as we approached them, she stopped,

---

*Schaller observed that the eyes, the lips, and the mouth were the best indicators of emotional state. By watching the eyes, he was frequently able to predict a gorilla's behavior.

stood motionless for a few seconds, and then suddenly as if noticing for the first time and recognizing something startling she rushed to me, seized me with both hands and clung to me as might a terrified child . . . To Cap Ricardo*, who close at hand was carefully observing all that happened, and also to me, the behavior suggested appeal to me for protection (p. 60).

In a humorous note, Yerkes added that: "It was indeed flattering to have the huge, powerful animal turn to me as defender against the lions which seemed to threaten her, but it was also amusing, for undoubtedly *Congo* could have killed me almost as readily as either of the lions could have destroyed her."

Furthermore, Yerkes hinted that conditions of captivity could distort the emotional behavior of apes, just as the behavior of people could be similarly distorted. Here again we quote directly from the 1928 monograph to illustrate this point. We should keep his words in mind when we later consider the be-havioral effects of captivity (cf. Chapter 8).

My accumulated observations clearly point to the conclusion that as in us, so in the gorilla, environmental factors which tend to induce, enhance, and perpetuate timidity and diffidence thereby render the organism extremely uncomfortable, inhibit, limit, and in a variety of ways determine the nature of self-expression, warp the development of behavioral capacities, and in considerable measure determine the dominant traits of individuality and personality, and limit or thwart social usefulness (p. 56).

COPULATORY EXPRESSIONS

In a study of the sexual behavior of captive lowland gorillas, Hess (1973) recorded characteristic facial expressions which were associated with copulations. For the female *Kati* he noted that:

K's lips are slightly pressed together with the edges drawn in forming a bulge. They remain, however, a trace apart. Her cheeks seem slightly puffed up and her eyes are closed at times (p. 561).

Table 3-1. Yerkes' shifting description of the "personality" of the gorilla *Congo*.

1926	1927	1928
Aloofness	Self-contained	Timidity
Superiority	Independent	
	Aloof	

*Congo's keeper.

The mature male, *Stefi*, was also observed to exhibit characteristic facial expressions during copulation as follows:

> Two to three times during copulation S screws up his eyes for a short while. His lips are pursed. The corners are pulled backwards and slightly downwards (p. 561).

The final phase in a copulation is inferred by a rising intensity of these expressions in both male and female. At ejaculation, the male is said to evince a "glazed" look.

Vocal sounds associated with copulation in these captive lowland gorillas included a long sequence of vibrating sounds in the female. Hess found these sounds to be similar to the male's strutting vocalization, although quieter, hoarser, and more "voiceless." The male emitted sounds only during the final moments of copulation, but not always. These sounds also resembled the strutting vocalization.

Thomas (1958), Marler and Tenaza (1977) and Schaller (1963) have all discussed gorilla vocalizations during copulation. Schaller described three types of copulatory vocalizations: a staccato call given by silverbacked males throughout copulation, a single instance of a short scream by a female, and growling and grunting by a captive pair preceding and during copulation. Nadler (1975a) has described a *dove-coo* vocalization in male gorillas involved in copulatory sequences. In our studies of group-living gorillas, in collaboration with Nadler, this male vocalization has occurred in the three instances of observed adult copulations, as well as in other sexual contexts (e.g., observation of female masturbation, or of infant sexual behavior).

AGGRESSION AMONG GORILLAS

An earlier review by Maple and Matheson (1973) provided a number of standard definitions for the concept aggression. A classic and useful definition, however, can be found in Carthy and Ebling (1964) who defined it as *behavior by an animal which inflicts, attempts to inflict, or threatens to inflict damage on another animal.* Pitcairn (1974) suggested further that aggression has two concomitants: (1) One animal may inflict damage on another which may be maladaptive; and (2) aggression eventually increases the physical distance between the animals involved.

Among fieldworkers studying gorillas, there is general agreement that little direct aggression is expressed among members of the same group. This finding of little contact aggression among gorillas has led Bourne and Cohen (1975) to characterize them as "gentle giants."

Despite this general amicability, however, gorillas do on occasion engage in aggressive activities. In his excellent review of pongid aggression, Pitcairn

Table 3-2. Dominance interactions between age and sex classes
(After Schaller, 1963).

Subordinate Animal / Dominant Animal	Silverbacked Male	Blackbacked Male	Female	Juvenile	Infant	Total
Silverbacked male	13	1	26	9	2	51
Blackbacked male	...	...	2	3	...	5
Female	...	4	12	13	11	40
Juvenile	...	...	...	4	8	12
Infant (one year or older).	...	...	...	...	2	2
Total	13	5	40	29	23	110

(1974) pointed out that it is necessary to distinguish between *aggressive acts* and *threat displays.* As Pitcairn correctly noted, displays are very important elements in the behavioral repertoires of all pongids. Schaller's monumental study of the mountain gorilla revealed both aggressive acts and two forms of threat displays.

Schaller has identified five basic modes of aggression in mountain gorillas. His categories included expressions, bodily postures, and overt contact, listed and edited as follows from the review of Pitcairn (1974):

1. *Stare.* This is a fixed, unwavering stare at another, sometimes with a furrowed brow. These stares are shorter in duration in *intra*group than in *inter*group confrontations, and are generally accompanied by short grunts.
2. *Jerk of head, or snap.* A jerk or thrust of the head toward the antagonist, it occasionally ends with an audible snap of the jaws.
3. *Foward lunge.* An incipient charge which is comprised of an abrupt advance of two or three steps toward the adversary.
4. *Bluff charges.* A charging display which was rarely observed by Schaller. Taking place at distances from 10–80 feet from the adversary, it generally consisted of a silent or *roaring* quadrupedal charge.
5. *Physical contact.* The major components of contact are grabbing and grappling, accompanied by biting and screaming, a relatively rare behavior during Schaller's period of study.

Additionally, as anger increased in an individual mountain gorilla, Schaller (1963) noted that the eyes remained hard and fixed, while the mouth opened, exposing the teeth and the curled lips. Van Hooff (1967) called these expressions the *staring open-mouthed face* and the *staring bared-teeth scream face.*

Figure 3-3. Aggressive interaction between male gorillas at the San Diego Zoo. This is an unusual photograph in that male gorillas are rarely permitted on display together. *(Photo courtesy Zoological Society of San Diego)*

In addition to aggressive acts, Schaller has identified two forms of threat displays in the gorilla: the chest-beating sequence and the strutting walk.   The chest-beating sequence consists of nine acts which may be performed separately or in almost any combination of two or more. The full sequence is displayed only by silverbacked males, and then only infrequently (see Table 3-3). When the acts occur in combination, there is a tendency for some to precede others, and for several to occur in a fixed sequence as follows:

1. *Hooting.*   The chest-beating display begins with a series of two to forty soft hoots, getting faster and slurred as it approaches a climax.
2. *Symbolic feeding.*   The hooting is sometimes interrupted as the gorilla plucks vegetation and puts it between its lips.

3. *Rising.* Just before the climax of the display, the animal rises bipedally for several seconds.
4. *Throwing.* As the gorilla rises, it often throws a handful of vegetation in the air.
5. *Chest-beating.* The standing gorilla slaps its chest, abdomen, or thighs alternately with open, cupped hands from two to twenty times (range) in the climax of the display. Beating typically begins with the right hand, and is usually composed of three to six beats.
6. *Leg kick.* The gorilla will sometimes kick one leg in the air while chest-beating.
7. *Running.* Toward the end or immediately following the chest-beat, the gorilla often runs sideways, first bipedally and then quadrupedally up to 20 meters.
8. *Slapping and tearing.* The gorilla will slap at and break vegetation as it runs.
9. *Ground thump.* The terminal act is a single ground thump with one or both palms.

According to Schaller, chest-beating is a ritualized display, commonly observed during a conflict between aggression and flight. Those events which seemed to precipitate chest-beating were the approach of people, the presence of other groups or lone males, general disturbances, other chest-beating displays, and play. Other gorillas are particularly responsive to the displays of the dominant male.

Fossey's (1972a) study of the communicative repertoire of the feral mountain gorilla also concerned display behaviors. Her results are similar to Schaller's. A series of *hoots* and species-typical *chest-beating* apparently functions in the context of intergroup communication. These behaviors occur more frequently between males, but as Schaller has shown both are also emitted by adult females. Such aggressive displays are frequently accompanied by *ground-thumping, branch-breaking, vegetation-tearing,* and a *sideways run.* The latter behaviors appear to be more probable than hooting/chest-bearing when males are closer together.

As Pitcairn (1974) has correctly pointed out, many of the same behavioral components of the gorilla chest-beating display also comprise the chimpanzee *explosive display.* Thus, we are compelled to argue that aggressive display behavior is, to a considerable degree, homologous in the African apes (cf. Table 3-4).

In addition to feral studies, chest-beating displays have been studied in captive animals. For example, Riess, Ross, Lyerley, and Birch (1949) observed that when captive lowland gorillas were together, chest-beating displays increased in frequency. In this study as in Schaller's, males were found to be more likely to beat their chests than females.

Table 3-3. Occurrence of the various elements of the chest-beating sequence
by age/sex class (After Schaller, 1963).

		Silverbacked Male	Blackbacked Male	Female	Juvenile	Infant 1-3 Years	Infant 0-1 Years
1	Hooting	XX	X	0	0	0	0
2	"Symbolic feeding"	XX	XX	X	X	X	0
3	Throwing	XX	XX	XX	XX	X	0
4	Rising	XX	XX	XX	XX	XX	XX
5	Chest-beating	XX	XX	XX	XX	XX	XX
6	Kicking	XX	XX	0?	X	0	0
7	Running	XX	X	X	0	0	0
8	Slapping and tearing	XX	XX	XX	XX	X	X
9	Ground-thumping	XX	XX	XX	X	0	0

XX: common.
X: infrequent.
0: not observed.
Copyright 1963 University of Chicago Press

Carpenter (1937) has also described captive gorilla chest-beating in some detail. He observed that in addition to chests, logs, other objects, and floors were
also beaten during situations in which the apes were aroused to activity. However, Carpenter contended that when chests or objects were rhythmically beaten,
it was an indication of playfulness and contentment.* Denying its likelihood in
the context of anger or disturbance, Carpenter went on to state that chest-beating
had a communicative significance:

> First, the behavior seems to be a form of playful *challenge* . . . Second, chest
> beating seems to be a form of *display* behavior . . . while assuming some un-
> usual posture he (Ngagi) would beat his chest . . . Chest beating also occurred
> when he seemed particularly anxious to attract the attention of a person to
> whom he was attached (p. 115).

An apparent derivation of the active chest- or object-beat is a slight tapping
on the body or substrate that we have often observed to precede chest-beating in

---

*About chest-beating, the Yerkes' wrote:

> The tendency to chest beating, even from early childhood onward, the tendency also to
> pound objects and to use these for noise production are as definitely suggestive of innate-
> ness as is nest building (1929, p. 420).

Figure 3-4. Juvenile gorilla *Jim (G. g. gorilla)* beating his chest at the San Diego Zoo. *(Photo courtesy Zoological Society of San Diego)*

captive animals. However, this behavior is apparently not completely idiosyncratic to captive gorillas, as the following passage* (attributed to Zenker) illustrates:

> If he suspects danger, he drums lightly at first upon his cheeks, opening his mouth and striking with his hands against it. This is a signal, commanding his company to flee (Yerkes and Yerkes, p. 462; Heck, p. 684).

This behavior was manifest in similar fashion in a mountain gorilla as recorded by Burbridge (1928):

> Often had I heard accompanying the muffled drum of a gorilla beating his chest in the forest another, metallic and penetrating, like that a small boy

---

*According to the Yerkes, this animal was a lowland gorilla.

Figure 3-5. Chest beating of Sacramento Zoo's lowland male *Kris*. *(S. Woo photo)*

makes when he beats with sticks upon a tin can. Until now I had supposed
this sound was produced by a small gorilla beating its chest. Usually there
are about sixteen beats, then a pause. A gorilla stands upright, manlike,
when producing these sounds . . . . He arose in plain view, mouth open,
cheeks drawn taut, and beat a rapid tatoo on each cheek with his open palms.
The sound was metallic and far-carrying. Another gorilla, like a jack-in-the-box,
popped up into an adjacent opening and drummed on his chin with a rapid
circular motion, striking the chin with the backs of his fingers. Often before I
had heard this teeth-rattling without seeing the performer. Whether it was a
signal or a note of defiance is a matter of conjecture. At least, its effect was
electric (pp. 234–235).*

A second form of threat display, which Schaller designated as the strutting
walk, is a very stiff short-stepped quadrupedal walk. In this exaggerated posture,

---

*Osborn (1963) also reported an observation of a mountain gorilla that beat
his cheek at the side of his mouth with one hand. The sound that it made was "a curious
loud hollow vibrating noise."

the arms are bent outward at the elbow, the body is stiffly held erect and the head is diverted to the side, with only brief glances directed at the opponent.* This pattern of behavior is similar in all age-sex classes. The strutting walk is also frequently accompanied by the lip-in (tense-face) facial expression (cf. Figure 3-6). In captivity, this display is frequently followed by a running sequence in which the enclosure barriers or a cagemate may be struck with its

Figure 3-6. Tight lips expression of *Kris*, male lowland gorilla at the Sacramento Zoo. *(T. Maple photo)*

---

*Sheldon Campbell (1978) clearly recognized the importance of visual stimuli in the life of gorillas when he formulated the following paragraph:

Gorillas are so sensitive about staring that they almost never stare at one another or at Zoo visitors. Their own method of watching a visitor is that employed by a middle-aged American male when he ogles bikini-clad girls while his wife is present. The secret, gorillas know, is to pretend to be looking at something else while taking in the true object of investigation out of the corner of the eye. Gorillas would no doubt find sunglasses a great boon (p. 75).

shoulder or forearm. Schaller has characterized this behavior as "playful," although it is certainly not exclusively so.

The tense-face of the gorilla, as Marler and Tenaza (1977) have suggested appears to be homologous with that expression in orang-utan and chimpanzee. Moreover, the lips are tightened in the same fashion when human beings are experiencing tension.* When a gorilla exhibits the tense face, it is generally accompanied by periodical quarter-turns of the head whereby the ape glances at the stimulus, looks away, then glances back out of the corner of its eye. Among captive gorillas, our observations suggest that this tight-lipped glancing is predominantly an adult male behavior. From the films of Hess, Jensen (personal communication) surmised that this behavior was a component of the male courtship display.

THE DEVELOPMENT OF AGGRESSIVE DISPLAYS

In our studies of captive group living gorillas we have examined aggressive displays in both the adults and infants (Hoff, Nadler, and Maple, 1978). The focus on normative infant development was supplemented by a group scan

Table 3-4. Probable homologs of great ape facial expressions.
(After Marler and Tenaza, 1977).

| Chimpanzee facial expression | Probable homologs in other apes | |
	Gorilla	Orang-utan
1a. Grin with mouth closed or only slightly open	None described	Grimace, fear face
1b. Grin with mouth wide open	Fear face and anger face	Wide-mouth grin
2. Open-mouth threat face	Annoyance face staring	Bare-teeth threat face
3. Tense-mouth face	Tense-mouth face	Tense-mouth face
4. Pout face	Light-distress face	Pout face
5. Play face	Pleasure face	Play face
6. Lip-smacking face	None described	Lip and mouth movements performed while eating particles removed from body of another individual during allo-grooming.

NOTE: Descriptions and terms for gorilla facial espressions are from Schaller (1963) and those for the orang-utan from Mackinnon (1974).

---

*An excellent example of the human tense face is the photograph of Richard Nixon which appears in Allison Jolly's book, *The Evolution of Primate Behavior* (1972).

focus on aggressive displays in the months surrounding the infant's second birthday. Adult male and female displays occurred throughout the study, although none of the animals exhibited the complete chest-beating sequence as described by Schaller.

A typical captive male sequence involved blowing through pursed lips while sitting, rising to a bipedal stand, tossing a rock into the air as he rose, and then chest-beating. The females exhibited an even more abbreviated chest-beat, involving pursing the lips, rising from the ground, and then chest-beating. The male exhibited individual components of the display at about 2.5 behaviors per hour; the females at half this rate.

Infants began showing an interest in male displays in early infancy, and began approaching the male at the conclusion of his displays at about one year of age. Shortly after this, various components of aggressive displays began appearing in play. Lunging appeared at 15 months, followed quickly by lunging with a terminal hit, and rudimentary chest- and wall-beating appeared. Several other individual display behaviors were ultimately identified. Figure 3-7 shows the ontogenetic progression of all infant aggressive displays through approximately two years of age. As can be seen, there was a precipitous rise in displays during the latter part of the second year of life.

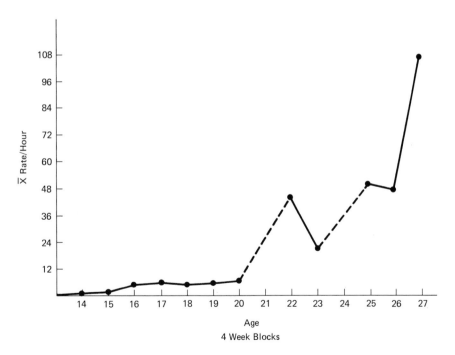

Figure 3-7. Mean rate per hour of all infant aggressive display behaviors as a function of age. (After Hoff, Nadler, and Maple, 1978b)

Aggressive displays occurred often during play bouts. As can be seen in Table 3-5, displays were often initiated and occurred during active ("rough and tumble") social play.

Infant displays most often occurred when infants were alone (Table 3-6). However, when directed towards another animal, displays occurred significantly more often toward another infant rather than adult. Additionally, infants directed more displays toward the adult male than all three adult females.

As we have seen, aggression is rarely expressed in gorilla groups. Similarly, dominance relationships (as measured by displacements; e.g., as in Schaller, 1963) are subtly expressed (see Chapter 1). For example, Schaller found that slight touches sometimes led to physical displacements. Of the 110 dominance interactions recorded by Schaller, 51 involved silver-backed males. Fifty percent of these interactions were directed toward females, while 25% were directed toward black-backed males. Aggressive behaviors are nonetheless characteristically low in mountain gorillas due, in part, to the fact that subordinate individuals avoid the dominant male when they detect his arousal (cf. Schaller, 1963; Pitcairn, 1974).

The complexity of dominance judgments is reflected in our aforementioned example of grooming in the mountain gorillas observed by Carpenter. As he suggested, an animal that is dominant in one modality may not be dominant in another. Carpenter also correctly noted that gorillas can maintain a stable relationship without resorting to fighting.

In temperament comparisons, as conducted by the Yerkes in 1929, the *Gorilla* was portrayed as less emotional than *Pongo* or *Pan*. In a second category, dispositional contrasts (moodiness), the Yerkes' ranked gorillas as the most moody. In the variety of their emotional patterns, they found that gorillas were the least shy of the apes, least aggressive, and least "agreeable." Furthermore, with respect to increasing evidence of "sorrow, grief, depression, sympathy, attachment, mutual and altruistic aid," *Gorilla* was intermediate between *Pongo*

Table 3-5. Infant aggressive displays as emitted by three captive gorillas during *active, moderate,* and *parallel* play bouts. (After Hoff, Nadler, and Maple, 1978)

	Active Social Play	Moderate Social Play
Precede	6	1
Initiate	54	16
During	104	7
Terminate	19	12
Parallel	36	

Table 3-6. Infant displays for 1020 behaviors.
(After Hoff, Nadler, and Maple, 1978)

Solitary	576
Toward infant	263
Toward adult male	102
Toward 3 Adult females	79

and *Pan*. In terms of their expressiveness via sound production, gorillas were found to be the least vocal but the most nonvocal; e.g., sound production by hand clapping and chest beating. With regard to intercommunicative skills, gorillas were again seen as intermediate between orangs and chimps. In their final category, motivation, gorillas were thought to be the most motivated of the apes. Nonetheless, their composite rankings indicated that *Gorilla* was somehow less "emotional" than the other apes.

The Yerkes' pioneering effort unfortunately suffered from a lack of objectivity. Because there were no precise studies to cite, they were forced to review the subjective literature, formulating conclusions in conjunction with their own personal impressions. In contrast, Schonwetter and Maple (cf. Maple, 1980a) attempted to examine temperament empirically by recording the emotional responses of chimpanzees, gorillas, and orang-utans to the presentation of food.

In our comparative study of temperament, gorillas were found to be calmer than chimpanzees, exhibiting the least amount of facial expression of the three taxa. However, gorillas were unique in that they alone grunted and beat their chests at the appearance of food, and exhibited the greatest amount of digit-sucking. They were also somewhat less active than chimpanzees or orang-utans during feeding periods.

In agreement with the Yerkes, our study revealed that gorillas were more emotional than orang-utans, but less emotional than chimpanzees. In the *variety* of their emotional expressiveness, a category in which the Yerkes found orangs exceeded gorillas, we determined that gorillas exhibited greater *types* and *amounts* of bodily movements and vocalizations. However, gorillas emitted slightly fewer facial expressions.

The portrait of gorillas as *withdrawn* and *stoic* is generally supported by the Schonwetter/Maple study. It is abundantly clear that both gorillas and orang-utans are poles apart from the loud and excitable common chimpanzee. A better understanding of their emotional makeup should contribute to improvements in their captive management. This is particularly important in view of the propensity of captive gorillas to exhibit signs of depression.

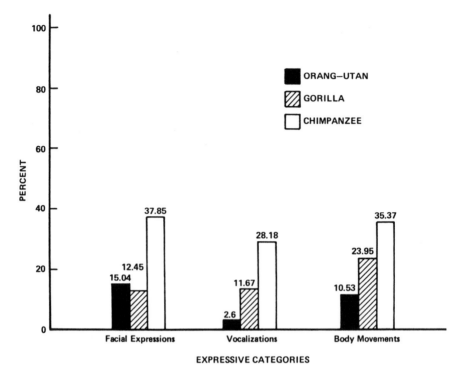

Figure 3-8. Percent of test that each general category of expressivity was observed. (After Maple, 1980a)

VOCAL BEHAVIOR IN MOUNTAIN GORILLAS

As Marler and Tenaza (1977) have shown, apes are well adapted for producing a variety of well-structured sounds. The gorilla, as we have already seen, is particularly inclined to emit nonvocal sounds. Chest-beating is facilitated by the air sac within its chest that resonates when inflated. Dian Fossey's (1972) list of vocalizations for the mountain gorilla is available in Table 3-7 together with the chimpanzee equivalent as provided by Marler and Tenaza for comparison. As can be readily seen, the repertoire is comprised of 16 distinct vocalizations. These vocalizations have been divided by Fossey into seven functional units:

1. *Aggressive*—three types
2. *Mild alarm*—two types
3. *Fear and alarm*—two types
4. *Distress*—two types
5. *Group coordination*—three types

Table 3-7. Gorilla vocalizations, and their characteristic context, as compared to chimpanzee equivalents. (After Marler and Tenaza, 1977, as derived from Fossey, 1972b)

Vocalization	Circumstances	Equivalent chimpanzee call Type	Equivalent chimpanzee call Circumstances
Wraagh	Sudden alarming situation; loud noise; unexpected contact with buffalo, with aggressive elements.	Waa bark and Wraaa	Same
Hoot bark	Alerting to mild alarm; group movement initiation.	Bark ?	Similar
Hoot series	Intergroup encounters with aggressive component.	Pant-hoot	Similar
Pig grunt	Mild aggression in moving group.	Grunt and cough	General arousal and aggression
Scream	Aggressive disputes within group; copulating female.	Scream	Same
Belch	Feeding; group contentment.	Rough grunt	Same
Question bark	Very mild alarm or curiosity.	Bark ?	Similar
Cries	Infant separated, in difficulty.	Whimper and squeak	Same
Roar	Strong aggression of silverback ♂ to predator or other group.	None	
Hiccup bark	Very mild alarm or curiosity.	Bark ?	Similar
Growl	Mild aggression in stationary group	None	
Pant series	Mild threat within group.	Pant-grunt?	Similar
Whine	Danger of injury or abandonment (?).	None	
Whinny	May be anomalous; ailing animal.	None	
Chuckles	Social play, tickling.	Laughter	Same
Copulatory panting	Male, copulating.	Pant	Same

6. *Intergroup communication*—one type
7. *Miscellaneous*—three types

Aggressive vocalizations of the mountain gorilla include at least four sounds as follows:

1. *Harsh grunt.* A series of two to five short grunts.
2. *Bark.* A loud and often high-pitched sound. (According to Pitcairn, 1974, it may be equivalent to the "Hwat, wat" call described by Kawai and Mizuhara, 1959).
3. *Roar.* A loud, intense call apparently made only by adult males.
4. *Harsh scream.* Young males and females were observed to make this call which is short, harsh, and usually emitted in a series (perhaps the "Kien" of Kawai and Mizuhara according to Pitcairn).

Other aggressive vocalizations such as *hooting* and the *panting ho-ho* of females occur in the context of chest-beating and other displays.

In Table 3-8, Marler and Tenaza have also compared chimpanzee and gorilla vocalizations by age and sex classes. As these investigators duly noted, whereas chimpanzees of all ages are apparently equally vocal, the adult male gorilla is much more vocal than any other age/sex class. More than 90% of all vocalizations recorded by Fossey were attributed to the adult males. Moreover, silverbacked males were considerably more vocal than blackbacked males.

Despite the differences in the distribution of calling within the two taxa, gorilla and chimpanzee vocalizations are quite similar in form and function. Fossey's original report on vocal behavior probably contained an overrepresentation of alarm calls since the groups were not yet sufficiently habituated to human observation. Fully 87% of the calls recorded were related to alarm or aggression. Marler and Tenaza reported that a later ranking by Harcourt, as personally communicated to them, led to the following revised rank order of usage:

1. *Belch*
2. *Chuckles*
3. *Pig-grunt*
4. *Hoot bark* or *hiccup bark*
5. *Hoot series*
6. *Whine* and *cries*
7. *Question barks*
8. *Screams*
9. *Pant series*

Table 3-8. A comparison of the frequency of gorilla and chimpanzee vocal behavior by sex and age classes. (After Marler and Tenaza, 1977).

	Gorilla*					Chimpanzee				
	Ad ♂	Ad ♀	Juv.	Inf.	Total	Ad ♂	Ad ♀	Juv.	Inf.	Total
Number of individuals in study population	31	36	20	19	106	15	12	10	7	44
Number of vocalizations of known individuals	1,583	77	7	33	1,700	831	633	506	343	2,313
Percentage of total vocal output	93	5	0.5	2		36	27	22	15	
Average vocal output per class member (B/A)	50.1	2.1	0.35	1.7	54.25	55.4	52.7	50.6	49	207.7
Percentage each class member makes of total	92	4	0.6	3		27	25	24	24	

*After Fossey, 1972; Tables 2 and 3.

10. *Copulatory pants*
11. *Growl*
12. *Wraagh*
13. *Roar*
14. *Whinny*

In this revised order the most common vocalizations relate to contentment and play. While certain calls were originally more frequent due to the wariness of the gorillas, others were doubtless inhibited for the same reason. Thus, after habituation, play sounds and other vocalizations of pleasure and leisure were more commonly recorded. Similarly, Marler and Tenaza suggested that laughing is probably over-represented in the repertoire of the chimpanzee population at Gombe National Park, since early provisioning permitted rapid habituation. Moreover, due to food competition, and resultant population stresses, aggressive vocalizations may have also been over-represented in this chimpanzee population. As we have argued, the way in which you carry out a study may greatly influence your results.*

An additional indication of the potential over-representation of alarm calls in Fossey's study may be found in the work of Schaller. While his descriptions of vocalizations are perhaps less precise than Fossey's, they are certainly worth examining. While Schaller found that gorillas are generally silent when left undisturbed, their vocalizations were quite varied and intense in the presence of people. However, and very important in view of Fossey's finding of a preponderance of alarm calls, Schaller found contentment vocalizations to be quite frequent among adults. In fact, he was able to subdivide them into four separate categories. Although complete quantitative data were not provided, these contentment vocalizations appear to have been heard at least as frequently as the various alarm calls:

> Thus, eight vocalizations occurred fairly frequently in the daily routine of free-living gorillas: a soft grumbling and grunting of contented animals; a series of abrupt grunts, functioning to keep the group together; a hoot preceding the chest-beating display in silverbacked males, a harsh staccato grunt of annoyance; a bark and harsh scream given by quarreling animals; and a screech by infants when in danger of falling behind the groups (p. 211).

In the captive situation, the wide range of gorilla calls identified by Fossey are apparently much less frequently expressed. In our studies of captive lowland

---

*As Schaller stated:

> Events and observers alike are rarely the same at the beginning and the end of any study. The longer the study, the greater the disparity in person and place, and perhaps results. We enthusiastically champion the recent emphasis on long-term field studies, but one must also acknowledge the drawbacks.

gorillas, the *belch* and the *pig-grunt* are most commonly heard with other forms of vocalizations occurring much less frequently. The full range of vocalizations described by Fossey has not been identified in the Yerkes group.

Carpenter (1937) also found a small range of vocalizations in the captive mountain gorillas he studied. This rather surprised him as he believed that vocalizations were closely related to the "higher mental processes" and emotional expression. Thus, he felt that the highly intelligent gorilla would have a more varied and extensive vocal repertoire. He found that *Mbongo* and *Ngagi* communicated vocally by a series of low-pitched grunts. The problem in communicating the essence of these sounds to the reader is obvious in Carpenter's description:

> Typically the grunts were of a similar pitch, volume, and intensity; however, when an animal was excited, his low pitched grunt of considerable intensity was gradually transmuted into one of considerably higher pitch. Variations in meaning, *judged from changes in the behavior of the associated animal,* could be made by changing the tempo with which the grunts were given. . . crude vocal descriptions of their vocalizations seem futile (p. 116).

Marler and Tenaza also commented on the vocal range of the gorilla in discussing the differences in chimpanzee and gorilla temperament, whereby the chimpanzee was portrayed as more emotional and expressive at all ages than the gorilla. As a cautionary note they added:

> . . .comparisons of temperament in the two species, which tend to emphasize the phlegmatic nature of the gorilla, should not overlook the remarkable vocal range of silverbacked males. If vocal output is indeed to be used as an index of temperament, then silverbacked males can hardly be viewed as any less expressive and emotional than chimpanzees, however phlegmatic other classes of individuals may appear. One wonders whether their restraint might not be correlated with the relative exhuberance and assertiveness of the silverbacked male (p. 999).

Finally, Jones and Sabater Pí (1971) discovered that Rio Muni lowland gorillas vocalized* during peak activity periods. Hence they were noisy in the early morning and late afternoon, but generally quiet during the midday hours. Gorillas persisted in making vocal sounds for about an hour after dark, but they were usually silent thereafter. Chest-beating occurred primarily during the morning activity period, but occasionally at other times. Chest-beating was not generally associated with vocal behavior, but it, too, occurred frequently while in the night nest.

---

*However, comparative data gathered by the same researchers indicate that gorillas are much quieter than chimpanzees.

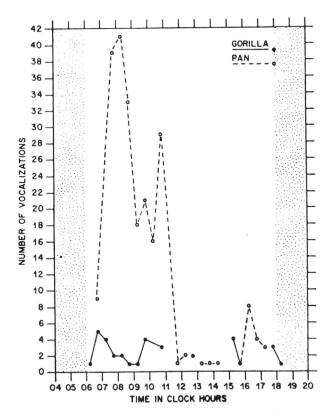

Figure 3-9. Vocalizations emitted during the daily activities of gorillas and chimpanzees in Rio Muni. (After Jones and Sabater Pí, 1971)

The expression of emotions has not been adequately studied in the genus *Gorilla*. It is our impression that their communicative repertoire is composed of many subtle gestures which have not yet been properly classified. Expression is best studied under consistent and unobstructed observational conditions. In a primate center or zoological park, an intensive study would be possible. We look forward to the acquisition of such data, trusting that the information herein will help to formulate and encourage such research.

4
Gorilla Sexual Behavior

In the beginning of his career, in independent life, the gorilla selects a wife with whom he appears to sustain the conjugal relations thereafter, and preserves a certain degree of marital fidelity. From time to time he adopts a new wife, but does not discard the old one; in this manner he gathers around him a numerous family, consisting of his wives and their children.

R. L. Garner, 1896

Of all the great apes, *Gorilla* has been the taxon most difficult to breed in captivity. This fact has been rendered more understandable by the finding that feral gorillas are rarely observed copulating (cf. Schaller, 1963; Harcourt and Stewart, 1977). Moreover, the courtship rituals of gorillas are relatively subdued, and expressed only during the narrowly prescribed period of female receptivity (actually "proceptivity" as we will see).

The reluctance to mate in captivity doubtless stems from a number of factors; e.g., prior social experience, environmental constraints, social stress, diet, incompatibility, etc. *Gorilla* behavior in general seems to be more easily disrupted than that of *Pan* and *Pongo*. When conditions are conducive to normal social interaction, as at the Basel Zoo for example, sexual activity is relatively common. However, even in the best conditions, gorillas appear to be considerably less sexual than chimpanzees and orang-utans. The gorilla repertoire is complex, but the frequency and duration of sexual activity in gorillas is comparatively low (cf. Short, 1977).

In spite of their lethargic libido, the sexual life of gorillas has been thoroughly described. The papers of Hess (1973) and Nadler (1975a) are particularly valuable. In this chapter, we will review that which has been written regarding gorilla sexual behavior. Currently, the captive work has provided a greater wealth of information about this behavior system. Further studies of feral sexual activity, particularly in the lowland taxon, should be encouraged. An especially promising line of research* would result from the formation of seminatural groupings of captive gorillas. Valid captive research is now possible at the San Diego Wild Animal Park, the Basel Zoo, and *Apenheul*, to name a few locations.

SEXUAL BEHAVIOR IN THE WILD

Schaller (1963) observed only two copulations by feral mountain gorillas, but Harcourt and Stewart (1978b) were able to record ninety-eight copulations during two and one-half years of research in the Virunga Volcanoes. In both of two groups, only the silverback copulated with parous females. However, a nulliparous female copulated with a resident blackback as well. The general trend was for adult females to mate with the silverback on different days. Daily rates of copulation ranged from 0.15 to 1.6 per hour (md = 0.4 per hour), with most occurring around midday.

In the field, nulliparous females first exhibited perineal tumescence at about seven years. They were first observed to mate with a silverback at about seven and one-half years, and first conceived at more than eight and one-half years of age. Judging from their copulation records, females exhibited estrous periods of about 1-2 days. The female's menstrual** cycles ranged from 22-38 days (md = 28; n = 9 cycles). Four of five females exhibited signs of estrus during pregnancy, but this was typically an infrequent phenomenon. In one animal, however, there was evidence of at least ten estrus*** periods.

In the Virunga Volcanoes, female mountain gorillas initiated copulations. Harcourt and Stewart observed a "soliciting approach" at 5 meters and 2 meters prior to a copulation. In their own words:

> Once the female was near the male, she stood facing him, with her body slightly sideways, as if waiting for a signal from the male, when she would abruptly turn and back into the normal dorso-ventral mating position. (p. 611).

---

*For a number of years, the Brookfield Zoo operated a summer research program for students in which stipends could be obtained for worthy projects. A cooperative summer research program has recently been instituted at the University of Vermont/Granby Park Zoo in which the behavioral effects of environments will be assessed. This program is supported by a grant from the National Science Foundation. A summer zoo research training program has been offered by Hal Markowitz at the Portland Zoo, Hilo (Hawaii) Zoo, and more recently, the San Francisco Zoo.

**In the apes, as in human beings, no distinction is made between *menstrual* and *estrous* cycles.

***Growth curves for six gorillas (one male and one female of the *gorilla* subspecies; two males and two females of the *graueri* subspecies) at the Antwerp Zoo indicates that there is a growth peak at 8-9 years in males, and 7-8 years in females, corresponding to the onset of puberty.

All observed copulations were dorso-ventral, with the exception of transitory ventro-ventral adjustments. Copulations ranged in time from 0.25-19.75 minutes (md = 1.6 min.). The median male thrusting length was only 2.0 seconds in duration. In half of the copulations, the female thrusted back onto the male, often thrusting before he was observed to do so.

In about two-thirds of the clearly observed bouts, both animals vocalized during copulation. Females typically started vocalizing before the male, and vocalized longer. Vocalization intensity and male thrusting increased toward the end of copulation, abruptly ceasing when the mount ended. The female departed at the end of 53 out of 62 copulations.

Copulations usually took place during travel-feed periods, when adults were widely dispersed. Although immature animals occasionally exhibited interest in adult mating, Harcourt and Stewart observed active interference only once.

Their valuable observations permitted them to interpret sexual behavior with regard to gorilla social organization. They argued that the reproductive success of males depended on the maintenance of exclusive rights to adult females. This is accomplished by forming a permanent bond with each female in the group. Bond formation minimizes competition with other males. Harcourt and Stewart further noted that the bond minimized selection pressure for "copulatory ability" during estrus. Thus, infrequent mating,* the male's evident "poor capacity for frequent, viable matings," and the prominent sexual role of the female may be related to this reduced selection pressure.

SEXUAL BEHAVIOR IN CAPTIVITY

The sexual interactions of captive group-living gorillas have rarely been studied. Only Hess (1973) has provided useful information within the context of a natural social group. Other data concerning sexual behavior in captivity have been derived primarily from pairs of gorillas (cf. Nadler, 1975). We strongly recommend that those institutions which maintain breeding groups carefully study them. Indeed, in every setting in which gorillas reside, it is important that they be observed. The variations which can be found in both physical and social environments contribute to our understanding of those variables which control sexual responsiveness. By studying compatible and reproductively successful gorillas, we may be able to correct situations in which reproduction has failed. In this section, we will review what is known about gorilla sexual behavior under captive conditions.

---

*The sexual reticence of male gorillas was recognized by C. R. Carpenter in his 1937 study of *Ngagi* and *Mbongo*. As Carpenter noted, not once in over 200 hours of observations did he observe the two male gorillas engaged in sexual activity. There were neither signs of self-interest nor interest in the genitalia of the other. Of special consideration here is Carpenter's suggestion that captivity and the lack of stimulation from females may have contributed to a delay in the onset of normal sexual activity.

Table 4-1. Duration of copulations (*Stefi* and *Kati*) and frequency of copulatory thrusting (*Stefi*) according to the observations of Hess (1973).

Duration of copulations (S + K)	
11 copulations were measured	
maximum in seconds	110
minimum in seconds	20
average	52.5
Frequency of copulation thrusts (S)	
23 measurements during 11 copulations	
maximum number of thrusts in 10 seconds	30
minimum number of thrusts in 10 seconds	14
average	24.2

Solitary Sexual Behavior in Adults

Masturbation with the fingers, hand, or foot is occasionally observed in the captive lowland gorilla. However, the reader should understand that it is by no means a daily behavior, given the comparatively low sexual motivation of this ape. Another interesting mode of solitary sexual behavior is the *rhythmic pelvic movements* emitted by both males and females. Hess' (1973) description of this behavior is especially instructive:

> The animal performs rhythmic upward and downward movements with the abdomen in a supine (female K only) or sitting (males M and J only) position. In the supine position K's legs are flexed and the feet hold onto the bars or door, or the wire netting, or are pressed against a firm object. In the sitting position, M and J hold onto the bars or an iron door with hands and feet; the knees are bent to an extent that the genital region is rubbing against the bars or the door while the whole body is continuously lifted and lowered. The direct rubbing-contact of the genitals is only observed in males. The frequency of movement in the female is higher than in males (p. 523).

Both males and females in the Basel group were observed to emit pelvic thrusting against inanimate objects (cf. Maple, 1977.)

Sexual Interactions

Among all of the Basel gorillas, Hess observed an interest in the genitalia of the others. They touched each other with their fingers, and also engaged in occasional oral-genital contact.   Often genital contact emerged from more general, nonsexual bouts of play.

In discussing the influence of estrus on sexual behavior, Hess detected a pre-estrus phase which begins 1-3 days prior to the onset of estrus. Of course, these are not dichotomous phases, since they are part of an overlapping continuum. However, it was possible to compare the behaviors which were correlated with each phase as defined. For example, during the pre-estrus period, both the female entering estrus and those around her evince behavioral changes.*   The female *Kati* "stared unwaveringly" at the male *Stefi*, and also exhibited an expression of "lips pressed together, with the corners slightly drawn in."   When the female *Kati* exhibited her pre-estrus behavior, the two younger males in the cage (aged ten and seven and one-half respectively) persistently followed her. Attempts to touch her genitalia and her armpits were frequent at these times. When they

Table 4-2. Copulatory positions of western lowland gorillas at the Basel Zoo (After Hess, 1973).

couple ♀ ♂		modus	further notes
A	S	dv and vv	inadequate personal observations (see additional notes of Lang)
K	S	dv and vv	couple separated: normally dv, rarely vv. couple in the group: normally dv and vv.
K	J	dv and vv	normally dv, vv very seldom. K does not offer herself to J in a variety of forms; J often takes the initiative by sitting behind her.
K	M	dv and vv	normally dv, M initially sits behind her or mounts her in a standing position; not all copulations seem to be accomplished; vv has only been observed in play context and K was the initiator in regard to the position.
G	J	dv	G normally offers herself by lying on her belly, therefore only dv positions occur.
G	M	dv	same as G/J

---

*There is also, according to Hess, a potent body odor associated with this period.

Figure 4-1. Ventro-ventral copulation posture of *Stefi* and *Kati* at Basel Zoo. *(J. P. Hess/ W. Angst photo)*

Figure 4-2. Dorso-ventral copulation. *(J. P. Hess/W. Angst photo)*

Figure 4-3. Dorso-ventral copulation. *(J. P. Hess/W. Angst photo)*

Figure 4-4. Awkward standing copulation posture of blackback male *Jambo* with female *Kati.* *(J. P. Hess/W. Angst photo)*

were successful in touching her, they responded by sniffing their fingers, indicating that it was these areas from which the strong odor was secreted.

During the estrus period (usually lasting about three days), the females *presented* in front of the adult male. At its most intense, these presentations and subsequent copulations occurred at 15-45 minute intervals. During one six-hour observation period, Hess counted a total of sixteen copulations.

Figure 4-5. Male-male mount at the Basel Zoo. Note *pursed lips* of *Stefi* (on top); *tense-lips* of *Jambo*. *(J. P. Hess/W. Angst photos)*

Presentations

Hess refers to this behavior as *inviting* and *offering*. *Kati* was observed to first make a clear hand gesture to *Stefi:*

> Her arm is stretched out, suspended in the air or lying on the floor, and is directed at S, the palm facing upwards. K's eyes always rest upon S. If S alters his position, K changes the direction of her eyes and arm accordingly.

Figure 4-6. Side view of *pursed lips* and *tense lips* facial expressions.

In some cases K touches S's forearm with her extended hand or even takes hold of him and pulls him slightly towards her. This gesture of invitation, with variations, has only been observed in Kati. It occurs in all forms of her offering behaviour (p. 540).

The extended arm with open hand has also been observed within the context of play in young gorillas (Hess, 1973) and other apes (cf. Maple and Zucker, 1978). Both Schaller (1963) and Fossey (1971) have observed similar behavior which apparently mediates contact in mountain gorillas.

Hess recorded two basic positions in which offering occurred: (1) the cowering, crouching, or prone position; (2) the supine position. In the former, the female generally orients her back toward the male. The stance resembled the presentation posture of chimpanzees except that the anogenital region is not elevated. In the second category, the female lays on her back and makes *rhythmic pelvic movements*. The hand is often extended in this position. About these pelvic movements, Hess explained:

> The activity may function as a stimulating signal for the males and probably as a surrogate for copulation. If S fails to join K, she continues these movements for quite a long time and then stops abruptly. Subsequently she reacts in the same way as after copulation (p. 543).

Among Basel gorillas, the mean duration of copulation was calculated at 52.5 seconds. A typical copulation was found to be composed of three to six sequences, with 30-60 thrusts. The rate of thrusting was calculated at about 2.4 per second. Facial and vocal expressions which characterize copulation have been described in Chapter 3.

Hess discovered that copulations at Basel were often preceded by mutual chasing. This was particularly true of instances when the adult pair were separated from the others. The female was found to be especially aggressive during such times.* In general, it can be said that among captive gorillas, females typically take the initiative in sexual interactions.

---

*An example of the manner in which zoo lore can be in conflict with scientific data is illustrated by the following assertions from Campbell (1978):

> Among gorillas particularly, well brought up young ladies learn the obedience and acquiescence to the will of their master that turns male gorillas on. Feminists can make of this what they will, but according to many knowledgeable observers, hand-raised female gorillas usually develop an independent nature which, when they are out with their own kind, leads them to believe they can willfully reject an amorous male. In a gorilla group there is no room for disdainful females (p. 148).

> Campbell is correct, however, in recognizing the overall dominance of males over females (cf. Chapter 1).

Labial Tumescence

Nadler (1975) recently investigated the variation in labial tumescence, essentially verifying the observations of Noback (1939) who recorded the linear dimension of the urogenital cleft of a female gorilla. Noback discovered that, through his subject's first eight menstrual cycles, the cleft consistently varied from 1-4 centimeters in size.

As Nadler pointed out, other observers have reported no detectable genital swelling among their animals (e. g., Thomas, 1958; Lang, 1959; Reed and Gallagher, 1963). These same authors have reported female gorilla cycle lengths based on copulations. Prior to Nadler's report, cycle lengths, using both genital swelling and periodic copulations, had been reported as ranging from 30-39 days.

Nadler used several methods to assess cyclical labial tumescence in his gorilla population. The initial methods, which were found to result in wide variability across individuals, involved noting the visibility to the observer of the pink labial mucosa. Two measurement techniques were used to assess swelling while the gorilla stood quadrupedally with its anogenital area facing the observer. The final, and recommended (by Nadler) method,* involved training the gorillas to climb the front of the cage and squat on their haunches while grasping the upper portions of the cage with extended arms.** This squatting position effectively exposed the labia in a uniform manner, allowing the technician to accurately measure the linear dimension of the urogenital cleft.†

Nadler found, using all three measurement techniques, a range of cyclic labial swelling approaching 31-32 days.†† This is considerably shorter than the thirty-nine days reported by Noback, but coincides with the copulation reports of female gorilla cycles. Nadler further reported that female receptivity in his subjects was largely confined to the days of labial tumescence.

---

*Nadler (1975) has included a photograph of a gorilla in this position while a technician measures labial tumescence with reference to a calibrated wire scale.

**Hoff, under the direction of Nadler, undertook to retrain female gorillas to assume this position after an abstinence of more than a year. Although ultimately successful in coaxing all three females to mount the fence, the course of retraining was, at best, trying. The method found to facilitate performance was one of successive approximations to the desired position, with each approximation rewarded by a favored food, typically orange slices. This gradual shaping led the animals to climb the fence, and to ultimately squat in the appropriate manner. The entire course of retraining took from one week for the female *Shamba* to approximately three months for the female *Segou*. All three females had their infants with them, and the reticence to mount the fence may well have been due to a protective response of keeping the infants at a distance from human observers.

†Nadler (personal communication) has since modified his measurement technique to include such measures as the width of the cleft, degree of pink color, and the presence or absence of mucus.

††A gorilla of the *graueri* subspecies (erroneously labeled "mountain" gorilla in the publication) at the Antwerp Zoo was found to exhibit a mean estrous cycle length of 33.24 days (n = 17 cycles).

While labial measurement is probably unnecessary for gorillas that regularly copulate, it would prove most useful to determine the onset of cycling in young animals, or to determine whether a female is cycling in the case of noncopulating pairs.

Hormonal Correlates

The sexual behavior of four male and nine female lowland gorillas was described in a 1976 paper by Nadler. Conducted at the Yerkes Primate Research Center, the animals were tested on a daily basis whereby a female was introduced into a male's cage for at least a 30-minute period. Nadler's three-year study produced 2000 tests of sexual behavior. An examination of the data revealed that copulations occurred in only 7% of the tests, and that pairs of animals varied considerably in their performance. For example, some pairs never copulated. As Nadler asserted, the variation in sexual behavior may have reflected individual partner preferences. Moreover, in line with their species-typical characteristics (cf. Hess, 1973), Nadler suggested that the females were the most likely source of partner selection, recognizing of course that the male also exerted some degree of influence.

In an analysis of those pairs in which copulations did occur, and normal female hormonal cyclicity was evident, Nadler discovered that as female labial tumescence increased, copulations were more likely. Furthermore, male ejaculations were more probable in the tumescent phase. In these gorillas, copulations typically occurred on four days per menstrual cycle. Males emitted from 2–346 thrusts per copulation, about 30 per bout in a typical interaction. Two patterns of thrusting were identified, labeled *continuous* and *discontinuous* by Nadler. In the first instance, thrusting was relatively constant, while in the second mode a series of thrusts was typically interrupted by positional adjustments. With both patterns ejaculation was observed.

Nadler also detected *cooing* vocalizations* before, during, and after copulations in both males and females. A sex difference in calling was manifest primarily in its characteristic duration. A low, guttural roar, idiosyncratic to one male, occurred only when he ejaculated. As Nadler further discovered, males vocalized more frequently than females in association with sexual activity. Both males and females vocalized more frequently during ejaculations as compared to incomplete copulations.

Male gorillas are capable of multiple ejaculations as indicated by Nadler's data. The Yerkes males experienced a delay of four to forty-two minutes (md = 15 min.) between successive ejaculations. While most males ejaculated only once per

---

*This "cooing like a dove" vocalization was also noted in the publication of Lotshaw (1971).

test, one of them ejaculated four times on one occasion, and three times on three other tests.

In Nadler's experiments, gorillas copulated in both the dorso-ventral and ventro-ventral mode. Approximately 80% of the copulations and 74% of the ejaculations occurred in the dorso-ventral posture. However, the data also suggest that particular gorillas may exhibit position preferences.

Nadler concluded that, among the apes, sexual behavior was most rigidly regulated in the gorilla. Nevertheless, experiential factors clearly influenced the propensity to mate. Moreover, the variability in the mode of copulation reflects the greater degree of flexibility in the behavior of this big-brained ape as compared to many other mammals.

Responses to Copulation

The interest in copulation by other animals has been well documented for chimpanzees (cf. Tutin, 1975) and other primates (cf. de Benedictis, 1973; Maple, 1977). Hess found that in the Basel gorillas, there was variation in the response to copulation according to sex and age. For example, the 24-year-old female *Achilla* responded to copulations with hostility:

> As a rule she tries to intervene, coughing aggressively, as soon as S copulates with K. She usually either advances on them with a strutting run and endeavors to tear K away or, if the pair is copulating on a platform, she tries to grab K's arms, jumping from below, and pull her down . . . It is obvious that the cause of her aggression . . . lies in S's intimacy with K (p. 573).

By contrast, the 3½-year-old offspring *Quarta* exhibited great interest in copulations and repeatedly attempted to touch the genitalia of the pair. Clearly, adult copulations were arousing to *Quarta* often instigating playful responses, including play-copulations.

The two young males at Basel, *Jambo*** and *Migger*, were also aroused in the presence of adult copulations. *Jambo* frequently attempted to copulate with the adult female *Kati*. However, *Kati's* interest was focused only on the fully adult *Stefi*. The following account is especially interesting:

> . . . it seems as though S's sexual motivation is increased by J's activity. On S's approach K walks away, leaving J sitting or standing . . . Moreover, I have observed K inviting S with a gesture of her hand, while copulating with J (p. 574).

---

*Somewhat later *Jambo* became famous as the captive-born sire of many offspring at the Jersey Zoo.

Both young males followed the consort pair and attempted to touch them during copulations. After touching them, especially in their genital region, they invariably sniffed their hands. As Hess explained:

Towards the middle and the end of a copulation phase the touching becomes more obtrusive and often causes great disturbance. Frequently, they try to tear S and K apart; they pass the pair with a strutting run and hit them or hurl themselves at K at full speed (pp. 574–575).

Incompatability

Perhaps more than in any other nonhuman primate, heterosexual pairs of gorillas have frequently experienced the problem of incompatibility. This has occurred even when animals have been matched according to knowledgable accounts of their respective "personalities." With so few gorillas remaining in captivity, incompatability is likely to frequently recur as a barrier to successful reproduction.

In the literature, there exists one report which discusses the problem in reasonable detail. Hardin, Danford, and Skeldon (1969) described the courtship of *Togo* and *Porta* which arrived as a pair at the Toledo Zoo in 1957. As the authors noted, the young gorillas "got along" while *Porta* was dominant. However, after the emergence of his canine teeth, *Togo* gradually asserted himself. The male's aggression increased to such a level that it eventually became necessary to provide separate quarters for each of them. Nevertheless, prior to their separation, mating frequently occurred. In each instance, however, mating was followed by *Togo's* attack on *Porta*.

After their separation, attempts to reunite the pair for mating always resulted in vicious attacks. Given these circumstances, it was decided to employ the tranquilizer *Mellaril*. As the investigators explained:

The pills were taken but were spat out as soon as the coating was licked off. Both forms of the drug were tried in various vehicles; the tablets were ground and then mixed in Pablum and milk, grape syrup, corn syrup or honey. Honey proved to be the most acceptable vehicle and Togo would take it from a spoon (p. 85).

The effects of the drug on *Togo* included the cessation of running about the cage and hitting the glass. Moreover, *Togo* did not exhibit the tight-lip expression when under the influence of the drug. After several successful introductions while drugged, *Togo* was united with *Porta* during an estrous period. He was administered 125 milligrams of *Mellaril* in syrup at 1600 hours on the day before the introduction. The next morning he received 150 milligrams in pablum, of which he consumed less than half. After he was given another 75 milligrams (eating about two-thirds of it), he and *Porta* were put together. Mating took place without incident. The gorillas were separated upon completion of mating, and the same procedure was followed on the next three days. These matings resulted in a successful pregnancy, and *Porta* properly cared for her infant.

Tranquilizers,* if used in the proper dosage, appear to have considerable potential in the modification of aggression. Another potential tool in the reproductive effort is computer technology. Already there are basic data on gorillas in the ISIS** storage system at the Minnesota State Zoo. Similar data can be found in the gorilla studbook. When it becomes possible to estimate behavioral propensities, i. e., "personalities," it may be feasible to computer match gorillas for breeding exchanges. Behavioral data are likely to improve the chances of achieving a compatible pairing.

The serious degree to which incompatiability can be taken is illustrated by the Sacramento Zoo pair, *Kris* and *Suzie*. The two had lived together in a small enclosure since their arrival as infants in 1965. As they reached adulthood, they exhibited no inclination to mate, and they periodically engaged in severe bouts of fighting. An especially fierce fight occurred on February 8, 1980, and intensified during the next two days. The female's wounds were so serious that she was removed to the Davis (California) Veterinary Medical Hospital for care. Several days later she died from extensive hemorrhage in both lungs.

DIET

The relationship of diet to breeding was suggested in popular accounts of the reproductive success of gorillas at the Cincinnati Zoo. All of the breeding at Cincinnati (eleven births to 1978) took place after the introduction of a foodstuff called rice bread, originally developed when the male *King Tut* became allergic to wheat. In a personal communication, John Miller described the bread as a combination of rice, rice cereal, raisins, Karo syrup,† and vitamin supplements. Rice bread has since become a substitute for bread and monkey biscuits in the diet of all the Cincinnati gorillas. However compelling the dietary argument, Miller suggested that the Cincinnati successes were rather "a combination of compatibility, diet and luck." The overall good health of the gorillas, attributable in part to the rice bread, indirectly facilitated breeding according to Miller. If the "Cincinnati love diet" has anything at all to do with breeding success, other zoos should take notice. One daily helping of food for Cincinnati males is listed in Table 4-3 as communicated to us by Miller.

---

*However, Turner et al. (1966) attempted to induce copulation in isolation-reared adult chimpanzees by the use of various tranquilizing agents. In these severely deprived animals, the drugs were not the least bit effective.

**International Species Inventory System.

†Given their tendency to obesity in captivity, sweet substances must be considered a risky food additive.

In his 1978 letter, Miller made another observation of value to students of gorilla sexuality. The pair *Hatari* (male, age fifteen) and *Mahari* (female, age fifteen) arrived at the Cincinnati Zoo in 1966, *Mahari* conceiving at the age of six and one-half years. According to Miller's observations the wild-born *Mahari* exhibits no cyclicity in her sexual behavior, copulating at any time during the month. Furthermore, copulations were observed a mere two weeks before she gave birth to her third infant.

THE MALE FERTILITY PROBLEM

Upon electro-ejaculation, a nineteen-year-old male lowland gorilla at the Brookfield Zoo was recently found to be sterile. Prior to the test, this animal had sired two offspring and had no history of serious illness. Dr. Ben Beck, the Curator of Research, subsequently attempted to locate a replacement, and in the process discovered that their problem was common to many other zoos. In response to this, Beck (1980) distributed a questionnaire to fifty-one North American zoos and primate centers which maintained lowland gorillas. At the time that he issued his report, forty-three institutions had responded by completing the questionnaire.*

In the forty-three institutions that responded to Beck's questionnaire, there were fifty-seven adult males in residence (defined as nine years of age or older). The mean age of these animals was computed to be 18.0 years. Eighteen of these were from 9–14 years of age, twenty-two were from 15–19, 6 from 20–24, and

Table 4-3. Daily diet for adult male lowland gorillas at the Cincinnati Zoo (From Miller, personal communication).**

---

3 cooked white potatoes
3 cooked sweet potatoes
4 raw carrots
7 bananas
1 hard-boiled egg
1 head lettuce
2 oranges
1/2 stalk celery
10 green beans
1 bunch grapes
1/2 pound cooked meat
8 pounds rice bread
2 apples

---

*Distributed thereafter as an unpublished report.
**Females get the same food in lesser quantities.

eleven were at least 25 years of age. Of the fifty-seven males, fifty were housed with mature females at some time or other in 1978 and 1979. Thirty of these animals copulated with intromission, according to the results of the questionnaire. However, only eleven of these males sired offspring in these years. When all institutions were considered, less than fifteen males reproduced in North American zoos in 1978 and 1979 combined. As Beck pointed out:

This seems not to result from lack of access to females, although not all female cagemates may have been fertile. Many males simply do not copulate, and less than half of those that do copulate have conceived in the last two years.

By comparing birth data for the years 1978 and 1979 (potentially underestimated due to the nonrespondent figures) to the previous seven years (1970–77), Beck determined that the encouraging increases up to 1975 have been followed by a disturbing reversal. Beck does not attribute this to changes in management policies. In fact, he asserts emphatically that "there has been a decrease in gorilla fertility in North America over the past four years." Whether the problem resides with males, females, or both is uncertain.

According to Beck, electro-ejaculation studies by Kenneth Gould, Stephen Seager, and C. J. Hardin have determined that twelve of twenty-two electro-ejcaculated gorillas were classified as sterile or highly suspect. As Beck concluded, organic infertility appears to be common among male gorillas.

Beck additionally asserted that males are maximally potent between the ages of nine and fourteen, when they produce the most young, although the later decline may have been due to female changes in fertility. Since there was no significant difference in the ages of fertile and sterile males, Beck urged that an evaluation of female fertility also be conducted.

To explain the findings, Beck hypothesized that environmental pollutants, viral disease, obesity, and repeated medication may be factors contributing to the effect. As Beck summarized the problem:

A declining birth rate, the failure of 80% of adult males to reproduce in the past two years, demonstrated organic sterility in a substantial proportion of adult males, and the inferential suggestion of widespread female sterility all indicate that there is a very real and a very serious fertility problem.

A problem with Beck's analysis is that as a gorilla breeding pair or group gets older, there is an increased probability that the female will raise her own offspring. Thus, early in their reproductive lives, if infants don't survive or are removed to nurseries, birth intervals are shorter. No wonder then that an adult male sires more young in his early reproductive life. One must also take into

Figure 4-7. Presentation posture of female *Kati* at Basel Zoo. *(J. P. Hess/W. Angst photo)*

Figure 4-8. Blackback male *Jambo* touches genitals of silverback *Stefi* at Basel Zoo. *(J. P. Hess/W. Angst photo)*

Figure 4-9. Basel female *Kati* touches genitals of silverback male *Stefi. (J. P. Hess/W. Angst photos).*

Figure 4-10. Basel infant *Quarta* touches the genitals of her mother *Achilla. (J. P. Hess/ W. Angst photos).*

Table 4-4. Reproductive data on the two female gorillas in the Jersey Collection (After Martin, 1977).

1. ♀ N'PONGO (M1)

Pregnancy Number	Date of Birth	Details of Offspring	Age at Conception	Age of Male at Conception	Inter-birth Interval	Date of last Mating	Likely Date of Conception	Gestation Period
1	11.9.73	♂MAMFE hand-reared	15y	11y	–	18.12.72 to 20.12.72	18.12.72 to 20.12.72	265–267d[1]
2	29.1.75	♂TATU hand-reared	17y	13y	505d	15.5.74	15.5.75	259d[1]
3	11.4.76	♂KUMBA hand-reared	18y	14y	438d	17.8.75	17.8.75	249d
4	21.6.77	♂N'GOLA mother-reared	19y	15y	435d	?	6.10.76[2]	259d

2. ♀NANDI (M2)

Pregnancy Number	Date of Birth	Details of Offspring	Age at Conception	Age of Male at Conception	Inter-birth Interval	Date of last Mating	Likely Date of Conception	Gestation Period
1	14.7.73	♂ASSUMBO hand-reared	14y	11y	–	18.10.72 to 19.10.72	18.10.72 to 19.10.72	269–270d[1]
2	23.10.74	♀ZAIRE hand-reared	16y	13y	466d	13.2.74[3]	29.1.74 to 30.1.74 (penultimate mating)	267–268d[1]
3	31.10.75	♀BAMENDA hand-reared	17y	13y	373d	17.12.74	?	?
4	14.1.77	♂-stillborn	18y	15y	441d	8.6.76[3]	mid-April 1976[3]	275d± 3 weeks[4]
5	29.11.77	spontaneous abortion of early foetus	19y	16y	(319d)	9.11.77[3]	not before end of July 1977	(maximum of 121d)

(1) data from Mallinson et al., 1976.

(2) estimated from oestrus dates in July, August and September 1976

(3) almost certainly dates of mating during pregnancy.

(4) estimate based on hormonal evidence.

consideration the greater willingness of institutions to permit mother-rearing. Thus, if a female raises the infant, she will not resume ovulating for at least three years. The statistics given in Beck's paper can therefore be interpreted in a different manner. As a general rule, zoos that successfully raise gorillas (with their parents) will experience a decline in birth rate.

We do not mean to diminish the central argument, however, since early sterility does appear to be a genuine problem. It is tempting to suggest that the stress of captivity may be affecting sperm production. To check this, researchers should electro-ejaculate free-ranging lowland gorillas, or gorillas that are living in less restrictive surroundings; e. g., the gorillas at *Apenheul* in the Netherlands. If a link were to be found, this would be another example of the complicated way that the environment affects behavior.

The literature which we have just reviewed indicates that the gorilla is an animal strongly influenced by the effects of circulating hormones. Yet members of this taxon also exercise intangible partner preferences for reasons known only to themselves. Characterized by most human investigators as the *least sexual* of the great apes, gorillas nonetheless engage in courtship and copulation in an efficient manner. Perhaps it is their great size which dictates this efficiency. It is very likely that the critical variables which largely determine their mode and schedule of interaction are to be found in their feeding habits and unique form of social organization. As we learn more about all of the apes, their specialized characteristics may be more readily organized into a general pongid scheme.

5
Birth and Parental Behavior

The increased need for research into ways to prevent neonatal deaths, in developing intensive care units for nurseries (or nurseries themselves), and using behavioral engineering techniques to train both inexperienced mothers and hand-raised children in the habits of their own species—all of these will continue to impose a greater burden of cost on the modern major zoos. But the cost, most zoo directors agree, will have to be borne if they are to be successful as the last preserves for many endangered species.

Sheldon Campbell, 1978

In reviewing the published information regarding the birth process in gorillas, it is encouraging to note that impending birth is becoming easier to predict. This is particularly true when urine or blood is regularly sampled in the course of animal management. However, in many zoological parks, and, of course, in the field, such procedures are impractical. In the absence of a blood or urine testing program, it is still possible to monitor relevant physical and behavioral indicators. While there are no *well-tested* indicators currently available, we have assembled in Table 5-1 a list of factors which have been associated with pregnancy by a number of authorities. Taken together, these factors account for the astonishing intuition of many skilled keepers who often accurately predict the onset of pregnancy and birth in the animals under their care.

Signs of pregnancy seem to appear about two and one-half to three months prior to birth. Distention of the abdomen and swelling of the breasts are the most obvious physical signs. Stewart (1977) noted that in the wild, two of five pregnant mountain gorillas had enlarged nipples, and one exhibited swollen breasts three months before parturition.

The most reliable behavioral changes during pregnancy are increased *irritability* and *nervousness*. They sometimes show a decrease in activity as well. Stewart mentioned that four mountain gorillas became unusually aloof during pregnancy, three maintained greater distances from the group, and one ceased all play soon after conception.

Table 5-1. Factors associated with pregnancy in gorillas.

1. Lethargy	Rumbaugh, 1965; Hardin et al., 1969
2. Increasing restlessness	Hardin et al., 1969; Fisher, 1972; Nadler, 1975a; Stewart, 1977; Fossey, 1979.
3. Avoidance of cagemates (in late pregnancy)	Rumbaugh, 1965; Lotshaw, 1971; Clift and Martin, 1978.
4. Increased irritability	Reed and Gallagher, 1963; Frueh, 1968.
5. Increasing lack of appetite	Clift and Martin, 1978.
6. Increased water intake	Clift and Martin, 1978.
7. Change in distribution of activity peaks throughout the day (no longer strictly bimodal)	Clift and Martin, 1978.
8. Attention to breasts and perineal region	Nadler, 1975a.
9. Distancing from the group	Fossey, 1979.
10. Change in estrous activity (becoming erratic)	Stewart, 1977.
11. Decreased play with cagemates	Clift and Martin, 1978.

The length of gestation in gorillas is fraught with confusion. Fossey (1979) mentions eleven captive records ranging from 238 to 295 days. She lists a mean of 263 and a median of 258. Unfortunately, she does not provide a frequency distribution for the determination of a modal interval. In her own observations of feral gorillas, copulations were observed from 212 to 289 days prior to parturition, appearing clumped at about the 260th day.

Stewart (1977) has pointed out that continued mating during pregnancy was not unusual among the wild mountain gorillas that she studied. In captivity, mating may occur at least through the first 6 months of pregnancy (cf. Hess, 1973; Nadler, 1975). As Stewart observed:

During the present study, four out of five pregnant females were seen copulating during pregnancy. One of these animals was observed mating about a week before she gave birth. She had several sexual interactions with other females throughout her pregnancy, one of which also occurred about a week before parturition. Such encounters consisted of embracing and thrusting in either ventro-ventral or dorso-ventral positions (p. 970).

If we can refer to these periodic sexual encounters by pregnant gorillas as estrous activity, as Stewart has done, then it is clear that estrous periods are erratic during pregnancy. Since other authorities agree that pregnancy affects the length of these interestrous periods, evidence of such change may be taken as an indicator of pregnancy (Stewart, 1978).

An estimate of seasonality, 1967-1974, has been recently calculated by Fossey (1979). Although births occurred throughout the year, she discovered a peak between July and August and a trough between September and December. Food resources apparently remain constant in the environment of the mountain gorilla and therefore are an unlikely influence on birth season. However, Fossey did find that the birth peak coincided with the dry season. Since feral gorillas are often sick during the wet season, there may be an advantage to births which occur in the drier months. Although Schaller (1963) found no convincing evidence for a breeding season, there was a trend to more summer births.

In the wild, infant mortality is high in the first year of life, 23% as estimated by Schaller. Within the first six years of life, mortality ranges between 25% (Fossey) and 40-50% (Schaller). Some mortality during the years of Fossey's research has been traced to violent encounters with lone silverbacks or a subgroup of gorillas. Three infants are known to have died from such causes. Both Schaller and Fossey reported that after infants died, mothers sometimes carried their bodies.

PERINATAL BEHAVIOR

An informative description of the events surrounding the first gorilla birth at the San Diego Zoo has been provided by Rumbaugh (1965). The pregnancy of *Vila* was indicated by changes in her behavior (cf. Table 5-1); she became less active outside, less inclined to interact with the other gorillas, less tolerant of contacts, more reclusive, and, using Rumbaugh's terms "temperamentally flat."

Although *Vila* handled her infant awkwardly at first, she exhibited increased proficiency within an hour after birth. The infant itself was vigorous and responsive to its mother. However, because of signs of weakness on the part of the infant and its failure to nurse, Zoo authorities reluctantly elected to remove the infant about twelve hours after its birth. *Vila* nonetheless exhibited good potential as a mother.

> . . . Vila, basically naive to infants of all kinds was potentially an excellent mother. Never once did she inflict harm upon her baby, and throughout the hours which followed delivery she became increasingly effective in handling and caring for it (p. 17).

Birth of a Feral Mountain Gorilla

The birth of a wild mountain gorilla was observed by Stewart (1977). This valuable account included details regarding the mother's behavior prior to the birth, the responses of other group members, and early mother-infant interactions. As Stewart stated, a visible birth among wild apes is an unusual event since most births apparently occur at night* (cf. Brandt and Mitchell, 1971). Moreover, since mountain gorillas only give birth once every three to five years, the probability of the observer being in the right place at the right time is dismally low. It is not surprising, therefore, that nearly all of our information about gorilla births is from captive accounts.

The observations pertaining to this birth were made by Stewart on December 3, 1975 at the *Parc des Volcans* in the Virunga Volcano region of Rwanda. The female under study, *Marchessa*, lived in a typical gorilla group composed of twelve individuals. *Marchessa* had two known offspring, *Pantsy*, a primiparous female with a two-month-old infant of her own, and the juvenile male, *Siz*, four years and nine months of age at the time of the study.

Curiously, *Marchessa's* appearance and behavior remained relatively unchanged during her pregnancy. According to Stewart, her abdomen and breasts appeared to be no larger than they had prior to conception. However, because of the normally large abdomens of mountain gorillas, Stewart considers abdominal changes to be a poor indicator of pregnancy. Prior to parturition, *Marchessa* traveled with the group, did not lag behind and apparently showed no signs of pain.

At the onset of labor, *Marchessa* began to finally exhibit restlessness. She often shifted her position, hastily constructed a nest, and began to alternately touch her perineum and lick her fingers. Somewhat later, she abandoned her blood-stained nest and made another. Amid some further movement and grunting she then assumed a squatting position, and reaching beneath her legs delivered the infant. At the emergence of the infant, which was initially held in a low *v-v* position, several group members approached her. She departed, out of sight of the observer, and did not return for 40 minutes. Since there were no signs of blood, fluid, or tissue on her lips, and no sign of the umbilical cord, little could be said about her manner of cleaning the infant.

The greatest interest in the birth was exhibited by the subadult male *Puck* who approached *Marchessa* and peered intently at the newborn infant. *Marchessa's* daughter, *Pantsy*, and a young silverback *Icarus* also approached, but *Marchessa* withdrew and briefly scuffled with them before disappearing in the brush.

At the next sighting of the infant, 42 minutes after its birth, its eyes were open, and it was gripping its mother's arm, flexing its fingers, and moving its mouth. Stewart's description of *Marchessa's* early handling of the infant is worth quoting here:

> Right after parturition when *Marchessa* left the birth site, she supported the infant in her left arm, with her hand under its head, holding it away from her body in a loose ventro-ventral position. The newborn's arms were held out in

---

*Fossey (1979) asserted that an advantage of night births (most mountain gorilla births are believed to occur at night) is that with the group inactive, the parturient female will not be left behind. Interestingly, in captivity, less than 30% of reported births occurred at night, while most occurred in the morning.

front of it, crooked at the elbow but not touching *Marchessa* . . . Over the next 32 minutes, she held the baby close to her ventrum in a high dorso-ventral position. The infant lay belly-down on her arm with its head turned outwards most of the time (p. 969).

Marchessa also groomed the infant, using her lips and bent forefinger. Stewart estimated that, during the thirty-seven minutes that they were observed subsequent to *Marchessa's* reappearance, at least 27% of the observation time was spent grooming the infant. Prior to the end of observations, the infant was held away from *Marchessa's* body, presumably for inspection. When the infant whimpered and emitted three high-pitched squeals, the mother made a belch vocalization and turned the infant to a ventro-ventral position with its head positioned next to her left breast.

Marchessa's labor was rapid and easy, as appears to be the case in the majority of recorded captive births. In discussing the stages of parturition, Stewart observed that there were essentially three stages as follows:

1. From the onset of contractions to the first appearance of the infant.
2. From the infant's first appearance to its complete emergence.
3. From the delivery of the infant to the complete emergence of the placenta.

The first two stages generally last from 30–150 minutes. These are the periods of typical restlessness and discomfort, during which time mothers are observed to strain and contract their muscles. Stage one is marked by the investigation of birth fluids by touching the perineum and licking and smelling the fingers. The second stage does not generally exceed 30 minutes, and is usually much shorter, often only a few minutes in duration. As the infant's head emerges, the mother typically reaches back and "guides" it through the birth canal.

The third stage of labor generally last from 10–30 minutes. The consumption of the placenta should not be considered a part of the actual birth process in gorillas according to Stewart. She noted that, although Brandt and Mitchell (1971) stated that most gorillas suck and nibble but do not eat the placenta, there is some evidence that wild mountain gorillas do consume it. This propensity must be considered incompletely verified and worthy of further investigation.

As Stewart and others have suggested, postnatal maternal behavior seems to progress from the early licking of the neonate to more advanced contact such as pushing or pulling the infant along the ground, picking it up and holding it out for visual inspection, and dorso-ventral contact. This progression culminates in appropriate ventro-ventral contact and prolonged suckling. It is the coordination of maternal positioning of the infant on the ventrum in response to reflexive grasping and vocalizing by the infant that results in nursing.

Among feral mountain gorillas, the evidence currently suggests that juveniles of both sexes and subadult females are the animals most attracted to newborns. As Stewart further argued:

> The attraction of immature animals to parturition, birth by-products, and neonates might simply be curiosity, i.e., the behaviour associated with novelty, typical of young primates. However, the fact that sub-adult females show greater interest than do male immatures suggests that some of their responses are related to maternal behaviour rather than curiosity (p. 972).

This argument is, of course, similar to the view that primates learn by paying attention to complicated events. Thus, by observational learning the acquisition of appropriate mating responses is facilitated. Maternal skills may be similarly transmitted through observation, although it must be considered only one of several ways in which these necessary skills are acquired.

In addition to this pure observation, Nadler (1974a) has demonstrated that prior experience contributes to the development of appropriate maternal skills. Stewart asserted that maternal experience was an important factor for wild gorillas as well:

> A primiparous female about one week postpartum handled her newborn clumsily, and the infant often whimpered while being transported. This was not noted in observations of multipara (p. 973).

In concluding her report, Stewart further discussed the importance of compensating for insufficient mothering. Noting that many captive gorillas arrived as infants in their first year or two of life, their later deficiencies as mothers may be due to deficiencies in their own early rearing history. The evidence indicates that while peer experience promotes normal development, this condition is not *optimal* in terms of complexity. In those instances where an inexperienced or previously ineffective mother is about to give birth, it may be useful to leave the animal in the group.* Maple (1980a) has argued this point elsewhere with respect to captive orang-utans. Stewart considers this to be important for gorillas as well, and expands upon our statement as follows:

> Maternal care might also improve if the females were caged with other animals. Nadler cites three occasions when mothers' mistreatment of their newborns was interpreted as resulting from "boredom." The abuse stopped when other

---

*According to a survey conducted by Keiter and Pichette (1979), thirty-four of forty-nine pregnant females in twenty-four institutions were isolated from their mates/group prior to delivery.

animals were moved into the cages. It is suggested here that these mothers were showing protective responses toward their infants because of the close proximity of other animals, in the same way that wild gorillas were observed to do. The close presence of conspecifics, particularly inquisitive immatures, might result, through protective responses in the mother, in the maintenance of closer mother-infant contact and, therefore, might facilitate the development of maternal care in captive animals (p. 974).

Birth of a Captive Lowland Gorilla

A 1974 report by Nadler is the most detailed description of the parturitional behavior of a lowland gorilla in captivity. In his introduction, Nadler identified two primary factors which made earlier accounts less useful to behavioral scientists. First, most gorilla births have occurred in zoos, where few personnel have been trained to "make systematic observations of behavior." The second factor is that most infants have been separated from their mothers shortly after birth. The first problem would have been a relatively easy matter to remedy. If zoos had earlier embraced research by establishing in-house programs, trained personnel could have been appointed to staff positions. This is now happening in many zoos. The simple addition of a video-tape system would, of course, greatly facilitate the acquisition of behavioral data. In the absence of an in-house research program, nearby universities can be employed in cooperative programs.*

The second problem, the early separation of mother and infant, is also a subject that we have discussed at some length elsewhere (cf. Maple, 1980a; Maple, Wilson, Zucker and Wilson, 1978). In fact, we would argue that had systematic observations of mother and infant been routinely carried out, many early separations could have been avoided. Thus, an active research program yields many benefits for the institution that supports it.

In Nadler's paper, the birth and first twenty-seven hours thereafter were described for the first gorilla born at the Yerkes Regional Primate Research Center. The mother was a primiparous female named *Paki.* Her offspring, born at 23 hours on August 7, 1972, was subsequently named *Kishina.* At the time of conception, *Paki* weighed 73.1 kilograms. She lost 6 kilograms during January-February, but steadily gained weight thereafter to a level of 79.7 kilograms in July. Within a 36-hour period postpartum, *Paki* lost 2.3 kilograms and within one month thereafter lost an additional 4 kilograms. The early weight loss

---

*Our research team has successfully established liaison between the Sacramento Zoo/ University of California, Davis, and the Atlanta Zoo/Emory University/Georgia Institute of Technology. Moreover, our program has received cooperation from personnel at various other zoos such as the San Diego Zoo, New Orleans Zoo, Oakland Zoo, and Los Angeles Zoo. To do research on the many rare or poorly described events which occur every day at a zoological park requires only creativity, enthusiasm, patience and, of course, cooperation. Behavioral research in zoo settings is rarely expensive.

recorded by the Yerkes staff coincides with an early symptom of pregnancy, loss of appetite, as illustrated in Table 5-1.

The first signs of *Paki's* impending labor, as reported by Jimmy Roberts (Superintendent of the Yerkes great ape facility) were restlessness and agitation. These factors are reminiscent of those reported by Stewart. *Paki* frequently changed her position from reclining to sitting to pacing. Moreover, the presence of a mucous discharge was detected, minimally visible in *Paki's* vulvar region. There were also signs of muscular tension. Nadler's superb photographic record, as portrayed in his 1974 paper, documents the emergence of the newborn and the postures assumed by the mother as the birth proceeded. Characteristic of *Paki's* behavior at this time was her repeated touching of her vulva and licking of her fingers. Her typical posture was to recline on her forearms and knees, side or back. The delivery occurred while she was positioned on one side. Of importance was the cautiousness of the mother during the first minutes after birth, a time in which she did not immediately establish contact with the infant. In ignoring the infant, *Paki* was preoccupied with the consumption of the excess blood and birth fluids. As Nadler noted, however, she soon returned to the infant, touching and manipulating it, and subsequently licking from her hands the additional birth debris.* To further illustrate this process, a direct quote from the author is appropriate:

> Although her initial handling of the infant appeared hesitant and cautious, she gradually began to manipulate the infant more intensively, including close examination of, and eventual mouthing and licking the umbilical cord and placenta and various parts of the infant's body. The head of the infant was the portion of its body that was licked most frequently, while the genital area did not receive notable attention (p. 58).

Nadler suggested that contact with the birth fluids facilitated early contact with the infant. Postnatal licking was therefore proposed as a mechanism that "facilitates the initial development of a social bond between the female and her firstborn." *Paki* neither severed the umbilical cord nor ate the placenta. Six hours after birth the placenta and cord detached, apparently due to the effects of dragging it about the cage.

During the first five minutes after birth, the infant was transported by sliding or pushing it along the floor. After five minutes had elapsed, *Paki* began to carry

---

*It is not known whether the reported early neglect of the infant while consuming birth debris is characteristic of feral gorilla births. As previously discussed in Stewart's observations, the female left the observer's sight with her infant almost immediately after the birth. As will be recalled, however, when the mother and infant reappeared some 40 minutes later, there were no visible signs of birth debris, this indicating that the mother did clean herself and the infant at some point.

the infant in one hand but *away* from her body. This behavior was replaced by appropriate ventral support, which first emerged in the second five-minute interval after birth. The erratic progress of this important maternal behavior is best illustrated in Nadler's own words as follows:

> . . . after the mother had cleaned and licked the infant rather thoroughly she picked it up with both hands and pressed it high on her chest and wrapped both her arms around it. That act occurred more and more frequently after the first 30 minutes and was the predominant position of contact observed by the end of the first hour (p. 61).

A dorso-ventral support position was also observed in which the infant was held with its back contiguous to *Paki's* ventrum. The ventro-ventral position was the preferred position once it had become established. *Paki* held her offspring in either a high or low position, the former being associated with the onset of nursing. Prolonged nursing was not observed until the second day of life. Another factor associated with the onset of nursing, according to Nadler, was reciprocal vocalization. While the mother first responded to infant vocalizations by growling, she subsequently responded by readjusting the infant's position. Infant search/suck behaviors also apparently influenced maternal readjustments.

In a brief examination of the infant, it was found to weigh 2.04 kilograms. It's foot and grasp reflexes were strong as measured by the test of Riesen and Kinder (1952). As Nadler indicated, at thirty-six hours postpartum, *Kishina* was able to support her weight with a one-handed grasp for three minutes, five seconds. She could hang suspended by one foot for only eight seconds.

Unfortunately, the infant eventually had to be separated from its mother due to a mistreatment "crisis." Clues to the probable sources of this mistreatment can be found in Nadler's description of previous indications of trouble:

> During the week prior to separation two similar crises occurred and were ameliorated; first by moving a female cage-mate of the mother to the cage adjoining the maternity cage, and then, by transferring the mother back to her original cage in the gorilla area. The first measure was taken three days postpartum and temporarily terminated a short period of agitation displayed by the mother. When the mother again became restless on the following day, she and the infant were moved to the mother's original cage where they resumed their harmonious interaction until four days later when the final crises developed (p. 67).

As Nadler pointed out, despite the emergence of mistreatment, Paki's early maternal behavior was adequate and appropriate. This is especially notable in view of the fact that she was obtained from the wild at about one year of age and raised with a peer. Thus, *Paki* had not interacted with or observed any socially experienced conspecifics since her removal from the wild. Nadler argued further that his observations provided evidence against the view that "extensive learning experiences prior to first deliveries, are necessary in higher primates to ensure adequate care and nurturing of firstborns (p. 67)."

This point requires elaboration. First, Rogers and Davenport's (1969) chimpanzee research indicated that female offspring with 18 months of normal parental care were likely to be good mothers later in life. *Paki* had received close to, if not an equivalent amount of such care. Moreover, by living with a peer, and interacting almost daily with other young gorillas in a play yard, *Paki* was acquiring a considerable degree of social experience. Thus "extensive learning experiences" were possible in an environment of peers. Harlow (1971) found as much with rhesus monkeys whereby peer experience adequately compensated for experience with a mother. Clearly, as Maple (1980a) has argued elsewhere, the development of adequate and appropriate maternal behavior is facilitated when input is received from a variety of sources; e.g., physical contact with adults, play with peers, observation of experienced others, sufficient physical space, novel stimuli, etc. Nadler is correct to state that "little experience with other births" is necessary for the acquisition of maternal behaviors. However, experience gained through interactions with other age-classes, either through observation or practice (e.g., aunting) *does* contribute something to the emerging maternal repertoire. Again, we must emphasize, it appears to be of paramount importance that apes be raised in *stimulating* surroundings if they are to be socially successful. Whether they interact with parents, peers, or people is probably less important than the requirement that they regularly receive social stimulation through all sensory channels. In this sense, adequate maternal behavior is more likely as learning experiences increase in both *complexity* and *quantity*. Increased experience with respect to one factor may compensate for deficiencies in another.

Additionally, as Nadler recognized, conditions of captivity appear to exacerbate maternal inadequacy. In particular, isolation of the mother seems to be associated with abuse, and efforts to socially modify mistreatment have shown some promise of success.

Nadler, like Stewart, found that separate stages in the birth process could be discerned. Stage one was about two and one-half hours in duration from the onset of observable labor pains (restlessness, grimacing, straining and bearing down, twitching of leg muscles, grasping of cage bars) to the complete dilation of the cervix. Stage two, from dilation to delivery, lasted only eighteen minutes. Paki's delivery was thus calculated at about three hours, comparable to the 1.5-2 hours as reported elsewhere (Rumbaugh, 1965; Fisher, 1972). Nadler further enumerated three minimal conditions which ensured the survival of the newborn gorilla:

1. The occurrence of initial contact between the mother and the infant, including those manipulations of the infant that may be necessary to enable it to breathe adequately.
2. The elaboration of that primitive state of contact to one that provides protection for the infant from the environment and also establishes the opportunity for feeding by the infant.
3. The commencement of nursing.

Maternal Competence

Nadler (1974b) surveyed ninety captive births of gorillas in order to evaluate the respective degrees of maternal competence. In this study, it was determined that more than 80% of all live-born infants had been separated from their mothers, many of these within the first week of life. For primipara, the primary reason for separation was maternal abuse or neglect. For multipara, most separations were carried out because of threat of injury or illness as indicated by prior experience. After one week of life with their mothers, infants were separated primarily because of mistreatment, injury, illness, or death.

As is the case with chimpanzees (cf. Davenport and Rogers, 1970), experienced mothers exhibited more adequate care than did inexperienced mothers. These

Figure 5-1. *Paki* and offspring *Kishina* at the Yerkes Primate Center. *(Photo courtesy Yerkes Regional Primate Research Center of Emory University)*

gorilla data mirrored the chimpanzee data in another way, as females exhibited a strong trend toward improvement in their maternal care with experience.

Nadler also discussed the interesting cases of the first two live-born captive gorillas, *Colo* and *Goma.* Separated from their mothers within thirty-six hours of birth, both were later housed with wild-born peers from the age of one and about two years respectively. When these animals reached sexual maturity, they successfully mated and delivered infants. *Colo* exhibited early signs of proper maternal care, but her first three infants were separated because of a fear of contracting tuberculosis. *Goma* properly raised her infant, the first *second-generation* captive-born gorilla.

Nadler pointed out that gorillas reared by their mothers in complex* social groups were more likely to develop appropriate maternal care. Peer-rearing, however, appeared to provide a degree of compensation for this complexity in animals separated from their mothers. As Nadler further asserted:

> The evidence available for primiparous females indicates that prior experience with births or with infant rearing by others is not necessary for the development of competent maternal behavior (p. 214).

Clift and Martin (1978) were uncertain about the generalization that the poor breeding record of captive gorillas was due to a lack of experience with infants in the context of a natural social group. As they pointed out:

> ... little attention has been paid to the possibility that in captivity certain factors differing from those in the natural environment (e.g., group composition, cage furniture, diet, unusual noise or other disturbance) might exert some *direct* influence on the mother's behavior, leading to infant rejection or later failure to rear (p. 165).

Recognizing the need for further research, Clift and Martin carefully studied a female lowland gorilla named *Lomie* which presumably had little "experience of infant rearing under natural conditions." The observations of *Lomie* were planned with the aim of: (1) identifying any features which might permit future assessment of impending birth, and (2) obtaining a detailed record of the success or failure of maternal behavior in the early stages. Clift observed *Lomie,* using a checklist to obtain frequencies of behavior. Data were acquired three weeks before the birth, during the twenty-three days that *Lomie* and her offspring were together, and for three weeks thereafter.

Clift and Martin found that as *Lomie's* pregnancy progressed, she exhibited frequent periods of lack of appetite. Moreover, she increased her water intake

---

*Additional factors which may be associated with adequate maternal care are the gradual improvements in the maintenance of captive gorillas, each of which is difficult to specify or define (cf. Chapter 7; Maple, 1979).

in the three weeks just prior to the birth as compared to levels during the three weeks after the infant's removal. Surprisingly, zoo staff reported that *Lomie* became less playful and less friendly to her juvenile male cagemate only one month after conception. She also reportedly rested more, but these were subjective impressions. Clift and Martin found it somewhat difficult to characterize some of the behaviors during the weeks prior to the birth, but their observations are worth quoting directly:

> During the three-week period of systematic observation just prior to birth, Lomie showed some signs of increased locomotion, but there was no clear trend over the observation period. However, there were more subtle signs of increasing restlessness, as indicated by fluctuating frequencies of adjustments in posture (p. 169).

Two clear trends did show up in the quantitative records. First, *Lomie* failed to exhibit her characteristic bimodal activity peaks during the three weeks prior to birth. Second, *Lomie* increasingly avoided her cagemate prior to the birth. In the last few days before birth *Lomie* was reluctant to leave her inside den. However, according to Clift and Martin, *Lomie* exhibited no conspicuous interest in her own nipples or vulva prior to birth. As the authors explained:

> . . . although it was possible to predict the date of birth with reasonable accuracy from mating observations and hormonal evidence, it was not possible to obtain a better estimate of the likely time of birth by detailed behavioral observation in late pregnancy. It may be that no such behavioral predictors exist. On the other hand, it is possible that they were simply not observed (p. 170).

Lomie's maternal behavior was studied during the twenty-three days that her infant remained with her. Clift and Martin observed that the earliest indication of "defective" maternal behavior was *Lomie's* failure to appropriately support the infant while in movement.* From day 3 onwards they report a rapid decline in such support. Support of the infant while stationary was adequate until the seventeenth day. Although the investigators reported an early reduction in appropriate maternal care, there was considerable day-to-day variation. One type of behavior which Clift and Martin considered inappropriate is especially interesting in light of our own research, so we will further quote them here as follows:

---

*With regard to clinging, Nadler made the important point that field reports (cf. van Lawick-Goodall, 1967) indicate that newborn apes do *not* grasp their mothers continuously. Thus, such signs may be unreliable indicators of infant weakness.

Inappropriate actions included placing the infant on the floor and squatting on it, which appeared in the first week following birth. Thrusting movements indicated a possible sexual component of this behavior (p. 170).

Lomie also spent a reduced amount of time moving about, but she did spend what the investigators termed a "fair amount of time in manipulation, and an increasing proportion of this time involved the infant, reaching a maximum of almost 80% just prior to removal (p. 171)." Clift and Martin suggested that this frequent handling of the infant may have been due to boredom. After the seventeenth day, the infant spent less time in ventro-ventral contact and was in fact placed on *Lomie's* back on the twenty-first day. This was considered to be inappropriate behavior.* The infant was removed on day 23 because "*Lomie's* maternal care was obviously inadequate, the infant had extensive but superficial abrasions on the head and was noticeably weak (pp. 165–166)." The authors also cite low body weight as a post hoc justification of the removal. At twenty-three days, the infant weighed 2.27 kilograms while four *hand-reared infants* with which it was compared weighed 2.52 kilograms. Despite their efforts, Clift and Martin were forced to conclude that there was no clear-cut explanation of the maternal failure which they observed.

While it is always hazardous to second-guess after the fact, we are nonetheless inclined to believe that in this case there was no maternal failure and hence no need to search for an explanation. Notice that we are not saying that *Lomie* was an *excellent* mother; she likely was *not*. However, in many ways she typified a primiparous mother. As the authors themselves admitted and as others have argued elsewhere (cf. Hess, 1973; Maple et al. 1978; Maple, 1980a), idiosyncratic infant-directed sexual behavior is not inherently abusive. Moreover, *Lomie's* interest in the infant should have been taken as a positive sign. Of course, in impoverished surroundings (we are not told whether Lomie was separated from her cagemate after the birth, but it has been standard procedure in zoos to do so) there is always a danger of excessive grooming and, contrariwise, abandonment of the offspring.

Moreover, the reported low body weight must be considered in light of the typically greater weight which characterizes hand-reared offspring. In other words, hand-reared norms should not be used to judge the adequacy of mother-reared infant weights, since the latter are typically smaller.**

In our view, the case reviewed by Clift and Martin is a perfect example of a premature removal of the infant. Of course, there may have been compelling

---

*In the Yerkes social group of gorillas, one infant was placed on its mother's back only a few days after birth. This mother subsequently raised her infant adequately through infancy.
**This is verified by the observations of Johnstone-Scott (1979) who observed that the female infant, *Kimba,* by three months of age, was two pounds heavier than the mother-reared *Kijo* at the same age (see also Maple, 1980a, Chapter 5).

health considerations as indicated by the abrasions, but the behavioral indicators, in our opinion, were insufficient to warrant removal.

Training for Maternal Care

Scollay, Joines, Baldridge and Cuzzone (1977) recently described an experiment with a female lowland gorilla (*Dolly*) at the San Diego Wild Animal Park. *Dolly* had rejected her first offspring *Jim* which was born in 1973. Thereafter, in conjunction with Steven Joines, Cathy Baldridge, and Ricky Cuzzone, Dr. Scollay and her associates attempted to train *Dolly* to exhibit appropriate maternal care. Scollay and her associates reasoned that maternal behavior* could be acquired in at least three ways:

1. Through experience with an infant
2. By observation and imitation
3. By operant conditioning

Once the team had determined that *Dolly* was again pregnant, they attempted to modify *Dolly's* habits through the use of motion pictures. Despite the availability of excellent films of gorilla maternal care, the projected images did not sustain *Dolly's* attention. The investigators concluded that the exclusive visual mode in which the information was presented was insufficient in its complexity. Because the touch, smell, and even sounds of motherhood might be important sources of stimulation, the San Diego scientists took a different (that is, operant) approach to the problem:

> The first weeks of the project were spent gaining Dolly's confidence and trust. This was vital as we would be introducing new and potentially frightening objects to Dolly. Gorillas are shy and gentle animals whose trust is not easily won. (p. 7)

Once the experimenter's determined that *Dolly's* confidence had been won, the team returned *Jim* to the proximity of *Dolly's* enclosure. Their rationale is contained within the following quotation:

> Each morning he was brought close to her, in order that she could observe him through the bars of her bedroom. During this time Dolly was told that this was a baby, and she could observe how to hold him properly and how to play with him. We thought this might serve the dual purpose of giving the

---

*At the Howlett's Park Zoo, Johnstone-Scott (1979) attempted to stimulate maternal care by anaesthetizing the mother and then placing the infant on her breast. Although this technique has previously worked with monkeys, in this instance it failed.

infant some much needed experience with an adult gorilla, as well as giving Dolly some experience with an older infant, even though at a distance (p. 8).

The effort was continued by the introduction of a pillow infant. This object was constructed of cream-colored canvas, approximating the size of a gorilla infant but without arms or legs. The doll was equipped with simple facial features. Within five minutes of the first introduction, *Dolly* accepted and played with her surrogate infant. While she manipulated the doll, she was told, in soft reassuring tones, that the doll was a baby and that she should treat it gently. The investigators were hopeful that *Dolly* would generalize her gentle doll-handling to her newborn offspring. To this end, one of the commands that Steven Joines taught *Dolly* was "Turn the baby around." Thus, when *Dolly* inappropriately held the doll with its face away from her, Steve would give the command. When *Dolly* responded correctly, she was given praise and a food reward. If she did not respond, the command was repeated. *Dolly* was taught other commands as follows:

1. Pick up the baby.
2. Show me the baby.
3. Be nice to the baby.

Within a few days after their initial presentation, *Dolly* was able to respond correctly to the commands. Training sessions were held daily for about three hours, interspersed with rest in order to accommodate *Dolly's* short attention span.

At the birth of the infant, *Dolly* at first seemed disturbed by its vocalizations. According to Scollay's report, however, she responded to the human prompting and within two weeks required no special treatment by her caretakers. The experiment was exclaimed an unqualified success. The importance of this work to the future of gorillas in captivity is emphasized by Scollay:

> The first step in establishing naturalistic, integrated social groups in captivity is raising young that have been socialized by adults and peers of their own species. This can only be accomplished if an infant is cared for by its own mother from the moment of birth (p. 9).

Keiter and Pichette (1977) followed up on the efforts of Scollay by preparing a pregnant gorilla at the Seattle Zoo. Their subject was a hand-reared six-year-old primiparous lowland gorilla named *Nina*. Preparations began during the third month of *Nina's* pregnancy. Her first surrogate was a simple rectangular cushion, 30 X 15 centimeters, covered with burlap, and containing two painted dark circles for eyes. Despite their efforts, however, *Nina* made no attempt to manipulate the doll. The investigators therefore introduced a more lifelike surrogate, 40 centimeters long, with arms and legs, covered with imitation fur. The head of the surrogate was constructed from a softball with two large brown buttons as eyes. *Nina* exhibited more interest in this figure, but she failed to actually pick it up. When her keepers picked up the doll, however, she watched intently. These demonstrations were accompanied by two commands, "pick up the baby," and "be nice to the baby." At no time did *Nina* respond to these commands. A third surrogate was then introduced, more complicated than the first two models. *Nina* was sufficiently interested in this doll to touch and stroke it but she again failed to pick it up.

Despite the failure to induce appropriate maternal care toward the surrogate, *Nina* correctly mothered her infant when it was born. Several days later, however, the infant was removed due to evidence of illness and it subsequently died.

In view of the events that preceeded the birth of the infant, it seems peculiar that Keiter and Pichette so readily concluded that *Nina* had profited from their efforts. As they concluded:

> In as far as the gorilla had learned from her exposure to the surrogate to accept a novel object in her cage, and had, by imitation and observation, been taught how to hold and support an infant, it was felt that this experiment had achieved a degree of success (p. 189).

While we would not dispute the outcome, it is impossible to know whether the training had anything to do with the animal's behavior. In fact, whenever studies of this type are carried out it is difficult if not impossible to determine the precise cause and effect relationship. Nevertheless, the procedure is a promising one and is doubtless worth the effort if there is reason to fear that the mother will neglect or abuse her infant.

As Sheldon Campbell (1978) so cogently pointed out:

> ... if the effective captive breeding of wild animals by zoos is to be called successful, all available resources will have to be used, including animals made abnormal by imprinting on humans. Increasingly, situations arise where the only obtainable male or female for a breeding program may be an imprinted animal. For this reason, the peculiar problems of sexual neuroses in hand-raised animals will have to be solved, perhaps in some instances through carefully tailored programs in behavior modification (p. 148).

VARIABLES AFFECTING SOCIAL DEVELOPMENT

Regarding the rearing conditions of great apes likely to promote normal social development, Lang (1959) offered the following advice:

> ... great apes are social animals, and it is important not to keep them isolated; especially when young they should be brought up in the company of their

own kind, or a closely related species, bearing in mind that the slow Orangs and Gorillas are favourably influenced by the lively Chimpanzees; otherwise the necessary distraction and stimulation must be provided through regular contact with human beings. Experience has shown that there is no fear of the animals becoming "humanized." Anthropoids and human beings resemble each other so closely, both in behavior and stature, that young apes accept their own kind later on without any trouble and quickly establish a social link (p. 3).

Of course, it is always difficult to specify the background of an imported ape. How long did it actually live with its mother? How long was it isolated? These are questions to which there often can only be guesses, not answers. However, it is possible in some cases to specify variables which, after the gorilla's arrival at the final destination, may influence later events. For example, in the case of *Achilla* who gave birth to the first gorilla born in a European zoo, her early social experiences were composed of close human contact and the companionship of a chimpanzee. Similarly, her eventual mate, *Christopher,* was raised in the company of a slightly older gorilla pair at the Columbus (Ohio) Zoo. When *Achilla* and *Christopher* were introduced, copulation, pregnancy, and the birth of an infant resulted. However, *Achilla's* initial parental behavior was apparently unsatisfactory, and her infant was removed. *Achilla's* prior social experience was sufficient to produce mating but the more complicated maternal repertoire was incompletely developed.

In Table 5-2, we have organized a list of the major variables which are likely to influence sociability, reproduction, and parental care. In some instances we have entered question marks if the effects of the variable on one of the three outcome measures are unknown or especially questionable. It should be admitted here that in relatively few instances are there quantitative data on any of these inferred relationships in gorillas. However, studies of rhesus monkeys and chimpanzees (e.g., Harlow, 1971; Rogers and Davenport, 1970) permit us to make inferences and educated guesses.

The experiments of Harry F. Harlow well illustrated the importance of contact comfort in monkeys. This motivation is also strong in infant gorillas as Lang (1959) observed in *Goma* at the Basel Zoo:

For hours on end she rests or sleeps on her feather bed, but with the first pangs of hunger she calls or shrieks until one of her foster-parents picks her up. This contact means a great deal to her, and usually she wants to be played with and caressed for quite a while before taking her bottle, even though she is ravenously hungry (p. 7).

During the hand-rearing phase of *Goma's* upbringing, Lang also witnessed the psychological phenomenon of *detachment.* Human infants who are separated from their mothers for medical reasons often exhibit aloofness when they return,

Table 5-2. Some variables affecting sociability, reproduction, and parental care.

	sociability	reproduction	parental care
Quality of environment	X	X	X
Genetic predisposition	X	X	X
Diet	???	X	???
Rearing history	X	X	X
Peer experience	X	X	X
Stimulus change	X	X	X
Hormonal status	X	X	X
Group composition	X	X	X
Environmental stress	X	X	X
Social status of parents	X	X	???
Disease history	X	X	X
Age	X	X	X
Subspecies	X	X	X
Length of captivity	X	X	X
Abnormal behaviors	X	X	X
Birth order	X	???	???
Compatibility	X	X	X
Prior parenting	???	???	X
Length of social relationship	X	X	X

X probable relationship

??? unknown relationship

seemingly failing to respond to their mother. As Lang noted, when *Goma's* care-taker was absent for ten days, she failed to recognize him. In one instance, it took three days before she would again permit him to feed her.

INFANT DEVELOPMENT IN THE WILD

For over ten years, Dr. Dian Fossey has studied the mountain gorilla while living more or less continuously in their midst. Very recently, Fossey (1979) described the early development of these gorillas in considerable detail. As she correctly asserted, detailed studies of great ape development have been few. Only Schaller (1963), Kingsley (1977), and Hoff, et al. (1981 a,b) have provided significant detail

Figure 5-2. Genital inspection of Basel infant *Tamtam* by its mother *Goma*. *(J. P. Hess/ W. Angst photo)*

regarding gorilla development.   When we have completely reviewed all these findings, we will be able to assess the strength of the data, compare them, and formulate some generalizations, however tentative.

As we have seen, in the wild, gorillas live in small and stable family groups. Under these living conditions, infant gorillas form long-term associations with their parents, peers, sibs, and others. This particular social organization appears to be unique among the apes (cf. Fossey, 1979) and resembles the familial

Figure 5-3. Closeup photo of *Goma's* hands manipulating the penis of infant *Tamtam*. *(J. P. Hess/W. Angst photo)*

organization of humankind. Infancy* was defined by Fossey as that time period from birth to thirty-six months.

The subjects of Fossey's observations were thirty-two infants residing in seven groups. The period of study was seven years, during which time twenty-four of the infants were born. Conducted within the two study locations in Zaire and Rwanda (cf. Chapter 1), Fossey based her report on 413 hours of direct observation of infants.

Fossey described both *physical* and *behavioral* stages of development in these young gorillas. Needless to say, these stages are not, in every case, rigidly dichotomous. As with all anthropoid characteristics, individual differences abound. According to Fossey, behavioral stages are subject to more individual variation than are physical stages. We will summarize her findings in the next several paragraphs.

Behavior of Newborn

In the first twenty-four hours, the wild infant mountain gorilla is capable of clinging unsupported for at least three minutes. When its body is vertically

---

*Fossey actually used the term *infanthood*.

supported, it is able to hold its head upright. Most of the time the infant appears asleep, but its rooting and nuzzling responses are intact at birth. At this age, infants are always carried in ventral contact with the mother. The infant's vocal behavior consists of "puppy-type whines."

Months 1-2. At this stage, the infant is able to ventrally cling for longer periods. Fossey observed that the leg and body movements appeared to be better coordinated than the arm movements. In general, the infant is still not capable of fine coordination. Solid food intake is limited to the chewing of debris left over from the mother's feeding session. It appears to be asleep about 75% of the time, and when in ventral contact it is supported only about half of the time. Vocalizations are more complex, consisting of whines and loud wails.

Months 2-4. The infant now clings ventrally unsupported for long periods of time. Because of its increased strength, the infant can better resist grooming, and maintain nipple contact. Awkward play is evident in the infant's manipulation of vegetation and the mother's body. In Fossey's own words:

> Arm movements, directed toward nearby foliage, are gross, jerky extensions with the fingers widely spread before the object is actually contacted, and then it is usually only grasped. Play on the mother's body consists mainly of unbalanced crawling, sliding, patting, and hair pulling (p. 146).

At this age, the mother gently reciprocates play and also disciplines with "mock-biting or pushing back." Fossey asserted that gorilla infants at this age can visually focus to at least forty feet, are able to follow moving objects, and visibly flinch at the sound of loud noises. At this age, too, brief dorsal riding is attempted. Fossey observed also that facial expressions of distress and play are by then clearly defined. The vocal repertoire of 2-6 month old mountain gorillas consists of whines, wails, screeches, and panting play chuckles.

4-6 months. Fossey estimated that while gorillas of this age travel in both ventral and dorsal positions, they travel ventrally about 50% of the time. Grooming protests* are less common at this age, but it is likely to strenuously object to prolonged bouts.** At this age the play repertoire is expanded from exploration to manipulation of vegetation. The infant's self-play is composed of "patting, clapping, and the whacking of its own body." Play with mother is more strenuous at 4-6 months. In the wild, the infant remains in proximity to the mother although sometimes out of contact. Parental restriction is frequently observed

---

*Young orang-utans also object to the grooming propensities of their mothers.
**Interestingly, in our studies, grooming of infants by their mothers was a relatively rare event, and these consistently of brief duration.

at this stage of the infant's development. Distant visual focusing is improved at this stage, and head and hand movements have noticeably improved also. Quadrupedal locomotion is first attempted at this stage of development, however awkwardly. Screeches and screams have, by this time, appeared in the vocal repertoire.

6–12 months. A dorsal travel position has by this time reached an estimated level of 80%. The infant at this age often follows in contact with the mother in a mode which Fossey has labeled rump-clinging. In this position, the infant follows with one or both hands clasping the hair of its mother's rump. Although wild infants in their second six months of life are still suckling, the mothers are then beginning to more forcefully prevent it. Self-play at this age includes awkward tree-climbing. Social play has increased, but self-play is still more frequent. The emergence of hoot cries and shriek vocalizations are characteristic of this age class.

12–24 months. The wild infant in its second year of life is almost exclusively a dorsal-rider. Other modes of traveling are quadrupedal following and rump clinging. Stressful situations apparently stimulate ventral-riding. Infants at this age more readily respond to maternal corrections concerning suckling, although the infants continue to try to gain nipple contact. At this age, social play has begun to overtake self-play in frequency. The latter modes of activity at this stage include swinging, twirling, and semibrachiating in trees. Awkward attempts to strip leaves from bamboo stalks and the wadding of vines has emerged by this age. Fossey has referred to this behavior as food preparation (cf. Chapter 1). For the first time, the infant exhibits grooming of its mother and attraction to the silverback male. In its second year of life, the young gorilla also begins to chest-beat, whack foliage, strut-walk (although clumsily) and exhibit tight-lip facial expressions (cf. Chapter 3). Vocal sounds at this age include temper tantrum screams, howls, and pig-grunts.

24–36 months. Independent following of mother has by two years of age supplanted dorsal-riding as the predominant mode of locomotion. Ventral-travel, however, is still occasionally seen in times of stress. Although suckling bouts still occur, the mothers do not generally permit lengthy bouts. Two- to three-year-old infants are more playful, seeking a wider array and greater number of play partners. More variable and risky tree play is at this time evident, and locomotion both on the ground and in the trees is generally more rapid. Food items are no longer plucked but prepared. At this age wild gorillas are more selective and competitive about food. Other gorillas soon become the focus of grooming efforts, and at this stage, more time is spent near the silverback male. Interestingly, the two- to three-year-old mountain gorillas observed by Fossey expressed interest

in adult copulations* (cf. Chapter 4; Maple, 1977). Newly emerging vocalizations include "basic disyllabic variants of the belch vocalization." At this age
the infant still sleeps in its mother's nest and may continue to do so until it is
five years old.

EMERGING INFANT INDEPENDENCE

As Hoff, Nadler, and Maple (in press) have pointed out, the development of infant
independence is a complex and multifaceted phenomenon. A reliable outcome
of independence studies is the decrease in mother-infant contact with the increasing age of the offspring. Using monkeys as subjects, many other studies have
reported decreases in ventro-ventral contact during the early months of life. These
reports also reveal increases in the amount of time that infants spend off mother
and an increasing distance traveled away from mother with age. Identified by
research on monkeys, variables which influence an infant's independence are
mother and infant departure (leaving and approach), maternal protection, nipple
contact, maternal punishment, weaning, other group members, and environmental
variables.

Few of the gorilla reports provide developmental data concerning mother-infant
contact. In the wild mountain gorilla, Schaller discovered that mother-infant
contact was initially broken at about three months of age. The maximal mother-
infant social distance gradually increased to approximately ten feet by four
months of age, and increased to about twenty feet by its eighth month. By one
year, infants were wandering away from their mothers and throughout the group.
Fossey (1974) initially reported that mother-infant contact in mountain gorillas
was first broken somewhat later, in approximately the fifth month. As previously
reviewed, Fossey's recent contribution (1979) contains contact data from the
first three years of life. By one year of age, infants and mothers that she observed
were in contact about half of the observation period. However, they were nearly
always within three feet of their mother. By two years, these infants were in
contact one-third of the time and within three feet about the same amount of
time. The remainder was spent beyond arm's reach. The same developmental
trends of less contact and increasing distance from the mother, often beyond
fifteen feet, were reported at three years. Fossey attributed to the mother the
major role in promoting infant independence.

There are two major reports of developing infant independence in captive
gorillas. The first of these was Kingsley's (1977) study comparing mother-infant

---

*We have observed three adult copulations in the Yerkes gorilla compound since the birth of
the infants. In all cases infants showed intense interest, approaching and staring at the adults
throughout the copulatory bouts. Adults, too, express interest in infant sexuality, see page
180.

interactions of a gorilla pair to a comparable orang-utan unit (cf. Maple, 1980a) at the Jersey Zoo. The gorilla subjects were the western lowland gorillas *N'Pongo* and *N'Gola,* the latter being the male offspring of *N'Pongo* who has been in captivity since 1959. Born on June 21, 1977, *N'Gola* was *N'Pongo's* fourth offspring but the first to be raised by her. Data were collected during three separate observation periods between days 10–16, 36–46, and weeks 17–19 after birth, for a total observation time of 41.5 hours.

In Table 5-3 Kingsley's contact data are depicted. Of four types of contact identified in this study, ventro-ventral (v-v) contact was initially high but had dramatically decreased by the third study period. By the eighteenth week of life v-v contact had increasingly given way to touch-contact whereby the mother and infant maintained contact by hand or foot.

While Schaller's (1963) earliest observation of an infant off of its mother was ten weeks, *N'Gola* was first observed off *N'Pongo* at six weeks, two days. As Kingsley pointed out, the safer captive habitat may account for this difference.

In calculating the responsibility for developing independence, Kingsley contended that the infant was primarily responsible for maintaining proximity with its mother. Separations, however, were initiated by the mother in 77.8% of the cases.

It is interesting to note that Kingsley observed few episodes of infant grooming by *N'Pongo,* and nearly all of these were instances of genital mouthing. The significance of this type of maternal contact will be discussed later in this chapter. As we have previously argued, a mother's interest in her infant's genitals may contribute to its sexual development (cf. Maple et al., 1978; Maple, 1979; 1980a).

Despite the importance of the previous data on both feral and captive infants, the reports are limited. Hoff, Nadler, and Maple (1981a) reported on the development of infant gorilla independence in an attempt to provide more quantitative data and detail in a captive, compound setting.

Three wild-born, primiparous female lowland gorillas, their one female and two male captive-born infants and one adult wild-born male were observed. The history and housing of this group are described in detail in Nadler (1976) and Tilford and Nadler (1978). Nadler initiated the study in 1976.

Our observations were made in either early morning or afternoon, both times of maximal activity in the mountain gorilla (cf. Chapter 1). Observations were

Table 5-3. Mother-infant contact as a percentage of total contact time (After Kingsley, 1977).

	Ventro-ventral	Ventral	Dorso-ventral	Touch
Period I:	69.3	19.4	10.2	1.1
Period II:	73.4	7.2	16.1	3.3
Period III:	28.4	1.0	26.5	44.1

Table 5-4.   Subject information for Hoff, Nadler, and Maple's study of infant development and social behavior.

Name	Sex	Born	Parentage
Rann	M	- 1963	Feral born
Choomba	F	- 1963	Feral born
Shamba	F	- 1959	Feral born
Segou	F	- 1963	Feral born
Machi	F	March 1, 1976	Rann or Calabar X Choomba
Akbar	M	March 9, 1976	Rann or Calabar X Shamba
Bom-Bom	M	March 30, 1976	Rann X Segou

conducted using both a modified Hansen checklist, and a continuous clock, sequential activity record.*   Research continued throughout the infants' first eighteen months of life excluding a six-week period (the eleventh four-week period) in which no observations could be made due to Georgia's extremely cold weather in late 1976 and early 1977.   At such times, the animals are confined inside.

Figure 5-4 shows the mean number of one minute intervals per thirty-minute test** to which ventro-ventral, dorso-ventral, ventro-dorsal, and other mother-infant contact positions occurred.   During the first eight months of life, ventro-ventral contact decreased and was largely replaced by the other contact positions. As can be seen there was a precipitous drop in ventro-ventral contact during the fourth month of life.   Over the next several months, other forms of contact increased.   At about one year of age, most types of contact had diminished to rather low levels.

Mother-infant pairs maintained constant contact throughout the first eleven weeks of life, at which time contact was broken but close proximity was maintained.   A dramatic increase in the proximate position corresponds to the fourth month decline, previously discussed, of ventro-ventral contact.   After first being observed distant in the sixteenth week, the infants began to stray farther from their mothers for longer periods of time.   However, through the first year, they remained within fifteen feet of their mothers.   At about one year of age, infants

---

*In light of the recent controversy regarding sampling methodology, correlations were performed between the one-zero frequencies and the actual frequencies for a variety of behaviors. The correlations were all significant, and ranged from .92 to .99.

**In the Hoff et al. paper, we used "lunar month" to refer to four-week blocks of data. Although these four week blocks do not *precisely* equal a month of life, we will refer to them simply as months in this chapter.   The discrepancy is obvious if we arbitrarily select the tenth four-week block for comparison.   Calculations clearly show that the tenth block is equal to only 280 days, about 28 full days short of a full ten calendar months.

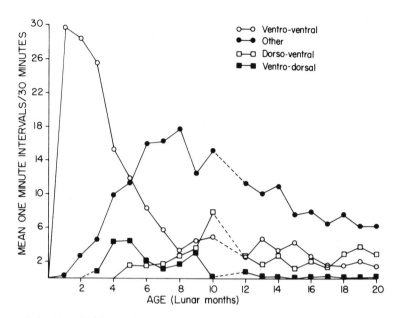

Figure 5-4.   Mean incidence of ventro-ventral, ventro-dorsal, dorso-ventral, and other contact as a function of infant age. (After Hoff, Nadler, and Maple, 1981a)

and mothers began moving more than fifteen feet apart, and toward the end of the study they were often observed an entire compound width from each other.

Both mothers and infants began leaving each other in the fourth month (Figure 5-5). However, the infants started and maintained a greater rate of leaving than did their mothers. As can be seen, infant leaving mother peaked in the first part of the second year, while mother leaving infant was still increasing at the end of the study. Both mothers and infants exhibited a pattern of returning to the other similar to that of leaving.

Throughout the study, Hoff observed that social approach was less frequent for mothers than for infants. In fact, it was an uncommon behavior of mothers, maintained at about the same level throughout the study. Social approach by infants began in the fifth month (as it did for mothers), increasing slowly to a high in the sixteenth month, and dropping thereafter.

Following was observed in both mothers and infants beginning in the fifth month. However, mothers did not regularly follow infants. Follow was both more common and reliable in infants. Its development was parallel to maternal leave (see Figure 5-5), but at slightly lower levels.

Both maternal restraint and the infant response of struggle (Figure 5-6) were short-lived behaviors, peaking at relatively high levels early in life, and occurring

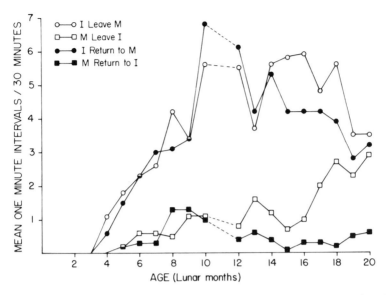

Figure 5-5. Mean incidence of leave and return as a function of infant age. (After Hoff, Nadler, and Maple, 1981a)

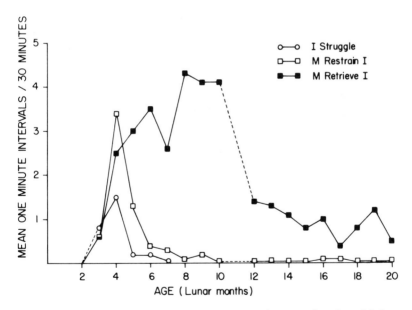

Fig. 5-6. Mean incidence of struggle, restraint, and retrieve as a function of infant age. (After Hoff, Nadler, and Maple, 1981a)

only rarely thereafter. These behaviors appeared at about the same time that infants were moving from v-v to other contact positions (Figure 5-4).

Both restrain and struggle were first observed in the third month. Both behaviors peaked rapidly in the fourth month. Maternal restraint decreased to low levels by the ninth month, subsequently occurring only infrequently. Infant struggle dropped also, and was completely absent after the sixth block.

Mothers began to retrieve their infants at about the same time the infants were being restrained. However, as restraint declined, mothers continued to retrieve infants to closer contact positions. This occurred most frequently in the first year, but mothers did consistently retrieve infants through the eighteen months of the study. Maternal retrieve began in the third month, peaked in the eighth month, and finally decreased through twenty lunar months.

Infant nipple contact with or without suckling, was observed throughout the study. The highest frequency of occurrence was in the first month at 3.5 intervals. Thereafter, this behavior decreased. Mothers did not begin to wean their infants until they were four months old. The manner typically employed was crossing a hand to the opposite shoulder, thereby gently pushing the infant's head away and momentarily blocking nipple access. Weaning remained at generally low levels throughout the study.

The mothers began inspecting their offspring at birth. Intense physical examination began at high levels of frequency, but became less frequent during the early months. By three months, physical examination largely gave way to visual examination. We found it particularly interesting that there was developing a close correspondence of mothers' and infants' examining the other. The rapid increase of social examination by both mothers and infants through six months corresponded to their initial movements away from one another.

Social examination of the infant by the mother began in the first month. Infant social examination of the mother did not occur until the fourth month. Once begun, however, it followed very closely the pattern of maternal social examination.

Infant object examination began early in life and quickly became the predominant infant activity. In the second half of the first year, the infants engaged in object examination during two-thirds of the total intervals observed. This level remained high throughout the study.

Protective behaviors by the mothers were almost exclusively due to attempts by the adult male to retrieve the infants. Under these circumstances, a mother typically retrieved her infant and turned her back on the male, sometimes pushing his hand away. A mother also protected her infant when any adult lunged toward the pair by retrieving it, crouching over it, and raising her arm to block any blows. No further observed instances of maternal protection of the infants occurred beyond the thirteenth month.

Our findings generally agree with the results of other studies of gorillas. For example, breaks in contact were first observed in these infants at eleven weeks, as compared with Kingsley's (1977) record of six weeks in an infant that lived alone with its mother. The slight difference may be due to the less complex social environment utilized by Kingsley (1977). As a result, less maternal restraint may have been necessary. Nicolson (1977) has thus explained a similar difference among chimpanzees living in various social situations. With respect to feral mountain gorillas, our results are similar to those of Schaller (1963), but somewhat different than those of Fossey (1979). Schaller (1963) reported breaks in contact at about three months, Fossey (1979) at five months. In addition, the gorilla infants which we studied were intermediate to those studied by Fossey (1979) and Schaller (1963) in moving to greater distances from their mothers. Schaller found infants beyond fifteen feet by eight months, Fossey at approximately eighteen months, while we detected it at approximately one year.

Fossey (1979) concluded that independence in wild mountain gorillas was maternally determined, but she provided no supporting data regarding variables such as leave, return, and restrain. Our study purposely employed many behavioral categories which allowed us to investigate the question of the relative contributions of mother and infant to developing independence.

We concluded that the development of independence in the infants that we observed was an interactive process between mother and infant. These findings suggest that infants were primarily responsible for decreasing contact throughout the study, as they always left the mothers more than they were left. Additionally, infants consistently struggled against (early) maternal restrictions. These early restrictions (restraint and retrieve) are indicative of the mother's role in maintaining contact. As these declined, infants began to take responsibility for maintaining contact as shown by an increase in infant following and approaching their mothers.

PATERNAL BEHAVIOR

Related to the foregoing review is a recent publication by Tilford and Nadler (1978) who described adult male parental behavior in this same captive group of gorillas. Tilford and Nadler preferred to view male care within the context of *parental investment* theory (e.g., Trivers, 1972; Alexander, 1974). Parental investment may be defined as the *parental act which increases the offspring's chances of survival.* Such acts on the part of males seem to be controlled by the degree of *paternity confidence.* Theoretically, when paternity confidence is high, the male will differentially respond in favor of his own offspring. Redican (1976) has determined that in monogamous pairs, where paternity is certain, male care of offspring is high, whereas in multimale groups, where paternity is very uncertain, male care is generally found to be lower and generalized to benefit all infants.

Since gorillas live in one-male families, and paternity certainty is high, then male care should also be high. Limited support for this prediction is found in Schaller's observation that, among mountain gorillas, the silverbacked male was attractive to offspring which sought to be proximate to and play with the male.

In their six-week study, Tilford and Nadler found that the adult male *Rann* approached and contacted each of the three infants.* An analysis of the data indicated that the male *Akbar* was the recipient of more paternal contact than either *Machi* or *Bom-Bom*. This preference of *Akbar* may have been in part, determined by the relatively higher degree of interaction between *Rann* and *Akbar's* mother *Shamba*. Indeed, the differential affiliation between *Rann* and the adult females correctly predicted his differential interactions with the respective infants. Another factor which was found to contribute to the male's behavior was the differential accessability of the infants. Thus, if an infant was relatively independent from its mother it was more likely to be in contact with the male. When compared, however, the superior predictor of the male's behavior was still the strength of his bond to the respective adult females.

In this captive study, the adult male was not a passive recipient of infant interest as in the case of Schaller's observations. Quite the contrary, *Rann* exhibited a considerable degree of interest in the infants. Several factors may account for this. Foremost, in our opinion, is that *Rann* had no prior experience with offspring and thus they were novel and presumably compelling social stimuli. Moreover, the captive environment in which *Rann* lived was considerably less complex than the Virunga Volcano region of Rwanda. With so much idle time, it is not surprising to us that *Rann* so frequently contacted the infants. Tilford and Nadler also made the point that the age of the Yerkes infants probably contributed to their early reticence to contact *Rann*. This receives support from later observations of the same group as reported by Wilson, Maple, Hoff, Zucker, and Nadler (1977). In this study, conducted when the infants had matured, somewhat less than 50% of the adult male-offspring interactions were initiated by *Rann*. This study also revealed a later emerging but strong preference by the adult male to contact male offspring.

Tilford and Nadler have further suggested that the affiliative bond between a male and particular females is a strategy for increasing paternity certainty. In the wild, this strategy apparently operates in conjunction with the male's propensity to repel competing males.

---

*Of interest, and previously discussed, is the maternal response to these contacts. Virtually all maternal protective responses occurred in response to *Rann's* persistent attempts to contact the infants. This resulted in increased maternal restrictiveness. This type and amount of maternal protection is not reported by either Schaller or Fossey for feral populations.

MATERNAL TRANSPORT OF INFANTS

Schaller (1963) reported that infants were continually supported by at least one hand very early in life, and possibly throughout the first month. The typical mode of early transport was a tripedal walk, with the mother holding her infant to her ventrum with one arm. By three months, infants began riding their mothers' backs for short periods, although they were pulled to the chest when the mother moved rapidly or rested. Beyond this age, infants were on their mothers' backs more often, and by one year were carried ventrally only infrequently.

Fossey (1979) has extended Schaller's observations, finding ventral travel about 60% of the time between four and six months, and back-ride travel about 80% of the time between six and twelve months. Beyond one year, infants almost exclusively travel on their mothers' backs, but increasingly follow along independently except when long distances are traveled.

Our own study of infants through eighteen months (Hoff, Nadler, and Maple, 1980) has shown the same general pattern of a predominance of infant transport against the mother's ventrum early in life (Figure 5-7: tripedal walk), this generally changing to back-ride transport in the second half of the first year (Figure 5-8: back ride). However, as can be seen in these two figures, there existed in this group a considerable individual difference in the amount each mother utilized these two transport modes.

We identified ten forms (see Table 5-5) of maternal transport of infants in this study. As can be seen in Figure 5-9, there were individual differences in the

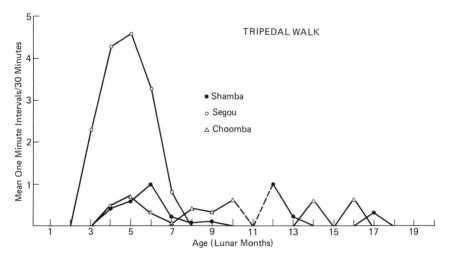

Figure 5-7. Development of the maternal transport mode *tripedal walk* as observed at the Yerkes Field Station by Hoff, Nadler, and Maple (1980).

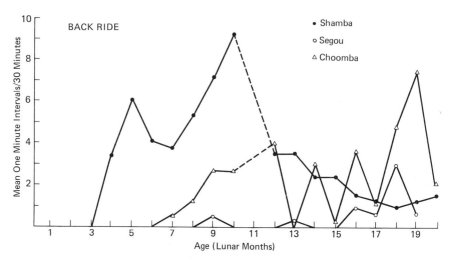

Figure 5-8. Development of *back ride* as a mode of maternal transport in the Yerkes gorillas. (After Hoff, Nadler, and Maple, 1980)

form of transport the mothers used, and the length of its utilization. For example, *Shamba* utilized exclusively, or predominantly, four modes of transport between four and eighteen months* of her infant's life, while the females *Choomba* and *Segou* each used two modes of transport between four and twenty, and three and nine months of their infants' lives respectively.

Throughout the study, the back-ride position was the most common form of transport. One infant was observed being placed on its mother's back very early in life. This same infant was often slung over its mother's shoulder and rode in a *dorso-dorsal* position throughout the early months of its life. By six months this infant was riding almost exclusively in a more typical dorso-ventral back-ride position.

During the eighteen months of observation, the various forms of maternal transport decreased both in type and in frequency. By the end of the study only two forms of transport, the back ride and the hanging walk, were being utilized, with the back ride predominant.

When a mother stirred and began to move, her infant generally returned spontaneously and climbed onto her back. Very often infants sat playing behind their mothers; when a mother moved, the infant simply grabbed the hairs of her back and was pulled up as the mother stood. Less often mothers signaled with a touch that the infant should climb onto her back.

---

*As on page 163, we again are using "months" in reference to lunar months.

Table 5-5. Forms of maternal transport of the infant as identified in Hoff, Nadler, and Maple, 1980.

AW—arm walk: infant sitting in mother's palm and holding her arm as she locomotes quadrupedally.

BR—back ride: infant carried on its mother's back as she locomotes quadrupedally.

CW—crutch walk: infant carried in its mother's lap as she locomotes bipedally using her arms as crutches.

DR—drag: infant dragged on ground near the mother's body as she locomotes either tripedally or quadrupedally.

EC—extended arm carry: infant held in one hand away from the mother's body while she locomotes tripedally.

ED—extended arm drag: as in DR, except infant held away from the mother's body.

HW—hanging walk: infant holding onto and hanging from the mother's ventrum as she locomotes quadrupedally.

LW—leg walk: infant holding onto the mother's rear leg as she locomotes quadrupedally.

TS—tripedal stand: mother motionless, holding infant against her body with one hand.

TW—tripedal walk: infant held against the mother's ventrum as she locomotes tripedally.

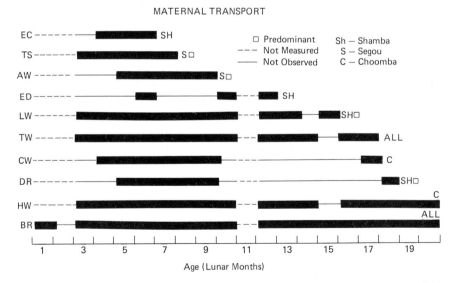

Figure 5-9. Forms of maternal transport in three captive lowland gorillas at the Yerkes Field Station. (After Hoff, Nadler, and Maple, 1980)

MOTOR DEVELOPMENT

The motor development of *Colo,* the first gorilla born in captivity, was studied by Knobloch and Pasamanick (1959a). In this pioneering study, *Colo,* a hand-reared infant, was first observed on day 18, and then examined and photographed every two weeks until up to the fortieth week. Thereafter, until the fifty-sixth week of life, it was examined and photographed once every month. Final study sessions were carried out at fifteen, eighteen, and twenty-one months. The *Gesell Developmental Examination* was employed. As the authors asserted, this instrument was thought at the time to be the "most detailed, complete, reliable, and best-standardized developmental and neurological examination available for use with human infants." Prior to a review of their results, the following general statement of Knobloch and Pasamanick is worth quoting here:

> Clear-cut qualitative differences from human development have been present from the beginning, but the similarities are perhaps greater than the differences. Progress has been more rapid and has tended to occur in spurts compared with the human patterns, with great strides being made in a short period and then a relative plateau being reached before another spurt is made. The first spurt occurred at 10 weeks of age, a less pronounced one at 16 weeks and after 20 weeks of age progress appeared to be relatively steady and slow. (p. 559)

The patterns of motor development were organized into the categories of supine and pull-to-sitting behavior, sitting behavior, prone behavior, and standing and walking behavior. In the first category, *Colo* exhibited symmetrical posturings of the head and body from birth to six weeks. However, from six to ten weeks of age, she reverted to an asymmetrical tonic neck reflex. This was an unusual development for a primate. *Colo* was able to bring her hands together at her midline at birth. Her feet could be brought together in this fashion at the age of fourteen weeks. As Knobloch and Pasamanick were able to show, human infants do not attain symmetrical posturing of the hands and feet until sixteen weeks of life. At ten weeks of age, *Colo* could roll over to a prone position. At birth she was able to lift her head in supine, a characteristic which does not appear in humans until the twenty-eighth week. Initially, she lifted her head and assisted in the pull-to-sitting task. However, from the fourth through the tenth week, she developed a head lag. This coincided with the previously mentioned tonic neck reflex change.

In sitting, there was also a regression between the sixth and tenth weeks of life. At first, she held her head steadily, but later developed bobbing, regaining her steadiness by the tenth week. By the sixteenth week, *Colo* was able to sit leaning forward on her hands. Knobloch and Pasamanick's views on sitting are quoted as follows:

> The transition to independent sitting was not sharply realized, probably for two reasons. Sitting was usually in the position of leaning on one hand or resting the

back against a support, a characteristic adult gorilla pattern; in addition, *Colo* was so active that she rarely sat still for a long enough period for *E* to be absolutely certain of whether she was sitting steadily or not. (p. 561)

Between twenty and twenty-four weeks of age, *Colo* was secure in sitting, was able to easily assume a prone position, and was capable of pivoting in the sitting position.

Head control was attained in the prone position later than in the supine position. This contrasts with trends in human development. At the age of ten weeks, *Colo* began pushing her feet and pivoting in prone, keeping her head down on the floor without the use of her arms. By twenty weeks of age, she was able to move about on her hands and feet in the characteristic locomotor pattern of her species. Unlike humans, *Colo* did not creep on her hands and knees.

The greatest difference between *Colo* and her human counterparts was in the area of standing and walking. Standing was accomplished at fourteen weeks of age. *Colo* was cruising at the railing at eighteen weeks, but she was inclined to swing with her arms. When held by her hands she typically withdrew her legs. She was generally more agile with her arms than her legs at twenty-eight weeks. *Colo* exhibited early bipedal progress, standing and toddling at thirty-eight weeks with good control at fifteen months. However, her walking posture was predominately quadrupedal, in keeping with the characteristic mode of her species. Her locomotion changed to a "stiff run" at twelve months, and a "very swift facile run" at eighteen months. As the investigators further explained:

At 18 months, also, Colo jumped with both feet off the ground simultaneously, and stood on her head. Perhaps an amusing aspect of the development of this behavior was observing how long she continued right on into the glass at the end of the cage when walking along the ladder or running about. Not until the 15-month examination did this persistent behavior disappear. (p. 562)

As Knobloch and Pasamanick pointed out, the development of gross motor patterns does not as closely follow the cephalocaudal progression of human infants. In this sense, *Colo's* progress is consistent with the findings for chimpanzees as determined by Riesen and Kinder (1952) using a slightly different instrument. As the investigators suggested:

The most outstanding difference in the gorilla is probably the appearance of prone progression considerably before the use of the lower extremities in standing, and the ability, albeit reluctantly, to use the lower extremities in erect progression before stable sitting is attained. (p. 562)

Knobloch and Pasamanick were unable to explain the reversion to the asymmetrical tonic nect reflex position. Perhaps it was due to some undetermined measurement error or was in some way influenced by unspecified but species-

Table 5-6. Comparison of age of appearance of motor behavior in human, gorilla, and chimpanzee infants. (After Knobloch and Pasamanick, 1959a)

Behavior Item	Human	Gorilla	Chimpanzee
Supine			
Asymmetrical tonic neck reflex position	4 w	6–10 w	(6)(5) w
Midpositions & symmetrical postures predominate	16 w	(2.5–6) 10 w	11 w
Hands engage in midline	16 w	2.5 w	>4 w
Feet engage in midline	–	14 w	–
Legs lift high in extension	24 w	12 w	–
Rolls to prone	24 w	10 w	11 w
Lifts head	28 w	2.5 w	4 w
Pull-to-Sitting			
Complete head lag	4 w	0	0
No head lag	20 w	(2.5–4) 10 w	>4 w
Lifts head, assists	24 w	(2.5) 10 w	14 w
Sitting			
Head predominately sags	4 w	0	–
Head predominately bobbing	8 w	0·	4 w
Head set forward, bobs	12 w	6–10 w	–
Head steady, set forward	16 w	(2.5–6) 10 w	9 w
Head steady, erect	20 w	12 w	>4 w
Trunk erect in supportive chair	24 w	10 w	–
Sits leaning foward on hands	28 w	16 w	24 w
Sits erect momentarily	28 w	–	24 w
Sits 1 min. erect, unsteady	32 w	18 w	25 w
Sits 10 min., steady	36 w	20 w	28 w
Leans forward, re-erects	36 w	20 w	23 w
Sits indefinitely steady	40 w	20–22 w	30 w
Goes to prone	40 w	20 w	20 w
Pivots in sitting	48 w	20–24 w	26 w
Prone			
Hips high, legs flexed, crawling movements	4 w	2.5 w	–
Lifts head to Zone I momentarily	4 w	0	0
Head droops in ventral suspension	4 w	0	–
Head rotates on placement	4 w	2.5 w	–
Head lifts to Zone II, recurrently	8 w	2.5 w	>4 w
Head compensates in ventral suspension	8 w	2.5 w	>4 w
Head in midposition on placement	8 w	4 w	–
Hips low, legs flexed	12 w	4 w	–
On forearms	12 w	4 w	>4 w
Lifts head to Zone II sustainedly	12 w	4 w	>4 w
Lifts head to Zone III sustainedly	16 w	6 w	>4 w
Legs extended	16 w	10 w	–
Arms extended	20 w	14 w	11 w
Pivots	32 w	10 w	12 w
Crawls, pushing with feet	[36 w]	10 w	14 w
Creeps	40 w	20 w	20 w
Creeps up stairs	15 m	40 w	–

174

Table 5-6. (Continued)

Behavior Item	Human	Age of Appearance Gorilla	Chim- panzee
Standing and Walking			
Supports small fraction of weight briefly	12 w	10 w	>4 w
Lifts one foot momentarily	12 w	10 w	>4 w
Supports large fraction of weight	28 w	14 w	20 w
Bounces	28 w	18 w	–
Maintains standing with hands held	32 w	14 w	22 w
Holds rail, supports full weight	36 w	14 w	20 w
Pulls to feet at rail	40 w	14 w	20 w
Lifts and replaces foot at rail	44 w	18 w	25 w
Cruises at rail	48 w	18 w	24 w
Cruises using arms only	–	18 w	–
Cruises easily, using arms only	–	30 w	–
Walks with 2 hands held	48 w	28 w	(26) w
Walks with 1 hand held	52 w	36 w	(26) w
Stands momentarily alone	56 w	38 w	39 w
(Toddles few steps)	[56 w]	38 w	43 w
Walks few steps, stops and starts	15 m	48 w	–
Falls by collapse	15 m	48 w	–
Creeping discarded	15 m	–	–
Walks, seldom falling	18 m	15 m	–
Runs stiffly	18 m	12 m	–
Walks up stairs, 1 hand held	18 m	40 w	–
Climbs into adult chair	18 m	15 m	–
Runs well, no falling	24 m	18 m	–
Jumps, lifting both feet	30 m	18 m	–

Note:—The behavior items are given as they appear on the Gesell Developmental Schedules (Gesell & Amatruda. 1941), and the age of appearance is the age at which the item is placed on these schedules. This is the normative age at which the pattern is found in human infants. The two items in brackets do not appear on the Developmental Schedules but are approximate ages of occurrence.

The ages in parentheses for the gorilla indicate the first weeks during which the behavior was seen temporarily.

The ages in brackets for the chimpanzee indicate the best estimations that could be made. A dash indicates no information is available.

typical movements of the gorilla. Because Riesen and Kinder used developmental items that were not directly comparable to those employed in the Knobloch study, a comparison of gorilla and chimpanzee was difficult to achieve. However, they were still able to assert that the gorilla progresses more rapidly than the chimpanzee in the development of gross motor patterns. From this and other findings, they ventured the following interesting conclusion which will be relevant to the material we shall consider in Chapter 6:

One hypothesis which might be brought forward is that the more prolonged the infancy, when one genus is compared to another, the higher the eventual attainment in terms of human intellectual functioning... The hierarchy would appear to be Homo sapiens, chimpanzee, and gorilla. (p. 563)

Although we did not study infant motor development as intensively as did Knoblock and Pasamanick, information concerning motor behavior does appear in our data. It is of interest to examine motor behavior as it developed in these infants who were raised in a large compound by their mothers.* Table 5-7 provides a brief summary of the age of onset of various motor behaviors.

Usher-Smith, King, Pook and Redshaw (1976) described the motor development of six hand-reared gorilla infants at the Jersey Zoological Park. Their data were based on the notes of each animals' respective caretakers, and appear in Table 5-8. The authors attribute *Tatu's* relative advancement to the week that he spent clinging to his biological mother. The other infants spent this time in an incubator.

Table 5-7. Approximate age of onset of motor behaviors in a captive social group of gorillas through eighteen months. (from Hoff, Nadler, and Maple, 1980)

Age (month)	Motor Behavior
1	Lie supine
1	Lie prone
1	Hold head up
3	Roll over
3	Sit
3	Kneel
3	Crawl
3	Quadrupedal walk
3	Quadrupedal stand
3	Bipedal stand with support
5	Run
5	Climb
5	Perch (motionless off ground)
7	Wall hit (one hand)
8	Gallop
12	Bipedal walk
15	Chest beat
15	Lunge
16	Lunge with hit
18	Quadrupedal stiff stance (threat)
18	Quadrupedal stiff walk (threat)

*Refer to "Infant Development in the Wild", page 160 for data concerning motor development in the feral situation.

Table 5-8. Development of motor patterns in six hand-reared lowland gorillas during their first year of life. (After Usher-Smith, et al., 1976)

Co-ordinated motor activity Stage of Development	Age first observed (weeks)					
	Assumbo	Mamfe	Zaire	Tatu	Bamenda	Kumba
Raised head while on back			1			
Lifted head while on stomach	2	2	8	3	6	4
Turned onto stomach or onto back	8	3	6	3	3	2
Attempted grasping of objects	6	7	7			6
Mouthing and chewing of objects encountered				5	8	
Crawls on stomach	10	13	10	2	11	9
Stood with support	13	14		8		9
Climbing	18	16	13	10	19	14
Holding and manipulating objects or solid food	20		12	15	12	10
Walking	21	19	14	15	17	19
First display to people			38	21	19	24
Use of horizontal bar	(26)	14	13	15		
Feeds self bottle	30	22	33		48	
Bipedal walking		34				
Bipedal standing		23	17	43	38	
Chest beating (one fist)			33	39	14	
Full chest beat	35			45		
Claps hands		51	38		52	

THE DEVELOPMENT OF INFANT PLAY

Although there have been several reports of play in infant gorillas, few of these have dealt with the development of play. Hess (1973) provided data regarding infant sexual play in captivity, reporting a female infant of one and one-half years engaging in copulatory play with a subadult male. Several months later this infant was seen to assume a copulatory position with her mother, and to exhibit sexual solicitation toward her father.

Schaller (1963) describes a few instances of play among his feral subjects, but provides little quantitative data. Fossey's (1979) study of free-ranging gorillas provides the most complete data on the developmental progression of play in infants. They were first observed to play on their mother's body in the early months of life. This was soon followed by solitary and then peer play. As infancy progressed, play became active and strenuous. In addition, infants engaged in social play more often, both with peers and older animals.

Hoff, Nadler, and Maple (1981b) have reported on the development of play in a captive group. Reciprocal mother-infant play was the first form of play observed

(Figure 5-10). It began in the fourth month, and was generally initiated and terminated by the mother. Mother-infant play was usually gentle, and never reached high levels of occurrence. Infant solitary play appeared in the fifth month. Solitary play began as ground slapping with one or both hands, and eventually included both gymnastic (tenth month) and locomotor (eleventh month) play.

Infant peer play began in the eighth month. We identified both active (rough and tumble) and moderate social play. Active social play typically consisted of chasing, lunging, tackling, wrestling, etc. Moderate social play was much less active. It included such behaviors as light bouncing on the play partner's stomach or mild tugging. Mothers were not involved in reciprocal peer play, although they frequently interrupted play bouts until the ninth month. Our data show the possibility of a sex difference in active (but not moderate) social play. Males began to play in this fashion at an earlier age and much more frequently than did the female infant. Due to the small sample size, we can, of course, only speculate about the existence of this sex difference. It is, however, consistent with findings for other apes.

SEXUAL DEVELOPMENT

In 1973 an important study of sexual behavior in captive lowland gorillas was published. The author of the report, Jörg Hess, initiated the study in 1968, observing a group of nine gorillas at the Basel Zoological Gardens. As Hess

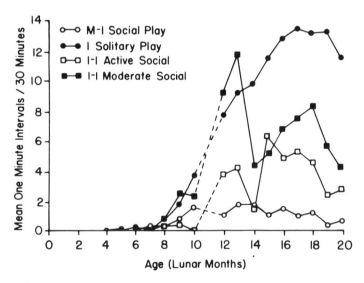

Figure 5-10. The development of play in three infant gorillas. M-I = mother-infant; I = infant; I-I = infant-infant. (After Hoff, Nadler, and Maple, 1981b)

correctly pointed out, Schaller's 1963 field study, impressive in every other way, provided little information concerning sexual behavior. Hess' informative report provided information on the following topics:

1. The behavior of one or more animals involving direct contact with its or their own genitals or genital region or those of a partner.
2. Behavioral sequences that correspond largely to the phases of copulatory behavior during an inter-oestrus phase.
3. Behavior which is clearly connected with the oestrus in females (p. 509).

While Hess' observations might at first glance suggest that his group is highly active sexually, Hess pointed out that all sexual behaviors were relatively rare in frequency. With respect to adult copulations, we have reviewed the principal findings of Hess' study in Chapter 4. The sections to follow concern the sexual development of young animals.

Almost immediately after birth, the newborn gorilla is carefully inspected and groomed by its mother. This picking, scratching, rubbing, plucking, poking, licking, sucking, biting, and nibbling occurred several times each hour. The areas of the body which attracted the mother's attention were the ears, shoulders, appendages, navel, and anogenital region. Hess described the mother's manipulation of genitalia as follows:

> The genitals are stroked, plucked at and poked or held and moved to and fro, mostly with the fingers (chiefly with the thumb or index finger . . . the little finger being employed for more delicate manipulations). Touching with the lips, teeth and tongue, combined with sucking, do occur but are less frequent (p. 513).

The infant's response to this contact was found to vary, and Hess organized these into the following list:

1) If the touching behavior is of brief duration, gentle and tender, the infant hardly reacts at the beginning; later it makes the same face as when being tickled by its mother.
2) If the touching lasts a long time or is rough, the newborn utters faint grunts and squeaks whereupon the mother's activity is discontinued.
3) Towards the end of the first month, the faint vocalizations become screams and are accompanied by increasingly violent arm and leg movements. As the locomotory faculties develop, sliding and crawling away, sitting up, turning, walking and finally running away can be observed. The mother may respond to these evasive movements by gripping the infant firmly when she wishes to touch its genitals. Moreover, she no longer necessarily reacts to its expressions of discomfort and resentment.

4) Towards the middle of the first year the mother sometimes uses genital touching as a training method; she thereby urges the infant to crawl, climb, walk and run; in certain cases it is used as a means of "getting rid of" the infant for a short time. Pulling at the genitals can also serve as a punishment (pp. 516–518).

Hess observed that this genital contact was effective in stimulating urination and defecation.* These excretory actions may have been somehow reinforcing to the mother. Moreover, genital erection also accompanied maternal stimulation. Hess reported that *Goma,* the mother of the male infant, *Tamtam,* engaged in more intensive and highly differentiated genital examination/manipulation than did *Achilla,* mother of the female infant, *Quarta.* He further suggested that the differential interest of the mothers may have been due to the sex of their respective offspring (see also Maple, 1977; Maple, 1980a)** rather than to individual differences (but see p. 181). As Hess explained it:

The erection of the penis and the wide arc described by the squirting urine in the male baby are reactions which are highly rewarding for G and which induce more intensive exploration (p. 518).

Another form of genital contact was observed which is similar, if not identical, to the behavior of orang-utan mothers (cf. Maple, Wilson, Zucker, and Wilson, 1978). Hess described this form of maternal behavior in the following passage:

During Quarta's first three years, Achilla repeatedly laid the infant on its back on the floor in front of her, placed her own genital region on that of the infant, then crouching down, either slid around with the child beneath her or performed rhythmic pelvic movements (p. 520).***

As Hess pointed out, the female *Delilah* engaged in similar behavior at the Bristol Zoo, and we have witnessed it both in the female *Hazel* at the Phoenix (Arizona) Zoo and the Yerkes group. The infant, too, seems interested in its own genitalia as it becomes accustomed to its body. In Hess' own words:

. . . its own genitals belong to the attractive parts for this kind of exploration. Touching of its own genitals may cause an erection. With increasing age the

---

*Hess reported that Fisher (1970) found a similar reaction to genital stimulation in a male infant at the Lincoln Park Zoo.
**Genital interest by mothers appears also to be characteristic of chimpanzees and orang-utans.
***This behavior was not idiosyncratic with *Quarta* as it had been directed toward *Achilla's* previous infants as well.

touching of the genital region with the hand becomes more direct and often occurs immediately before or during urination and defecation. At no moment during the first two years of life may the touching of the genital region, in the cases I observed, be called "masturbation" (p. 521).

After one year of life, however, Hess observed that the gorilla female *Quarta* was for the first time seen to engage in play-copulations with the subadult male *Migger*. At two years and two months, *Quarta* first assumed a copulatory position of her own, and she later seemed to "offer" herself to her father during play.*

In our own studies of mother-infant interactions and infant development in a captive group of lowland gorillas we have reported on infant sexuality (Hoff, Nadler, and Maple, 1979). The first to occur and most common behavior related to any form of infant sexuality was manual and/or oral-genital examination of an infant by another animal. Maternal genital manipulation began early in the first month of life. This behavior occurred infrequently throughout the first year, and became very rare thereafter. Interestingly, in light of Hess' finding of an apparent sex difference in maternal manipulation of infant genitalia, we found no difference, either qualitative or quantitative in the mothers' inspection and/or manipulation of their offsprings' genitals. This raises the possibility that the difference that Hess observed between the mothers *Goma* and *Achilla* were in fact idiosyncratic.

Much as Hess reported, we also found maternal mountings of an infant. In such cases, the infant was typically laid on its back by the mother, and she squatted and made rhythmic pelvic movements against it.

Infant-infant sexuality began with genital examinations. These were typically manual although two instances of oral manipulation were recorded. In both cases the female infant, *Machi,* examined the male infant, *Bombom.* Infant-infant sexuality typically occurred in the midst of play bouts. Pelvic thrusting began at about one year of age.** The first observed instance of infant male to female pelvic thrusting was terminated by an adult female retrieving the male infant and engaging him in sexual activities. Although both male-male and male-female thrusting bouts were observed, male-female bouts accounted for more than 70% of the fifty-three bouts observed. Early thrusting was awkward, the infant thrusting against the other's stomach, legs, arms, or back. Through the following months, thrusting became more sophisticated, including manipulating the partner and appropriate ventro-ventral and dorso-ventral positioning.

Keiter and Pichette (1979) have written about the sexual activity of juvenile and subadult lowland gorillas. At the Woodland Park Zoo in Seattle, they observed a social group composed of two females (5–6 and 6–7 years of age) and two males (5–6, and 7–8 years of age). Classifying labial tumescence as slight, moderate, or

---

*An excellent film on the subject of infant development has been produced by Dr. Hess.
**Schaller has reported copulatory play in a captive two-year-old male.

marked, Keiter and Pichette observed that in the slight phase, the females initiated increased play activity with the males:

> Both females engaged in activities which attracted the attention of the males, such as twirling from the end of the rope in close proximity to them, coming to rest either sitting or leaning against one of the males following her release of the rope . . . The female "Nina" engaged in a play-chase game where she would run up to the males punch them or push them with closed fist, and then run off a few feet inviting a chase. At the conclusion of the chase, she initiated the slow wrestling or gentle caressing of the male (p. 221).

Thereafter, the two females typically presented to the males, and characteristic back-riding and play-biting emerged. Among the Seattle gorillas, Keiter and Pichette observed 300 instances of back-riding, all but four of which involved the females riding the males. As the investigators learned, however, the males initiated back-riding by backing up to the females, exhibiting slight piloerection and in a stiff posture jiggling their bodies several times. A more vigorous form of riding-inducement occurred when a male backed up to a female, forcefully contacting her abdomen with his buttocks and thereby inducing her to climb onto his back. Moreover, these "presents" by the male were sometimes preceded by a stiff-walk approach and subsequent reaching back by the male presumably in order to facilitate her climbing effort.

During back-riding, both males bounced up-and-down in a kind of bucking motion, while the females assumed a variety of postures. The majority of the 300 back-riding episodes were accompanied by penile erections during the ride or immediately thereafter. Copulation frequently followed.

During the moderate phase of the cycle, both females exhibited an increasing amount of chest-beating prior to engaging in more typical courtship behaviors (see Chapter 4). They also were observed to lay on their backs, slap the soles of their feet, or slap their own buttocks while standing. Rolling about the floor also occurred in this phase as did mouth grooming. This behavior involved the female *Caboose* orally exploring the face and mouth of the males, inserting her tongue into their mouths. According to Keiter and Pichette, *Caboose* was observed kissing the males. In this phase too, genital probing with the digits by the males increased, and oral investigation of the perineum by the males emerged. Back riding increased during this phase.

Finally, in the labial tumescence phase, the females manually/orally explored the penis of the males. In addition, both of them presented to the males. Digital probing, oral investigation, and back-riding reached a peak level of frequency in this phase of the cycle. As Keither and Pichette summarized:

> During estrus a great deal of probing, licking and sniffing by the males occurred, occasionally with the male Kiki using both hands to part the lips of the vulva

before proceeding with his investigation. These examinations were more often digital (80%) than oral (20%) and simultaneous 10% of the time (p. 222).

The Seattle investigators also identified a type of *flehmen* expression which occurred in one female after she had manipulated herself and sniffed/licked her finger. Whether this behavior represents a species-typical or individually idio-syncratic expression remains to be confirmed by subsequent investigation.

Keiter and Pichette recorded eight variants in the copulatory posture of the Seattle gorillas. The two males exhibited preferences for different postures, further indicating the flexibility of this species as compared to so many other mammals. The vocalizations associated with copulation in these young gorillas were described as follows:

1. Female *Nina* – low, semirumbling growl.
2. Female *Caboose* – grunting, growl, low hooting or oooing.
3. Male *Kiki* – short hoots, grunting, chuckling or low growl.
4. Male *Pete* – grunting, low semirumbling growl.

Pursed lips facial expressions were emitted by both males and females during back-riding. The male *Kiki* exhibited pursed lips during copulation, but also kept his mouth open at such times. An open mouth was common to all of the gorillas in the context of sexual activity.

As Keiter and Pichette pointed out, in the absence of experienced adults, the Seattle gorillas exhibited courtship play, precopulatory, and copulatory activity which closely resembled that of feral gorillas (cf. Chapter 4). However, to further emphasize our argument (see page 143), these gorillas received the early stimula-tion of human contact and very soon thereafter were introduced to peers. Thus, they were not socially isolated and had an opportunity to acquire sexual behaviors through relatively trial-and-error interactions with each other. Their relative degree of inexperience is apparent in Keiter and Pichette's description of their sexual repertoire. Clearly, it is *not* necessary for gorillas to learn to copulate from adults, but it *is* sufficient for them to acquire such skills through peer interaction. The more enriched (complex) the social environment, the smoother will be this process of acquisition.

RESPONSES TO SEPARATION

Hoff, Nadler, and Maple (1978a) recently carried out a study in which the adult male was systematically separated from the group residing at the Yerkes Field Station. Prior to the separation period, which lasted for two weeks, behavioral baselines were established. Post separation data were then compared to these base-lines according to standard separation procedures (cf. Maple, Brandt and Mitchell,

1975). We hypothesized that in the absence of the control role of the male, *Rann*, aggression in the group would increase. Additionally, we expected that the stress of this heightened agression would result in increased mother-infant and group affiliative behaviors. We found, in support of our hypotheses, dramatic effects on the behavior of the group in the absence of the adult male. Adult female aggressive behaviors increased significantly, then declined upon the return of *Rann* (Figure 5-11). Additionally, mother-infant ventral contact increased at separation to more than *fifteen* times its baseline level. Although this form of contact did not decline to preseparation levels upon the return of the male, this was largely due to the extremely high score in the first post separation week. Following this, ventral contact did drop to approximate preseparation levels (Figure 5-12). Similarly, the following behaviors, among others, also increased during the separation of the adult male: mother-infant proximity, nipple contact, and infant contact with others. Additionally, infant play decreased during *Rann's* absence. These behavioral changes indicate, as we expected, that the loss of the

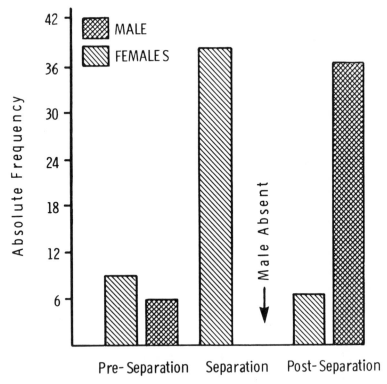

Figure 5-11. Absolute frequency of adult agressive displays prior and during removal, and after the adult male's return. (After Hoff, Nadler, and Maple, 1978a)

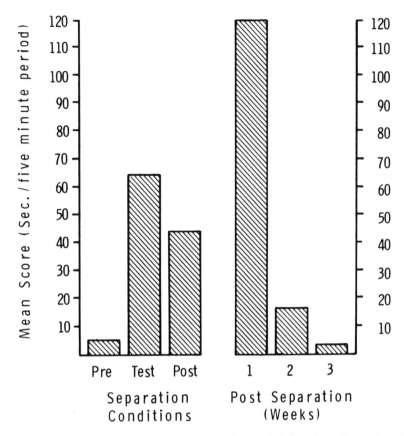

Figure 5-12. Ventro-ventral contact between mothers and their infants during the adult male separation experiment. (After Hoff, Nadler, and Maple, 1978a)

adult male is a stressful event for the entire group. Furthermore, the male's control role in maintaining group stability and minimizing intragroup agression is indicated by the results. Finally, we found evidence that the return of the adult male is discomforting. During the first hour of reintroduction, the adult male was apprehensive, tense and avoided contact. He even exhibited signs of the commonly observed (human) infantile response to early separation from its mother: *detachment* (Bowlby, 1969). The adult females followed the male, but did not actually contact him until one of the young males, *Bom-Bom,* successfully approached and touched the male. At that moment the others moved forward and the reunion tension was over. This remarkable interaction resembled the agonistic buffering which occurs in the Barbary macaque and other monkeys. However, in this instance, the buffering was opportunistically utilized from a distance.

Clearly, this experiment does not totally generalize to conditions in nature. However, at the sudden loss of an alpha male, a wild group of gorillas might be expected to respond in a manner similar to this captive group. Moreover, it is quite possible that when new males successfully take over a group it may generate behaviors similar to those observed at reunion in the Yerkes group. An important application of our findings, however, is in understanding group dynamics in captivity. Clearly, membership changes in captivity are stressful. Therefore, when the composition of a gorilla group must be altered, it is an especially difficult time for all concerned, gorillas and staff alike.

The separation and reunion of a mother and infant gorilla was earlier described by Nadler and Green (1975). The case concerned the removal of *Patty Cake,* the first gorilla born in New York City. The birth of *Patty Cake* to *Lulu* and *Kongo* at the Central Park Zoo, was a surprise to all concerned. After the infant's birth, *Lulu* exhibited signs of conscientious motherhood. However, she also became temporarily indifferent, sometimes leaving the infant to scream alone on the floor of the cage. The male *Kongo,* separated at the time of the birth, was later reintroduced in order to induce further maternal care in *Lulu.* However, at a later date during a brief separation from *Kongo, Patty Cake's* arm was somehow broken, and so she was removed for a three-month separation.

After the three-month period had passed and the infant's health had improved, a reunion was attempted. *Patty Cake* initially resisted her mother's attempts to retrieve her but eventually the reunion was accomplished. Thereafter, the male was successfully reintroduced to the mother and her infant. Although lactation apparently returned spontaneously (no suckling was actually observed), it sub-sided soon thereafter and evidence of cyclic sexual behavior was revealed. During the several days of *Lulu's* subsequent estrous periods, *Patty Cake* was routinely re-moved and housed with a young chimpanzee. These procedures were successfully carried out by Zoo staff and sufficiently protected the infant, according to the 1975 report of Nadler and Green. Despite the rather lengthy separation and the trauma associated with it, it is clearly possible to reunite offspring with their mothers. To do so successfully, however, the development of extreme forms of behavioral pathology must be prevented (cf. Puleo, Zucker and Maple, in press; Maple, 1980a) and the infant ideally should be weaned. Where offspring must be supplementally fed, conditioning procedures can be used whereby the mother is trained to permit the infant to receive food from caretakers. In fact, it is conceivable—albeit difficult—that gorillas could be taught to bottle feed their own offspring.

Moving beyond the report of Nadler and Green, our research team (Hoff, Nadler, and Maple, 1979) examined the effects of mother-infant separation and reunion in the Yerkes gorilla group. This separation was *not* due to any form of maternal neglect or abuse. It was undertaken in early summer, 1978, to facilitate the females' resumption of cycling. In the feral situation, these females would have soon begun cycling spontaneously. It was therefore decided to artificially accelerate this process to minimize the possibility of infants being born during the winter months. Newborn infants were likely to do poorly in the cold, damp atmosphere of the winter, and there existed the strong possibility of illness leading to early removal from the mother or possibly even to the death of an infant born at this time. The three infants were therefore removed as a group and were kept together during separation.* They were fully capable of independent feeding, and were not subject to additional human intervention or manipulation. They should, in no way, be considered hand-reared.

The infants were separated at twenty-seven months of age for a period of six months. Baseline behavioral levels indicated that the infants were rather independent of their mothers prior to separation. The great majority of observed interactions of the infants were composed of peer play.

The immediate responses to separation were loud screams and cough threats. Through the first two days, other measures also indicated active infant protest at separation. Following this period of agitation, behavioral depression ensued and continued throughout most of the first separation month. There was a striking increase in infant-infant contact, and a decrease in peer play (Figure 5-13). Object

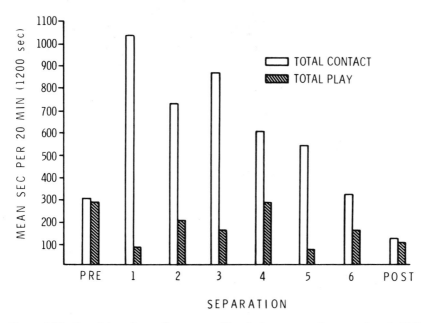

Figure 5-13. Peer interactions of young gorillas during a separation experiment. (After Hoff, Nadler, and Maple, 1979)

---

*It should be emphasized here that this procedure was carried out when the offspring were twenty-seven months of age. The separation was arranged as an experimental manipulation which held minimal risk for the infants due to their advanced age and the opportunity for continual peer housing. We continue to strongly advocate mother-rearing and advise against premature separation from the natal group.

Figure 5-14. Bottle feeding at the Yerkes Regional Primate Research Center. *(Photo courtesy Yerkes Regional Primate Research Center of Emory University)*

examination and, solitary play also showed dramatic declines (Figure 5-15). Through the five remaining months of separation there was a gradual amelioration of these indices of behavioral depression.

The infants were returned to the large compound simultaneously. They entered the compound in a "choo-choo" formation (see Harlow, 1969). Throughout the first days of reunion the infants spent a good amount of the time closer to each other than to their respective mothers. This series of behaviors are indicative of possible detachment occurring in all infants. Subsequent to this, infants returned to their mothers. Within several weeks, the infants exhibited few behavioral differences from the preseparation period. However, despite the apparent full recovery of the infants, the long-range effects of this separation are presently unknown.*

HAND-REARING PROCEDURES

Elsewhere, Maple (1980b) has discussed the problems posed by hand-rearing apes. In gorillas, hand-rearing has been the rule rather than the exception. An

*Further details will appear in a fourthcoming publication.

account of hand-rearing was recently published by Mallinson, Coffey, and Usher-Smith (1976). The two female primipara from which the infants were taken failed to exhibit appropriate maternal care. It is interesting to note here that both females arrived at Jersey past the age of eighteen months. As Rogers and Davenport (1970) concluded for chimpanzees, female infants that live with their mothers for eighteen months or more are likely to be adequate mothers. Of course, for these gorillas, the records do not indicate how long they were isolated prior to their shipment from the French Cameroons.

One of the females, *Nandi,* hald the infant properly but did not permit it to nurse.* On the second day the decision was made to remove the infant. As Mallinson and his associates explained:

> In our experience gorilla infants are slow starters and provided the mother holds her infant in a maternal fashion and it appears to be strong, we consider that it can safely be left with the mother up to 40 hours. If, however, it has not suckled by that time, it must be removed (p. 190).

A nursery equipped for hand-rearing procedures is completely described in Mallinson, Coffey, and Usher-Smith, 1974. Further hand-rearing details are also provided in Taylor and Bietz' 1979 handbook. A very interesting statement regarding overfeeding is found in the Mallinson et al. publication. In *Orang-utan Behavior,* Maple** (1980a) also warned of the dangers of overfeeding. We find particular comfort in quoting Mallinson et al. as follows:

> Advice was given by Sister Robbins of the Jersey Maternity Hospital, who particularly stressed the dangers of overfeeding. Overfed infants can develop vomiting and diarrhea with consequent loss of weight and it is better therefore to slightly underfeed (p. 192).

We have also reproduced herein two tables from Mallinson et al. which depict the diets for two Jersey gorillas during their first week of hand-rearing (Table 5-9), and first 236 days of life (Table 5-10). A complete table of ape diets from three other experienced institutions can also be consulted in Maple (1980a).

---

*Medical authorities have asserted that, in humans, babies have been known to survive five days without feeding (cf. Fisher, 1972). Since, in apes, nursing can be infrequent or even nonexistent for several days, observers should not be too quick to remove the infant. Previously, on the recommendations of the veterinarian at the Yerkes Primate Center (Swenson, personal communication), Maple has argued that staff should be patient but vigilant during the first few days after the birth of an ape (1979). If the infant's grasping reflexes remain strong, some undetected suckling may be taking place. In Fisher's patient vigil, definite nursing was not observed until the fifth day postpartum. Thereafter, it was observed to occur about six times per day, lasting from two to six minutes each time. Similarly, the infant *Kishka* was not observed nursing until its third day of life (Johnstone-Scott, 1979).

**The observations of Tijskens (1971) suggest that captive gorillas grow at a faster rate than orang-utans. This trend is apparent in both body weight and the eruption of deciduous teeth.

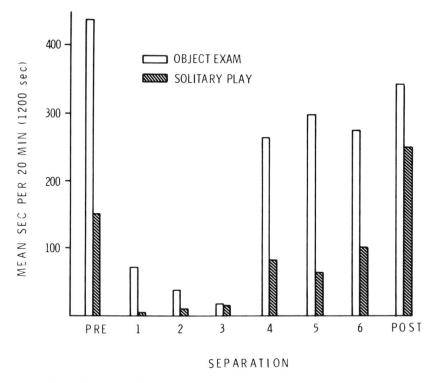

Figure 5-15. Solitary behaviors of young gorillas during a separation experiment. See text for details. (After Hoff, Nadler, and Maple, 1979)

King and Rivers (1976) also discussed the problem of obesity in relation to hand-rearing. It was noted that gorilla milk contains between 50 and 20% of the fat content found in human or cow's milk, or milk substitutes. They suggested that hand-reared gorilla infants may therefore be receiving milk with an excessive caloric density. There is evidence that bottle-feeding contributes to obesity later in life. Breast-fed baby apes, like their human counterparts, have been found to be lighter in weight at comparable ages than bottle-fed infants (Maple, 1980a). King and Rivers were also concerned with the captive diet of the adults in the Jersey colony. We list their recommendations as follows:

1. Obesity was considered to be a major risk, possibly of sufficient importance to ultimately threaten the survival and longevity of the colony.
2. Action should be taken to increase activity, and hence energy expenditure,
   particularly in the obese females. Failing that, the diet should be redesigned to reduce the caloric density.
3. For the health of both mother and infant, breast-feeding should be encouraged when at all possible.

Table 5-9. Diet for gorilla infants during week one of hand rearing at the Jersey Wildlife Preservation Trust (After Mallinson, Coffey, and Usher-Smith, 1976).

AGE (days)	INFANT	TOTAL VOL. OFFERED VOLUME PER FEED (ml)		FREQUENCY	WEIGHT (kg)
1	Assumbo	84	2×7 ml 5% Dextrose sol[1] 10×7 ml SMA	2 hourly	At 40 hrs 2·200
	Mamfe	96	1×12 ml 5% Dextrose sol[1] 7×12 ml SMA	3 hourly	At 7 hrs 2·550
2	Assumbo	120	8×12 ml SMA $(+ 1 \times 5$ ml 5% Dextrose sol)[2]	3 hourly	2·230
	Mamfe	152	8×19 ml SMA	3 hourly	2·400
3	Assumbo	160	8×20 ml SMA $(+ 1 \times 5$ ml 5% Dextrose sol)[2]	3 hourly	2·240
	Mamfe	200	8×25 ml SMA $(+ 1 \times 1$ tsp brown sugar)	3 hourly	2·365
4	Assumbo	200	8×25 ml SMA	3 hourly	2·240
	Mamfe	248	8×31 ml SMA $(+ 3 \times 1$ tsp brown sugar)	3 hourly	2·360
5	Assumbo	240	8×30 ml SMA	3 hourly	2·265
	Mamfe	296	8×37 ml SMA $(+ 6 \times 1$ tsp brown sugar)	3 hourly	2·370
6	Assumbo	280	8×35 ml SMA	3 hourly	2·275
	Mamfe	360	8×45 ml SMA $(+ 8 \times 5$ ml 10% Fructose sol)[3]	3 hourly	2·435
7	Assumbo	320	8×40 ml SMA	3 hourly	2·280
	Mamfe	440	8×55 ml SMA $(+ 8 \times 5$ ml 10% Fructose sol)	3 hourly	2·450

[1] 5% Dextrose solution given as first feed/feeds.
[2] 5% Dextrose solution given to provide more volume without increasing food content.
[3] 10% Fructose solution used as a laxative until day 10.

Table 5-10. The daily food intake of the western lowland gorilla *Assumbo* from day 8–236 (After Mallinson, Coffey, and Usher-Smith, 1976).

AGE (days)	TOTAL VOLUME SMA OFFERED (ml)	NUMBER FEEDS	SMA VOLUME PER FEED	DAILY SMA INTAKE (average)	SOLIDS GIVEN (tsp) mashed/strained/solid	TIMES OF FEEDS
8/9	350	7	50	350	1 tsp Farex	0100, 0500, 0900, 1200[1] 1500, 1800, 2100.
10/12	420	7	60	420	1 tsp Farex	
13	525	7	75	525	1 tsp Farex	
14/16	540	6	90	540	2 tsp Farex	0100, 0500, 0900, 1300,[1] 1700, 2100.
17/20	630	6	105	630	3 tsp Farex	0100, 0500, 0900, 1300,[3] 1700, 2100.[1]
21/23	720	6	120	720	3 tsp Farex	
24/25	810	6	135	740	2 tsp Farex 1 mashed banana Farex discontinued see note[3]	
26/36	675	5	135	670	3 msh banana	0600, 1000,[1] 1400, 1800, 2200.[1]
37/44	700	5	140	700	3 msh banana	
45/46	720	{3 / 2	{140 / 150	720	3 msh banana	
47/48	735	{2 / 3	{140 / 150	735	3 msh banana	
49/51	750	5	150	750	3 msh banana	
52/57	770	{3 / 2	{150 / 160	770	3 msh banana	

Table 5-10. (Continued)

AGE (days)	TOTAL VOLUME SMA OFFERED (ml)	NUMBER FEEDS	SMA VOLUME PER FEED	DAILY SMA INTAKE (average)	SOLIDS GIVEN (tsp) mashed/strained/solid	TIMES OF FEEDS
58	780	{2 / 3	{150 / 160	780	3 msh banana	
59/60	800	5	160	800	3 msh banana	0600, 1000,[1] 1400, 1800, 2200.[1]
61	820	{3 / 2	{160 / 170	820	3 msh banana	
62	830	{2 / 3	{160 / 170	830	3 msh banana / str fruit[4]	
63/81	850	5	170	800	3 str fruit	0700, 1100,[1]1500, 1900, 2300.[1]
82/106	840	4	210	810	3-4 str fruit	
107/125	880	4	220	800	4-5 str fruit	
126/139	920	4	230	880	6-8 str fruit	
140/154	960	4	240	950	8-12 str fruit	
155/185	1000	4	250	800	12-16 str fruit	0700, 1100,[2] 1200, 1800, 2300.
186/204	1040	4	260	800	16-20 str fruit	
205/224	1080	4	270	810	20 str fruit	
225/235	810	3	270	810	24 str fruit	0700, 1100,[2] 1700, 2300
236[5] onwards	690	3	230	630	3 × 24 str fruit/vegetable	0800,[1] 1200,[1] 1700[2] 2300.

[1] Both fruit and SMA feed given.
[2] Fruit feed only.
[3] Wheat and rye cereals excluded from diet to avoid the possibility of the gorillas developing coeliac disease (a malabsorption condition due to an idiosyncrasy to the gluten fraction of protein in wheat and rye).
[4] Tinned fruit and fruit/rice desserts given for variety (Heinz strained baby food).
[5] Milk reduced and more fruit and fluid (glucose solution and/or pure orange juice) given because both infants, in particular Assumbo, were constipated.

4. Blood samples should be obtained for serum cholesterol and tri-glyceride content determinations at every opportunity.

5. Accurate weights of specimens was considered sufficiently important to justify considerable effort and expenditure in devising systems for routine weighing. It would be useful to go to the extent even of anaesthetising specimens regularly for weighing and blood sampling.

6. Components of animal origin should be removed from the diet, at least on a trial basis, with subsequent dietary monitoring to check the effect of such changes.

7. The diet should be redesigned to increase the role of fruits, vegetables and other foods of plant origin, and to decrease that of animal products, taking care to maintain the quality of the diet in other respects.

ADOPTION OF A FERAL INFANT

Some potential for adoption apparently exists in feral gorilla groups. Our research associate, John Fowler, participated in a reintroduction study in Rwanda during the early months of 1980. The reintroduction was necessary because an infant female had been found apart from her natal group. She was brought to Dian Fossey's camp for a rehabilitation period, during which time John lived with her in a forest camp, "teaching" her to forage on her own. After this intermediate phase, a first introduction attempt ended in near disaster. On March 1, an effort was made to introduce the infant to Fossey's group 5. The response of this group was aggressive, and John and his young charge were obliged to flee. A few weeks thereafter, Stuart Perlmeter attempted to introduce her into group 4. This effort has apparently succeeded. As this book goes to press, the infant (named *Bonne Anneé*) has resided in group 4 for over three months, spending a considerable amount of her time in proximity to the silverbacked male, *Peanuts*. Thus, it appears that feral gorillas are capable of "adopting" a young member of their own kind. Since *Bonne Anneé* has no mother, the key to her successful introduction has been her ability to obtain food on her own.

In this chapter, we have examined the events surrounding birth, the subsequent development of offspring, and the behavior of both mothers and fathers. There is now a considerable literature on these subjects as a glimpse at the bibliography quickly reveals. What are the subjects which need most to be investigated in this new decade? We think that there are several. First, it is important that we learn more about parity and how it affects birth. Ideally, we need to observe and quantify a greater number of births of individual mothers. In this way, we document the progress of mothers as they gain experience. Second, we have yet to observe a sufficient number of offspring to be able to determine the behavioral effects of gender. We have so little data on this important topic that, for this anthropoid taxon, it would be foolhardy to generalize. Finally, it would be extremely useful if a successful field study of feral lowland gorilla development could be accomplished. The ideal study would be coordinated with captive observations so that direct comparisons could be made. There is still far too little communication among field and captive workers, and this makes comparisons and generalizations very hazardous indeed. If gorilla research continues at its rapid pace, we are in for an exciting ten years of new findings.

6
Intellect of Gorillas

... I am still of the opinion that our ability actually to gauge the intelligence of most of these wild creatures is based largely on the intelligence of the individual making the observations and I have never felt yet that a statement of comparative intelligence of great apes, or any other animals based largely on the study of a few individuals, is a fair comparison.

Belle Benchley, 1949

There has been surprisingly little research concerning the intellectual powers of the gorilla. This is so despite the fact that Robert and Ada Yerkes (1929) intuitively ranked the gorilla as superior to both *Pan* and *Pongo* in intelligence. Objectively, the Yerkes' ranked the gorilla ahead of the chimpanzee and orang-utan in the following dimensions: attention, memory, and imagination. The Yerkes furthermore believed that the gorilla bore the greater intellectual resemblance to humankind. In their view, if it lagged behind the chimpanzee in the other eight intellectual categories that they identified, it was because gorillas had not yet been so well studied as chimpanzees. Today, we still know less about gorillas than chimpanzees, but we now have much more objective data than the Yerkes had available to them. With these facts in mind, we will review what is known about gorilla intellect and then, with the Yerkes' as our model, we will do our best to make comparative generalizations. In this effort, perhaps we can improve upon the judgment of the humorist Will Cuppy (1931) who wrote:

> If the scientist places a banana in a box the chimpanzee will go and get it and eat it . . . [;] the gorilla will bite the Professor's cousin (p. 33)

TEMPERAMENT

The temperament differences to be found among chimpanzees, gorillas, and orang-utans extend to the realm of problem-solving. Gorillas are not as exhuberent when challenged as are chimpanzees. According to Benchley:

196

I have seen chimpanzees open a door by beating and striking, pulling and shoving, turning it back and forth and apparently having no conception of what any of their movements have accomplished, but finally forcing or breaking it open by sheer strength (pp. 127-128).

As argued elsewhere (Maple, 1980a), the orang-utan is by contrast a masterful manipulator of objects. This propensity to patiently "fool" with the objects* is not so nearly developed in gorillas. Here again, Benchley makes the point clear:

Our gorillas apparently are not interested in anything of a mechanical nature. When we put impediments in the way of their doing what they desire, they appear to lose that desire (p. 127).

It is quite likely that the perception of the gorilla as an uncooperative and disinterested creature has discouraged investigators from properly scrutinizing their intellectual powers. An added deterrent has been their great strength and alleged ferocity. Gorillas make short work of any experimental apparatus which has not been strengthened to withstand their blows. In captivity, as we have seen, gorillas incorporate the built environment into their agressive displays. They will drum, pound, and kick against any surface that reverberates the sound. Their use of the environment to create noise may be seen as a kind of tool use, and in gorillas the behavior is clearly an extension of their natural chest-beating display. As must be apparent, the species-typical temperament of any animal will put constraints upon those behaviors which can be readily acquired. As we will see, however, given the "personality" of the gorilla, there are many behaviors which it learns as easily as any chimpanzee. No more nor less dangerous than a chimpanzee, gorillas can also be trained and controlled, but few trainers have dared to try. For this reason, the gorilla's captive reputation is one of relatively greater dignity.

ADAPTIVE BEHAVIOR

Knobloch and Pasamanick (1959b) followed up on their study of motor development (cf. Chapter 5) with a report on the adaptive behavior of *Colo*. Since these investigators could not rely on their motor behavior data to assess intellectual functioning, they selected tests of adaptive behavior in order to do so. Knobloch and Pasamanick asserted that, although their instrument did not actually test for conceptualization, it did predict later ability for abstract thinking. Thus, according to these investigators, their study successfully tested the infant precursors to cognition.

---

*Schaller observed no tool using in his year of study, suggesting that a vegetarian amidst plentiful forage has no need for tools.

We have extracted intact Knobloch and Pasamanick's original data in Table 6-1. Like motor behavior, adaptive behavior developed early in *Colo* and progressed in a series of spurts and plateaus. At ten weeks of age, she could approach and grasp objects within her reach. At sixteen weeks, many behaviors not seen in human infants until much later appeared in *Colo*. The *one-hand approach and grasp* appeared at twelve weeks, while hand-to-hand transfer did not appear until twenty-four weeks. In human infants, both occur at about twenty-eight weeks. Thus, *Colo's* development was erratic by human standards. A special gorilla adaptation became evident within these first six months of life:

> When Colo became more interested in small things, she was very inept at securing them, and she began to develop the use of her mouth as a third prehensile organ. This pattern of mouth reaching she elaborated, and in many instances she seemed to prefer it, for example, as a method of removing the cube from the cup or of securing the pellet (p. 702).

Colo achieved a sort of asymptote in her adaptive behavior patterns by the twenty-eighth week of life. Knobloch and Pasamanick noted, however, that many of the test activities were never mastered. For example, she never matched together two objects held in her hands, and could not be induced to thrust a cube into the cup or to attempt to build a tower. Furthermore:

> When presented with three inverted cups under one of which her favorite fruit, a grape was placed, she would either reach indiscriminately for all three at once in pursuit of the cups themselves or ignore them. Only if she actually saw the grape being put under a cup would she go for it directly. In view of these responses, no attempt was made to employ some of the other tests which have been used with Zoo or laboratory-raised subhuman primates (p. 702).

Knobloch and Pasamanick further described *Colo's* behavior as *autistic,* although their reasoning is difficult to comprehend, since their elaboration on this point is so vague. Because she failed to progress beyond a certain point, they suggested that she may have been retarded (her mother had been diagnosed as toxemic prior to her birth), or that her association with humans may have somehow disturbed her performance. Comparison with another calmer gorilla, however, revealed that *Colo's* performance was indeed representative of her species. As Knobloch and Pasamanick concluded:

> There is little question that the chimpanzee is capable of conceptualization and abstraction that is beyond the abilities of the gorilla. It is precisely because of these limitations, which are apparently genetically determined and which make him a gorilla rather than a chimpanzee or human, that it is more difficult to work with him [sic] (p. 703).

Table 6-1. A comparison of the age at which *Adaptive* behavior occurs in human, gorilla, and chimpanzee infants. (After Knobloch and Pasamanick, 1959b)

Behavior Item	Age of Appearance		
	Human Norm	Gorilla (Colo)	Chimpanzee[a] (Viki, Gua)
Supine			
Regards line of vision only	4 weeks	2.5 w	6 w[b]
Follows to midline		2.5 w	
Drops rattle immediately		2.5 w	
Diminishes activity at bell-ringing		10 w	
Supine			
Delayed midline regard	8 weeks	4 w	
Regards examiner's hand		2.5 w	
Follows past midline		6 w	6 w
Retains rattle briefly		8 w	
Facial response to bell-ringing		—[b]	
Supine			
Prompt midline regard	12 weeks	10 w	
Follows 180°		10 w	
Glances at rattle in hand		12 w	
Sitting			
Regards cube & cup more than momentarily		10 w	
Supine			
Regards immediately	16 weeks	10 w	
Arms activate on sight		10 w	
Regards rattle in hand		12 w	
Rattle to mouth		10 w	6 w
Free hand to midline		10 w	
Sitting			
Looks down at TT or hands		10 w	
Looks from hand to object		10 w	
Regards pellet		10 w	
Supine or Sitting			
2 hand approach	20 weeks	10 w	
Grasps only if near hand		10 w	
Visual pursuit lost rattle		10 w	
Sitting			
Holds 1st cube, regards 2nd		16 w	
Grasps 1 of multiple cubes on contact		14 w	
Supine or Sitting			
Approaches and grasps	24 weeks	10 w	
Prehensile pursuit dropped rattle		12 w	
Sitting			
Regards 3rd cube immediately		18 w	
Takes cube or bell to mouth		12 w	
Resecures dropped cube		16 w	
Holds 1 of multiple cubes, approaches another		18 w	

Table 6-1. (Continued)

Behavior Item	Age of Appearance		
	Human Norm	Gorilla (Colo)	Chimpanzee[a] (Viki, Gua)
Supine or Sitting			
1 hand approach and grasp	28 weeks	12 w	
Shakes rattle definitely		12 w	
Transfers		24 w	
Sitting			
Holds 1 of multiple cubes, grasps another		18 w	
Holds 2 cubes more than momentarily		16 w	
Bangs bell		18 w	
Retains bell		16 w	
Transfers bell adeptly		24 w	
Sitting			
Grasps 2nd cube	32 weeks	16 w	
Retains 2 cubes as 3rd presented		18 w	
Holds 2 cubes prolongedly		18 w	
Holds cube, regards cup		16 w	
Secures ring by string		20 w	14 w
Sitting			
Grasps 3rd cube	36 weeks	24 w	
Hits and pushes cube with cube		24 w	
Hits cube against cup		24 w	
Approaches bottle first, with pellet & bottle		18 w	
Manipulates string while holding ring		18 w	
Sitting			
Matches 2 cubes	40 weeks	Never Seen	
Touches cube in cup		26 w	
Index finger approach to pellet		28 w	
Approaches pellet first with pellet & bottle		26 w	
Regards pellet if drops out of bottle		20 w	
Grasps pellet & bottle simultaneously		18 w	
Grasps bell by handle		18 w	
Spontaneously waves or shakes bell		24 m	44 w
Sitting			
Removes cube from cup	44 weeks	28 w[c]	
Thrusts cube into cup without release after demonstration		Never Seen	44 w
Points at pellet thru glass of bottle		26 w	
Regards and pokes clapper of bell		48 w[d]	
Approaches string of ring-string first		20 w	

Table 6-1. (Continued)

Behavior Item	Age of Appearance		
	Human Norm	Gorilla (Colo)	Chimpanzee[a] (Viki, Gua)
Sitting			
Sequential play with cubes	48 weeks	36 w[e]	
Takes pellet only with pellet and bottle		30 w	
Removes round block from formboard easily		26 w	
Sitting			
Tries tower of 2, fails, after demonstration	52 weeks	Never Seen	
Releases 1 cube in cup, after demonstration		Never Seen	44 w
Tries to insert pellet in bottle, releases, fails		Never Seen	
Dangles ring by string		32 w[e]	
Looks selectively at round hole of formboard		Never Seen	
Sitting			
Cube into cup without demonstration	56 weeks	Never Seen	44 w
Vigorous imitative scribble		Never Seen	52 w
Inserts round block in formboard without demonstration		Never Seen	52 w
Sitting			
Tower 2 cubes	15 months	Never Seen	48 w
Indicates wants by pointing		Never Seen	48 w
Sitting			
Scribbles spontaneously	18 months	Never Seen	56 w
Looks at pictures		Never Seen	14 m
Eats with spoon		Never Seen	48 w

[a] Ages for the chimpanzee can only be approximated, since either the items reported were not strictly comparable nor specifically defined or the time of appearance was given in general terms, e.g., "Spring."

[b] Uncertain about time of appearance.

[c] With mouth first before with hand.

[d] With mouth; with finger at 21 m.

[e] Behavior seen only on this one occasion.

As far as intellectual functioning was concerned, this study concluded that gorillas were most likely inferior to both chimpanzees and human beings. Knobloch and Pasamanick were apparently unwilling to admit the possibility that some degree of human error could influence their findings. Since they had little appreciation for the natural propensities of gorillas (in all fairness, there was no literature in 1959 with which to acquire such an appreciation), their conclusion was misguided. In re-examining their data, we could just as easily conclude that *Colo* was not sufficiently habituated to the testing situation, or that the tasks were inappropriately administered. Gorillas, like children, do not perform optimally when overly stressed. To be sure, Knobloch and Pasamanick's early study provide us with some valuable data, but more recent studies have given us another picture of the gorilla. The modern literature reveals that gorillas are clever creatures, intellectual equals of *Pan* and *Pongo*.

Manipulativeness

The manipulative skills of lowland gorillas were described in a comparative study by Parker (1969). Maple (1980a) reviewed this study in some detail, so we will concentrate here on the major results which pertain to our subject taxon. Although gorillas were found to be less responsive to manipulable objects than orang-utans,* they persisted at manipulation longer than did their Asian counterparts. Gorillas tended to explore objects visually, whereas orang-utans were more tactual in their mode of exploration. In terms of the specific kinds of manipulations, Parker noted that gorillas were inferior to orangs in the variety and number of responses. Gorillas, like chimpanzees, cautiously touched the objects with fingertips and backs of hands before grasping them.

Parker developed two further techniques for the examination of initial motor responses, and the perception of the respective species. The *dip* problem required the insertion of a piece of rope into a hole to extract banana mash. The *hoe* problem required the acquisition of fruit by the use of a J-shaped tool. Parker attempted to relate problem success and mode of solution to the degree of responsiveness and the initial response repertoire of his subjects. Gorillas were found to be superior to chimpanzees but inferior to orang-utans on both problems. On the hoe problem, the mode of solution for gorillas was to throw and strike the hoe, and to strike the apparatus with the hoe. Solution was therefore a matter of trial and error. As Parker suggested, the gorillas properly oriented their behavior toward the incentive, but they exhibited less awareness of the solution than did orang-utans.

The manipulation of objects seems not to be as highly developed in gorillas as compared to chimpanzees and orang-utans. In our observations, gorillas

---

*Gorillas were found to be more responsive than chimpanzees however.

Figure 6-1. *Bata,* a western lowland gorilla, engaged in test of intelligence as carried out by Joan Kelly at the San Diego Zoo. *(Photo courtesy Zoological Society of San Diego)*

were observed to place clods of dirt, sticks, and foliage on their heads and shoulders. Both adults and infants manipulated these objects playfully. Gorillas are also known to employ objects in the course of intimidation displays. However, in keeping with Benchley's early observations, gorillas do not appear to be as interested in objects as do the other apes. This generalization, however, needs to be more carefully studied. Carpenter also observed a form of cooperation in the San Diego mountain gorillas as they worked together in moving an 800-pound log inside their cage. He also suggested that their water-sliding behavior, and their mutual grooming roles were essentially cooperative in nature.

Problem Solving

In studies of learning set, in which subjects acquire a pattern or set by experience with a series of discriminations, Rumbaugh and McCormack (1967) found that lowland gorillas performed at the 65-90% correct levels on all tests. This performance was essentially equivalent to that of chimpanzees and orangs. Similarly, a patterned-string study conducted by Fisher and Kitchener (1964) also determined that gorillas performed as well as chimps and orangs.

COGNITIVE DEVELOPMENT

In 1975, Redshaw reviewed her findings on the cognitive, manipulative, and social skills of captive lowland gorillas. The four infant subjects of her investigation were all hand-reared at the Jersey Zoo. Redshaw's initial studies (Hughes and Redshaw, 1974; 1975) had determined that the gorillas *Mamfe* and *Assumbo* generally developed in a fashion parallel to, but in advance of, the development of human infants. However, as Redshaw pointed out, there were some exceptions to this generalization. For example, there was a lack of reciprocal play over objects which is so clearly evident in the play of human infants. Between gorillas, there were no give and take games, and no handing back of toys to the caretaker. On the contrary, gorillas focused their attention on the toy itself, biting and manipulating it, and throwing it about.

All four of the young gorillas exhibited a tendency to imitate simple gestures, but this behavior developed later than is the case in human infants. During their first year of life, none of the gorilla infants were able to use a rake as a tool nor did they successfully place one block onto another. Redshaw confidently noted in her 1975 paper that in cognitive development there is less variability in the performance of gorillas than in comparable human infants. Redshaw's conclusions on the first year of development are worth quoting here:

> The pattern of early psychological development found in gorilla infants is similar to, and in a few very particular ways, different from, the development of human infants during this period. After this point however, the divergence which was already underway, goes ahead by leaps and bounds, each infant becoming very much a member of its own species. The human infant learns to talk, to play symbolically and to walk bipedally, while the gorilla knuckle-walks, chest-beats, wrestles, climbs and builds nests (p. 56).

As Redshaw suggested, young gorillas can be difficult subjects for cognitive testing, but with patience on the part of the experimenter, results are eventually forthcoming. In a category which she labeled *thinking and problem solving,* Redshaw used both paper-and-pencil and videotape apparatus to record her data. To induce her subjects to cooperate, she used dried fruit, nuts, or grapes as rewards. During her second year of testing, Redshaw worked exclusively with the subjects *Mamfe* and *Assumbo*.

Discrimination studies were carried out by hiding rewards beneath containers which varied in color, shape, and size. In the initial stages of testing, the differences in the containers were large, but with experience the problems were increased in

Table 6-2. Comparative development of operational causality in gorilla
and human infants. (After Hughes and Redshaw, 1974)

	Age Observed (weeks)		
Step	Assumbo	Mamfe	Human
1. Hand watching behavior observed	6	6	8
2. Immediate repetition of an action resulting in interesting input	10	6	13
3. Use of a specific action to activate (restart) a spectacle	14	14	25
4. Use of a specific action to restart a familiar game with another person	42	38	ni
5. Touches the examiner's hand after demonstration (e.g. hitting blocks together)	ny	ny	21
6. Hands a mechanical toy back to the examiner, following a demonstration	ny	ny	52−65
7. Attempts to activate a mechanical toy by direct action, following a demonstration . .	46	50	91

ni: no information.   ny: not yet observed.

difficulty. In a general way, the results indicated that gorilla infants, like human infants, admirably succeed with the simpler problems but experience difficulty with finer discriminations.

In latch box problems, Redshaw analyzed the fashion in which gorillas were required to open a box. These boxes were graded in difficulty of entry, much like the early puzzle boxes that Thorndike (1898) constructed to investigate problem solving in cats. Both gorillas worked enthusiastically on this problem, unlike human subjects which generally cried or enlisted the assistance of an adult. The gorillas were of course suitably gorillalike in their approach to the problem, as Redshaw has shown:

. . . between the gorillas there was a clear difference in strategy, with Assumbo very much concentrating on manipulating of the mechanism gently, while Mamfe, if success did not occur after the first few vigorous attempts, would intersperse further efforts with beating the box very severely . . . On this problem it seemed that the gorillas were considerably more persistent than the human subjects, though the latter could follow a series of verbal instructions to bring about the solution of the problems and obviously the gorillas could not. If equally matched, without any helpful verbal hints for the humans, the gorillas would be more likely to succeed on this task (p. 58).

Table 6-3. Comparative development of ability to construct object
relations in space. (After Hughes and Redshaw, 1974)

	Age Observed (weeks)		
Step	Assumbo	Mamfe	Human
1. Alternates glance slowly between two visual targets	ni	2	8
2. Alternates glance rapidly between two visual targets	ni	6	13
3. Localizes sound source	10	6	13−21
4. Grasps an object presented in visual field	14	14	17−21
5. Reconstructs the trajectory of a falling object	14	14	26
6. Leans forward, actively searching for fallen object	18	22	30
7. Recognizes the reversal of an object	22	22	39
8. Uses one object as a container for another	32	30	39
9. Builds a tower of at least two blocks	ny	ny	65
10. Uses string as an extension of an object vertically, compensating for gravity	38	34	56−65
11. Takes account of the effect of gravity by releasing a wheeled toy on an inclined plane	ny	54	ni
12. Interest in the phenomenon of 'the fall', systematically dropping objects and watching them fall	46	46	ni
13. Makes detours in order to obtain objects	ni	ni	ni
14. Indicates knowledge of whereabouts of familiar persons	na	na	75

ni: no information.   ny: not yet observed.   na: not applicable.

In *spatial-mechanical* problems, the subjects had to operate a lever or a pulley to obtain the reward. These problems determined whether the subject could differentiate between two types of levers. At this task, the two gorillas were not equally successful:

By about two years of age, Assumbo has succeeded on this task when e.g. a series of trials involve the same lever and then a following series of trials involve the other lever. However, when the trials were mixed, he tends to move the lever "any old how," without looking very carefully to see the location of

Table 6-4. Comparative development of visual pursuit and object permanence in gorilla and human infants. (After Hughes and Redshaw, 1974)

	Age Observed (weeks)		
	Assumbo	Mamfe	Human
1. Follows object thro' 180° arc smoothly . .	4	4	4
2. Gaze lingers at point of disappearance of slowly-moving object	8	6	8
3. Searches for a partially hidden object . . .	14	14	16–20
4. Gaze returns to starting-point on disappearance of a slowly-moving object	14	14	20–32
5. Finds object completely hidden by a single screen	18	18	28
6. Finds object hidden under one of two screens	22	22	28
7. Finds object hidden under one of three screens	30	30	30
8. Finds object hidden under a number of superimposed screens	30	34	39–43
9. Finds object after visible displacement under 3 screens	34	38	ni
10. Finds object after 1 invisible displacement under a single screen	38	38	48–56
11. Finds object after one invisible displacement under one of 2 screens	38	38	56
12. Finds object after 1 invisible displacement with 2 screens alternated	38	38	60
13. Finds object following 1 invisible displacement under one of three screens	42	42	60
14. Finds object after a series of invisible displacements	42	46	82

ni: no information.

the reward . . . Mamfe, on the other hand, has yet to understand the problem at all. The lever has to be moved sideways, either to the right or to the left, but Mamfe insists on pulling it towards him, pushing it down or pulling it upwards or even chewing it . . . (p. 58).

In another task utilized by Redshaw, the gorillas were required to use a lever and switch simultaneously. Both gorillas quickly learned to operate the switch or lever separately. The simultaneous operation of the two manipulanda were learned just as quickly by *Assumbo*, however, *Mamfe* only learned to operate them in sequence.

Rake problems, as described by Köhler* (1925; see also Maple, 1980a) and utilized in the Yerkes' early experiments with *Congo*, were not successfully solved until *Assumbo* succeeded at twenty-six months of age. Redshaw remarked that it seemed as if, for the first time, the little gorilla had become aware of what he was trying to do. Thereafter, he readily solved rake problems. *Mamfe's* performance on rake problems was notably deficient by comparison.

As for memory for the location of rewards, a level of 80% correct was reached by both subjects by the age of fourteen months. *Mamfe*, deficient on so many other tasks, was superior to *Assumbo* on this one. When delays were increased from five seconds to longer periods (15 seconds to 5 minutes), the subjects were often successful but also lost motivation.

Tube problems, in which the gorillas had to tilt the objects to receive the rewards enclosed, were also readily learned by both subjects. Both gorillas exhibited hand preferences with *Assumbo* exhibiting a slight left-hand preference, and *Mamfe* an overwhelming right-hand preference (see also Chapter 1).

This research, although preliminary in scope, has demonstrated that young gorillas are responsive to the test situation, exhibiting an ability equal to that of chimpanzees and, in some instances, human children. As Redshaw determined, the young gorilla can no longer be derogated as the "dim-witted" relative of the chimpanzee.

From the recent work of Redshaw and her colleagues, it is appropriate to look back at the early experiments of Robert Yerkes. Using as his subject the mountain gorilla *Congo*, Yerkes was the first scientist to objectively evaluate the learning skills of this taxon. It is interesting to note that every subsequent test has employed the western lowland gorilla. Whether Yerkes' results were influenced by the taxonomic variable cannot be determined until rigorous comparative studies are conducted. It is unlikely that there will ever be enough captive representatives of *beringei* to even begin to answer the question.

Memory For People

Yerkes was convinced that *Congo* remembered him and certain experimental situations even after an interval of ten to eleven months. Planned as a test of recognition, Yerkes (dressed in his testing garb) appeared without warning before the ape's cage after an absence of ten months, and as he described it:

> No sooner had I appeared beside the cage than Congo approached me and, pressing her face against the wire netting which separated us, protruded her

---

*The feral gorilla's use of sticks to acquire out of reach food has been reported by Phillips (1950) and Pitman (1931; as cited in Schaller, 1963).

Table 6-5. Comparative development of means by which gorilla and human infants acquire objects. (After Hughes and Redshaw, 1974)

	Age Observed (weeks)		
	Assumbo	Mamfe	Human
1. Hand watching behaviour observed	6	6	8
2. Attempts to keep toy in motion by repeated movements	6	6	13
3. Grasps toy when both hand and toy are in view	10	10	13–17
4. Grasps toy when only toy is in view (hand out of visual field)	14	14	17
5. Lets go of one object in order to reach for another	18	18	34
6. Pulls a support to obtain an object	30	22	34
7. Uses locomotion to retrieve a toy	18	18	39
8. Resists pulling the support when an object is held 4 ins. above it	34	34	43
9. Uses string tied to an object to obtain the object on a horizontal surface	30	22	52
10. Uses string to obtain an object suspended vertically	38	34	56
11. Uses a stick to obtain a toy which is out of reach on a horizontal surface	ny	ny	65–78

ny: not yet observed.

lips as if in salutation. Simultaneously she made a deep throaty grunting sound, which previous experience enabled me to interpret as indicative of satisfaction . . . The animal made me feel that she was glad to see me. In deed, her welcome was more than my experience a year previously had led me to expect (p. 13).

This behavior was not elicited when *Congo* was approached by strangers, and thus Yerkes concluded that she had indeed remembered him.

Box and Pole Test

In this problem, the ape was required to obtain food from a long box by means of a wooden pole. This task is also quite similar in demand to the insight experiments of Wolfgang Köhler (1925). When first introduced to the problem, *Congo* immediately ran to the pole, carried it quickly to one end of the box and, using the stick properly, pushed the food into reach in only twenty-eight seconds. In three thirty-minute trials, ten months after the original mastery of the problem, *Congo* failed to evince memory of the solution.

Platform and Stick

A classical insight problem, *Congo* was presented a stick with which to reach out-of-reach food items. This problem was solved only with extreme difficulty and the "tuitional aid" of the experimenter himself. However, when tested ten months later, *Congo* promptly solved the problem acting "with at least as great a measure of skill and proficiency as at the completion of this experiment in the previous winter" (p. 17).

Roundabout Course with Stick

This problem was somewhat more challenging in that *Congo* was required to use a stick to first move the object away from her body, and then toward it. In the winter of 1927, *Congo* failed to solve the problem during three trials of thirty minutes each. Nearly one year later, she failed just as miserably as before, this time failing to solve the problem in four lengthy trials. As Yerkes (1928) concluded:

> According to the findings of Kohler, the young chimpanzee may promptly solve a roundabout-course-with-stick problem, thus indicating a measure of superiority in behavioral adaptivity to *G. beringei,* as represented by Congo (p. 21).

COGNITIVE PROBLEM SOLVING

Robbins, Compton, and Howard (1978) attempted to assess the cognitive processes of lowland gorillas by using an extradimensional versus reversal shift comparison. In this procedure, one of two stimulus dimensions is the relevant cue which must be learned. As the investigators explained:

> . . . let us assume we have stimuli varying on two dimensions, size and shape. A simultaneous discrimination task is used and subjects are presented with a large triangle and a small square on one trial type and a small triangle and a large square on the other trial type. If the relevant "concept" or dimension is size and large is positive, then the large triangle of one and the large square of the other trial type are the positive stimuli. During an extradimensional shift, the same stimuli are presented, but now shape is relevant, e.g. triangles are positive (p. 231).

Depending on the experimenter's choice of right or wrong dimensions, the animal is faced with two subproblems, one that is changed and one that is unchanged. Thus, in the preceding example, although the dimension has changed or shifted, the subject need not change its response on the large triangle-small square trial (the unchanged subproblem) because the large triangle is still correct. On the changed subproblem, however, they must reverse their previous choice. There are published data which show that animals tend to make few errors on the unchanged problem, and most of their errors on the changed problems. The learning of two independent subproblems is considered noncognitive or nonconceptual behavior. This is in contrast to the behavior of human subjects who show no differential behavior on changed and unchanged subproblems. Thus, human beings exhibit cognitive or conceptual behavior.

The study conducted by Robbins and his students employed two female lowland gorillas, *Oko* and *Katoomba,* each of which were residents of the Yerkes Primate Center. The investigators used a modified Wisconsin General Test Apparatus (WGTA). The gorillas were exposed to a series of six problems incorporating a two-choice simultaneous visual discrimination task. Each problem was comprised of four phases: original learning, an extradimensional shift, an intradimensional shift, and another extradimensional shift. Each phase continued until the subject made twenty consecutive correct responses. The reward for participation was Hershette (M&M type) candy. Robbins described a typical trial as follows:

> The experimenter turned the light on above the two stimuli; the subject responded by breaking a photocell beam in front of one of the two stimulus pictures; the response terminated the light above the stimuli and reward was delivered if a correct response was made. Since a noncorrection procedure was used, incorrect responses terminated these error trials. The experimenter recorded the subjects' choice and reward (or nonreward) and set up the stimuli and reward conditions for the next trial during a 30-45 sec intertrial interval. The position of the stimuli was randomly determined within blocks of 10 trials (p. 233).

The results of the study indicated that these two gorillas developed a "cognitive solution style" after initially solving the problems in a noncognitive manner. Robbins compares the phenomenon to the "learning to learn" set as first reported by Harlow (1949). Thus, with experience gorillas exhibit cognitive behaviors in much the same way as do human beings who are faced with similar problems.

A PIAGETIAN MODEL

Chevalier-Skolnikoff (1977) recently described an ongoing study in which five infant and five adult western lowland gorillas were studied. In this project, the investigator assumed that socialization potential is dependent upon intellectual capacity. She further assumed that this capacity changed during development and varied according to species. The gorilla data were directly compared to macaque and chimpanzee data which were also acquired during the course of her research.

In the model developed by Piaget (1952), human infants were found to pass through six stages of development in each of two series: (1) the Sensorimotor Intelligence Series, and (2) the Imitation Series. The stages of these two series occur from birth up to the age of two years in human infants. Specific characteristics of each stage include such items as increases in voluntary control, increased numbers of motor patterns and contextual variables within a single event, and increased variability of motor patterns. Chevalier-Skolnikoff modified Piaget's model when it was necessary to do so, developing some new categories and behaviors appropriate to the study of nonhuman primates.

Gorillas were found to complete the entire Sensorimotor Intelligence Series in both the *tactile/kinesthetic* and *visual/body* modalities. Like human infants, they also completed the higher stages in the *visual/gestural* mode. According to Piagetian terminology they are initially characterized as at the stage of *primary circular reactions*. This stage includes the repetitive coordination of their own body, and manual secondary circular reactions (e.g., repetitive interactions with objects). In these ways, gorillas are able to learn about the effects of their actions. They also show signs of stage 4 *coordinations of secondary behaviors;* e.g., bringing objects to their mouths during running and chest-beating displays. Stage 5 *tertiary circular reactions* are evident when they use sticks to poke free inaccessible food items. Stage 6 behavior, classical examples of insight, was also recorded in these gorillas. The higher stages of Piaget's visual/facial modes were also reached by gorillas, but vocal modes reached only stage 1 in the Piagetian series. As Chevalier-Skolnikoff explained:

> . . . They fail to manifest stage 2 repetitive self-vocalization (cooing), and stage 3 repetitive vocal attempts to effect changes in the environment (babbling, or vocal "games"), or stage 4 combinations of sounds, or stage 5 experimentation with sounds. In the auditory modality, apes appear to be intermediate between monkeys and humans. . . (p. 168).

In gorillas, according to Chevalier-Skolnikoff's report, the sensorimotor period is completed sometime between twenty months and four years of age.

The Imitation Series, which measures cognitive development, was completed by gorillas in all six stages. Gorillas are able to learn new bodily, facial, and manual motor patterns by repeated imitative matching behaviors. Moreover, they can imitate new motor patterns on the first try without prior practice. Gorillas also exhibited delayed imitation, in which they imitated new motor patterns when the model was absent. In the vocal mode, gorillas reached only stage 3 for socially facilitated imitations of emotional cries. In the auditory

Table 6-6. Characteristics of the sensorimotor intelligence series in human infants (After Chevalier-Skolnikoff, 1977, as adapted from Piaget and modified by Sugarman Bell).

STAGE	AGE (MOS.)	DESCRIPTION	MAJOR DISTINGUISHING BEHAVIORAL PARAMETERS	EXAMPLE
1 Reflex	0–1	Stereotyped responses to generalized sensory stimuli	Involuntary	Roots and sucks
2 Primary circular reaction	1–4	Infant's action is centered about his *own body* (thus "primary") which he learns to repeat ("circular") in order to reinstate an event.	Repetitive coordinations of own body occur First acquired adaptations occur Recognition of various objects and contexts	Repeats hand-hand clasping Exhibits conditioned reflexes
3 Secondary circular reaction	4–8	Repeated ("circular") attempts to reproduce *environmental* ("secondary") events initially discovered by chance	Environment-oriented behaviors Establishment of object/action relationships Semi-intentional (initial act is not intentional, but subsequent repetitions are). Active attempts to effect changes in environment Simple orientations toward a single object or person	Swings object and attends to the swinging spectacle, or to the resulting sound; repeats
4 Coordination of secondary behaviors	8–12	Two or more independent behavioral acts become intercoordinated, one serving as instrument to another	Intentional Goal is established from the outset Establishment of relationships between two objects Coordination of several behaviors toward an object or person Objects explored as well as acted upon Familiar behaviors applied to new situations Infant begins to attribute cause of environmental change to others	Sets aside an obstacle in order to obtain an object behind it

Table 6-6. (Continued)

STAGE	AGE (MOS.)	DESCRIPTION	MAJOR DISTINGUISHING BEHAVIORAL PARAMETERS	EXAMPLE
5 Tertiary circular reaction (experimentation)	12–18	Child becomes curious about an object's possible *functions* and about object-object relationships ("tertiary"); he repeats his behavior ("circular") with variation as he explores the potentials of objects through trial-and-error experimentation	Behavior becomes variable and nonstereotyped, as the child invents new behavior patterns Repetitive trial and error experimentation begins Interest in novelty for its own sake Coordination of object-object, person-object, object-space and object-force relationships Considers others entirely autonomous	Experimentally discovers that one object, such as a stick, can be used to obtain another object
6 Invention of new means through mental combinations (insight)	18 +	The solution is arrived at mentally, not through experimentation	The child can mentally represent objects and events not present	Mentally figures out how one object can be used to obtain another object

Table 6-7.   Progress of the stages in Piaget's *Sensorimotor Intelligence*
and *Imitation* Series in macaque, gorilla, and human infants.
(Adapted from Chevalier-Skolnikoff, 1977)

STAGE NO.	STUMPTAIL MACAQUE	GORILLA	HUMAN
1	0–2 weeks	0–1 month	0–1 month
2	2 weeks–3 months	1–3 months	1–4 months
3	about 3 weeks (1–4)– 3 months	3-less than 7 months	4–8 months
4	2 months–	Less than 7– about 14 months (13½–14½)	8-12 months
5	about 4½ (4–5) months	About 14-more than 20 months and less than 4 years	12-18 months
6	?	Less than 18 months– less than 4 years	18 months–

mode, gorillas imitated nonvocal noises (stage 3), and incorporated them into
their displays (stage 4).

During the first three months of life, gorillas evince repeated hand-mouth,
hand-hand, and hand-foot manipulations. Chevalier-Skolnikoff suggested that
these *primary circular reactions* enable infant apes to acquire a high degree of
hand-eye coordination. The cognitive and social attributes of the apes may, in
turn, derive from these early developments.

Emotional facial expressions and vocalizations occur during the next four
months of life, the period of *secondary linear* and *secondary circular reactions*
and socially facilitated self-imitation. Moreover, gorillas at this stage are beginning
to acquire their mothers' food repertoire through imitation. *Secondary circular
reactions* are also evident in play, during which time gorillas sometimes imitate
the behavior of their playmates.

In stage 4, gorillas begin to incorporate *secondary circular reactions* into their
play, and to imitate new motor behaviors using body parts they cannot see (e.g.,
touching the ear).

In the stage of *tertiary circular reactions,* infant gorillas "experiment" with
gravity by repeatedly placing a stick on an incline and letting it roll down, or
by tossing sticks down a slope. Object-object and object-space relationships
are demonstrated by the repetition of poking a stick into a hole. These reactions
are also incorporated into play when gorillas employ sticks to hit each other

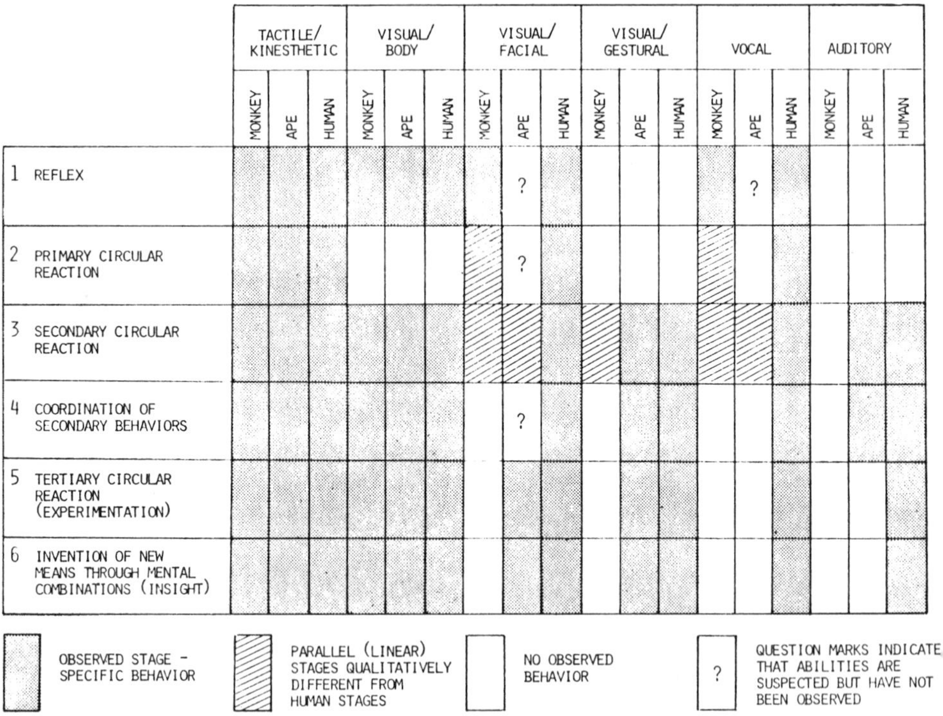

	TACTILE/ KINESTHETIC			VISUAL/ BODY			VISUAL/ FACIAL			VISUAL/ GESTURAL			VOCAL			AUDITORY		
	MONKEY	APE	HUMAN	MONKEY	APE	HUMAN	MONKEY	APE	HUMAN	MONKEY	APE	HUMAN	MONKEY	APE	HUMAN	MONKEY	APE	HUMAN
1 REFLEX							?						?					
2 PRIMARY CIRCULAR REACTION							?											
3 SECONDARY CIRCULAR REACTION																		
4 COORDINATION OF SECONDARY BEHAVIORS							?											
5 TERTIARY CIRCULAR REACTION (EXPERIMENTATION)																		
6 INVENTION OF NEW MEANS THROUGH MENTAL COMBINATIONS (INSIGHT)																		

OBSERVED STAGE - SPECIFIC BEHAVIOR

PARALLEL (LINEAR) STAGES QUALITATIVELY DIFFERENT FROM HUMAN STAGES

NO OBSERVED BEHAVIOR

? QUESTION MARKS INDICATE THAT ABILITIES ARE SUSPECTED BUT HAVE NOT BEEN OBSERVED

Figure 6-2. The Sensorimotor Intelligence Series as manifested by apes (gorillas), human infants, and monkeys. (After Chevalier-Skolnikoff, 1977)

during play. The use of tools to obtain food may also be acquired through the socialization process. According to Chevalier-Skolnikoff:

Among the captive gorillas at the San Francisco Zoo, the use of tools for obtaining out-of-reach food is a regular occurrence and appears to be a social tradition passed from one generation to the next through the socialization process. It was probably first "invented" by one of the animals through stage 5 or 6 imitation of the new motor pattern (p. 179).

Tertiary circular reactions apparently occur in the wild as well, as Dian Fossey's observations have demonstrated (cf. Chevalier-Skolnikoff, pp. 179-180).

LANGUAGE

The issue of language acquisition in apes is very controversial. Studies with chimpanzees have demonstrated that a vocabulary of arbitrary signs can be learned and utilized by an ape. Whether this is a form of language acquisition

Table 6-8.   Characteristics of Piaget's Imitation Series as exhibited by
human infants (After Chevalier-Skolnikoff, 1977).

STAGE	AGE (MOS.)	DESCRIPTION
1 Reflexive contagious imitation	0–1	Reflexive behavior (e.g., crying) is stimulated by the behavior in a model.
2 Sporadic "self-imitation"	1–4	Imitation by the model of the infant's own motor patterns (self-imitation) stimulates diffuse vocal activity in the infant. It is unclear whether the infant distinguishes the model's behavior from his own.
3 Purposeful "self-imitation" (social facilitation, or stimulus enhancement)	4–8	Self-imitation in which matching becomes more precise. For visual imitation, the infant's acting body part must be visible to him.
4 Imitation using unseen body parts	8–12	Imitation using unseen body parts. Infant attempts to imitate new behavioral acts, but often fails to precisely match the model.
5 Imitation of new behavior patterns ("true" imitation)	12–18	Imitation of new motor acts, precisely accommodating behavior to that of the model through repeated attempts at matching.
6 Deferred imitation	18 +	Child precisely imitates new motor acts, without preliminary attempts at matching, through symbolic representation. Child manifests deferred imitation.

or merely discrimination learning is subject to debate. Benchley addressed the question in 1940.

Do gorillas communicate? Of course they do . . . But do they speak a language? No more than any other animal does . . . The spoken words of birds are merely imitations, but if the gorilla has the muscular machinery of words, it must still be that he lacks the mental power which is the first necessity of the spoken word (p. 127).

This was the prevailing view until the chimpanzee *Washoe* burst upon the academic scene in the 1960s. To consider the gorilla's competence, let's examine the behavior of *Koko,* a lowland gorilla.

Dr. Francine Patterson has for eight years labored to teach American Sign Language (ASL or Ameslan) to a female lowland gorilla named *Koko* (Patterson,

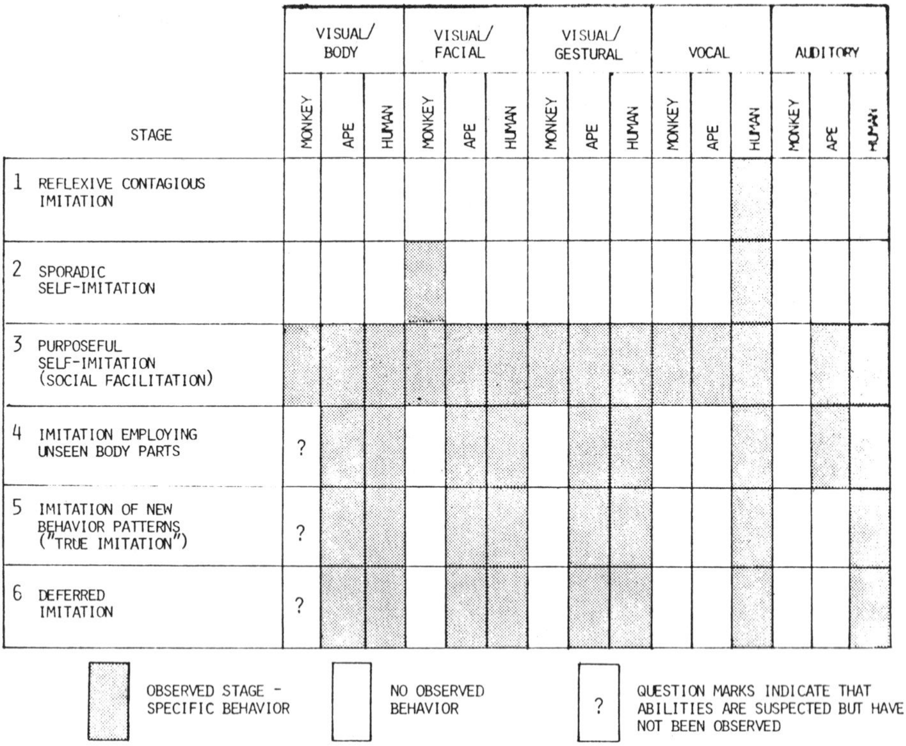

STAGE	VISUAL/ BODY			VISUAL/ FACIAL			VISUAL/ GESTURAL			VOCAL			AUDITORY		
	MONKEY	APE	HUMAN	MONKEY	APE	HUMAN	MONKEY	APE	HUMAN	MONKEY	APE	HUMAN	MONKEY	APE	HUMAN
1 REFLEXIVE CONTAGIOUS IMITATION															
2 SPORADIC SELF-IMITATION															
3 PURPOSEFUL SELF-IMITATION (SOCIAL FACILITATION)															
4 IMITATION EMPLOYING UNSEEN BODY PARTS	?														
5 IMITATION OF NEW BEHAVIOR PATTERNS ("TRUE IMITATION")	?														
6 DEFERRED IMITATION	?														

OBSERVED STAGE – SPECIFIC BEHAVIOR

NO OBSERVED BEHAVIOR

? QUESTION MARKS INDICATE THAT ABILITIES ARE SUSPECTED BUT HAVE NOT BEEN OBSERVED

Figure 6-3. The Imitation Series as manifested by apes (gorillas), human infants, and monkeys. (After Chevalier-Skolnikoff, 1977)

1978).* She is the only gorilla to have been so instructed, beginning when Patterson acquired her on loan from the San Francisco Zoo in 1972. Like other pioneering workers in ape language (Gardner and Gardner, 1969; Fouts, 1973), Patterson molded *Koko's* hands; teaching her 184 signs in thirty-six months of training. By the age of six and a half, *Koko* had actually used 645 different signs as judged by Patterson, but her then *working* vocabulary—those signs that were used regularly and appropriately—was estimated to be about 375 signs at age seven.

In addition to her considerable linguistic ability, *Koko's* IQ has been tested by means of the Stanford-Binet Intelligence Scale. During several tests, the gorilla's IQ varied from 85-95, nearly equivalent to that of an average human child. Interestingly, Patterson has discovered a human cultural bias in the test which puts gorillas at a distinct disadvantage. For example, when *Koko* was

*Readers who are interested in *Koko* and Patterson's language project may wish to become members of their supporting organization: *The Gorilla Foundation, 17820 Skyline Boulevard, Woodside, California 94062.* Members receive a semiannual newsletter, *Gorilla.*

Figure 6-4. *KoKo* signs *bite* on her finger (a variant of the iconic sign she invented for the activity) in response to the approach of an alligator puppet held by Francine Patterson. *(Photo by Dr. R.H. Cohn, courtesy of the Gorilla Foundation)*

asked where she would run to seek shelter from rain, she selected "tree" from the available list of "hat, spoon, tree, and house." The correct answer was "house." Thus, the logical choice for the gorilla was incorrect as far as the Stanford-Binet was concerned.

Patterson has also maintained that *Koko* exhibits a sense of past and future. More extraordinary, perhaps, Patterson asserted that *Koko* also prevaricates with some degree of regularity. We quote here from Patterson's 1978 article in *National Geographic:*

> At about the age of 5 Koko discovered the value of the lie to get herself out of a jam. After numerous repeat performances I'm convinced that Koko really is lying in these circumstances and not merely making mistakes. One of her first lies also involved the reconstruction of an earlier happening. My assistant Kate Mann was with Koko, then tipping the scale at 90 pounds, when the gorilla plumped down on the kitchen sink in the trailer and it separated from its frame and dropped out of alignment. Later, when I asked Koko if she broke the sink, she signed, "Kate there bad," pointing to the sink. Koko couldn't know, of course, that I would never accept the idea that Kate would go around breaking sinks (pp. 549–461).

In relation to this claim, it is interesting to note that Yerkes (1928) also recognized a deceitful tendency in the gorilla *Congo:*

> Whatever one imagines the intent of the organism to be, the value of the behavior is to hide or obscure purpose, motive, objective, and to mislead the observer.   Perhaps this type of ability and behavioral tendency is more necessary to the gorilla than to most other highly organized primates because of its relative slowness of action and of wit (p. 64).

Recently, Terrace (1979) has criticized studies reporting language-acquisition in apes.   Briefly, Terrace's argument suggests that there is too much room for interpretation in the signing studies.   Thus, Fouts' (1973) report of *Washoe* signing the innovative "water-bird" for a swan was considered by Terrace to be nothing more than a temporal recognition of the elements of "water" and "bird".   As Terrace convincingly argued, there is really no objective way to determine which interpretation is correct.   There is little doubt, however, that the argument of Terrace is the more parsimonious of the two.

Sebeok and Umiker-Sebeok (1979) go one step further in suggesting that, in some instances, overzealous trainers may be cueing their subjects with unconscious bodily movements.   In either case, some degree of observer bias seems to be inherent to sign language studies.   Certainly Patterson's gorilla study can be criticized along the same lines.   For example, where *Koko* uses the phrase "white tiger" to describe a zebra she may merely be discriminating between two stimulus properties of the organism.   There can be no doubt, however, that her perception of these properties is quite remarkable.   She also has applied the terms "elephant baby" to describe a Pinocchio doll, and "eye hat" to describe a mask.

That gorillas are capable of perceiving minute intention movements on the part of people, and presumably, other gorillas is well known to anyone who has carefully observed them.   For example, every primate keeper is familiar with the difficulty of separating one ape from another.   They always know when it is about to happen.   Carpenter observed that the gorillas *Ngagi* and *Mbongo* responded to the slightest movements which indicated that a separation was about to be attempted.

> If lured into the room for food, the animal would snatch it and dash out again.   If I was successful in beginning to lower the door, the animal would catch it and raise it up again to its original position.   He would always catch the experimenter and the slightest move towards the remote control device would produce an immediate attempt at escape (p. 119).

According to Patterson (1980), *Koko* is very different from Terrace's chimpanzee *Nim* in that *Koko's* frequency of imitation and spontaneous signing is relatively greater.   While *Nim* emitted spontaneous utterances only 12% of the time, *Koko* averaged a 41% rate of spontaneous utterances. Patterson has furthermore determined that *Koko's* imitation and expansion more closely resemble the behavior of human children than that of *Nim.* Unlike *Nim, Koko* apparently imitated less as her training continued. As Patterson explained in her newsletter *Gorilla:**

> We believe, along with Nelson and other researchers, that it is important to determine the limit of the ape's linguistic capability and the ways in which it may enhance their cognitive functioning. Thus, we are continuing our efforts to trace the development of creative language phenomena which Terrace failed to find. The gorilla Michael has within the last year exhibited most of the innovative patterns which we have been observing for some time in Koko.

To eliminate nonverbal cues to the gorillas, Patterson employs mirrored sunglasses (eliminating eye-pupil and gaze direction cues). The gorillas have also been deliberately mislead by the researchers, but their subjects persist in responding to the questions rather than the misleading cues. Finally, Patterson has observed that both gorillas sign to strangers, to themselves, and to each other, further evidence that their signing is not controlled by cueing.

It is very difficult to evaluate Patterson's work. Clearly, Terrace's findings raise some questions about the way to interpret all signing studies. However, since there has been no attempt to replicate Patterson, her data remain as the only record of gorilla signing. Even if we are conservative in granting *Koko's* achievements, her remarkable abilities must be conceded. The reliability and the validity of these findings must ultimately be established by replication. Thus, further research with gorillas, and other apes, should be encouraged.

An additional point needs to be made here. Studies which concern the intellectual abilities of gorillas contribute much to their conservation. The more intelligent a given species, the more likely that humankind will bestow upon it a greater degree of protection. The movement to save the whales gained momentum with the evidence that whales are highly intelligent. By this criterion, gorillas are promising candidates for the same sympathetic protection.

IMITATION

Carpenter noted that certain behaviors of one gorilla were invariably followed by the same behavior in the other. Carpenter preferred the term "copying" when the behavior of one animal set off similar behavior in another, but the stimulated behavior was a part of the second's action system. He finely distinguished between this "simpler" form and true imitation. We find this distinction somewhat difficult

---

*1980, volume 3, number 2.

to make, in that the latter implies a cognitive construct of some sort. Carpenter recognized copying in the following examples:

> One of the gorillas would begin to dash water from the pool and the other one would follow suit . . . Furthermore, simple forms of behavior such as playing with objects, swinging ropes or rings are copies from one animal by another (p. 117).

At the Atlanta Zoological Park, we have often observed the lone male *Willie B.* responding to a horizontal run by his keeper. This twenty-one-year-old lowland gorilla responds to this as if it were a game, running back and forth in synchrony with his distant human playmate. A signal that effectively stimulates this activity is a gentle but rhythmic tapping of the fingers onto the chest, emitted by either *Willie* or the keeper.

Great apes can be socially facilitated to carry out an unfamiliar task and chimpanzees are especially prone to the imitation of human behaviors. However, gorillas are somewhat less inclined to imitate human action, although Patterson has had great success in shaping sign-language, employing in part the gorilla *Koko's* imitative propensities. Drawing on her years of experience at the San Diego Zoo, Benchley further amplified the differences between orang and gorilla as follows:

> Our gorillas have never attempted to imitate our actions as chimpanzees will. Orang-utans are not so imitative, but are natural engineers, taking anything apart that is not in a solid piece. They understand the principles of leverage. I have never seen one that did not. Recently Ngagi obtained from some unknown source a short piece of reinforcement steel. He carried it around and, except for our fear that he might accidentally strike Mbongo with it, we felt that there was nothing dangerous in his holding it. After a while, he lost interest in it and dropped it within easy reach of the outside of the cage. The same weapon in the hand of an orang-utan would have been used immediately to pry the wire off the cage (p. 128).

CONDITIONING COOPERATION

At the Woodland Park Zoo in Seattle, Veterinarian James Foster and his associates, Mary Keiter and Violet English, have had considerable success in conditioning gorillas to accept veterinary examinations. In a personal communication, Keiter described the conditioning procedure of the female *Nina* as follows:

1. A cotton tipped swab approximately 6 inches long was shown to the female and she was allowed to touch and sniff it in order to become familiar with it. The swab was then placed gently on the arm/hand of the trainer, rubbed back and forth several times, and the swab than placed onto two glass slides and rolled on each.

2. Once the female was assured that the swab was harmless, it was no longer necessary to have her touch and sniff it, and the swab/body contact was transferred from the trainer to the animal, placing the swab at first on the hand/arm of the animal and then rolling it onto the glass slides.
3. Gradually, the swab/body contact was shifted from the hand/arm to the shoulder, abdomen, back, legs and thighs, and finally the perineal area. Only when the animal felt completely at ease with the swab/body contact in one area was it shifted to the next. Again, following each contact the swab was rolled onto the glass slides.
4. Prior to insertion of the swab into the vagina, several days were spent gently rubbing and placing the swab adjacent to the vaginal opening, again rolling the swab onto the glass slides at completion of body contact.
5. Insertion of the swab into the vagina was done gently and quickly, and the swab was rolled onto the glass slides at withdrawal.

Following each of the training sessions, as outlined above, *Nina* was rewarded with a tidbit of her favorite food. While the original training took place while staff were actually in the gorilla's cage (see Figure 6-5), it is now necessary to test *Nina* through the bars of the new enclosure.

Less formal, but equally effective, were the efforts of English (personal communication) who began collecting urine from the adult female *Timbo* eighteen days after a recent copulation. *Timbo* was tested prior to her morning feeding. She was first moved into a cage with a bare floor where she urinated. Thereafter, she was moved to a familiar cage with hay on the floor and then fed. After several months of conditioning, *Timbo* could urinate in the bare cage within a few minutes, and thereafter move to the door and wait to be let into the feeding cage.

Clearly, given the promising success of the Seattle staff, there is every reason to believe that gorillas in other zoos could be similarly conditioned to submit to routine physical examination. With such techniques, the dangers of anesthesia would be greatly reduced by its less frequent application.

With respect to show training, captive gorillas have rarely been subjected to such rigors as have chimpanzees and, occasionally, orang-utans.* Indeed, their imposing size would make training difficult. However, Bourne and Cohen (1975) described a Japanese trainer whose performing act included several subadult gorillas. A contrary and commendable attitude was exhibited by San Diego

---

*An interesting form of "tool use" was attributed to the captive gorillas *Ngagi* and *Mbongo* by Carpenter (1937). As he described it:

It was interesting to observe the apes swinging by means of ropes from one perch to another. Repeatedly I have seen one of the animals carry the swinging rope by holding the end between his chin and chest and then, having gained his elevation in the tree, swing off in the direction of an elevated platform and land on it. (p. 111)

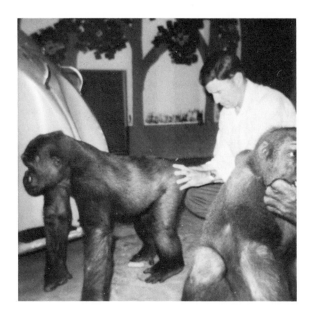

Figure 6-5.   Veterinarian obtaining vaginal smear from female *Nina* at the Woodland Park Zoo in Seattle. *(Photo courtesy J. Foster, and Woodland Park Zoo).*

Zoo authorities who were determined to bring up their mountain gorillas with minimal human intervention. According to Benchley (1940):

> Our plans for dealing with them were laid out then, and there has been no deviation. They were to be allowed as much freedom from human interference as they could be given; they were to be treated like gorillas. By this experiment that has never been tried before, we hope to have them live out a natural span of life in captivity (p. 117).

This early experiment in the exhibition of gorillas was notable in another way; two gorillas were displayed in the same enclosure. This may be contrasted to the traditional exhibition of lone male gorillas such as Ringling Brothers' *Gargantua,* London's *Guy,* Chicago's *Bushman,* Philadelphia's *Massa,* and Atlanta's *Willie B.* There is no modern justification for solitary displays, but a few are still exhibited this way owing to the difficulty of acquiring companions, and enlarging out-moded quarters. A final comment in the training potential of gorillas was provided by the Yerkes' as follows:

> Domestication of the gorilla, in the ordinary sense of the term, is impossible. It may be rendered gentle and amenable to human control but never has a specimen been known so far to subject itself to human desires as to render monotonous service. We have failed to find any record of specimens trained

for exhibition purposes. On the one hand, they may be, and we believe are, resistant to ordinary methods of tuition or instruction; and on the other, they may be, and we believe are, unsuited by temperament to stage or exhibit their uses (p. 425).

VISUAL STIMULI

Chimpanzees studied by Menzel and his associates (1978) are capable of perceiving a video-tape image as real. If they are given information through this medium, they successfully employ it to solve a problem. Prior to this empirical study, their ability to perceive a televised image was supported by a wealth of ancedotal information. Gorillas, too, have been the subjects of considerable speculation in this regard. In Sacramento, California, Zoo gorillas were exposed to a 16 millimeter film of other captive gorillas copulating. The responses of the animals indicated that elements of the film were perceived as real. For example, when projected onto the cage wall, the adult male *Kris* attempted to grasp a fallen log as if it were a branch. The desired objective, the stimulation of copulation, was not achieved. Similarly, as we have seen, films of maternal behavior have failed to be instructive. When the gorilla *Koko* viewed the Hess' film on gorilla sexual behavior, she reportedly fell asleep (Patterson, personal communication). A presumed problem in the use of film as instruction is the difficulty of inducing attention. As with chimpanzees, some shaping of attention is helpful.

In both American and European Zoos, televisions have been provided for isolated gorillas. Numerous ancedotes have resulted, but no objective study of their propensity to attend has been accomplished. Recently a study was carried out at the Atlanta Zoo in which the gorilla *Willie B.* was provided with various prime time programming. When the novelty wore off, it became perfectly clear that television was a source of little stimulation. As a public relations device, a television for a gorilla is a marvelous acquisition, but it is a poor substitute for genuine habitat improvements. In our opinion, television—as currently employed—is of no value to captive apes. If utilized creatively, however, it might be used to give apes visual access to their keepers, other apes, food preparation, or the outside world. If televised stimuli are made meaningful to an ape, attention should be vastly improved.

In summary, the literature indicates that the genus *Gorilla* is at least the intellectual equal of its anthropoid cousins *Pan,* and *Pongo.* To be sure, its great size and strength, reticence to be dominated, and stoic disposition are challenging barriers to testing and training. However, young gorillas are considerably more cooperative and, from them, we have learned that gorillas are clever and capable creatures. These giants can be brutish, but their intelligence has frequently been woefully underestimated. A careful survey of the literature reveals the essential accuracy of the Yerkes' educated hunch. Gorillas are the most intelligent of the nonhuman primates, even if we must grant that they share this distinction.

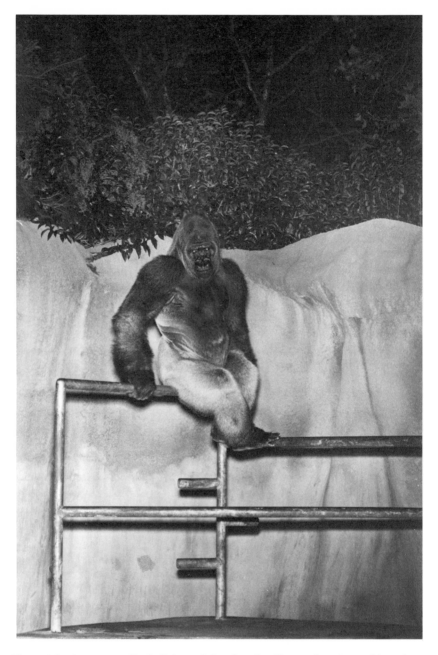

Figure 6-6.   Sacramento Zoo's *Kris* carefully observing films projected onto his enclosure wall at night. *(S. Woo photo)*

7
Gorillas in Captivity

There is not the slightest reason to hope that an adult gorilla, either male or female, will ever be seen living in a zoological park or garden.

W. T. Hornaday, 1915

In this chapter, we will review the conditions in which gorillas live in captivity, and offer some recommendations for their management. Much of what has been written about captive orang-utans (cf. Maple, 1980a) will apply here, and we will try not to be redundant. While the special requirements of gorillas need to be considered, we will attempt to discuss their indiosyncrasies in terms of only practical solutions. While there has recently been considerable research conducted on wild mountain Gorillas, only a few are currently exhibited in captivity. However, as there are about 400 western lowland gorillas on display throughout the world, it is this subspecies which is the subject of our concern in this chapter.

In captivity, the gorilla is considerably less active than the chimpanzee, has been difficult to breed, and is especially prone to coprophagy. In the earlier years of their exhibition, gorillas often were fed to excess, leading to extreme obesity.* The gorilla *Gargantua* attained the incredible weight of 550 pounds, while the two mountain gorillas displayed at the San Diego Zoo both attained weights of over 600 pounds. Even when trim, gorillas are huge creatures, with males typically weighing from 350–400 pounds. The muscular features and stern facade of the gorilla have given it a reputation for ferocity and great strength (Bourne and Cohen, 1975; Morris and Morris, 1967; Chapter 2, this volume).

There are a number of important differences in the respective ape taxa and these affect the manner of their exhibition. For example, chimpanzees appear to be more responsive to humans than are gorillas or orang-utans. The gorilla by comparison is quiet, and apparently easily bored. Special care must therefore be taken to ensure that gorillas are provided with stimulating surroundings.

---

*Weight gain and longevity have both been associated with health in captivity, but as Sommer (1974) points out: "It is true that some species will gain weight in captivity and live longer than they would in the wild, but the quality of life is so different it is hard to speak of size or longevity as benefits." (p. 56).

In Table 7-1 we have organized a list of factors which may affect the quality of the captive habitat. Each of these factors is relevant to the display and management of all nonhuman primates. The manner in which they are varied will determine the total effectiveness of a respective enclosure. The difficulties of properly maintaining gorillas in captivity were acknowledged by the Yerkes' in their 1929 volume:

> . . .as we review the history of certain well known captives we feel increasingly assured that timidity, distrust, slowness of adaptation to novel environmental conditions, and lack of natural companionship are primarily responsible for the peculiar difficulties which man meets in attempting to tame and domesticate the gorilla (p. 423).

Thus, by this statement we learn that it is only partly the natural inclinations of the gorilla that contribute to their uncooperative reputation. More importantly, it

Table 7-1. Factors which may affect the quality of habitat.

1. Size:
   a. height
   b. width
   c. length
   d. flight distance

2. Cover:
   a. refuge
   b. escape/denning

3. Climbing structures

4. Sitting places

5. Browse

6. Sunlight

7. Ventilation/fresh air

8. Humidity

9. Exercise/work

10. Cleanliness

11. Novel objects/variety of food

12. Social opportunities

13. Visual contact with humans/other animals

14. Schedule of caretaker manipulations

15. Regularity of feeding

16. Geographical region

has been the failure of institutions to appropriately meet its needs that has so seriously affected its survival in captivity.

CAPTIVE DEMOGRAPHICS

According to the most recent edition of the gorilla studbook (Kirchshofer, 1979), 635 western lowland gorillas have been registered in 137 zoos and research institutes during a fifteen year period from January 1, 1962 until December 31, 1976. From this population, 479 were wild-caught, and 138 captive-born specimens. An interesting statistic is the difference in the number of captive births between the two studbook reporting periods. From January 1, 1962 to June 30, 1970, only 33 gorillas were born in captivity. However, 105 gorillas were born during the six years thereafter; a ratio of 1:3, a remarkable improvement.

There have been 293 male and 342 female western lowland gorillas in captivity according to the studbook register. The mortality rate of all western gorillas during the studbook period was calculated at 24%. Many of these deaths occurred during infancy, especially in the first month of life.

During the studbook reporting period, twenty-four gorillas have been registered as *beringei*; however, it now appears that as many as eight are actually the *graueri* subspecies, and nine others are of undetermined origin. One of the original twenty-four was later proved to be a western gorilla. Currently, the studbook does not provide for a *graueri* entry, lumping under *beringei* all reputed "mountain" gorillas. Given the strength of the recent evidence (cf. Chapter 1), it is desirable that the studbook now be further subdivided. The sex distribution of the mountain gorilla registrants is seven males, fourteen females, while two were undetermined. As of 1976, only sixteen of these animals survived. Within the reporting period, not one true *beringei* has been born in captivity!

Currently the responsibility of the Frankfurt Zoo, the studbook is an important document, including data on date and place of birth, arrival, death, and names of the parents. All institutions which maintain gorillas receive the studbook in exchange for information about their animals.

SPATIAL REQUIREMENTS

No captive enclosure can approach the dimensions of natural habitats (cf. Chapter 1). Nevertheless, with ingenuity, it is possible to construct environments which evoke activities that normally occur in the wild. For all of the apes the vertical component is an important habitat dimension. Orang-utans are overwhelmingly arboreal and require elevated pathways in order to locomote in their characteristic fashion. Habitats which do not permit arboreal locomotion

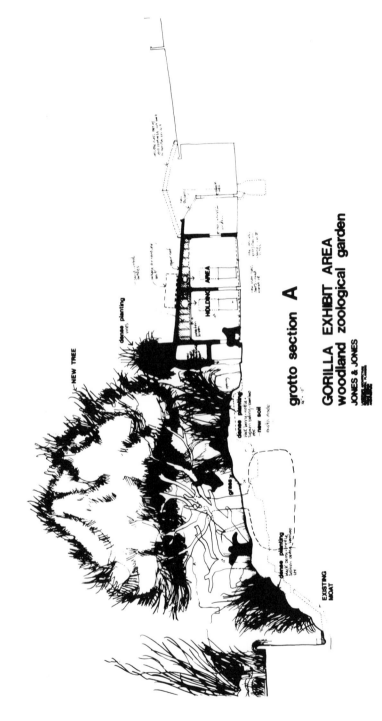

Figures 7-1 and 7-2. Details of the new gorilla enclosures at the Woodland Park Zoological Gardens, Seattle. *(Courtesy David Hancocks, and Jones & Jones, Architects and Landscape Architects, Seattle, Wa.; drawings by Johnpaul Jones).*

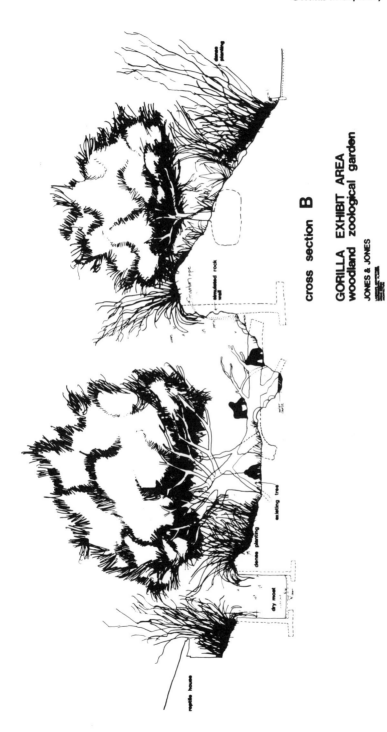

cross section **B**

GORILLA EXHIBIT AREA
woodland zoological garden

JONES & JONES

Figure 7-2.

Table 7-2. Locations reporting gorillas in residence according to the 1979 studbook and register (After Kirchshofer, 1979).

Aalborg, Den.	Fukuoka, Jap.	Osnabruck, Aust.
Albuquerque, U.S.A.	Gelsenkirchen, W. Ger.	Ozoir la Ferriere, Fr.
Amsterdam, Neth.	Granby, Can.	Paris, Fr.
Antwerp, Bel.	Hamburg, W. Ger.	Philadelphia, U.S.A.
Apeldoorn, Neth.	Hanover, W. Ger.	Phoenix, U.S.A.
Arnhem, Neth.	Hiroshima, Jap.	Pittsburgh, U.S.A.
Asheboro, U.S.A.	Honolulu, U.S.A.	Prague, Czech.
Atlanta, RPRC*, U.S.A.	Houston, U.S.A.	Pretoria, S.A.
Atlanta, Zoo, U.S.A.	Howletts/Bekesbourne, G.B.	Rome, It.
Baltimore, U.S.A.	Ibadan, Nig.	Rostock, E. Ger.
Barcelona, Sp.	Inuyama PRC*, Jap.	Rostov, U.S.S.R.
Basel, Switz.	Jerez de la Frontiera, Sp.	Rotterdam, Neth.
Beaverton, OPRC,* U.S.A.	Jersey, G.B.	Saarbrucken, W. Ger.
Berlin, E. Ger.	Johannesburg, S.A.	St. Louis, U.S.A.
Berlin, W. Ger.	Kaliningrad, U.S.S.R.	St. Paul, U.S.A.
Birmingham, U.S.A.	Kansas City, U.S.A.	Salt Lake City, U.S.A.
Blackpool, G.B.	Kiev, U.S.S.R.	Salzburg, Aust.
Boston, U.S.A.	Kobe, Jap.	San Antonio, U.S.A.
Bristol, G.B.	Kolmarden, Swe.	San Diego, U.S.A.
Brownsville, U.S.A.	Krefeld, W. Ger.	San Francisco, U.S.A.
Buffalo, U.S.A.	Kyoto, Jap.	Sao Paulo, Braz.
Calgary, Can.	La Fleche, Fr.	Seattle, U.S.A.
Chessington, G.B.	La Plata, Arg.	Sendai, Jap.
Chester, G.B.	Leipzig, E. Ger.	Seoul, Kor.
Chicago, Lincoln Park, U.S.A.	Les Mathes/La Palmyre, Fr.	Southampton, G.B.
Chicago, Brookfield, U.S.A.	Lisbon, Port.	Stuttgart, E. Ger.
Cincinnati, U.S.A.	London, G.B.	Sukhumi, U.S.S.R.
Cleveland, U.S.A.	Los Angeles, U.S.A.	Sydney, Aus.
Colombo Dehiwala, Sri Lanka	Manchester, G.B.	Takamatsu, Jap.
(Ceylon)	Melbourne, Aust.	Tampa, U.S.A.
Colorado Springs, U.S.A.	Memphis, U.S.A.	Tarpon Springs, U.S.A.
Columbus, U.S.A.	Miami/Goulds, U.S.A.	Tel Aviv, Iz.
Copenhagen, Den.	Milwaukee, U.S.A.	Tokyo, Tama, Jap.
Dallas, U.S.A.	Moscow, U.S.S.R.	Tokyo, Ueno, Jap.
Denver, U.S.A.	Munich, W. Ger.	Toledo, U.S.A.
Detroit, U.S.A.	Munster, W. Ger.	Topeka, U.S.A.
Dresden, E. Ger.	Nagoya, Jap.	Toronto, Can.
Dublin, Ire.	New Iberia, GSRI*, U.S.A.	Turin, It.
Dudley, G.B.	New Orleans, U.S.A.	Twycross, G.B.
Duisburg, W. Ger.	New York, Bronx, U.S.A.	Washington, U.S.A.
Dvur-Kralove, Czech.	New York, Central Park, U.S.A.	Wassenaar, Neth.
Edmonton, Can.	Nuremburg, W. Ger.	Weybridge, G.B.
Erie, U.S.A.	Oklahoma City, U.S.A.	Wroclaw, Pol.
Fort Worth, U.S.A.	Omaha, U.S.A.	Zurich, Switz.
Frankfurt, W. Ger.	Osaka, Jap	
Fresno, U.S.A.		

*Primate Research Centers

contribute to the lethargy which often characterizes them in captivity. While gorillas are predominantly terrestrial, they too utilize trees on occasion, particularly when they are young. In fact at *Apenheul*,* the gorillas which inhabit this unique enclosure have regularly used trees for resting as high as forty feet from the ground (cf. Figure 7-3). All of the great apes construct sleeping nests, and they will spend many hours at this task if they are given branches, hay, or some other form of browse. This activity is good for the animals and stimulating to the public. Platforms or raised sitting areas provide an opportunity for elevating these nests, which further contributes to increased activity.

By attending to vertical** as well as horizontal space, an entire enclosure can be more effectively utilized. Climbing and sitting apparatus (furniture) increases the *complexity* and therefore the *quality* of the environment. In addition, when a group of animals can be housed together, an increase in spatial volume will re-

Figure 7-3. Gorillas climbing the tall pine trees within the enclosure at *Apenheul*, Appeldoorn, the Netherlands. *(Photo courtesy W. Mager)*

---

*Located in Appeldoorn, the Netherlands.
**The Lincoln Park Zoo has also constructed a very commendable orang-utan enclosure which provides complex vertical pathways for arboreal locomotion. Readers who are familiar with *Captivity and Behavior* (1979) may have noticed that a caption in Chapter 10 (Figure 9-12) erroneously identified the Lincoln Park enclosure as inadequate. We regret this error and herein set the record straight.

duce crowding and subsequent social stress. Internal habitat construction should also take into account the need for cover. As Erwin et al. (1976) have pointed out, cover can effectively remove an animal from view, thereby providing a means to shorten conflict. Modified cement culverts, protruding walls, and room partitions are especially effective in providing refuge and privacy. Open sleeping dens have also been employed in this manner.

Water as a Source of Enrichment

Even in its earlier days, the San Diego Zoological Park provided rather progressive habitats for gorillas. This is evident in Carpenter's (1937) description of the enclosure which housed *Ngagi* and *Mbongo*:

> The animals were found housed in quarters which made it possible to observe them very satisfactorily. Throughout most of the day they lived in the out-of-door cage which was forty feet by twenty feet by twenty feet in size. Within the cage there were many objects with which the animals could occupy themselves. There was a tree, a pool of water large enough for the animals to bathe in, a swinging rope, a chain with a hoop three feet in diameter attached to the end, a stump with a considerable log, automobile tires, and several elevated corner platforms. Connected with the cage were two small sleeping rooms with elevated floors (p. 109).

Figure 7-4. Gorillas which must be hand-reared require "contact comfort" from human caretakers. *(Photo courtesy Yerkes Regional Primate Research Center of Emory University)*

An especially interesting dimension of this enclosure was the availability of water, an important consideration according to Carpenter:

> Their response to water was always positive for purpose of drinking, playing and bathing.   In fact, it seems evident that constant access to a plentiful supply of water is one of the important factors in the success of the San Diego Zoological Gardens in keeping these animals in captivity healthy, contented and growing normally (p. 112).

The genuine importance of this factor may not lie in its intrinsic characteristics but instead can be attributed to its stimulus value.   In this way water, as well as other fixtures, adds to the overall complexity of any captive habitat. With the absence of any given component, the stimulus complexity of the environment is diminished accordingly.

As early as 1876, Falkenstein noted that young gorillas exhibited a fondness for water as a medium for play (cf. Yerkes and Yerkes, 1929).   Garner (1896), however, commented on their aversion to *deep* water and their doubtful swimming ability.   That gorillas have drowned after falling or running into deep water is a well-known historical fact. (cf. Maple, 1979).   Robert and Ada Yerkes summarized the early evidence surrounding this issue thus:

> Granting the inconclusiveness of the evidence we venture the tentative inference therefrom that the gorilla possesses neither fondness for water as a surrounding medium nor natural ability to swim.   In these respects we have discovered no reason to suppose that it differs essentially from man, orangutan, or chimpanzee.   Whether like man the great apes can readily learn of their own initiative or be taught to swim we do not know (p. 410).

According to Schaller's (1963) observations, mountain gorillas avoided water, refusing to cross even small streams except in those instances when fallen tree trunks provided an easy access.   The reaction of great apes to water has been more recently reviewed by Don Cousins (1978) who is perhaps the most prolific of all contemporary observers of captive apes.

In considering the use of water-filled moats to confine apes, Cousins noted that they do not seem to *instinctively* fear water.   As he correctly pointed out, lacking previous experience with such barriers, entry into a moat can be fatal. For example:

> Some years ago Arnhem Zoo's male gorilla, "Robbie" jumped into his moat after only an hour of first access to his outdoor enclosure.   Fortunately he was being watched and was safely landed with a long pole.   After this experience neither he nor any of the other apes, who must have been watching, ever approached the water again (pp. 8–9).

There have been many notable deaths of apes by drowning. Four chimpanzees drowned in the Holloman Air Force moat within a six-month period. The Bronx Zoo gorilla *Makoko* drowned in six feet of water in 1951. In both of these instances, observers noted that the apes quickly sank to the bottom.

However, when captive apes are exposed to water during their youth they often become fond of entering it. For example, Cousins discussed the case of the male gorilla *Phil.* At the St. Louis Zoo, *Phil* would not only willingly enter the four feet of water which was available to him, but would sit quietly upon the bottom with the water up to his neck. The male *Joe* also plays in water at the Twycross Zoo in England.

Golding (1972) described the case of the two young gorillas which entered the moat surrounding their enclosure in the Ibadan Zoo, Nigeria. Both of these animals learned to enthusiastically leap into the water, and the male would glide through the water after propelling himself forward with a kick on the bottom.

From these examples, it is clear that, in captivity, water can be used as a kind of "tool" for enriching the environment. However, with inexperienced animals the presence of a deep water source can be risky. Judicious planning can take out the guesswork and lead to innovations in the effective use of this medium. In general, it is to be recommended that moats be filled to a shallow depth, not in excess of twenty-four inches. The depth and width of moat/wall combinations has been reviewed by Reuther (1976) and extracted for examination in Table 7-3. As can be readily seen, there is great variation in the dimensions of these barriers throughout the world. With respect to depth, the actual depth has equaled the recommended standard in all but one of the institutions queried. In considering the recommended range only, the maximum projection is 490 centimeters (about 16 feet). The minimum achieved standard depth is 170 centimeters (about 5 feet) at the Dudley Zoo. As Reuther noted, gorillas have been observed reaching to a height of 210 centimeters (about 7 feet). Regarding moat width, the range of recommended dimensions was 240–460 centimeters (9-12 feet). The smallest actual width was 240 centimeters reported by the Twycross Zoo.

Width dimensions must be derived that they cannot be leapt across by agile apes. If the width is too narrow, safety is compromised. Moreover, a shallow moat reduces the space available for furniture. In many modern enclosures where island space is minimal, vertical space enhancement is limited by its contiguity to the moat. With a vigorous swing on a pole, branch, or rope, the animals can easily escape. Thus, failure to properly plan ahead reduces later building options.

INNOVATIONS AT THE HOUSTON ZOO

As Werler (1975) has pointed out, captive gorilla exhibits traditionally have been "stereotyped cages of tile and concrete, with thick bars separating animals from

Zoo	Actual* Depth (cm)	Recommended Minimum Depth (cm)	Actual Width (cm)	Recommended Minimum Width (cm)	Comments
Dudley (GB)	170		460		wet moat, hot wire
Frankfurt (GER)	180		500		wet moat led to accident; since filled in and replaced by 400 cm high glass wall
Kyoto (JAPAN)	210		500		wet moat with 10 v. electrical potential
Ibadan Univ. (NIGERIA)	260		490		water level 200 cm at public side, 60 cm dry wall above, hot wires at 105 cm depth
NY Bronx (USA)	270	270	430		water level 60–75 cm
San Diego Animal Park (USA)	300	300	300	300	
Munich (GER)	320	320			glass wall
Toronto Metro (CAN)	320	490		300	
Phoenix (USA)	340	300	400	400	
Jersey (GB)	370	370	340		
Oklahoma (USA)	370	370			
San Francisco (USA)	370		460		
Twycross (GB)	370	240–270	370		animals have reached up to 210 cm
Houston (USA)	370	300–370	380–430	240-300	dry moat
Kansas City (USA)	430	370–430	430	430	
Antwerp (BEL)			400	360	wet moat
Chester (GB)			430–520	460	wet moat, hot wire

*Depth of moat/wall at outer perimeter

Figure 7-5. Begging by lowland gorilla in outmoded barred enclosure. *(T. Maple photo)*

viewers." In the late fifties, tempered glass had begun to be substituted for steel bars as a barrier between the apes and the public. Glass was an improvement, but had drawbacks as well. The most serious drawback in our view, is that glass brings the public closer to the gorillas themselves, a potential violation of their personal space. As we have previously suggested (Maple, 1979), the intrusion of human spectators frequently results in aggression on the part of the apes. They may hit or kick the glass or in other ways indicate their irritation with public intrusion. In our opinion, this is neither healthy for the animals nor the spectators.

At the Houston (Texas) Zoo, Werler and his associates developed an enclosure with a dry moat which not only separated the gorillas from the people, but from a planted area at the rear of the exhibit. Since apes tend to consume their organic environment, the Houston authorities argued that a distant but contiguous plantation would successfully enhance the appearance of their man-made habitat. As Werler stated:

> This jungle serves much the same function as the backgroup scenery on a theatrical stage, and as it is separated from the animals by a 2.7 m wide moat (which is visible to the viewer), the landscaping is safe from damage (pp. 258–259).

The public has been especially responsive to this innovation as they perceive the habitat as a wilderness rather than a prison. Within the enclosure itself is a platform, about 16 x 11 meters (35 x 50 feet). The moats are about 3.7 meters (12 feet) in depth. The levels of the platform are variable, encouraging the occupants to climb up and down. Pools and waterfalls are included and, as the Houston authorities confirmed (M. Barr, personal communication), the gorillas frequently play in them.

Climbing apparatus are available in the specially constructed concrete trees. In the Houston enclosure, vertical space is especially well utilized. Forks in the large branches were designed to provide natural resting places, and lengthy sections of wild grape vines were acquired in the local woods for use in the enclosure. Suitably anchored by short chains and anchored to eye-bolts in the habitat ceiling beams, these vines have been a favorite swinging and climbing toy. Since the apes also eat the bark, the Houston staff must periodically replace the vines.

In Houston, the gorillas are also given each morning up to two dozen branches of hedge bamboo, *Bambusa multiplex*, which grows in abundance on the zoo grounds. They also receive sunflower seeds. These tidbits are continually manipulated throughout the day, satisfying both resting and feeding needs.* Elsewhere, Maple (1980a) has listed the shrubs utilized as browse at the Philadelphia Zoo. The use of such items contributes to the well being of the animals by stimulating foraging activity. In addition, it is likely that its presence inhibits the development and expression of coprophagy and regurgitation.

The Houston facility was innovative in another way. It initially contained free-flying birds (pigeons, turacos, weavers, and starlings), and a pair of Talapoin monkeys, none of which were harmed by the gorillas.** A sketch of this enclosure, as it appeared in the original report, is provided in Figure 7-6.

In 1976, Richard Quick followed up on Werler's report on the Houston exhibit. Three years after its opening, Quick found that the gorillas were chasing and wrestling with each other on a daily basis, using the complex environment in precisely the way that it was intended. The male especially enjoyed the effect of a spectacular splash made by dropping six to eight feet from a swinging vine into the pools. Quick considered water for play as a "must" for gorilla enclosures.

Another very important aspect of enclosure design was also discussed by Quick. In his report, he lamented the potential for escape when it becomes necessary to deviate from an original plan. In his own words:

Original design of the dry moat barrier's called for dimensions of 14 feet in width and 12 feet in depth with a 15 foot wall on the public viewing side. Unfortunately the widths were reduced by cost factors to 12 feet, 6 inches

---

*Harper Leather Goods Manufacturing Company (Chicago) produces a "rawhide chewie" for dogs which is about thirty inches long and suitable as a manipulable/consumable toy for apes. Atlanta's *Willie B.* has enjoyed these objects on several occasions.

**Eventually, the birds and monkeys destroyed the vegetation and had to be removed. For others planning a similar habitat, Werler recommends an area of planting at least twenty-five feet deep.

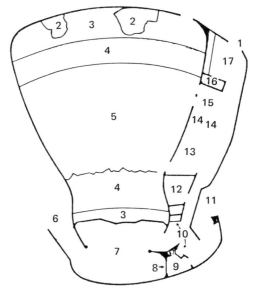

1. Service entrance
2. Waterfalls
3. Planted areas
   rear: 20.2 x 3.4
   front: 9.8 x 0.6-0.9
4. Moat
   front: 9.8 x 3.8-4.3 x 3.7
   rear: 19.5 x 2.7 x 3.7
5. Exhibit platform: 15.9 x 10.5
6. Exit
7. Public viewing area: 9.8 x 6.1

8. Rear projection screen
9. Projection room: 2.8 x 1.4
10. Display cases
11. Entrance
12. Office: 3.0 x 3.0
13. Holding cage
14. Shift cages
15. Squeeze cage
16. Restroom
17. Kitchen: 4.3 x 3.7
(measurements in metres)

Figure 7-6. Gorilla habitat display at Houston Zoo. (After Werler, 1975)

for the front moat and 8 feet, 9 inches for the unique rear moat which separates the gorillas from the heavily planted background and waterfalls. The gorillas have not crossed either of the spans directly, but both moats have been scaled by our imaginative apes after dropping into them, twice using ladders which they were able to reach from the rear moat and place properly, and twice presumably, by wedge-climbing up corners at the ends of the moats (p. 16).

THE ARCHITECTURE OF ESCAPE

In Figures 7-7 and 7-8 details of a naturalistic enclosure under construction can be examined. What is revealed by these photographs is the ever present danger

Figure 7-7. The naturalistic background walls in this enclosure initially provided opportunities for escape. With a few modifications, this enclosure ultimately proved to be both safe and attractive. When properly planned, aesthetics need not be compromised to ensure safety. *(T. Maple photo)*

of building escape routes into a naturalistic background. As we have seen, given their lengthy and powerful arms, apes can readily negotiate a corner, pushing against the sides in order to elevate themselves upward. The sharper the corner, the worse the problem. Moreover, rockwork often contains unintended handholds which can aid in propelling the occupants up and out. Thus, we cannot overemphasize the value of planning for security. Walls must not be too short, moats must not be too narrow, and designers should test an enclosure before they certify it as safe. A way to do this is to challenge a disinterested and acrobatic third party to escape. If a human being can get out of an enclosure, the odds are heavily in favor of the ape being able to do so.

An example of how troublesome this problem can be was illustrated in another context. A zoological park had designed an island habitat for a highly arboreal primate. The surroundings were natural and beautiful, but the moat was frightfully narrow. Compounding the problem, the island itself was very small, necessitating an elaborate climbing structure. Moreover, the scope of the arboreal furniture was severely limited by the moat width. Thus, one problem area affected the solution for another, such that in several dimensions the habitat problems had no remedy at all.

Figure 7-8. This naturalistic corner provides hand holds and an opportunity for long-armed apes to scale the wall. *(T. Maple photo)*

COMFORT

Another habitat dimension which is characteristically neglected is that of resting places. In many enclosures, there are few suitable places for an animal to comfortably sit or recline. Where they have been installed, they are generally stiff and straight in construction (benchlike). Why not mimic the buoyant and rounded qualities of the natural habitat by constructing *nestlike* resting places? This could be especially helpful in aiding in the comfort of females in labor. Knowing that human females in labor have difficulty getting comfortable, one must have empathy for apes that give birth on concrete and steel benches and floors.

THE "NATURALISTIC" TREND

At the 1980 conference of the American Association of Zoological Parks and Aquariums, a workshop was held to discuss recent advances in the management of great apes. At the workshop and in conversation thereafter, descriptions of new gorilla enclosures at San Francisco and Seattle were provided. These two facilities were especially innovative in their deployment of natural grass and trees. In San Francisco's *Gorilla World*, Kikuyu grass, eucalyptus, and Maple trees have been blended with a stream, waterfalls, and extensive rock work over a one-half acre area.

The Woodland Park Zoo in Seattle was opened before its San Francisco counterpart, and has been inhabited for a sufficient period to determine the efficacy of live trees. The destruction of foliage in both areas has been minimized by the provision of supplementary foliage. As this book goes to press, these habitats appear capable of withstanding frequent use and occasional abuse.

In both San Francisco and Seattle, the public has been favorably impressed with the natural terrain. Clearly, people enjoy seeing gorillas in surroundings of trees and grass. The image of the zoo is enhanced by such enclosures, and their aesthetic value is without question.

The Topeka Zoo will soon join their community of innovators with the opening of a new gorilla habitat (cf. Figure 7-9). In this enclosure, a protected tunnel will be constructed so that viewers may enter the gorilla's domain. Heavily planted, Topeka's gorilla habitat will resemble a genuine rain forest.

Even more spectacular is Chicago's Brookfield Zoo *Tropic World*. This huge facility (475 ft. long, 110 ft. wide, and 70 ft. high) is designed to completely enclose both African and Asian rain forests. In the gorilla portion, their spatious home range contains a stream, man-made rock and tree work, and a complex of trails, all within easy but distant view of the elevated public pathways. Inside this high temperature, high humidity building, thundershowers have been engineered. It rains near but not onto the gorillas, providing a fantastic element of realism.* Influenced by the thinking of Dr. Ben Beck, Brookfield's Curator of Primates, *Tropic World* will represent a fantastic research opportunity as the apes explore and adjust to their incredibly complex surroundings. Ten years in the making, this unique enclosure has cost 9.4 million dollars to build. It is indeed a great ape facility which has been built to endure both time and cold weather. The only serious drawbacks of an enclosure of this type are the price tag and the potential expense of its energy requirements. There can be no doubt that the Brookfield enclosure will be good for its gorillas and its public.

_____

*One of the hidden advantages of a naturalistic enclosure was suggested to me by Jon Charles Coe, an architect who contributed to the innovative enclosure at Seattle's Woodland Park Zoo. Coe argued that in a well-landscaped viewing area, the public is put into a subordinate position. The "jungle" habitat is alien to us, but comfortable for the apes. People appear to be more respectful, quieter, and less inclined to vandalism. Thus, a naturalistic enclosure may stimulate positive behaviors in both apes and people.

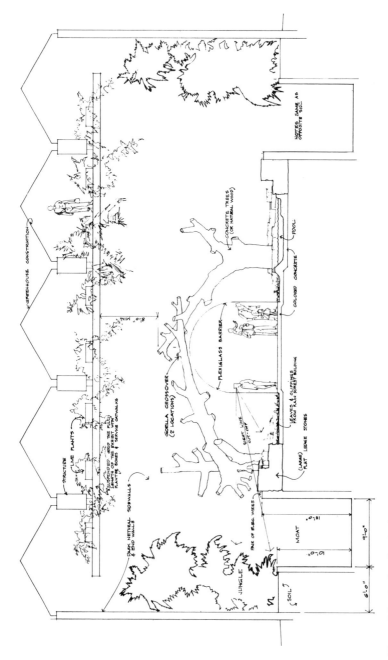

Figure 7-9. Design for the innovative gorilla exhibit at the Topeka Zoological Park. *(Courtesy Gary K. Clarke, Director and Zooplan Associates, Inc., Wichita, Kansas)*

Finally, the National Zoo has recently completed a 2.8 million dollar great ape house which resembles the effective Lincoln Park facility. Complex and spatious, the National Zoo will soon take its rightful place among the leaders in great ape habitat design. In all of these facilities, and others like them, great apes will doubtless lead more active and interesting lives. It is a promising trend.

BEHAVIORAL ENGINEERING

In the wild, apes must travel great distances in order to acquire sufficient sustenance. Foraging for food is a type of work in which all wild animals must

Figure 7-10. Lowland gorilla *Pogo* as she appears in the natural foliage of the San Francisco Zoo's new Gorilla World. *(Photo by S. Allyn Keller)*

engage.   To encourage exercise, it is necessary to devise ways of stimulating activity.   Yerkes recognized the importance of this in his book *Almost Human* (1925):

> Undoubtedly, kindness to captive primates demands ample provision for amusement and entertainment as well as for exercise. If the captive cannot be given opportunity to work for its living, it should at least have abundant chance to exercise its reactive ingenuity and love of playing with things . . . The greatest possibility of improvement in our provisions for captive primates lies in the invention and installation of apparatus which can be used for play or work (p. 229).

Captive apes need activity in order to prevent boredom and promote health. Without such opportunities they will engage in unhealthy behaviors such as excessive self- and social grooming, repetitive regurgitation of food, and coprophagy. The latter two behaviors are, in part, the result of reduced food intake which is necessary in order to prevent obesity. Were the animals active, restricted food intake would be unnecessary and coprophagy and regurgitation would be unlikely to develop. One of the more promising solutions to such problems is the technology developed by Hal Markowitz (cf. Erwin, Maple and Mitchell, 1979). These devices (tic-tac-toe; reaction games, etc.) can induce locomotion, cooperation, and problem-solving efforts when designed properly. Games devised by Markowitz to permit public-animal interactions are safe and indeed, beneficial for the animal. These innovative techniques clearly fulfill a need which has previously been satisfied through public feeding, petting zoos, and animal rides. For the animals that are provided such manipulanda, it is advisable to change the game from time to time. In fact, where objects are introduced for play, it is helpful to change the objects periodically. As has previously been emphasized, a *changing* environment is to be preferred over a static one. An added benefit of many games is that the cognitive abilities of the apes can be studied in the context of entertainment. Morris (1960) has pointed out the value of testing chimpanzee intelligence in full view of the public, and Reynolds (1967) has further extended this view to include other forms of training:

> . . .young tractable apes can be used in training programs, circus-style, to brighten their lives and amuse the public. There is absolutely no reason why zoos should be shy of using circus techniques. These may result in healthier animals and greater subsequent breeding success, and zoos should embrace them as a valuable management aid (p. 246).

Regarding fatigue from overtraining, Morris added:

> Far from being overworked, exhausted chimpanzees, these demonstration chimps are by far the healthiest, most intelligent, and most alert that I have

ever seen in captivity. They obviously benefit tremendously from their varied and complicated activities and one is immediately struck by the need for introducing some similar kind of occupational therapy for adult chimpanzees and for other primates (p. 22).

Jack Throp's efforts to develop the gorilla tug-of-war apparatus at the Honolulu Zoo were described in his 1975 article as follows:

Our most recent adventure into the field of people involvement has made it possible for the visitor to "feel" a live gorilla. A woven nylon rope stretches between the guardrail and the gorilla enclosure, passing through four guideposts. The middle two posts allow for a 1 m play in either direction. Our extroverted male gorilla "Cameroun" is a willing participant in this "tug-of-war" between human and animal and is eager to test the strength of any challenger. To make contact with a fully grown adult male gorilla in a form almost as intimate as a hand-shake is a memorable experience (p. 268).

Thus the need of visitors to somehow make intimate contact with an exotic animal can be sublimated through this ingenious form. The major problem with this idea is in its implementation. Tugging with a gorilla can be risky for the people who undertake the challenge. A better method might be to construct intermediate constraints so that a limited and even safer contact could be made. Such a device will await further technical inventiveness.

As we have seen, Foster (personal communication) has had considerable success in the training of gorillas to accept routine veterinary examinations. By daily working with the apes at the Woodland Park Zoo in Seattle, Foster and his associates have used conditioning techniques to acquire blood samples, and to carry out other clinical tasks. In the former procedure, Foster's gradual procedure calls for *desensitizing* the ape to tactual contact by stroking and stimulating the arm. By providing social and food rewards, the animal gets used to the procedure, and blood can eventually be drawn. The same procedure was originally pioneered in baboons (cf. Chapter 6).

MODE OF HABITAT

Throughout the world, a variety of habitats have been created for the purpose of exhibiting apes. In many cases, temporary isolation of an animal which is in need of care can actually contribute to its demise from the combined effects of its ailment and stress. Gorillas are especially sensitive to such stress.

In research facilities, the major housing problems are the limits in physical size, and the effects of social deprivation. Moreover, Reynolds (1967) has differentiated between the "hygiene" and "natural" schools of ape-keeping. The former is advocated by laboratory specialists. The benefits of a hygienic habitat are obvious, but the stark cement and steel enclosures are rarely engineered for social activity. This is not to say that cement and steel per se are to blame, as it is certainly possible to successfully utilize these building materials. The problems of the zoo habitat are similar to those of the laboratory (cf. Maple, 1979). However, some of these common problems are even more difficult to manage in a zoo setting. For example, the health of captive apes is difficult to protect when the public is permitted close access to them. The modern solution to this problem has been to install glass-fronted enclosures. When the surface is strong and clean, a satisfying view of the animals is created, and they are relatively well-isolated from human disease. A glass front also serves to protect the public from flying fecal projectiles, spitting, and water throwing which are common features of captive ape behavior. However, as we previously asserted, a drawback of these windows is that they result in reduced barrier distances. Apes often respond to these public invasions by kicking and hitting the glass which in turn encourages further public teasing. Glass-fronted enclosures therefore may inadvertently violate flight distance requirements.

Within the zoo enclosure, whatever barriers may be constructed, various forms of furniture may be utilized to enrich the space. Especially functional are large wooden climbing frames such as those recently erected at the San Diego Zoo for orang-utans and a complicated, but smaller, version which has been standing at the Phoenix (Arizona) Zoo for several years (cf. Maple, 1980). Although vulnerable to teeth and the elements, wood lends a natural appearance to any enclosure. Even in the construction of human playgrounds, wood structures have become very popular. In the construction of wooden apparatus, volunteers from the community may be employed as was recently accomplished by Lee White at the San Francisco Zoo. A useful manual for constructing such structures has been written by Hewes (1974). At the Zurich Zoo in Switzerland, bamboo has been utilized to construct arboreal pathways for a variety of species. Another way to use bamboo is as a background, where it can be separated from the animals by wire or glass. Although an illusion, the use of growing foliage as a background creates a superior educational display, and the growth may be culled periodically to obtain browse.

In addition to the primary functions of feeding, care, and capture, the captive habitat should be constructed so that public viewing and daily observations are unobstructed. The former is complicated by the animal needs which we have previously reviewed. The latter can be facilitated by building into the enclosure observation areas, closed-circuit television access points, and/or one-way observation windows. A well-equipped research program is an essential feature of successful captive animal management, and clinical judgments can be enhanced when the veterinarian is supplied daily behavioral data. With regular observation, problems can be objectively verified and appropriate solutions are more likely to be discovered.

As early as 1896, Garner formulated several steps which he surmised would assure the survival of captive gorillas. We will paraphrase and summarize his views in the list of suggestions that follow:

1. The habitat should be highly humid and contain decaying vegetation.
2. The temperature ought to be variable, not constant.
3. A pool of water should be always accessible.
4. The water and indoor shelter should be kept from 60°-90°F.
5. Fresh air, sunlight, and shade should be provided.
6. The animals should not be overly attended.
7. There should be variety in their diet and they should be permitted to select the foods that they desire.
8. Facilities for amusement, companionships, and entertainment must be supplied.

Garner added further that when gorillas become sullen or obstinate "they should not be coaxed or indulged, nor yet used with harshness. They should either be left alone at the time or diverted by a change of treatment" (p. 270). We have already discussed points 3, 6, 7, and 8. The others have never been empirically evaluated. A reasonable range of humidity can be readily achieved in subtropical or tropical regions. Elsewhere, humidity can be manipulated artifically. The value of variable temperatures has been frequently suggested, but we know of no experimental evidence to recommend it. In the rain forests of Africa, temperatures vary from 50°F to 100°F for western lowland gorillas.

Social Deprivation

For gorillas, captivity has not been conducive to reproduction, although there has been rapid improvement in recent years. For all of the great apes, it has been implied that a lack of early social experience is responsible for these breeding problems. This argument appears plausible in light of the fact that most captive apes were captured in the wild as infants and raised by human caretakers.* Since the work of Harlow (1971) has so clearly demonstrated that social deprivation can affect sexual behavior in monkeys, the same results may be expected in apes. However, it has turned out that although Rogers and Davenport (1969) found

---

*Early advances in the nurturance and care of captive gorillas were made by Garner (1914), Hornaday (1915), Reichenow (1920), and Cunningham (1921).

chimpanzees to be greatly affected by isolation, they also found some potential for recovery:

Distortion of the environment in infancy and early childhood, including social isolation and substitute maternal care, has a drastic effect on the sexual behavior of the chimpanzee. It appears that the critical variable is early social experience. Second, some chimpanzees reared in total isolation can, in contrast to similarly reared rhesus monkeys, recover from behavioral injury to the extent that they can copulate (p. 203).

The authors of this paper explained the chimpanzee's ability to recover as a function of its less rigid and less stereotyped pattern of sexual behavior. Moreover, Rogers and Davenport found that the sexual behavior of isolation-reared chimps was *less* drastically affected than that of a human-reared animal. The authors further related this finding to Hediger's (1950) concept of *zoomorphism*; whereby animals develop a sexual preference for human caretakers over conspecifics (see also Maple, 1977). It should be noted, however, that human contact does not preclude normal development or appropriate species identification. Rather it seems that failure to exhibit sexual behavior in hand-raised gorillas is due to social neglect. This stems perhaps from the western propensity to isolate infants, whereas normal gorilla maternal care is continuous. In nurseries, where human care is required, it is possible to maintain more continuous contact by the use of specially constructed carriers.* This type of contact simulates normal continuous mothering, and is likely to improve social development. This idea has been more completely discussed in Maple (1980b). Hand-raising a gorilla should be accomplished over a brief period of intensive contact. As early as possible, the animal should be introduced to peers or a suitable conspecific aunt.

STRESS OF CAPTIVITY

Cousins (1972) also noted that captive gorillas suffered from emotional stress. Aggressiveness toward offspring was cited by Cousins as one aspect of emotional instability. As he suggested:

Rejection of the offspring through lack of knowledge of how to look after it is understandable in captive animals but when aggression is the reaction to the infant something is seriously wrong (p. 215).

---

*A very versatile device for carrying human infants can be adapted to infant apes, thus freeing the caretaker's arms for other nursery work. These infant carriers bear the name *Snugli* and can be obtained by writing: Snugli Inc., Consumer Relations, 1212 Kerr Gulch, Evergreen, Colorado 80439.

The things wrong, according to Cousins' account, could be any of the following early experiences:

1. A brutal capture.
2. Ill-treatment in infancy.
3. Human proximity during parturition.
4. Reactions to an unnatural way of life.

Persistent body-scratching, lethargy, fur plucking, masturbation, and sexual advances to humans were all products of loneliness and boredom in the opinion of Cousins. Elaborating on the behaviors of regurgitation and coprophagy (cf. Chapter 1), the author pointed out that neither had been witnessed to occur in free-ranging gorillas. Sabater Pi's (1967) observations at the Ikunde Centre in Equatorial Guinea revealed that newly captured gorillas developed coprophagy within eight to ten days thereafter. Remarkably, brief removal from the cage served to reduce the habit but did not eradicate it.

The trauma which accompanies a change in environment is due, in part, to a lack of familiar social partners. Yerkes recognized the complexity of the problem, as reflected in the following passage:

> Probably the most serious change of all in the transfer of circus quarters was social environment. With me the gorilla was familiar and friendly, but otherwise she was among strangers. In place of her caretaker Charles Welsh, of whom evidently she had become fond during her months at Ca'd'Zan, she now had a new and experienced attendant, who, however wise and skillful his ministrations, in order adequately to replace his predecessor must win the confidence and affection of his charge. The little chimpanzee did not accompany Congo to Circus Quarters because it was deemed unnecessary. In yet another important respect the social environment of the old and the new locations differed radically . . . at Quarters there was an endless procession, and often a continuing gallery, of curious and at times officiously disturbing visitors (1928, p. 10).

In general, primates do not respond well to such changes in routine or setting. Mitchell (1979) has referred to this as a kind of attachment process whereby the animal becomes attached to its surroundings. Gorillas are no exception to the rule and, as Benchley (1949) has written about *Ngagi* and *Mbongo:*

> They are set in their habits of living; any innovation such as a change in sleeping quarters, diet or keeper is resented for several days (p. 118).

However, this fact should not discourage staff from introducing novel objects. Although we really don't know exactly how to characterize the effects of novelty, most psychologists consider it to be an important dimension in protecting the well-being of captive animals. The process of introduction should, of course, be gradual, and care should be taken that the items be nontoxic, reasonably wear-resistant, unusable as tools for escape or attack, etc. In introducing playthings, we should be as careful with apes as we are (or should be) with our own children.

The Transport of Gorillas

One procedure which requires further study is the breeding loan. There are few rules to guide such arrangements, and, peculiarly, no one has ever endeavored to study the process. This is all the more surprising when one considers the fact that the animals frequently prove to be incompatible. Perhaps, we have found ourselves thinking, the problem is not in the primates themselves, but rather *in the process*. What happens when an ape is moved from familiar to unfamiliar surroundings? Are special precautions taken to gradually introduce the animal to the enclosure? Is its new diet to be a radical departure? Will it be fed at the same time? How is the adjustment to be facilitated? And what about the insult to the resident gorillas? How are they to respond to the intruder?

The only published description of an actual gorilla move is that of Seal and his associates (1970). They described the transport of *Casey* who was acquired by the Como Zoo, St. Paul, Minnesota, in 1959. During his eight years at the zoo, he lived in an enclosure with an orang-utan named *Yogi*. As Seal explained, *Casey* became increasingly assertive with *Yogi* during their last year together. As the Como authorities were seeking a female gorilla, an arrangement was made to loan *Yogi* to the Middlesex Falls Zoo in Stoneham, Massachusetts, thereby providing an opportunity to pair up *Casey*. However, as the facilities at Como were not ideal for gorillas, the zoo authorities very nobly decided to lend *Casey* to a zoo that could effectively attempt to breed gorillas. This was a most commendable decision and a sacrifice which is worthy of our praise. Any zoological park which cannot themselves properly house or breed an endangered species should be willing to seek a more suitable home for the animals.

The Como authorities succeeded in locating a home for Casey at the Henry Doorly Zoo in Omaha, Nebraska. Arrangements were made for him to join their group of two six-year-old females, and one four-year-old male.

In making these arrangements, it was necessary to solve the problem of moving the then 572-pound *Casey*. A decision to move the animal by air was made after a successful trial immobilization. At this time, *Casey's* response to the drugs was monitored and bodily measurements were acquired. The actual move took place on August 16, 1968. *Casey* was initially given 140 milligrams

Phencyclidine HCl (*Sernylan*)* and 75 milligrams *Promazine* (Sparine)** administered through a dart fired from a Palmer CO_2 powered pistol. Sixteen minutes later, caretakers entered the cage, placed him onto a special pallet and moved him by truck to the airplane. At the time of takeoff, 57 minutes after receiving the drugs, *Casey's* temperature was $38°C$ ($100°F$). Four minutes later, he received another 20 milligrams *Phencyclidine*. A third dose of 20 milligrams was administered seven minutes after the second dose in response to increased movement. *Casey's* body temperature varied during the flight between 37.4 and $38°C$ (98.8-$99.8°F$), hovering around $37.7°C$ ($99.4°F$). Altitude affected his heart rate such that it increased to 140 beats/minute at 2140 meters (7000 feet), dropping during descent to 100. At 0836 hours, nearly two hours after the initial dose an additional 20 milligrams *Phencyclidine* was administered. A final 20 milligrams dose was injected at 0858 hours. The plane arrived in Omaha at 0930 hours whereby Casey was transferred to another truck for the trip to the Zoo. The entire operation required 3.5 hours of immobilization.

The foregoing is the extent to which we have documented gorilla translocations. The veterinary procedures are fairly straightforward, although conducted at considerable risk. However, we still have few guidelines regarding behavioral responses to separation, isolation and subsequent reintroduction. Learning more about these responses would aid in specifying advisable procedures and precautions. Transporting an adult gorilla is a hazardous, but often necessary, procedure, and a subject worthy of further careful study.

Lincoln Park's Otto

In an excellent film produced by Dugan Rosalini of Film Associates in Evanston, Illinois the translocation of the Lincoln Park apes from old to new surroundings was documented on film.*** The film focuses on the transition of the lowland gorilla *Otto*. His apprehension when encountering unfamiliar surroundings, however superior, is especially evident in this film. The improved habitats contain an especially stimulating array of cage furniture. There are elevated sitting places, and suspension ropes which can be utilized as a kind of hammock. Surprisingly, one of *Otto's* early responses to the ropes—as portrayed in the film—was to walk upon them. Thus, the vertical component of the enclosure was effectively utilized by a primarily terrestrial organism. Maple has emphasized elsewhere the importance of this spatial dimension (1979; 1980a).

---

*Parke, Davis and Co.
**Wyeth Laboratories Inc.
***Otto: Zoo Gorilla* can be rented through Films Inc., 1144 Wilmette Avenue, Wilmette, Illinois.

The Lincoln Park officials were careful to monitor the change, and the documentary which was produced should be viewed by everyone concerned with improving captive habitats. Here again, the value of an in-house research program cannot be overemphasized. Recently, we had the opportunity to evaluate the new enclosures for gorillas and orang-utans at the Audubon Zoological Gardens in New Orleans. The evaluation is still in progress as this book goes to press, but the methodology can be outlined here. The intent of the study is the same as in so-called postoccupancy evaluations of newly constructed public institutions, such as office buildings, schools, prisons, etc. In a zoo enclosure evaluation, the occupants are observed first in the old enclosure. The major dependent variables which should be employed are activity and social interaction, although there are many other behaviors which may be affected by a change in the surroundings. For example, we expect that, at the Audubon Zoo, activity and social interaction will increase in the new enclosure. Moreover, because of enhanced opportunities for arboreal locomotion, the animals should spend more time in an elevated position. To test these expectations, we observed the animals* at the time of their release into the new quarters and for several days thereafter. A third sample will be undertaken thirty days later. At the time of the third test, the elevated target variables should have decreased and leveled off. More importantly, however, *activity* and *interaction* should remain at higher levels than the norms for the old enclosure.

Evaluation is an important part of zoo management and enclosure design, and should be encouraged. Unfortunately, it is more likely that enclosures will be subjectively evaluated, leading to endless controversy about their true effects.

In a unique study carried out by Susan Fisher Wilson (personal communication), 127 gorillas housed in forty-three enclosures were studied in twenty-six zoological parks in Europe and Great Britain. In this study the dimensions and characteristics of the respective enclosures were quantified. The degree of correlation between the respective variables and activity was subsequently calculated. The results revealed that there was a very strong correlation between activity and the number of animals per enclosure, movable and temporary objects in the enclosure, and stationary objects in the enclosure. As Wilson pointed out, it is somewhat surprising that the amount of space was not a more important factor in stimulating activity. However, the fact that stimulation from the social and physical environment in some way influences activity is a very valuable finding. This study provides strong evidence that the quality of the habitat (in quantitative terms, no less) contributes to the well-being of captive gorillas. As Wilson concluded:

> What I am suggesting is that when new enclosures are built or old ones are enlarged, it may be extremely important to also exponentially increase the num-

---

*We are grateful to Janet Kerley, Jill Yakubik, Robin O'Neil, David Anderson, Betsy O'Donoghue, and Dr. Elizabeth Watts for assistance in the completion of this project.

ber of objects within the enclosure. Space is not enough; there must be something in the space.

There are many elements to consider in the design of optimal gorilla habitats. Despite our advanced technology, it is difficult to improve upon the Yerkes' (1929) insightful summary of the requirements for successfully maintaining gorillas in captivity:

> Essential undeniably in the successful handling of captives are avoidance of injury or shock, the speedy establishment of mutual confidence or sympathetic rapport, training to the acceptance of unusual foods and new habits of feeding, suitable companionships and amusement or entertainment, and adequate measure of freedom with appropriate shelter and a hygenic and otherwise healthful environment (p. 425).

This sage advice is being followed by modern zoo designers. Within this chapter we have reviewed the many exciting enclosures which are being developed. With a greater knowledge of their natural habitat and an understanding of their habits, these apes need not be housed in shameful gorilla ghettoes.

As we have seen, the gorilla is difficult to exhibit in captivity but adequate habitats are becoming more common as a new generation of superior facilities have been designed and constructed. Chicago's Lincoln Park Zoo, The San Diego Wild Animal Park, Seattle's Woodland Park Zoo, the Houston Zoo, and the Audubon Park Zoo are particularly notable examples of innovative designs for functional gorilla habitats. They retain the essential features of a complex, stimulating, and naturalistic habitat. Privacy is also possible in these enclosures, as gorillas seem to need privacy more than any other ape. In Europe, we have the splendid *Apenheul* to admire. No better gorilla habitat has been constructed in this world. The only apes that live better are free in the African rain forest. The trend today is a positive one, and we are optimistic that one day soon, there will be no captive gorillas residing in impoverished surroundings. We owe them and our children at least that outcome.

8
Conservation of Gorilla

Human rights are triumphing over animal rights, and it would be hard to determine which rights are really superior or most worthy to survive.

Henry Fairfield Osborn, 1923

Field workers have long fought to provide greater protection for the gorillas of Africa. Efforts have been primarily focused on the mountain gorillas since their numbers are so dangerously low, and human encroachment has been so rapid and obtrusive. With regard to captive populations, improvements in the breeding records, so disgracefully poor a decade ago, have been dramatic and encouraging. This improvement parallels our greater and still growing understanding of the requirements of gorillas in captivity. Thus, we continue to work on two fronts, striving for the protection and expansion of their natural habitats, while we continue to seek improvements in the conditions of captivity. We have reviewed progress and problems in the latter category in Chapter 7; here we can address in some detail the problems which face conservationist and gorilla alike. The reader should again remember that the conservation issues for all primates are similar. For a review of the conservation issues in Indonesia and Malaysia, the reader is referred to the companion to this volume (Maple, 1980a). Clearly, the problems which confront the Asian and African apes are essentially the same.

Gorillas have been historically exploited as a source of food, as a trophy, and for exhibition abroad. They were once ruthlessly hunted by outsiders, but they are today also the victims of the local people. In addition, gorillas compete with people for the scarce resources of space and food. Where gorillas and humans compete, depending upon the seriousness of the competition, gorillas rarely win. Make no mistake; gorillas that come into contact with crops can be formidable pests.* Nonetheless, much more gorilla food has been destroyed by people, than conversely.

---

*One of the ways in which gorillas can damage crops is discussed in a technical report by Stephen Bullock (1978). In the Campo subdistrict of Cameroon, the investigator noted that cultivated *Musa* plants were handled by gorillas in three different ways: 1. Longitudinal shredding while standing; 2. Pulling/pushing down with breakage of the petioles near the base; 3. Pulling/pushing over with no breakage but partial uprooting. As Bullock determined, the first technique resulted in less damage. In all cases, fruit regrowth is delayed by gorilla feeding. Of greater concern is Bullock's observation that an entire crop of *Musa* may be lost if the grower abandons the field to weeds after the initial gorilla damage.

EASTERN GORILLAS

The conservation of eastern gorillas has been reviewed in detail by Goodall and Groves (1977). Noting that the two recent census efforts (Emlen and Schaller, 1960; Schaller, 1963) had produced widely divergent population estimates of 5,000 and 15,000, the authors suggested that short-term census work is inadequate for the acquisition of accurate figures. While the pockets of African gorillas distributed throughout a total range of 35,000 square miles are doubtless growing smaller, and the floral composition of their habitats is changing, most gorillas are found in Zaire, where there are many national parks. Nonetheless, the designation of additional parks is needed. There is also a great need for further long-term census work, some of which is currently being carried out in West Africa by Gartlan and his associates from the University of Wisconsin.

Population figures for eastern regions also suggest that gorillas are on the decline in some areas, although in at least one, the Kahuzi-Beiga region, after the imposition of safeguards against hunting, recruitment levels improved. While capture for zoos and museums has been a historical threat to gorilla survival, other sources of population decline have been habitat destruction by fuel industries and local peoples, cattle grazing, poaching for meat and byproducts of the gorilla body, competition with humans for space, and disturbances by tourism. An additional and even more formidible challenge to the gorilla's existence is the practice of large-scale deforestation in order to produce larger agricultural areas, and additional cash crops.

Recommendations by Goodall and Groves have included the formulation of realistic land-use management plans, cessation of habitat incursions by cattle, creation of gorilla research headquarters staffed by local personnel, detailed censusing, rapid information exchange and dissemination, habitat creation, gorilla relocation experiments, and the strict enforcement of all existing national park statutes and regulations.

Protection in Rwanda

In 1978 the Fauna Preservation Society launched a campaign to raise funds for the protection of mountain gorillas in the *Parc National des Volcans* in Rwanda. This effort followed publicity concerning the killing of a wild gorilla named *Digit* which had gained fame by appearing in a television documentary about the research of Dian Fossey. A. H. Harcourt and Kai Curry-Lindahl discussed the problem in a 1979 publication.*

---

*Sabena Airlines is a company which should be heartily commended for its commitment to the welfare of the mountain gorilla. Population surveys and conservation efforts have been facilitated by Sabena's financial support and cooperation. We urge other corporations to do likewise.

The death of *Digit,* and later *Uncle Bert* and *Macho,* were the result of a growing trade in gorilla heads and hands which began in 1976. Although little is known about the mechanics of this trade, it appears to be dependent on the interaction of poachers, middleman entrepreneurs, and white residents and touring trophy hunters. This is a serious problem in view of the fact that the use of high velocity weapons has led to greater efficiency in killing these animals. Since the Virunga Volcanoes may be the last refuge of the mountain gorilla, the danger of rapid extinction is very real.

By 1973, Fossey estimated that there were no more than 260-290 gorillas in the Virunga Volcano region, down considerably from Schaller's 1960 estimate of 400-500 animals. With these data in mind, Harcourt and Curry-Lindahl made the following observations:

1. There are only 31 guards to patrol the whole of the Parc National des Volcans. Given that all patrolling has to be done on foot, and that at any one time a number of the guards will be on leave or sick, this is too small a number for the present system of patrolling, although with more effective management, 30 guards would probably be enough.

2. The system of patrolling the park is inadequate and inappropriate, although at the moment no other may be feasible. The guards live in ten two-man huts distributed around the park boundary, and themselves organize their own patrols into the forest each day. With well paid, well equipped, highly trained and motivated men, such a system would probably be ideal, but it is quite unrealistic when the discomforts and supposed dangers of the forest, and the guards' own lack of motivation are taken into account. What is needed are small, mobile, overnight patrols of about four men led by a senior guard. But two factors make this difficult. First, lack of equipment. For example, all we saw in the way of gear at the post we visited was boots, World War I rifles, and knapsacks; otherwise the guards' dress was indistinguishable from that of the local people. Waterproof clothing and, especially, facilities for overnight patrols, such as tents, are necessary; second, the siting of the National Park Headquarters, which has no radio link with any of the huts, far towards the eastern end of the park, near Sabinio. This makes effective central control of guard movements nearly impossible. A substation near the park border between Karisimbi and Visoke is needed, and ORTPN has this high on their list of priorities, along with equipping and training of the guards.

3. Cultivation reaches right up to the national park boundary, and between the park and the local peoples and their livestock there is no barrier whatsoever; no ditch, no fence, no boundary posts or notices, and no entrance gates. Provided the eyes of the guards can be avoided, people can come and go into the park at will. The only existing demarcation is a line of planted conifers that not only merges into the backdrop of the forest, but can easily be moved and replanted. Shortly before we arrived a further 400 ha of the park had been taken by a high official in the area, and the conifers merely replanted along the new edge of the man's field, scores of metres further into the park.

4. The Rwandan Ministry of Agriculture is planning to excise a further 3000–4000 ha from the western end of the Parc National des Volcans to provide pasture for cattle, in addition to the 10,000 ha already appropriated for pyrethrum.

Moreover, they advised that the Rwandan tourist efforts were inadequate, permitting more tourists to enter the Park illegally than legally. Without reorganization, the Rwandans were daily losing essential revenue. While in the park, the lack of information and supervision has already led to injury:

On the day we arrived at the park, a French tourist was bitten on the leg by a gorilla, and it was abundantly clear from the guide's account that they had been severely antagonising the animals. To put this incident into perspective, it should be remembered that during all the years the gorillas were being censused by Dr. Fossey and her assistants, mostly undergraduates from American and European universities, who worked with totally unhabituated animals *after training at the Karisoke Research Centre,* not one person was ever harmed by any gorilla (p. 320).

In reviewing the problems of the *Parc National des Volcans,* Harcourt and Curry-Lindahl advised that the number of park personnel be greatly increased, and receive better training and improved equipment. They also recommended that more gorilla groups be habituated to tourists, that the park should be better publicized at home and abroad, and that a research program should be developed within the park. On this latter recommendation, given its importance, we quote as follows:

The only research station working in the Virunga Volcanoes is the Karisoke Research Centre at the south base at Visoke. It is, for example, *solely* due to the work carried out from there that we even know how many gorillas there are in the park. The Research Centre is gaining an international reputation as a source of knowledge on the mountain gorilla and the Virunga Volcanoes, and it would be a tragedy, both for science and the Virunga Volcanoes, if this research were to be stopped (p. 322).

The importance of the forest ecosystem was emphasized in the conclusion of Harcourt and Curry-Lindahl's paper. As they declared, the forest acts as a giant sponge, storing water in the wet season and slowly releasing it through the dry season. By destroying their forest, the Rwandan people are unwittingly "severing their lifeline." By preserving the park for tourism, the two scientists believe, the area could be as economically important to Rwanda as the national park system is to Kenya.

Virunga Translocations

In a 1976 issue of the conservation journal *Oryx,** John MacKinnon suggested that authorities should consider the movement of gorillas from the Kahuzi-Biega** National Park to the Virunga National Park. Such a move, in his opinion, could serve to introduce "new blood" into the potentially inbred Virunga population. Harcourt (1977) disagreed with this suggestion in view of the potential dangers that it presented.

Harcourt acknowledged that the eastern gorillas were split into small, isolated areas. Their scattered distribution, as he pointed out, leaves them especially vulnerable to human encroachment. In addition, isolation does contribute to the risk of inbreeding (MacKinnon, 1976). However, according to Harcourt, translocating gorillas would likely endanger both the resident and the translocated populations. Moreover, Harcourt argued that there is currently no evidence that deleterious inbreeding has been occurring in the Virunga gorillas. The possibility that Virunga gorillas may be able to successfully withstand inbreeding has also been suggested:

A population is likely to *suffer* from inbreeding if it was initially outbred and then started to inbreed. MacKinnon repeats Schaller's supposition that gorillas only recently moved into the Virunga region. If so, and if they were once part of a larger population from which they are now separated, they fulfill this criterion for being prone to deleterious inbreeding. However, because of their social structure, and for the very reason that they originated as part of an expanding population, it is not unlikely that they have been selected to withstand the damaging effects of inbreeding. (Harcourt, 1977, p. 470).

As he further noted, the Virunga population contains no evidence of physical defects or decreased viability attributable to inbreeding. In addition, Harcourt pointed out that these gorillas have proved adaptable to very different environments, whereas inbred animals would likely be unable to do so.***

With respect to translocation itself, Harcourt highlighted the dangers of such an operation. The capture, transport, and release of an alien population would doubtless be traumatic for both residents and newcomers. Moreover, the ecological

---

*Published by the Fauna Preservation Society. Subscriptions to this excellent publication can be obtained by writing FPS, c/o Zoological Society of London, Regent's Park, London NW1, 4RY, England.

**As Groves and Stott (1979) noted:

. . . the Kahuzi gorilla . . . must rank as the only gorilla population anywhere which seems to be flourishing, and whose future seems—as of now—secure. (p. 174).

***An additional and fundamental objection to translocating Kahuzi gorillas is that they may not belong to the same taxonomic group as the Virunga subspecies (see Chapter 1 for a further discussion of this issue). Thus, purposefully inbreeding *beringei* and *graueri* would forever damage the integrity of the respective subspecies.

adaptations of Kahuzi gorillas would be of little use in the Virunga environment. In particular, Virunga is much colder than Kahuzi and the resident animals of the former are consequently much hairier. The major food plants are also very different, and translocated animals might have considerable difficulty locating sufficient food. There is also a danger that the Kahuzi gorillas might succumb to local diseases or parasites, or introduce new pathogens which would endanger the Virunga population. Harcourt also suggested a potential effect on the local people. In his view, the capture of gorillas by conservationists encourages locals to likewise enter the boundaries of the park. Thus the park/gorilla sanctity may need to be *totally* protected.

In summary, Harcourt has determined that human encroachment, e.g., habitat destruction, is a far more immediate danger than inbreeding. Efforts to protect existing populations must first be made. In the future, as Harcourt suggested, an interbreeding effort may become necessary, but authorities currently lack the knowledge and expertise to assure that such action will be successful. Thus, translocation would seem to be an inadvisable strategy at this time.

WESTERN GORILLAS

As we mentioned in Chapter 1, Gartlan's* IUCN report split western gorillas into four groups as follows:

1. Originally classified as the Gabon gorilla (*P.g. gorilla*), Groves (1970a) mapped Group 1 as deme A. Extending south from the Nyong River in south-central Cameroon, these animals occur in Rio Muni and Gabon almost to the mouth of the Congo River. Inland they are found along the Ogowé River in Gabon to its headwaters, and east to the hilly west-central Congo region in the Ivondo-Ogowe watershed.
2. According to Gartlan, Group 2 has been previously characterized as the *Plateau* gorilla (*P.g. matschiei*). Groves identified this population as deme B. This group is found exclusively in Cameroon at over 2000 feet. The northern boundary of their range is thought to be between the Pangar and Djerem River valley, not farther than 6°N. This group was formerly found south through savanna and forest islands which are now the sites of the towns of Yaoundé, Obala, Nanga Eboko, and Abong Mbang. The western range was formerly as far as Ebolowa, while to the east and south, they extended to Batouri and the Dja River (between Sangmelima and Lomié), respectively.

*Donations to Gartlan's conservation efforts can be directed to IUCN/WWF Joint Project #1089, c/o World Wildlife Fund, 1601 Connecticut Avenue, N.W., Washington, D.C. 20009.

Figure 8-1. Young western gorilla exhibiting injuries sustained from the effects of a wire snare. Note gangrenous left foot. *(Photo courtesy J. Stephen Gartlan)*

3.   Gartlan's third group has been previously identified as *P.g. castaniceps*. Groves mapped this group as deme C. According to Gartlan, they are the least "clear-cut" of the four groups, and may have derived from interbreeding between the first two groups. Distributed along the riverine banks of the Sangha, Ngoko, Bouma, and Likoula aux Herbes Rivers, these animals once extended from the southeastern Cameroon into southwestern regions of the Central African Republic, and north-eastern regions of Congo.

4.   The final group in Gartlan's scheme is *P.g. diehli,** known previously as the West Cameroon gorilla. Gartlan noted that it was incorrectly mapped

---

*Although Gartlan used the genus name *Pan* in this report, he agrees with us that *Gorilla* is today the preferred genus name for this taxon.

as deme D in Groves' 1967 paper (cf. Chapter 1). Ecologically and geographically isolated from all other populations of western gorillas, the recent range of this group was from south-east of the Ogoja Hills (Eastern Nigeria) to the westernmost part of the Northwest Province of Cameroon. The Cross River to the south, Katsina Ala River to the north, Benoné Valley to the west, and Bamenda Highlands to the east are considered to be the limits of this population. Gartlan estimated their total range to be about 150 by 50 miles in size.

Accordingly, Gartlan proposed that Group 1 was the most extensive and least endangered of the four. However, they are not to be considered safe from the increasing pressures represented by human population growth, logging, and economic development. A relatively abundant population can be found in the Campo Reserve of Cameroon according to the observations of Julie Webb (unpublished). This region is rich in gorilla food plants and local hunting is still rare. Gartlan considers it logistically feasible to protect this area and thus conserve a gorilla population of substantial numbers. Specific dangers to such a plan include a 25-year logging permit held by a French company, a government project which identifies Campo as a potential site for perennial plantations, and persistent rumors of petroleum deposits.

As Jones and Sabater Pí (1971) estimated, the total population of gorillas in Rio Muni did not exceed a few hundred prior to the country's independence in 1968. Today, Gartlan doubts that any gorillas remain in this country. One of the reasons for their demise has been the skillful hunting* and trapping of the Fang tribe. In this country, whether under Spanish dominion or independent, conservation laws have never been effective. The political turmoil of the seventies decimated the remaining gorillas, as people exploited the local fauna in order to survive.

For the gorilla subspecies, Gabon is the country with the greatest amount of suitable habitat. Gabon's low human population density is in contrast to its relatively high gorilla population. Gartlan determined that they were generally absent from regions lower than 500 meters in altitude. The three main population centers for Group 1 are:

1. South of the Ogowé River, inland along the coast to the Congo, east to the N'Goumé River (about 150 kilometers inland).
2. The highlands between the N'Goumé and the upper headwaters of the Ogowé, south of Booué town.
3. Northern Gabon immediately south of the Cameroon border, extending west from the Rio Muni border to north-central Congo in the east.

---

*Jones and Sabater Pí (1971) noted that local people in Rio Muni believe that gorilla hunting is necessary due to their reputation for raiding crops. However, it appears that gorillas only selected fields that provided the cover of regenerating indigenous vegetation.

Areas of abundance are Mitzic in the west and the Belinga Mountains in the east.

In Gabon, gorillas are also hunted and trapped as sources of food, but Gartlan believes that it is less of a problem in this country than elsewhere. The greater threats to their survival, in his view, are industrialization, mineral extraction, and railway construction. Logging is also considered to be a factor in the gorilla's southern population centers. As Gartlan elaborated:

> As an example of the deteriorating situation in Gabon, I was told in 1974* that in the region of the Lopé Okanda National Park, in the second of the southern centers of gorilla abundance in Gabon, that gorillas were then both numerous and easy to observe and follow. Five years later it was reported** that two logging operations were being conducted within the confines of the villages. Hunting and trapping of gorillas was extensive, and in contrast to the situation five years earlier, they were both shyer and rarer. (p. 5)

There are six areas where gorillas are officially protected in Gabon: The Lopé Okanda National Park, the Wonga Wongue National Park, the Domaine de chasse de Iguela de N'gove N'dogo, the Domaine de chasse de Moukalaba, the Domaine de chasse de N'dendé, and the Reserve de Ipassa. However, as Gartlan asserted, "It seems that these are little better than paper parks."

In Gabon, Gartlan recommended that the laws be better enforced in the existing sanctuaries, and that new areas of protection should be established in the far northeast and northwest sections of the country. As in other parts of Africa, the long-term prognosis for gorilla survival is not promising.

In summarizing the findings for Group 1 gorillas, Gartlan surmized that they may have been reduced by 45% in the past 100 years. He estimated that the Cameroon population numbers around 500 animals, while there may be 2000 in Gabon, and 500 in the Congo. Thus, by these estimates, only about 3000 *G.g. gorilla* may remain in these areas today.

As we noted in Chapter 1, Group 2 gorillas can be found only in Cameroon. Gartlan characterized these populations as relict, located primarily in the southwest and perhaps in the north of that country. Although gorillas were formerly common in the Dja Reserve, Julie Webb and Thelma Rowell (unpublished), in separate surveys, found few gorillas in this region. Gartlan suggested that many of the gorillas of this part of Cameroon have been pushed south. The pressures

---

*By Dr. A. Borosset.
**By Giuseppe Vassallo.

which have been exerted on Cameroon gorillas are familiar ones: logging, agriculture, hunting, and trapping.

Gartlan estimated that 85% of the range of these gorillas has been eliminated during the past century. In Gartlan's opinion, the southwest area near Ebolowa and the Pangar Djerem region of Cameroon should quickly be surveyed and the remnant populations be protected. The latter location has been enhanced as a conservation area by its recent designation as a National Park.

The Group 3 gorillas, subspecies *castaniceps,* is now apparently extinct in the Central African Republic. They are still found in Cameroon near Mouloundon and Keka, but these are also prime logging regions. A gorilla sanctuary at Lac Lobeke has been proposed by the Cameroon government, but this region is mainly a swamp forest with little likelihood of a resident gorilla population. Gartlan has accordingly suggested that the sanctuary be relocated.

Although gorillas probably survive in northcentral Congo, little information has been gathered to support the claim. 250,000 hectares of protected land are contained in the Parc d'Odzala, the Réserve de la Lekoli, and the Domaine de M'Boko. However, the effectiveness of this protection is in doubt. Reduced by as much as two-thirds in this century, there are probably no more than 1000 of Group 3 gorillas in the three countries combined.

Group 4, the western highland gorilla in Gartlan's terminology, has been extinct in Nigeria for at least fifteen years. Julie Webb located a few individuals of this type in Cameroon within the Takamanda Reserve. Here there is extensive hunting pressure. Gartlan suggested that this unique subspecies has been reduced by as much as 80% in the last century. The current population is put at 200 individuals or less. Here we must quote Gartlan:

> It is clear that a survey should be carried out swiftly in order to assess the status of this race, and if a viable population still exists, all efforts should be made to protect it either within the boundaries of the Takamanda Reserve, or if populations exist outside this region, to protect it where it exists. It would be ironic if this race were to become extinct before it has been properly described and studied. (p. 8)

In summarizing the status of western gorillas, Gartlan estimated the total population at less than 5000 animals.* He furthermore asserted that, at the present accelerating rate of loss, the western gorilla will be completely extinct within twenty to twenty-five years.

---

*Peculiarly, Reynolds (1967) reported that western gorillas were not endangered in an alarming way by hunting, collecting, or habitat destruction. As Jones and Sabater Pí (1971) subsequently determined, "the complete converse was true."

Protection in Cameroon

In a recent publication, Awunti (1978) discussed the conservation policies of the United Republic of Cameroon where populations of the western lowland gorilla reside.
As Awunti stated:

> We are conscious of the endangered state of this very precious rare species. Consequently, every effort is being made to conserve it. Thus the gorillas are protected by law and up to 1974 capturers were strictly restricted in the exportation of gorillas and chimpanzees despite the highly attractive prices paid by the developed countries for these animals. (p. 77)

In 1971, the Cameroon government converted the Douala-Edea and Korup Reserves into national parks and created within their boundaries a primate research center. Recent efforts have resulted in the protection of another 400 Km^2 in the southeast area near Mouloundou, surrounding Lake Lobeke. In addition to these, important gorilla sanctuaries in Cameroon are the Dja, Campo, Takamanda, and probably the Pangar-Djerem Reserves.

The principle conservation problem for Cameroon has been the tradition of shifting agriculture. This pattern not only affects the wildlife habitats, but it also encourages illegal trapping and hunting. According to Awunti, the major need in Cameroon is for conservation education. In his own words:

> People are now familiar with the general principles and concepts. They still have to reconcile this new idea with their entrenched traditional ideas, that forests and wildlife are God-given and should be used as required, to satisfy man's needs. Thus the old traditional thinking has no room for conservation. (p. 78)

Awunti goes on to point out the sad fact that for many African children, their first glimpse of many African animals is in the zoological parks of western nations. Anyone who has traveled in Africa has learned that far too many Africans are ignorant of the indigenous wildlife which surrounds them.

The protection of the rain forests has proved to be more difficult in Cameroon than the protection of savanna. Costly research programs are a necessary starting point in the proper management of these forests. The government of Cameroon has proved to be willing to carry out such programs, and this is an attitude which should be commended. Since the bulk of the human population of Cameroon lives in the forested zones, there is always pressure on the wildlife and the indigenous flora, especially on the hardwood trees for which there is a continuing demand in the western world. As Awunti concluded, the developing countries are becoming rapidly aware of the value of sound conservation:

> We in the Republic of Cameroon are convinced that the wildlife in our country is our natural heritage which if properly conserved and managed could be-

come a source of foreign exchange through touristic attraction. It is an important base for research and education. Given time, knowledge and money, the few problems confronting our wildlife management will certainly be overcome (p. 79).

THE FOREST ECOSYSTEM

As Gartlan (1974) has pointed out, the differentiation of the African forest from the savanna is ancient, dating at least from the Miocene epoch. Pliocene climatic conditions apparently led to the extension and diversification of the savanna at the expense of forests. Perhaps 95% of tropical evergreen forest has been lost in the last 65 million years, according to an estimate by Napier (1970).

Crucial to the problem of maintaining viable numbers of primates within the dwindling forest ecosystems is the acquisition of accurate information on their distribution. Moreover, it is equally important that the extant vegetation be properly classified. Thus *zoogeography* and *phytogeography* can be employed in order to specify target areas of concern to conservationists. Once the geographical regions and their inhabitants are properly identified, it is possible to discuss the problems of these areas.

A major constraint on the size of the African forests is agricultural expansion. Human population growth puts people and animals in direct competition for scarce resources. Experts are in agreement that the forest ecosystem is too fragile to withstand large scale agricultural intrusions.*

A second major threat to the rain forest is the logging industry. Indirectly, road construction for logging opens the forest to hunters and to cultivation for subsistence (e.g., yams, plaintains, cassava) or cash (cocoa, coffee, rubber, palm oil) crops. The direct effects of logging can be catastrophic for the indigenous inhabitants of rain forests. Frequently, reforestation has been attempted subsequent to massive logging operations. Because these efforts generally employ alien fast-growing softwoods, the composition of the indigenous hardwood forest is invariably altered. As Gartlan (1974) pointed out:

> The plantations are useless as far as the native mammal fauna is concerned. Even when indigenous species are involved there is a tendency to plant monospecific stands of hardwood, which again are of minimal value to the indigenous fauna (p. 515).

Thus, the major pressure on gorillas, as with other primates, is from *habitat destruction*. In the coastal forests of the Lower Guinea area, timber activity has greatly increased. The International Primatological Society has promoted this

---

*Readers of this book who want to contribute funds to the mountain gorilla's protection can write to: The Honorary Secretary, Fauna Preservation Society, c/o London Zoo, Regent's Park, London NW1 4RY, England.

area as an official conservation target and two National Parks (Korup and Doualy-Edea) have recently been established. The total area under protection is 1000 square miles. A forest block in Eastern Zaire (also including portions of Rwanda and Uganda), extends from the right bank of the Lualaba River to the Rift Valley, bounded north by the Ituri River and south by the Lutaka River. The forests which comprise this area are lowland, montane, and bamboo. The most extensive type of rain forest in this area is the lowland type. Formerly even more extensive, lowland forests have declined due to human encroachment in the form of slash-and-burn agriculture. It is an interesting irony that as Schaller first noted and Gartlan reiterated, gorillas probably benefit from *limited* slash-and-burn efforts as secondary vegetation increases.

Even more vulnerable are the moist montane and bamboo forests. Since, as Gartlan asserted, these areas are rich enough for continuous cultivation, they support dense human populations. Overgrazing by domestic cattle has been troublesome for the Virunga Volcano region in Zaire and Rwanda. The bamboo forests are threatened by this and the deforestation which has accompanied the increase in home construction. These events are amplified by the concomitant erosion of national park boundaries in Zaire, Rwanda, and Uganda. The Kahuzi and Mwenga-Fizi regions are similarly threatened by human expansion. Gorilla populations are clearly threatened in these regions.

As Gartlan further warned:

> The undisturbed rain-forest maintains its own high humidity and moisture as long as the canopy remains intact. Once disturbed by extensive logging or agricultural incursions, degeneration may be rapid. It is particularly important therefore that areas of rain-forest are preserved intact during periods of climatic change. The current change in the prevailing wind systems can be potentially disastrous if the forest canopy were to be breached on a large scale (p. 521).

Some general recommendations for the protection of the rain-forest ecosystem can be derived from Gartlan and organized into the following list:

1. The genetic and ecological diversity of the rain-forest must be preserved in order to protect the system from natural insults such as disease, insects, earthquakes, climatic shifts, and human incursions.
2. Some biologically viable forest units must be chosen for *total protection*.
3. Developed countries must assist in financing protection for the forests of developing nations.

4. The price of tropical hardwoods should be increased to reflect the actual cost of acquisition.*

5. Forest national parks should become centers of research on the forest ecosystem, providing practical information about the effects of logging, reforestation, etc.

6. Forest parks should be an integral part of the nation's educational system so that the citizens can learn to appreciate and preserve their fragile forest ecosystem.

7. The tourist potential of protected areas should be further developed as a source of revenue.

In this volume, we have endeavored to provide the most up-to-date information concerning gorilla behavior. In emphasizing the captive gorilla, we have tried to successfully integrate the findings of both field and captive studies. Hopefully, the facts are clear, and the gaps in our knowledge are well defined. We will attempt to fill some of these gaps ourselves, and we trust that as research continues the pages within this volume will be periodically altered. In ending this effort, we can find no better way than to quote the scientists who are most responsible for our inspiration, and for the development of a great ape psychology. We concur with Robert and Ada Yerkes in hoping that our book, like theirs, will serve the public well. It pleases us to let them have these last words:

> If it serves to inform the layman authoritatively and acceptably, to conserve the time of the investigator, to improve historical perspective, to increase respect for those who effectively use and generously acknowledge the contributions of their predecessors, to suggest problems, to reveal important opportunities for verifying or supplementing knowledge, to encourage and inspire more determined, enthusiastic, objective, and efficient study and use of the anthropoid apes for the enlightenment of mankind and the improvement of his lot; our regrets for the hours which have been lost to research will have been dissipated and our labors abundantly rewarded (p. 591).

---

*As Gartlan observed:

Currently the bulk of the profits from the timber industry go, not to the producer countries, but to European, American and Japanese middlemen. It has been aptly observed that the need for economic assistance to the developing countries would be minimized if the developed countries would merely stop exploiting them. This is particularly true in the case of the tropical forests. (p. 522)

References

Akeley, C. E. 1923. *In Brightest Africa.* New York: Doubleday.

Alexander, R. D. 1974. The evolution of social behavior. *Ann. Rev. Ecol. Syst.,* 5, 325-383.

Awunti, J. 1978. The conservation of primates in the United Republic of Cameroon. In: Chivers, D. J. and Lane-Petter, W. (Eds.). *Recent Advances in Primatology,* Vol. 2. London: Academic Press, 75-79.

Baumgartel, M. W. 1958. The Muhavura gorillas. *Primates,* 1, 79-83.

Baumgartel, W. 1959. The last British gorillas. *Geogr. Mag. Lond.,* 32, 32-41.

Baumgartel, W. 1976. *Up Among the Mountain Gorillas.* New York: Hawthorn Books.

Beck, B. B. 1980. Fertility in North American male lowland gorillas. Unpublished.

Benchley, B. J. 1949. *My Life in a Man-Made Jungle.* Boston: Little, Brown.

Bernstein, I. S. 1969. A comparison of the nesting patterns among the three great apes. In: Bourne, G. H. (Ed.). *The Chimpanzee,* Vol. 1. Basel/New York: Karger, 393-402.

Bernstein, I. S. 1970. Primate status hierarchies, In: Rosenblum, L. A. (Ed.) *Primate Behavior: Developments in Field and Laboratory Research,* Vol. 1, New York: Academic Press, 71-109.

Bingham, H. C. 1932. Gorillas in a native habitat. *Carnegie Inst. Washington Publ.,* 426, 1-66.

Bingham, L. R. and Hahn, T. C. 1974. Observations on the birth of a lowland gorilla. *Int. Zoo Yearbook,* 14: 113-115.

Bolwig, N. 1959a. A study of the behavior of the chacma baboon. (*Papio ursinus*). *Behaviour,* 14, 137-163.

Bolwig, N. 1959b. A study of the nests built by mountain gorillas and chimpanzees. *S. Afr. J. Sci.* 54, 195-217.

Bourne, G. H. and Cohen, M. 1975. *The Gentle Giants.* New York: Putnam and Sons.

Bowlby, J. 1969. *Attachment and Loss. Vol. I, Attachment.* New York: Basic Books.

Brandt, E. M. and Mitchell, G. 1971. Parturition in primates: Behavior related to birth. In: L. A. Rosenblum (Ed.). *Primate Behavior,* Vol. 2. New York: Academic Press, 177-223.

Brehm, A. 1922. *Tierleben,* Vol. 4. Leipzig.

Bullock, S. H. 1978. Regeneration of *Musa* after feeding by *Gorilla*. *Biotropica,* 10, 4, 309.

Burbridge, B. 1928. *Gorilla.* New York: Century Company.

Campbell, S. 1978. *Lifeboats to Ararat.* New York: Times Books.

Caro, T. N. 1976. Observations on the ranging behavior and daily activity of lone silverback mountain gorillas (*Gorilla gorilla beringei*). *Anim. Behav.,* 24, 889-897.

Carpenter, C. R. 1937. An observational study of two captive mountain gorillas (*Gorilla beringei*). *Human Biology,* 9, 175-196.

Carter, F. S. 1974. Comparison of baby gorillas with human infants at birth and during the postnatal period. *Rep. Jersey Wildlife Preservation Trust,* 10, 29-33.

Carthy, J. D. and Ebling, F. J. 1964. *The Natural History of Aggression*. London: Academic Press.

Casimir, M. J. 1975a. Some morphological data on the systematic position of the Mt. Kahuzi gorilla. *Z. Morph. Anthrop.*, **66**, 188–201.

Casimir, M. J. 1975b. Feeding ecology and nutrition of an eastern gorilla group in the Mt. Kahuzi region (Republique de Zaire.) *Folia Primat.*, **24**, 81–136.

Casimir, M. J. 1979. An analysis of gorilla nesting sites of the Mt. Kahuzi region. *Folia Primat.*, **32**, 290–308.

Casimir, M. J. and Butenandt, E. 1973. Migration and core area shifting in relation to some ecological factors in a mountain gorilla group (*Gorilla gorilla beringei*) in the Mt. Kahuzi region (Republique de Zaire). *Z. Tierpsychologie*, **33**, 514–522.

Chaffee, P. S. 1967. A note on the breeding of orangutans at Fresno Zoo. *Int. Zoo Yearbook*, **7**, 94–95.

Chevalier-Skolnikoff, S. 1977. A Piagetian model for describing and comparing socialization in monkey, ape, and human infants. In: Chevalier-Skolnikoff, S. and Poirier, F. E. (Eds.). *Primate Bio-Social Development*, New York: Garland, 159–187.

Clift, J. P. and Martin, R. D. 1978. Monitoring of pregnancy and postnatal behavior in a lowland gorilla at London Zoo. *Int. Zoo Yearbook*, **18**, 165–173.

Coffey, P. and Pook, G. 1975. Breeding, hand-rearing and development of the third lowland gorilla. *Gorilla g. Gorilla* at the Jersey Zoological Park. *Rep. Jersey Wildlife Preservation Trust*, **11**, 45–50.

Conroy, G. C. and Fleagle, J. G. 1972. Locomotor behavior in living and fossil Pongids. *Nature*, **237**, 103–104.

Coolidge, H. J., Jr. 1929. A revision of the Genus *Gorilla*. *Mem. Mus. Comp. Zool. Harvard*, **50**, 295–381.

Coolidge, H. J., Jr. 1933. Notes on a family of breeding gibbons. *Human Biology*, **5**, 288–294.

Corbet, G. B. 1967. Nomenclature of the eastern lowland gorilla. *Nature*, **215**, 1171–1172.

Cousins, D. 1972. Diseases and injuries in wild and captive gorillas. *Int. Zoo Yearbook*, **12**, 211–217.

Cousins, D. 1973. Classification of captive gorillas. *Int. Zoo Yearbook*, **13**, 155–159.

Cousins, D. 1976. The breeding of gorillas in zoological gardens. *Der Zoologische Garten*, **46**, 215–236.

Cousins, D. 1978. The reaction of apes to water. *Int. Zoo News*, **25/7**, 8–13.

Crook, J. H. 1970. The socio-ecology of primates. In: Crook, J. H. (Ed.). *Social Behavior in Birds and Mammals*. London: Academic Press, 103–166.

Cunningham, A. 1921. A gorilla's life in civilization. *Bull. N. Y. Zool. Society*, **24**, 118–124.

Cuppy, W. *How to Tell Your Friends From the Apes*. New York: Liveright, 1931.

Darwin, C. 1859. *On the Origin of Species by Means of Natural Selection, or the Preservation of Favored Races in the Struggle for Life*. London: John Murray.

Darwin, C. 1871. *The Descent of Man and Selection in Relation to Sex*. London: John Murray.

Darwin, C. 1872. *Expression of the Emotions in Man and Animals*. London: John Murray.

de Benedictis, T. 1973. The behavior of young primates during copulation: Observations of a *Macaca irus* colony. *Am. Anthrop.*, **75**, 1469–1484.

Donisthorpe, J. 1958. A pilot study of the mountain gorilla (*Gorilla g. beringei*) in S. W. Uganda. *S. Afr. J. Sci.*, **54**, 195–217.

Du Chaillu, P. B. 1861. *Explorations and Adventures in Equatorial Africa*. John Murray: London.

Duckworth, W. L. H. 1915. *Morphology and Anthropology*, Vol. 1, Cambridge, Mass.: Cambridge University Press.

Elliot, D. G. 1913. A review of the primates. *Monogr. Am. Mus. Nat. Hist.*, 3, 206-223.

Elliott, R. C. 1976. Observations on a small group of mountain gorillas. *Folia Primat.*, 25, 12-24.

Ellis, J. 1974. Lowland gorilla birth at Oklahoma City Zoo. *The Keeper*, 7/8, 9-10.

Emlen, J. T. and Schaller, G. 1960. In the home of the mountain gorilla. *Anim. Kingdom*, 63, 98-108.

Erwin, J., Anderson, B., Erwin, N., Lewis, L., and Flynn, D. 1976. Aggression in captive groups of pigtail monkeys: Effects of provision of cover. *Percept. Mot. Skills.* 42, 319-324.

Erwin, J., Maple, T., and Mitchell, G. (Eds.). 1979. *Captivity and Behavior: Primates in Breeding Colonies, Laboratories and Zoos*. New York: Van Nostrand Reinhold.

Falkenstein, J. 1876. Ein Iabender gorilla. *Z. Ethn.*, Berlin, 8, 60-61 (cited in Yerkes and Yerkes, 1929).

Fick, R. 1926. Massverhaltnisse an den oberen gliedmassen des menschen und den gliedmassen der menschenaffen. *Sitzber. preuss Akad. Wiss. Berlin*, 417-451. (cited in Yerkes and Yerkes, 1929).

Fischer, R. B. and Nadler, R. D. 1977. Status interactions of captive female lowland gorillas. *Folia Primat.*, 28, 122-133.

Fischer, R. B. and Nadler, R. D. 1978. Affiliative, playful and homosexual interactions of adult female lowland gorillas. *Primates*, 19, 4, 657-669.

Fisher, L. E. 1972. The birth of a lowland gorilla at the Lincoln Park Zoo, Chicago. *Int. Zoo Yearbook*, 12, 106-108.

Fisher, G. and Kitchener, S. 1965. Comparative learning in young gorillas and orang-utans. *J. Genet. Psych.*, 107, 337-348.

Fitzgerald, F. L., Barfield, M. A., and Grubbs, P. A. 1970. Food preferences in lowland gorillas. *Filia Primat.*, 12, 209-211.

Forbes, H. O. 1897. *Monkeys: A Handbook to the Primates*. London: Edward Lloyd Ltd.

Ford, H. A. 1852. On the characteristics of the Troglodytes gorilla. *Proc. Acad. Nat. Sci. Phila.*, 6, 30-33.

Fossey, D. 1971. More years with mountain gorillas. *Nat. Geo. Mag.* 140, 574-585.

Fossey, D. 1974. Observations on the home range of one group of mountain gorillas. *Anim. Behav.*, 22, 568-581.

Fossey, D. 1979. Development of the mountain gorilla (*Gorilla gorilla beringei*): The first thirty-six months. In: Hamburg, D. A. and McCown, E. R. (Eds.). *The Great Apes*. Menlo Park, Calif.: Benjamin/Cummings, 139-186.

Fossey, D. 1972a. Living with mountain gorillas. In: *The Marvels of Animal Behavior*. Washington, D. C.: National Geographic Society, 208-229.

Fossey, D. 1972b. Vocalizations of the mountain gorilla (*Gorilla gorilla beringei*) *Anim. Behav.*, 20, 36-53.

Fossey, D. and Harcourt, A. H. 1977. Feeding ecology of free-ranging mountain gorilla (*Gorilla g. beringei*). In: Clutton-Brock, T. H. (Ed.). *Primate Ecology: Studies in Feeding and Ranging Behavior of Lemurs, Monkeys and Apes*. London: Academic Press, 415-447.

Fouts, R. S. 1973. Acquisition and testing of gestural signs in four young chimpanzees. *Science*, 180, 978-980.

Franks, D. 1963. The blood groups of primates. *Symp. Zool. Soc. London*, 10, 221-250.

Freeman, H. E. and Alcock, J. 1973. Play behavior of a mixed group of juvenile gorillas and orangutans. *Int. Zoo Yearbook*, 13, 189-194.

Freuh, R. J. 1968. A captive born gorilla at St. Louis Zoo. *Int. Zoo Yearbook,* 8, 128–131.

Galdikas, B. M. F. 1979. Orangutan adaptation at Tanjung Puting Reserve: Mating and ecology. In: Hamburg, D. A. and McCown, E. R. (Eds.). *The Great Apes.* Menlo Park, Calif.: Benjamin/Cummings, 195–222.

Gardner, R. A. and Gardner, B. T. 1969. Teaching sign language to a chimpanzee. *Science,* 165, 664–672.

Garner, R. L. 1896. *Gorillas and Chimpanzees.* London: Osgood McIlvaine and Co.

Garner, R. L. 1914. Gorillas in their own jungle. *Zool. Soc. Bull.* (N. Y.), 17, 1102–1104.

Gartlan, J. S. 1974. The African forests and problems of conservation. *Symp. Fifth Congr. Int. Primat. Soc.,* 509–528.

Golding, R. R. 1972. A gorilla and chimpanzee exhibit at the University of Ibadan Zoo. *Int. Zoo. Yearbook,* 12, 71–76.

Goodall, A. G. 1974. Studies on the ecology of the mountain gorilla (*G. gorilla beringei*) of the Mt. Kahuzi-Biega region (Zaire) and comparisons with the mountain gorillas of the Virunga Volcanoes. Unpublished Ph.D. dissertation, Liverpool University.

Goodall, A. G. 1978. On habitat and home range in eastern gorillas in relation to conservation. In: Chivers, D. J. and Lane-Petters, W. (Eds.). *Recent Advances in Primatology,* Vol. 2. London: Academic Press, 81–84.

Goodall, A. G. 1979. *The Wandering Gorillas.* London, Collins.

Goodall, A. G. and Groves, C. P. 1977. The conservation of eastern gorillas. In: Rainier, Prince and Bourne, G. H. (Eds.). *Primate Conservation.* New York: Academic Press, 599–637.

Goodman, M. 1964. The specificity of proteins and the process of primate evolution. In: Peeters, H. (Ed.). *Protides of the Biological Fluids.* Amsterdam: Elsevier.

Gregory, W. K. 1927. How near is the relationship of man to the chimpanzee-gorilla stock? *Quart. Rev. Biol.,* 2, 549–560.

Groves, C. P. 1970a. *Gorillas.* New York, Arco.

Groves, C. P. 1970b. Population systematics of the gorilla. *J. Zool.,* 161, 187–300.

Groves, C. P. 1971. Distribution and place of origin of the gorilla. *Man,* 6, 44–51.

Groves, C. P. and Humphrey, N. K. 1973. Asymmetry in gorilla skulls: Evidence of lateralized brain function? *Nature,* 244, 53–54.

Groves, C. P. and Stott, K. W., Jr. 1979. Systematic relationships of gorillas from Kahuzi, Tshiaberimu and Kayonza. *Folia Primat.,* 32, 161–179.

Gruber, H. E. and Barrett, P. H. 1974. *Darwin on Man and Darwin's Early Published Notebooks.* New York: Dutton.

Halperin, S. D. 1979. Temporary association patterns in free-ranging chimpanzees: An assessment of individual grouping preferences. In: Hamburg, D. A. and McCown, E. R. (Eds.). *The Great Apes.* Menlo Park, Calif.: Benjamin/Cummings, 491–500.

Hamburg, D. A. and McCown, E. R. (Eds.). 1979. *The Great Apes.* Menlo Park, Calif.: Benjamin/Cummings.

Hancocks, D. 1979. A note on using natural artifacts in zoo exhibits. *Int. Zoo News,* 26/5, 22.

Harcourt, A. H. 1977. Virgunga gorillas—the case against translocations. *Oryx,* 13, 469–472.

Harcourt, A. H. 1978. Activity periods and patterns of social interaction: A neglected problem. *Behaviour,* 66, 121–135.

Harcourt, A. H. 1979. Contrasts between male relationships in wild gorilla groups. *Behav. Ecol. Sociobiol.* 5, 39–49.

Harcourt, A. H. and Curry-Lindahl, K. 1979. Conservation of the mountain gorilla and its habitat in Rwanda. *Environ. Conserv.,* 6, 143–147.

Harcourt, A. H. and Stewart, K. J. 1977. Apes, sex, and societies. *New Scientist,* **76,** 160–162.

Harcourt, A. H. and Stewart, K. J. 1978a. Coprophagy by wild mountain gorilla. *E. Afr. Wildlife J.,* **16,** 223–225.

Harcourt, A. H. and Stewart, K. J. 1978b. Sexual behaviour of wild mountain gorillas. In: Chivers, D. J. and Herbert, J. (Eds.) *Recent Advances in Primatology,* Vol. **6.** New York: Academic Press, 611–612.

Harcourt, A. H. and Stewart, K. J. 1980. Gorilla-eaters of Gabon. *Oryx,* xv, 3, 248-252.

Harcourt, A. H., Stewart, K. J., and Fossey, D. 1976. Male emigration and female transfer in wild mountain gorillas. *Nature,* **263,** 226–227.

Hardin, C. J., Danford, D., and Skeldon, P. C. 1969. Notes on the successful breeding by incompatible gorillas at Toledo Zoo. *Int. Zoo Yearbook,* **9,** 84–88.

Harlow, H. F. 1949. The formation of learning sets. *Psych. Rev.,* **56,** 51-65.

Harlow, H. F., 1971. *Learning to Love.* Chicago: Aldine.

Hayes, K. J. and Hayes, C. 1951. *The Ape in Our House.* New York: Harper.

Hediger, H. 1950. *Wild Animals in Captivity.* London: Butterworth.

Hess, J. P. 1973. Some observations on the sexual behavior of captive lowland gorillas. In: Michael, R. P. and Crook, J. H. (Eds.). *Comparative Ecology and Behaviour of Primates.* New York: Academic Press, 508-581.

Hewes, J. J. 1974. *Build Your Own Playground.* Boston: Houghton-Mifflin.

Hinde, R. A. 1969. Analyzing the roles of the partners in a behavioral interaction: Mother-infant relations in rhesus macaques. *Ann. N. Y. Acad. Science,* **159,** 651–667.

Hladik, C. M. 1978. Adaptive strategies of primates in relation to leaf-eating. In: Montgomery, G. (Ed.). *The Ecology of Arboreal Folivores.* Washington, D. C.: Smithsonian Institution Press.

Hobson, B. 1975. The diagnosis of pregnancy in the lowland gorilla and the sumatran orang-utan. *Rep. Jersey Wildlife Preservation Trust,* **12,** 71–75.

Hoff, M. P., Nadler, R. D., and Maple, T. L. 1981b. The development of infant play in a captive group of lowland gorillas. *Am. J. Primatology,* **1,** 1, 65-72.

Hoff, M. P., Nadler, R.D., and Maple, T. L. 1978a. Group response to removal of the alpha male in a captive group of gorillas. Paper presented at the Southeastern Psychological Assn., Atlanta, Georgia.

Hoff, M. P., Nadler, R. D., and Maple, T. L. 1978b. Aggressive displays in infant gorillas. Paper presented at the Southeastern Conference on Human Development, Atlanta, Georgia.

Hoff, M. P., Nadler, R. D., and Maple, T. L. 1978c. Development of captive gorillas: The first two years. Paper presented at the American Society of Primatologists, Atlanta, Georgia.

Hoff, M. P., Nadler, R. D., and Maple, T. L. 1979. Separation and depression in infant gorillas. Paper presented at the Animal Behavior Society, New Orleans, La.

Hoff, M. P., Nadler, R. D., and Maple, T. L. 1980. Infant motor development in a captive group of gorillas. Paper presented at the American Society of Primatologists, Winston-Salem, N. C.

Hoff, M. P., Nadler, R. D., and Maple, T. 1981b. The development of infant independence in a captive group of lowland gorillas. *(G.g. gorilla). Developmental Psychobiology,* **14,** 251-265.

Hornaday, W. T. 1915. Gorillas, past and present. *Zool. Soc. Bull.* (N. Y.), **18,** 1181–1185.

Horvat, J. R., Coe, C. L., and Levine, S. 1980. Infant development and maternal behavior in captive chimpanzees. In: Smotherman, W. and Bell, R. (Eds.) *Early Experience and Behavior.* Jamaica, N.Y.: Spectrum, pp. 285-309.

Hoyt, A. M. 1941. *Toto and I: A Gorilla in the Family*. Philadelphia: Lippincott.

Hughes, J. and Redshaw, M. 1974. The psychological development of two infant gorillas. *Rep. Jersey Wildlife Preservation Trust*, **10**, 34–36.

Hughes, J. and Redshaw, M. 1975. Cognitive manipulative and social skills in gorillas. Part I. The first year. *Rep. Jersey Wildlife Preservation Trust*, **11**, 53–60.

Hutchins, M., and Barash, D. P. 1976. Grooming in primates: Implications for its utilitarian function. *Primates*, **17**, 145–150.

Imanishi, K. 195. Gorillas: a preliminary survey in 1958. *Primates*, **1**, 73–78.

Ishida, H., Kimura, T. and Okada, M. 1975. Patterns of bipedal walking in anthropoid primates. In Kondo, S., Kawai, M., Ehara, A., and Kawamura, S. (Eds.) *Proc. Symp. Fifth Congr. Int. Primat. Soc.*, Tokyo, Japan Science Press, pp. 287–302.

Johnstone-Scott, R. 1979. Notes on mother-rearing in the western lowland gorilla. *Int. Zoo News*, **26/5**, 9–20.

Joines, S. 1977a. A training program designed to induce maternal behavior in a multiparous female lowland gorilla at the San Diego Wild Animal Park. *Int. Zoo Yearbook*, **17**, 185–188.

Joines, S. D. 1977b. The effects of experience on the maternal behavior of a multiparous female lowland gorilla. Unpublished M. A. thesis, San Diego State University.

Jolly, A. 1972. *The Evolution of Primate Behavior*. New York: The Macmillan Company.

Jonch, A. 1968. The white lowland gorilla at Barcelona Zoo. *Int. Zoo Yearbook*, **8**, 196–197.

Jones, C. and Sabater Pi, J. 1971. Comparative ecology of *Gorilla gorilla* (Savage and Wyman) and *Pan troglodytes* (Blumenback) in Rio Muni, West Africa. *Bibliotheca Primatologica*, **13**, 1–96. Basel: Karger.

Kagawa, M. and Kagawa, K. 1972. Breeding a lowland gorilla at Riibsuren Park Zoo, Takamatsu. *Int. Zoo Yearbook*, **12**, 105–106.

Kawai, M. and Mizuhara, H. 1959. An ecological study on the wild mountain gorilla. *Primates*, **2**, 1–42.

Keiter, M. and Pichette, P. 1977. Surrogate infant prepares a lowland gorilla for motherhood. *Int. Zoo Yearbook*, **17**, 188–189.

Keiter, M. D. and Pichette, P. 1979. Reproductive behavior in captive subadult lowland gorillas. *Zool. Garten*, **49**, 215–237.

Keith, A. 1896. An introduction to the study of anthropid apes. *Nat. Sci.*, **9**, 372–379.

Keith, A. 1899. On the chimpanzees and their relations to the gorilla. *Proc. Zool. Soc. London*, 296–312.

Keith, A. 1923. Man's posture, its evolution and disorders. *Brit. Med. J.*, **1**, 451–454.

Kellogg, W. N. and Kellogg, L. A. 1933. *The Ape and the Child*. New York: McGraw-Hill.

Kennedy, K. A. R. and Whittaker, J. C. 1978. The ape in stateroom 10. *Natural History*, **85** (9), 48–53.

King, G. J. and Rivers, J. P. W. 1976. The affluent anthropoid. *Rep. Jersey Wildlife Preservation Trust*, **13**, 86–95.

Kingsley, S. 1977. Early mother-infant behavior in two species of great ape. *The Dodo*, **14**, 55–65.

Kirchshofer, R. 1979. *International Register and Studbook of the Gorilla*. Frankfurt Zoological Garden.

Kirchshofer, R., Fradrich, H., Podolczak, G., and Podolczak, D. 1967. An account of the physical and behavioural development of the hand-reared gorilla infant born at Frankfurt Zoo. *Int. Zoo Yearbook*, **7**, 108–113.

Knobloch, H. and Passamanick, B. 1959a. Gross motor behavior in an infant gorilla. *Journal Comp. and Physiol. Psych.*, **52**, 559–563.

Knobloch, H. and Passamanick, B. 1959b. The development of adaptive behavior in an infant gorilla. *J. Comp. Physio. Psych.,* **52,** 6, 699–704.

Köhler, W. 1925. *The Mentality of Apes.* New York: Harcourt, Brace, and Co.

Lang, E. M. 1959. The birth of a gorilla at the Basel Zoo. *Int. Zoo Yearbook,* **1,** 3–7.

Lindburg, D. G. 1973. Grooming behavior as a regulator of social interactions in rhesus monkeys. In: Carpenter, C. R. (Ed.). *Behavioral Regulators of Behavior in Primates,* Lewisburg, Pa.: Bucknell University Press, 124–148.

Lindburg, D. G., and Hazell, L. D. 1972. Licking of the neonate and duration of labor in great apes and man. *Amer. Anthrop.,* **74,** 318–325.

Lotshaw, R. 1971. Birth of the two lowland gorillas at Cincinnati Zoo. *Int. Zoo Yearbook,* **11,** 84–87.

MacKinnon, J. 1974. The behavior and ecology of wild orang-utans *(Pongo pygmaeus).* *Anim. Behav.,* **22,** 3–74.

MacKinnon, J. 1976. Mountain gorillas and bonobos. *Oryx,* **13,** 372–382.

Mallinson, J. J. C. 1974. Wildlife studies on the Zaire River expedition with special reference to the mountain gorillas of Kahuzi-Biega. *Ann. Report Jersey Wildlife Preservation Trust,* **11,** 16–23.

Mallinson, J. J. C., Coffey, P., and Usher-Smith, Jr. 1976. Breeding and hand rearing lowland gorillas at the Jersey Zoo. *Int. Zoo Yearbook,* **12,** 189–194.

Maple, T. 1973. Introduction to the scientific study of aggression. In: Maple, T. and Matheson, D. W. (Eds.). *Aggression, Hostility and Violence,* New York: Holt, Rinehart, & Winston, 1–7.

Maple, T. 1977. Unusual sexual behavior of nonhuman primates. In: Money, J. and Musaph, M. (Eds.). *Handbook of Sexology.* Elsevier: North Holland Biomedical Press, 1167–1186.

Maple, T. 1979. Great apes in captivity: The good, the bad, and the ugly. In: Erwin, J., Maple, T., and Mitchell, G. (Eds.). *Captivity and Behavior.* New York: Van Nostrand Reinhold, 239–272.

Maple, T. 1980a. *Orang-utan Behavior.* New York: Van Nostrand Reinhold.

Maple, T. 1980b. Breaking the hand-rearing syndrome in infant great apes. *AAZPA Regional Proceedings,* Wheeling, W. Va.

Maple, T. 1980c. *Chimpanzee Reproduction, Rearing, and Rehabilitation in Captivity.* Report presented to the Ad Hoc Task Force, National Chimpanzee Breeding Program, Tanglewood, N. C. Atlanta: Georgia Institute of Technology Publication.

Maple, T. In Press. *Chimpanzee Behavior.* New York: Van Nostrand Reinhold.

Maple, T., Brandt, E., and Mitchell, G. 1975. Separation of preadolescents from infants *(Macaca mulatta). Primates,* **16:** 141–153.

Maple, T. and Matheson, D. W., (Eds.) 1973. *Aggression, Hostility, and Violence.* New York: Holt, Rinehart and Winston.

Maple, T., Wilson, M. E., Zucker, E. L., and Wilson, S. F. 1978. Notes on the development of a mother-reared orang-utan: The first six months. *Primates,* **19,** 593–602.

Maple, T. L. and Zucker, E. L. 1978. Ethological studies of play behavior in captive great apes. In: Smith, E. O. (Ed.). *Social Play in Primates.* New York: Academic Press, 113–142.

Maple, T., Zucker, E. L., and Dennon, M. B. 1979. Cyclic proceptivity in a captive female orang-utan *(Pongo pygmaeus abelii). Behavioral Processes,* **4,** 53–59.

Marler, P. 1965. Communication in monkeys and apes. In: Devore, I. (Ed.). *Primate Behavior.* New York: Holt, Rinehart, & Winston, Inc., 544–584.

Marler, P. 1976. Social organization, communication and graded signals: The chimpanzee and the gorilla. In: Bateson, P. P. G. and Hinde, R. A. (Eds.). *Growing Points in Ethology,* Cambridge: Cambridge University Press, 239–280.

Marler, P. and Tenaza, R. 1977. Signaling behavior of apes with special reference to vocalization. In: Sebeok, T. A. (Ed.). *How Animals Communicate*. Bloomington, Indiana: Indiana University Press, 965-1033.

Martin, R. D. 1975. Application of urinary hormone determinations in the management of gorillas. *Rep. Jersey Wildlife Preservation Trust*, 12, 61-70.

Martin, R. D. 1976. Breeding great apes in captivity. *New Scient.*, 72, 100-102.

Martin, R. D., Kingsley, S. R., and Stavy, M. 1977. Prospects for coordinated research into breeding of great apes in zoological gardens. *The Dodo*, 14, 45-55.

Matschie, P. 1903. Über einen Gorilla aus Deutsch-Ostafrica. *Sitzber, Ges. naturf. Fr. Berl.*, 253-259 (cited in Yerkes and Yerkes, 1929).

Maxwell, M. 1928. The home of the eastern gorilla. *J. Bombay Nat. Hist. Soc.*, 32, 436-449.

McWhirter, N. and McWhirter, R. 1974. *Guinness Book of World Records*. New York: Sterling.

Mears, C. E. and Harlow, H. F. 1975. Play: Early and eternal. *Proc. Nat. Acad. Sci.*, 72, 1878-1882.

Menzel, E. W. 1973. Chimpanzee spatial memory organization. *Science*, 182, 943-945.

Menzel, E. W., Premack, D. and Woodruff, G. 1978. Map reading by chimpanzees. *Folia primatol.*, 29, 241-249.

Merfield, F. G. 1956. *Gorillas Were My Neighbors*. London: Longmans, Green and Co.

Mitani, J. C. and Rodman, P. S. 1979. Territoriality: The relation of ranging pattern and home range size to defendability with an analysis of territoriality among primate species. *Behavioral Ecology and Sociobiology*, 5, 241-251.

Mitchell, G. 1979. *Behavioral Sex Differences in Nonhuman Primates*. New York: Van Nostrand Reinhold.

Mitchell, G. and Tokunaga, D. H. 1976. Sex differences in non-human primate grooming. *Behavioral Processes*, 1, 335-347.

Mollison, T. 1908. Rechts and links in der primaten reihe. *Korrbl. deuts. Ges. Anthrop.*, Braunschweig, 39, 112-115. (cited in Yerkes and Yerkes, 1929).

Montagu, A. 1970. Another trait common to the pongidae and man. *Amer. Anthrop.* 72, 1447.

Montgomery, G. (Ed.) 1978. *The Ecology of Arboreal Folivores*. Washington, D. C., Smithsonian Institution Press.

Morris, D. 1960. The new champanzee den at London Zoo. *Int. Zoo Yearbook*, 1: 18-20.

Morris, D. 1964. The response of animals to a restricted environment. *Symp. Zool. Soc. London.* 13, 99-118.

Morris, R. and Morris, D. 1967. *Men and Apes*. New York: McGraw-Hill.

Nadler, R. D. 1974a. Periparturitional behavior of a primiparous lowland gorilla. *Primates*, 15, 53-73.

Nadler, R. D. 1974b. Determinants of variability in maternal behavior of captive female gorillas. *Symp. 5th Congr. Int. Primat. Soc.*, 207-215.

Nadler, R. D. 1975a. Sexual cyclicity in captive lowland gorillas. *Science*, 189: 813-814.

Nadler, R. D. 1975b. Cyclicity in tumescence of the perineal labia of female lowland gorillas. *Anat. Rec.* 181, 791-798.

Nadler, R. D. 1976. Sexual behavior of captive lowland gorillas. *Arch. Sex. Behav.* 5, 487-502.

Nadler, R. D. 1977. Sexual behavior of orang-utan. *Arch. Sex. Behav.* 6, 457-475.

Nadler, R. D. and Green, S. 1975. Separation and reunion of a gorilla infant and mother. *Int. Zoo. Yearbook*, 15, 198-201.

Nadler, R. D. and Jones, M. L. 1975. Breeding of the gorilla in captivity. *AAZPA Newsletter*, 12–17.

Napier, J. R. 1970. *The Roots of Mankind*. Washington, D. C.: Smithsonian Institute Press.

Napier, J. R. and Napier, P. H. 1967. *A Handbook of Living Primates*. London: Academic Press.

Nicolson, N. A. 1977. A comparison of early behavioral development in wild and captive champanzees. In: Chevalier-Skolnikoff, S. and Poirier, F. (Eds.). *Primate Bio-Social Development*. New York: Garland, 529–560.

Noback, C. R. 1939. The changes in the vaginal smears and associated cyclic phenomena in the lowland gorillas (*Gorilla gorilla*). *Anat. Record, 73*, 209–225.

Oki, J. and Maeda, Y. 1973. Grooming as a regulator of behavior in Japanese macaques. In: Carpenter, C. R. (Ed.). *Behavioral Regulators of Behavior in Primates*. Lewisberg, Pennsylvania: Bucknell University Press, 149–163.

Osborn, H. F. 1923. Preface to Akeley, C. F. *In Brightest Africa*. New York: Doubleday.

Osborn, R. M. 1963. Observations on the behaviour of the mountain gorilla. *Symp. Zool. Soc. London, 10*, 29–37.

Parker, C. 1969. Responsiveness, manipulation, and implementation behavior in chimpanzees, gorillas, and orang-utans. *Proc. 2nd Int. Congr. Primat., 1*, 160–166. New York: S. Karger.

Patterson, F. 1978. Conversations with a gorilla. *National Geographic, 154* (4), 438–466.

Phillips, T. 1950. Letter to the editor. *Man, 50*, 168.

Piaget, J. 1952. *The Origins of Intelligence in Children*. New York: International Universities Press.

Pilbeam, D. R. 1972. *The Ascent of Man, an Introduction to Human Evolution*. MacMillian: New York.

Pitcairn, T. D. 1974. Aggression in natural groups of Pongids. In: Holloway, R. L. (Ed.). *Primate Aggression, Territoriality, and Xenophobia*. London: Academic Press, 241–274.

Pitman, C. R. S. 1931. *A Game Warden Among his Charges*. London: Nisbet and Co.

Plowden, G. 1972. *Gargantua: Circus Star of the Century*. New York, Bonanza.

Puleo, S. P., Zucker, E. L., and Maple, T. L. In Press. Social rehabilitation and foster mothering in captive orang-utans. *Zool. Garten*.

Pusey, A. 1979. Intercommunity transfer of chimpanzees in Gombe National Park. In: Hamburg, D. A. and McCown, E. R. (Eds.). *The Great Apes*. Menlo Park Calif.: Benjamin/Cummings, 465–479.

Quick, R. 1976. Gorilla habitat display. *Int. Zoo News, 23/6*, 13–16.

Raven, H. C. 1936. Genital swelling in a female gorilla. *J. Mammal. 17*, 416.

Raven, H. C. 1950. Regional anatomy of the gorilla. In: Gregory, W. K. (Ed.). *The Anatomy of the Gorilla*. New York: Columbia University Press, 15–188.

Redican, W. K. 1976. Adult male-infant interactions in nonhuman primates. In: Lamb, M. E. (Ed.). *The Role of the Father in Child Development*. New York: Wiley, 345–385.

Redshaw, M. 1975. Cognitive, manipulative, and social skills in gorillas: Part II, The second year. *Rep. Jersey Wildlife Preservation Trust, 12*, 56–60.

Redshaw, M. and Locke, R. 1976. The development of a play and social behavior in two lowland gorilla infants. *Rep. Jersey Wildlife Preservation Trust, 13*, 71–85.

Reed, T. H. and Gallagher, B. F. 1963. Gorilla birth at National Zoological Park Washington. *Zool. Gart., 27*, 279–292.

Reichenow, E. 1920. Biologische Beobachtungen an Gorilla und Schimpanse. *Sitzber. Ges. Naturf. Fr. Berl.* 1–40 (cited in Yerkes and Yerkes, 1929).

Riess, B. F., Ross, S., Lyerly, S. B., and Birch, H. G. 1949. The behavior of two captive specimens of the lowland gorilla. *Gorilla gorilla gorilla* (Savage and Wyman). *Zoologica* 34: 111–118.

Reuther, R. 1976. Barrier dimensions for lions, tigers, bears, and great apes. *Int. Zoo Yearbook,* 16, 217–222.

Reynolds, V. 1967. *The Apes.* New York: Dutton.

Riesen, A. H. and Kinder, E. F. 1952. *The Postural Development of Infant Chimpanzees.* New Haven, Conn.: Yale University Press.

Robbins, D., Compton, P., and Howard, S. 1978. Subproblem analysis of skill behavior in the gorilla: A transition from independent to cognitive behavior. *Primates,* 19, 231–236.

Rogers, C. M. and Davenport, R. K. 1969. Effects of restricted rearing on sexual behavior of chimpanzees. *Dev. Psychol.,* 1, 200–204.

Rogers, C. M. and Davenport, R. K. 1970. Chimpanzee maternal behavior. In: Bourne, G. H. (Ed.). *The Chimpanzee,* Vol. 3. Basel: S. Karger, 361–368.

Rosenblum, L. A., Kaufman, I. C., and Stynes, A. J. 1966. Some characteristics of adult social and autogrooming patterns in two species of macaques. *Folia Primat.,* 4, 438–451.

Rothschild, L. W. 1923. Exhibition of adult male mountain gorilla. *Proc. Zool. Soc. Lond.,* 176–177.

Rumbaugh, D. M. 1965. The birth of a lowland gorilla at San Diego Zoo. *Zoonooz,* 38 12-17.

Rumbaugh, D. M. and McCormick, C. 1967. The learning skills of primates: A comparative study of apes and monkeys. In: Stark, D., Schneider, R., and Kuhn, H. J. (Eds.). *Progress in Primatology.* Stuttgart: Gustav Fischer, 289–306.

Sabater Pí, J. 1966. Gorilla attacks against humans in Rio Muni, West Africa. *J. of Mammalogy,* 47, 123–124.

Sabater Pí, J. 1967. An albino lowland gorilla from Rio Muni, West Africa, and notes on its adaptation to captivity. *Folia Primat.,* 7, 155–160.

Sabater Pi, J. 1979. Feeding behaviour and diet of chimpanzees in the Okorobiko Mountains of Rio Muni (West Africa). *Z. Tierpsychol.,* 50, 265–281.

Sade, D. S. 1965. Some aspects of parent-offspring and sibling relations in a group of rhesus monkeys, with a discussion of grooming. *Am. J. Phys. Anthro.,* 23, 1–18.

Savage, T. S. 1847. Notice of the external character and habits of a new species of *Troglodytes* (*T. gorilla,* Savage) recently discovered near the River Gaboon, Africa. *Proc. Boston Soc. Nat. Hist.,* 2: 245–247.

Savage, T. S. and Wyman, J. 1847. Notice of external characters and habits of *Troglodytes gorilla.* A new species of orang from the Gaboon River–Osteology of the same. *Boston J. Nat. History.* 5, 417–443.

Schaller, G. B. 1963. *The Mountain Gorilla.* Chicago: University Chicago Press.

Schultz, A. H. 1927. Studies on the growth of gorilla and other higher primates with special reference to a fetus of gorilla, preserved in the Carnegie Museum. *Memories Carnegie Museum,* Pittsburgh, Vol. II, 1–86.

Schultz, A. H. 1934. Some distinquishing characters of the mountain gorilla. *J. Mammal.* 15, 51–61.

Scollay, P. A., Joines, S., Baldridge, C., and Cuzzone, A. 1975. Learning to be a mother. *Zoonooz,* 6-9.

Seal, U. S., Anderson, J., Farnsworth, R., and Fletcher, J. 1970. Airborne transport of an uncaged immobilized 260 kg (572 lb) lowland gorilla. *Int. Zoo Yearbook,* 10, 134–136.

Sebeok, T. A. and Umiker-Sebeok, J. 1979. Performing animals: Secrets of the trade. *Psychology Today,* 13 (6): 78–91.

Seyfarth, R. A. 1977. A model of social grooming among adult female baboons. *Anim. Behav.* 24, 917-938.

Short, R. V. 1977. Sexual selection and the descent of man. In: Calaby, J. H. and Tyndale-Biscoe, C. H. (Eds.). *Reproduction and Evolution.* Netley, Australia: Griffin Press Ltd., 3-19.

Simons, E. L. 1972. *Primate Evolution, an Introduction to Man's Place in Nature.* New York: MacMillian.

Simpson, M. J. A. 1973. The social grooming of male chimpanzees. In: Michael, R. P. and Crook, J. H. (Eds.). *Comparative Ecology and Behaviour of Primates.* London and New York: Academic Press, 411-505.

Smith, E. O. (Ed.) 1978. *Social Play in Primates.* New York: Academic Press.

Snyder, R. D. 1978. Strategies for feeding captive omnivorous animals. *Proc. AAZPA Conf.* 127-140.

Sommer, R. 1974. *Tight Spaces.* Englewood Cliffs, N. J.: Prentice-Hall.

Sonntag, C. I. 1924. *Morphology and Evolution of the Apes and Man.* London: John Bate, Sons and Danielsson Ltd.

Steiner, P. E. 1954. Anatomical observations on a *Gorilla gorilla. Am. J. Phys. Anthrop.,* 12, 145-180.

Stewart, K. J. 1977. The birth of a wild mountain gorilla. *Primates,* 18, 965-976.

Szalay, F. S. and Delson, E. 1980. *Evolutionary History of the Primates.* New York, Academic Press.

Taylor, S. H. and Bietz, A. D. 1979. *Infant Diet/Care Notebook.* Wheeling, W. Virginia: American Association of Zoological Parks and Aquariums.

Terrace, H. S. 1979. Can an ape create a sentence? *Science,* 206, 891-900.

Terry, R. L. 1970. Primate grooming as a tension reduction mechanism. *J. Psychol.,* 76, 129-136.

Theobald, J. 1973. Gorilla pediatric procedures. *Proc. Am. Assoc. Zoo. Vet.,* 12-14.

Thorndike, E. L. 1898. *Animal Intelligence.* New York, MacMillan.

Thomas, W. D. 1958. Observations on the breeding in captivity of a pair of lowland gorillas. *Zoologica,* 43, 4.

Throp, J. L. 1975. People involvement innovations at the Honolulu Zoo. *Int. Zoo Yearbook,* 15, 266-268.

Tijskens, J. 1971. The oestrus cycle and gestation period of the mountain gorilla. *Int. Zoo Yearbook,* Vol. 11.

Tilford, B. L. and Nadler, R. D. 1978. Male parental behavior in a captive group of lowland gorillas. *Folia Primat.,* 29, 218-228.

Trivers, R. L. 1972. Parental investment and sexual selection. In: Campbell, B. (Ed.). *Sexual Selection and the Descent of Man.* Chicago: Aldine, 136-179.

Tutin, C. E. G. 1975. Exceptions to promiscuity in a feral chimpanzee community. In Kondo, S., Kawai, M., and Ehara, A. (Eds.). *Contemporary Primatology.* Basel: Karger, 445-449.

Tuttle, R. H. 1967. Knuckle-walking and the evolution of hominoid hands. *Am. J. Phys. Anthrop.* 26, 171-206.

Tuttle, R. H. 1969. Knuckle-walking and the problem of human origins. *Science,* 166, 953-961.

Tuttle, R. H. and Basmajian, J. V. 1975. Electromyography of *Pan gorilla:* an experimental approach to the problem of hominization. In Kondo, S., Kawai, M., Ehara, A., and Kawamura, S. (Eds.) *Proc. Symp. Fifth Congr. Int. Primat. Soc.,* Tokyo, Japan Science Press, pp. 303-314.

Tullner, W. W. and Gray, C. W. 1968. Chorionic gonadotropin excretion during pregnancy in a gorilla. *Proc. Soc. Exp. Biol. Med.,* 128, 954-956.

Usher-Smith, J. H., King, G., Pook, G., and Redshaw, M. 1976. Comparative physical development in six hand-reared lowland gorillas (*Gorilla g. gorilla*) at the Jersey Zoological Park. *Rep. Jersey Wildlife Preservation Trust*, 13, 63-70.

van Hooff, J. A. R. A. M. 1967. The facial displays of the catarrhine monkeys and apes. In: Morris, D. (Ed.). *Primate Ethology*. Chicago: Aldine, 7-68.

van Lawick-Goodall, J. 1967. Mother-offspring relationships in chimpanzees. In: Morris, D. (Ed.). *Primate Ethology*. Chicago: Aldine, 287-346.

Vogel, C. 1961. Zur systematatischen untergliederung der gattung *Gorilla* anhand von untersuchungen der mandibel. *Z. F. Säugetierk* 26, 65-76 (cited in Schaller, 1963).

Vogt, P. 1977. Tropical house for apes at Krefeld Zoo. *Int. Zoo Yearbook*, 17, 225-228.

Washburn, S. L. 1950. The analysis of primate evolution with particular reference to the origin of man. *Cold Spring Harbor Symp. Quant. Biol.* 15, 67-78.

Washburn, S. L. 1967. Behavior and origin of man. *Proc. Roy. Anthrop. Soc.* pp. 21-27.

Washburn, S. L. and DeVore, I. 1961. Social life of baboons. *Sci. Amer.*, 204, 62-71.

Washburn, S. L. and Moore, R. 1974. *Ape into Man*. Boston: Little, Brown & Co.

Werler, J. E. 1975. Gorilla habitat display at Houston Zoo. *Int. Zoo Yearbook*, 15, 258-260.

Wiener, A. S., Moor-Jankowski, J., and Gordon, E. B. 1966. Blood groups of apes and monkeys. *Folia Primat.*, 4, 81-102.

Williams, C. A. 1964. Immunochemical analysis of serum proteins of the primates: A study of molecular evolution. In: Buettner-Janusch, J. (Ed.). *Evolutionary and Genetic Biology of Primates, Vol. II*. New York and London: Academic Press, 25-74.

Willoughby, D. B. 1979. *All About Gorillas*. Cranbury, N. J.: A. S. Barnes and Co.

Wilson, M. E., Maple, T., Nadler, R. D., Hoff, M., and Zucker, E. L. 1977. Characteristics of paternal behavior in captive orang-utans (*Pongo pygmaeus abelii*) and lowland gorillas (*Gorilla gorilla gorilla*). Paper presented at the Inaugural Meeting of the American Society of Primatologists, Seattle, Washington.

Wilson, S. F. Unpublished. *Environmental Influences on the Activity of Captive Apes*.

Wolfe, K. A. 1974. Comparative behavioral ecologies of chimpanzees and gorillas. *Univ. Oregon Anthroplogical Papers*, 7, 53-65.

Wrangham, R. W. 1979. On the evolution of ape social systems. *Social Science Information*, 18, 335-368.

Yerkes, R. M. 1925. *Almost Human*. New York: Century.

Yerkes, R. M. 1927a. The mind of a gorilla. *Genet. Psychol. Monog.*, 2, 1-193.

Yerkes, R. M. 1927b. The mind of a gorilla. Part II. Mental development. *Genet. Psychol. Monog.*, 2, 375-551.

Yerkes, R. M. 1928. The mind of a gorilla. Part III. Memory. *Comp. Psychol. Monog.*, 5, 1-92.

Yerkes, R. M. 1933. Genetic aspects of grooming, a socially important primate behavior pattern. *J. Soc. Psychol.*, 4, 3-25.

Yerkes, R. M. 1943. *Chimpanzees: A Laboratory Colony*. New Haven, Conn.: Yale University Press.

Yerkes, R. M. and Yerkes, A. W. 1929. *The Great Apes*. New Haven, Conn.: Yale University Press.

Zucker, E. L., Wilson, S., Hoff, M. P., Nadler, R. D., Maple, T., and Dennon, B. 1977. Grooming behaviors of orang-utans and gorillas: Description and comparison. Paper presented at the Animal Behavior Society, University Park, Pennsylvania.

Zuckerman, S. 1932. *The Social Life of Monkeys and Apes*. London: Kegan Paul.

Author Index

Subject Index